OTHER BOOKS WRITTEN BY TERRY L NEWBEGIN:

Genesis: Your Journey Home, 2nd Edition

The Book of Revelation: A New Beginning

Terry's Website Address: www.terrynewbegin.com

Unlocking the Consciousness of Your Soul

Terry L Newbegin

BALBOA PRESS
A DIVISION OF HAY HOUSE

Unlocking The Consciousness of Your Soul

Copyright © 2012 Terry L Newbegin

All rights reserved. No part of this book may be used or reproduced by any means, graphic, electronic, or mechanical, including photocopying, recording, taping or by any information storage retrieval system without the written permission of the publisher except in the case of brief quotations embodied in critical articles and reviews.

Balboa Press books may be ordered through booksellers or by contacting:

Balboa Press
A Division of Hay House
1663 Liberty Drive
Bloomington, IN 47403
www.balboapress.com
1-(877) 407-4847

Because of the dynamic nature of the Internet, any web addresses or links contained in this book may have changed since publication and may no longer be valid. The views expressed in this work are solely those of the author and do not necessarily reflect the views of the publisher, and the publisher hereby disclaims any responsibility for them.

The author of this book does not dispense medical advice or prescribe the use of any technique as a form of treatment for physical, emotional, or medical problems without the advice of a physician, either directly or indirectly. The intent of the author is only to offer information of a general nature to help you in your quest for emotional and spiritual well-being. In the event you use any of the information in this book for yourself, which is your constitutional right, the author and the publisher assume no responsibility for your actions.

Any people depicted in stock imagery provided by Thinkstock are models, and such images are being used for illustrative purposes only.
Certain stock imagery © Thinkstock.

ISBN: 978-1-4525-5866-0 (sc)
ISBN: 978-1-4525-5868-4 (hc)
ISBN: 978-1-4525-5867-7 (e)

Library of Congress Control Number: 2012917074

Printed in the United States of America

Balboa Press rev. date: 10/02/2012

	Acknowledgments	vii
	A Note From the Editor.	ix
	A Word From the Author.	xiii
	Introduction	xix
1.	Opening Up To Your Soul	1
2.	The Challenge	10
3.	The Beginning	21
4.	The Spirit Of One	35
5.	Leaving Your Divine State.	55
6.	Moving Into A Divided Consciousness	70
7.	The Structuring Of The Second Creation	85
8.	The Divine Plan	94
9.	Earth Bound	113
10.	Uniformty Of The Physical Body	127
11.	The Search For God	138
12.	You Are A Divinine Being.	159
13.	The Creation Of Many Personalty-Aspects	171
14.	Belief Systems, And How They Affect Your Reality .	192
15.	How Susceptibility, Vulnerability, And Belief Systems Led To Control And Death Of The Soul . .	204
16.	Misunderstanding Lucifer's (Satan) Role	216
17.	How Energy Works	241
18.	Understanding Your Soul	267
19.	How To Create Miracles.	284
20.	The Importance Of Deep Breathing	302
21.	Learn To Be A Conscious Creator	316
22.	Moving Beyond Perception And Lies	334
23.	True Freedom.	349
	Epilogue	373

Acknowledgments

I give thanks to my parents, Frederick and Florence Newbegin – for they have given me the foundation that transformed my outlook on life to meet whatever obstacles that came in my path. Their display of courage and total love became the standard for me in optimizing my opportunities that came my way without showing any fear of loss or failure because of my education and position in life. Their selfless endeavors were all that I needed to encourage me to become what I am today.

I give my love, respect, and thanks to my dear wife Diane for her love, support, patience, and devotion – for she gave me the space, time, and trust to stay committed to what I feel within, and then write about it.

I give thanks to all who work for Newbegin Enterprises, notably to my sons Troy and Toby Newbegin, my daughter Tanya Dufore and her husband James, along with Zhiqiang (Ralph) Cui, Thomas Ritter, and Andrew Crunkleton. These individuals made it possible for me to write about my passion for truth and awareness by taking care of my business.

I give my love, gratitude, thanks, and my blessing to Nancy Salminen. Nancy's editing has made it possible for me to express my writing in a clear and precise manner. Nancy has now worked with me on two of my books and her contribution has proven to be invaluable. Nancy's resolve has made the production of this book possible.

My dear friends, we are all faced with situations everyday in life that don't look like blessings or miracles. But how we choose to meet these challenges and conditions in life determines the reality we will experience. Therefore, I dedicate this book to a unique and special friend, my own "I AM Soul" – for it was my soul that came forward in helping me "unlock my consciousness," introducing me to my personal journey through time and space.

It was my "soul" that awakened me to the insights of it not being about where I was born, about my education, my religion, my intellect, or even about money. It was, and still is, about the wisdom that I have learned from every experience and encounter that I have had with myself, with my family, with others, and with my many past lifetimes.

So with that, my desire is to help my readers discover their own "soul" and their own journey of lifetimes and blessings – for we are all here on earth by choice even though we may not think so.

A Note From the Editor

After the completion of this book, Terry asked if I would write down a few comments of my own to his work. I was so delighted to have this opportunity as I wanted to explain my own discovery and personal journey while absorbing the content of his book. Never in my wildest dreams did I ever expect to receive such enrichment and confidence from this experience which I can now share with you.

Although I thought my life was in good order, I never realized just how much better it could still be with more freedoms from any power that judges or controls my true being. I have learned to embrace my true strength and clearly understand the following:
- I am my own God
- how to embrace the moment on this earth with love, health, and abundance that I create
- judgment, jealousy, and fear with belief systems that will not control me
- my future will be exciting as I now have the ability to create it
- ultimate trust within is my true power

One may say these are miracles, which in fact, they are not! Happily, you will discover why they are not "miracles" as you read this book and learn about your true soul. As I have recognized these abilities and

embraced them, I have also watched happenings in my life unfold with ease. Some of them include:
- my retirement was a very easy transition
- my medical status is in my power and I live pain free
- my house sold instantly
- my new house fulfills my desires
- my bank account holds the amount I envisioned
- my pets selected me and we share an unconditional bond and love
- I travel with no fears
- my family personalities are not judged and I enjoy the company of all my relatives and many fine friends

I also observed that I am no longer influenced by:
- negative news
- the complexity of almost everything
- the illnesses of our societies and systems
- the struggles of other individuals
- the irregularities of earth's characteristics

Now I realize how simple it was for me to experience all these beautiful happenings. All I did was provide a quiet and comfortable space for myself with little disturbances. Then I rested my mind and asked it not to make any judgment or busy itself with past knowledge. And finally, I allowed the content of the book to do its work. With the help of deep breathing I began to feel a transformation take place that was warm, and weightless. My emotions that were personally tested at the beginning of this book began to soften and that is when my "being" began to feel my true self.

My life did not just "turn a corner"…it was far more than that. The challenge falls in wording this feeling as there are no words that exist beyond "the ultimate elation of existence". Therefore, my experience was indescribable!

I feel freedom and confidence like never before. I allow the power of my heart, and not my mind, to guide me. I feel the energy of my limitations become released, and the energy of my freedom become increased. I know that all my experiences on earth are gifts to gain wisdom in whatever forms that may be, and I know this journey is mine and only mine.

Lastly, I also recognized that it was not necessary to feel that I must try to retain all the information in this book at once. The author provides repetition for reinforcement and justification. I learned to trust myself, and feel my own energy guide me through the book. As a result, I better understood myself as my own God and that I am the creator of my future in all ways. I realized I am just an ordinary person who found my true being and you can do the same.

Happy reading!
Nancy Salminen

A Word From the Author

From my two earlier books, Genesis: Your Journey Home, 2nd Edition and the Book of Revelation: A New Beginning, I revealed the deeper metaphysical (beyond the literal) meaning behind what was transcribed in the Bible as physical creation and the ending of the world. And now, I present to you my new book, "Unlocking the Consciousness of Your Soul." The book introduces you to the wisdom of your soul and to who you truly are instead of who you think you are.

The book pertains to my experiences with my soul, and how it was by means of by building my business that led me to the wisdom of my soul. It is a story regarding where I truly began as a child of God, who I thought I was because of where I was born, and how I became enlightened to the most profound kept secrets that were ever devised in the history of mankind. It is a story about how to succeed in all aspects of your life.

Without you realizing it, your soul has been hiding from you for many lifetimes, and by choosing to open up your heart and put aside your dogmatic beliefs for awhile, your soul will reveal to you the whys of you choosing the route of sin, physicality, earth, brainwashing, forgetfulness, and suffering as the means to remember "who you truly are."

If you are looking for clarity in life and how to overcome distress, grief, anger, and the pain you are feeling right now, then it becomes very important to understand "who you truly are, where you truly come from, how miracles are created, and why you do the things you do." It is a story that touches on the human struggles of life and how to overcome them just by learning to connect to the wisdom of your very own soul.

The story takes you all the way back to the first creation, known in the Bible as the Garden of Eden, and how it relates to you. It does not matter if you are a king, a queen, a president of a country, or that you are a pauper, a drunk, a drug addict, or even a non-believer of God, or just an ugly sinner, all your soul wants is to join you and show you how divine you are no matter what you have done in life.

From my research I have learned that not only did we go all the way back to the Garden, we actually lived in the Garden. However, because of not knowing who we were and our connection to the Spirit of One, we purposely left the Garden with the intent to learn about life, love, who we truly are, and to help us take full responsibility for our choices in life as a sovereign creator in our own right.

Because of my willingness to open my mind to other possibilities, I have discovered secrets so profound that when I was awakened to them I felt a spiritual frequency of such a high degree deep within my being that it ended up as my soul. Once I became aware of my soul, I then became aware of my soul's wisdom and how to open up to it. Now my life has transformed into me being a true master in my own right. A master that knows "who I truly am," where I stand in this material world, and "how energy works" (God) to create the miracles of your heart.

The chaos you see around the world today is a sign that deep within, you want a change because religion, the bible, your family, the media, and the governments of the world cannot offer you anything more because now they are all broken and outdated.

Therefore, to master your own life and to bring in the miracles you seek, including the healing of the mind and body, you must take a good look and see why you confined yourself to a prison-like mentality of reasoning, dogmatic beliefs, and logic as the means to understand God, yourself, and life. I did, and to my surprise, I have learned that my prison was that I was hiding from my very own soul – for this is my soul's untold story.

I know that many of us have been going through health issues, job worries, money problems, family problems, worrying about loved ones, and on top of it all, wondering what this world is coming to. And yes, many of you are scared to death about what government is doing and what might befall on you because of some issue you are experiencing. I know that you can get very emotional and mental with all of these things that are going on right now. What a combination this is when our emotions and mental state come together in trying to figure this mess out.

My friends, when you live and make decisions from the mind of reason, logic, judgment, and from others long-established interpretations of God's written words, not counting what government has established what is best for you, your soul cannot bring forth the wisdom that you hold deep within your consciousness. Thus, you become more and more separated from your soul and to the wisdom it possesses.

It is not about intelligence, or your ability to be smarter than someone else, or if government, religion, and others know more than you, or if they can help you. It is not even how much you know about God or how much you do for your church. It is about knowing and being aware of your soul, who you truly are, and how the body and mind relates to your soul's wisdom. It is about being aware of your creations, from the food you eat, to what you believe are your truths and everything in-between.

If you believe in destiny, that you are a sinner, that you have to belong to a religion, or go to church, or that you are unworthy of miracles because of what you think you did, then you are processing who you truly are in an intellectual way, through the rational mind and not through your soul and "I AMness."

In what my soul has conveyed to me since my awakening is more than astonishing, so astonishing, that I felt that I needed to write this book in an effort to awaken you to the real truth about who you truly are and where you truly come from. You did not come from your human parents as you might think. Also, to the statement of who you truly are. Well! No matter your station in life or the name given you by your parents, you are indeed equal to God. Understanding this could lead to a wonderful life.

Because of my persistence in learning about myself, who God is, and what He wants for me, compared to someone else's point of view, I began to question the why of it all, including the creation of the universe and of Earth.

Now, as first, I was confused about what I was feeling. My head was even trying to push those feelings out because of what I was taught by my parents, the church, by science, and what I learned about physicality in school. However, by staying open minded to what I was receiving from my soul, I learned to unravel the mystery and the uncertainty behind it all, including God, his purpose, and the why we all bought in to religion and sin.

"Unlocking The Consciousness of Your Soul" is a book that reveals the deep secrets behind your suffering, the whys of wars, and that power and manipulation by government and religion have been the method used for brainwashing. It is a book that opens up the real truth about God, Satan, and Christ, including who you truly are, where you truly come from, and that you, no matter your station in life, are indeed equal to God and not less than.

This book will challenge you to the very core of your being. It will help you come face to face to what you have always accepted as your truths. A book that will certainly challenge your mind-set about everything that you have always been taught by your parents, by their parents before them, by government, by the educational system, and by the churches, for it all has been a big lie. Lies that have become so deeply hidden and rooted within your heart, that it took your soul to come up with a divine plan to unlock the memories of those lies.

The consensus of my soul, and that of the angelic realm, is that you have been journeying through time and space for a long time. However, now is the time for you to wake-up from your sleep and see how your beliefs, and those in power, have been lying to you? What Jesus mentioned over two thousand years ago was not about Him coming for your salvation. It was about the divine you suddenly coming out from behind your own ignorance, for the mystery of God can no longer be hidden from you because your soul is now willing to lay out God's covert plan for you to see. All that is left is your willingness to take the leap in consciousness to see it.

However, to see it, you must become a true master, like Jesus, in your own right and let go of your belief that you are only human, and that you only came from your parents. For this is your soul's untold story as much as it is mine. Your soul has been waiting for the "human ego" for a long time to evolve in consciousness to where you, while in the flesh, understand that the truth about who you truly are lies in understanding that you have no mind because all thoughts and beliefs come from a mental disposition, and not only from this lifetime but lifetimes past. .

We have forgotten that our soul has never ventured out beyond the gates of our divine oneness. It is only a mental perception on our part that we did, which is why we have this belief that we have sinned. Of course, that is the gift and the love that came from our spirit because our spirit desired to know all things.

From reading my soul's story, you too will walk away feeling that you are not trapped in a world of chaos and confusion because you will know exactly what to do next in creating all the miracles you can stand.

From what I have learned from my soul, and that of the angelic realm, is that we have actually overlooked our beliefs and how they have actually came from others, including our family, our religion, and what we were taught in our schools. And now, these beliefs have shaped our thoughts in to creating the world that we are experiencing today therefore, leaving out the desired life that we have always dreamed of experiencing.

So, if you are ready to move beyond your suffering, your concerns about life, and your pain forever, then by all means buy this book, and then stay tune to my website at www.terrynewbegin.com for more updates on expanding your consciousness beyond your physical senses.

Also, while you are on my website, and if you are ready to learn the real wisdom behind the Bible's Genesis and the Book of Revelations, then please read the template on them, watch their related videos, and you will learn how fear, punishment, and sin became the vehicle for power and control.

Now, allow me to help you open up to your soul and see what your soul has for you, for your journey and mine are similar, other than your soul's narrative account in what you chose for your divine plan.

Introduction

If I asked you your name, whether you are a male, female, black, white, yellow, red, or brown, if you believe in God and Satan, what your point of view is on sin and religion, and what you think about money, health, and power? What would be your answer? I do suggest that you think about these questions for a moment because how you choose to answer them could reveal the mystery behind why you suffer and cry out for miracles.

In fact, if you say that you believe in God, then in what way do you think about God, his laws, and how he allocates his miracles? Do you even feel worthy of God's miracles or do you believe that miracles only come to those that are good and upstanding people that go to a place of worship on a regular basis? How about the belief that God is fair when it comes to allotting his blessings and his miracles?

Dear reader, do you really believe that you were born a sinner? Have you really put any thought into that question? Do you believe, since you give your loyalty to a church, and because you are without money, that you will go to heaven? What about those that never attend church, visit a synagogue, and always have money, are they destined to a place of hell or somewhere in-between because of it? When religions say that you are part of God do they mean that you are equal to God or do they mean something totally different?

How do you view Jesus, or any holy name for that matter, that declare themselves, God? Are you a person that views what the church has declared as God as being the one and only Supreme God that is all-powerful, all-knowing, and the creator of all life, including the creator of you and your soul? Moreover, how do you view your soul, mind, and physicality anyway?

Were you given a soul and a mind when you were born on earth or has your soul and mind been around since your awakening back in the Garden? Or, for that matter, do you even believe that you were in the Garden?

How about a divine plan, not just for mankind, but for you too? Do you believe in a divine plan or are you one of those people that believe man was an accident and therefore just wondering around in life hoping things will turn out okay?

What about reincarnation? Do you believe that you come to earth over and over again in a different physical body? I have heard some people say that reincarnation does answer the questions when it comes to God's fairness in dealing with his creations and his blessings.

How about those that don't believe in God, heaven, hell, Jesus, or for that matter, any holy person, even the belief that one doesn't have a soul? Are you a person that is confused about what your soul does or is, or do you just believe that once you die that's it?

When I was baptized as a young boy I took on the belief that I belonged to the Catholic Church. Now, why is that? Do you think it was because of my parents and their parents before them being Catholic? I believe it was, and you know it was the same for you. I believed, since I was born into the family religion, that I was expected to observe, follow, and support the convictions of the Catholic Church. Isn't this true for most everyone that is born into a family religion?

The teachings I received from the Catholic Church were based on the promise made by Jesus that the church is guided by the Holy Spirit and protected from falling into any personal viewpoints that would distort or misrepresent those teachings. Therefore, everything that I was taught was based solely on the Catholic faith in what was written in the Bible and how it was presented to me by my parents, grandparents, and the church. As you can see, I know this would be true for most that is born into a family religion.

Now, when I reached the age where I attended public schools, I was taught that the mind, science, and mathematics were all that were needed to understand physical earth, to measure my life, what I wanted in life, and how to obtain what I wanted. Well! I have read and studied the Bible, and I have revisited what I was taught in school about the mind, mathematics, and how science rationalizes the physical world around me. What I have found is that Scripture, and what I have learned in school, is not what it is all made-out to be, for we all have been brainwashed.

For example: I have found that our religious leaders have been lying to us since the time man has been introduced to God, Satan, and Christ, and what God wants for us. I have also found that the more I studied Scripture, and revisited what I was taught in school, the more I discovered the divine plan and how the vibrational energy of good and evil, sin, and our rational mind has all been a big lie. It was my soul that revealed to me God's greatest kept secrets, and your soul can do the same for you.

I have discovered secrets so profound that when I was awakened to them I felt a spiritual frequency of such a high degree deep within my being that it ended up as being my soul. What my soul conveyed to me was more than astonishing, for my soul laid out before me my true beginning, where I truly came from, and that it was me, and not science, religion, or even God, who shaped and laid out my divine plan.

What I learned that day coming from my soul is that my real beginning was not from my parents or from a single white male God but went all the way back to the Garden. Now, at first, I was confused about what I was feeling coming from my soul. My head was trying to push that feeling out because of what I was taught by the church about God, and what I have learned about physicality in school.

However, because of my persistence in learning about myself, who God is and what He wants for me, compared to someone else's point of view in what is best for me, I began to question the why of it all, including what I was taught in school. In fact, studying of Scripture and revisiting what I was taught in school led me to ask myself a big question. "Who am I, really?" This question then led to another question. "Why was I born and for what purpose?" I even had thoughts about why there is so much suffering in the world. However, my big question was why is God such a mystery?

As you can see, our schools and our religions are a mess today. The biggest reason is because today's schools and religions are structured around old ideas and old beliefs. What do you think is going to happen when children are forced in a classroom approach where one teacher stands in front of many students trying to get each student to learn the same thought on a particular subject? What we, as adults, fail to see is what might be good to learn for one student may not be relevant to another.

Look, I have been an entrepreneur for a long time, and there is one thing that I have learned about having a room full of people having a discussion about something that may be relevant to one individual but is irrelevant to another. What happens is, if one does not understand, or is not interested, or how something may relate or don't relate to one's own goal or future, then one will not care about what you are discussing, and therefore will not work toward the benefit of the whole.

If one cannot see the relevance of the material covered in the meeting and has no desire to score political points with the boss, one will just sit there and tune out. Thus, the discussion becomes very boring to the one that cannot see the relevancy of the material, and therefore will show no interest or desire to learn.

If a child does not understand how knowing history, himself, or knowing why he needs to understand math, or know about his physicality, will help to address the concerns of his life, and he is not really interested in pleasing the teacher, then what do you think the child is going to do? You see, it is not so much about trying to please the teacher or understand who one is. It is about the teacher addressing the subject to fit into the concerns of the child, or in a business case, the employee.

As we all know, most children, as they work through their school years, do find topics of study that they really enjoy as well as not enjoy. However, no matter what the topic of study is, one can be poles apart from what the teacher is teaching them. The idea of matching individual interests to the schools fixed curriculum these days might seem impossible. The reasons are that students, as well as adults, clearly have different backgrounds, beliefs, and objectives, all because of one's religious training.

Of course, we can force the subject matter down the student's throat just like we do religion. But this only makes it appear relevant; however it does not make it beneficial to the student. Why? It is due to the student, after being taught by the teacher, forgetting about it. It is the same with religious training. Once the student becomes an adult they leave the church.

Therefore, instead of me pushing this repetitive high energy frequency out of my heart because of what I was taught by my parents, religion, and my school, I, without thinking, took a deep breath and invited in my soul to come closer to me. That is when I began to ask my soul even more questions than what I just asked you in the first few paragraphs.

Nevertheless, by reading the Bible myself, instead of someone telling me what it says, and then questioning what I was taught by my parents, religion, and government, as well as learning institutions, it actually became one of the best things that I ever did in my life. Not because of its spiritual message according to the views of my parents, or the church, or what I thought that I learned in school. It was because it developed a formula for me to question my core beliefs. At the same time, it set up a challenge for me to learn the real truth about who I am, what my purpose here on earth is all about, and why is it that I have to suffer.

Many of us overlook our purpose here on earth, why we suffer, and why religion present God as being such a mystery. Maybe it is because we are overshadowed by the stress of life, or some illness, or accident, or not having enough money, or maybe not having a good relationship with someone. You see, we overlook our purpose and what it means because we fail to notice the purpose of our own soul and why it was created in the first place.

Most of us look at our soul as a gift from God at birth and, if not at birth, then when we die. Because of my examining of these things, I have found the Bible, and what we are taught in school, as outdated. Why? It is because of how it leaves out the importants of our soul, our many lifetimes past, and how everything, including family, friends, government, businesses, and religion, interacts with our mind and human ego personality.

However, I do admit here, studying biblical scripture was what actually created the first step in me interacting with my own soul, which I must say happened quite unexpectedly. Now, I did not experience my soul through my human senses as if my soul was talking to me like it was standing next to me. I felt my soul intuitively through my thought patterns, and because of the knowledge and the wisdom being displayed in those thought patterns, it could only have come from a place of a much higher consciousness than my human ego consciousness.

That is when I realized I was more than what religions, my parents, the government controlled schools that I attended, and what science say about what I am made off. I have found that I am more than my human name and the education that I received in this lifetime. For instance: Most everyone is familiar with Genesis 1:27, *"God created man in his image; in the divine image he created him; male and female."*

Just by reading this verse you can see that it is your birthright and duty to question all authorities including your priest, rabbi, minister, or all religious leaders and teachers, even the Bible, God, Jesus, and all translators of the Bible, including your parents and family traditions when it comes to God, your government controlled schools, and what science say about the big bang. My dear friends, it all comes down to understanding that you have been brainwashed by our leaders for centuries.

Look, if Genesis 1:27 is indeed correct, then God created you, me, and everyone else, no matter if one is good or bad, in the divine image of Himself. It says that in the verse. If you are in God's divine image, then this makes you, me, and everyone else worthy of His love unconditionally, no matter what we do or did, even if it was appalling.

So, instead of me fighting, ignoring, and doubting my soul, I invited my soul (higher Christ self) in to join me in my human consciousness. And when I did, it was amazing, even to the point of mind-boggling, because that was the day when I learned the wisdom behind all of my choices, my experiences, and my suffering. I even asked my soul about this long confusing question that I know that everyone has asked. "Why does it seem like God overlooks those of questionable character and allows those that are of good character to suffer or die young?" And yes, my soul answered that question too.

What it comes down to is that we are so connected with our human name, our parent's traditions, our education and our intellect, and how we interpret our experiences because of our religious training. We actually overlook our beliefs and how they shape our world, therefore our experiences. If we are attached to our beliefs then we cannot know life other than what we are experiencing today, therefore leaving out the wisdom of our very own soul.

Chapter 1

Opening Up To Your Soul

The consensus of my soul is that we have been journeying through time and space for a long time, and now it is time for us to wake-up from our sleep and see how our beliefs, and those in power, have been lying to us. The lie is about us being only human, being unworthy of God's miracles, that we are sinners, that we need supervision, and about prayer. Praying, according to my soul, is a mental and emotional activity of the rational mind that says that we don't have it within ourselves to know and understand who we truly are at the human level, which is generally why prayers go unanswered, and why we don't heal.

My dear friends what Jesus mentioned over two thousand years ago was not about Him coming for your salvation. It was about the real you suddenly coming out from behind your own ignorance because the mystery of God can no longer be hidden from you. Your soul is now willing to lay out God's covert plan for you to see. All that is left is your willingness to take the leap in consciousness to see it.

For instance: When we look at something, anything, even our physical body, what we do not see is how it all splits up in to infinite possibilities, all of which exists simultaneously in other dimensions. We even have other etheric bodies in those many dimensions that are very healthy and know how to create miracles for us, and all that we have to do is bring them into our current reality; because reality is only energy in motion, therefore it is an illusion.

Most of you believe that God is a white, male personality unto himself, who created all things, including mankind; your soul, and that He lives in a heavenly place that is far from your reach. However, God is closer than you think. Religions, your parents, and governments have been lying to you for centuries about God's true identity, and where he lives. Of course, it was all done on an unconscious level.

You see, we have been trained to function in a certain way that tells us that we are only human, and that is why we understand matter or material substance as all that there is because of the way we perceive it. My dear friends, God is not a mystery, and He never was, for God's greatest secret is that we, as humans, are God, for the real God is our soul in disguise!

Now, let me make myself clear! The mystery of God and how we look at our physicality was introduced to us a long time ago by religion, science, and our governments (rulers) because of where we were in understanding ourselves and the world around us. However, it was appropriate for its time since the belief gave us stability and moral direction. Nevertheless, we have grown in consciousness since then because what we describe as God today is actually the consciousness of our soul and "all that we are" at all levels of our existence.

You see, the "human you," which is nothing but the ego personality disguised in the flesh, helps you blend into your environment without you knowing "who you truly are." It is your human ego and your rational mind that supports the feeling of being separate from your soul, from everyone else, and from everything that surrounds you, including your understanding of being solid.

My fellow searchers, your physical body is not as solid as you think, and this was proven by Einstein himself and other physicists. We all know that the physical body and physical reality is not real. In truth, it appears that you are both solid and non-solid, and therefore it becomes a question of how you perceive your ability to view your reality.

Reality only behaves according to universal laws and your perception of things because your higher divine mind is non-physical and non-mental, and therefore not subject to universal laws or physicality, which is very important for you to understand. The illusion of physicality allows the disguised human ego to express a belief in something that actually causes it to feel real so you can experience it. That's all!

By allowing the disguised human ego to feel separate from your soul and higher, divine mind, your soul gains the wisdom of your experiences at the human level, both good and bad. Once the human ego formulated this separateness from your soul and that of universal divine mind eons ago, the human ego ultimately became limited only to the belief systems of group consciousness and what you picked up through your experiences as you journeyed through time and space in many physical bodies.

Now, the question is how do you open up and reconnect to your soul and to this higher universal divine mind, for, my dear friends, your soul is the Christ you seek.

Now, I do not mean to confuse you here, but the truth is that God is really a Goddess. God is just a symbol of your connection to universal divine mind and to the wisdom of your soul. You see, what gives the universal, divine mind life, or life to God if you will, is your spirit consciousness, the Goddess. This concept will be explained more as you read on in the book but for now allow my soul to continue.

The only way to open up and reconnect to your soul consciousness is for you to connect to your wisdom and to the Christ that you are. How do you do that? You do it by the human you raising its vibrational signature to meet up with your soul's vibrational signature. It would be like your physical body traveling less than the speed of light and your soul traveling at the speed of light.

So, if you learn to raise your human consciousness to a higher level, you then reconnect to your soul that is traveling at the speed of light. To do this, you have to have the courage to let go of all of your beliefs, everything that you have been taught by your parents, teachers, and especially your religion. By letting go of your beliefs you will find the greatest truths. Once you move into your divine or Christ consciousness, you can actually move faster than the speed of light.

For example: The human rational mind is nothing but the center for mental impressions that are only based on opinion and thought patterns that carries within them a dense impenetrable intellectual vibrational energy signature that only perceives you as a human who is unworthy of being a divine expression of the Spirit of One. This is why you suffer and create the things you experience in life.

This dense, impenetrable, intellectual energy signature is of a mental process that deals only with rational thought, analyzing, duality, judgment, emotions, and the belief that intelligence only comes from education, and of the mind. However, what we are not aware of in what we perceive as our mind is that this is actually a mental version of a mind that we identify as real. My dear friends, we, in truth, have no mind. What we do have is our connection to universal divine mind or what we all happen to call God.

You see, you have forgotten that the universe is not really solid but is nothing but a mental manifestation, and therefore not truly real. So, what you consider as your mind is nothing more than your brain, for the brain belongs to this world of duality and that of flesh, which is why you have a left and right brain hemisphere. Therefore, the only way for you to overcome this dense energy dualistic signature of a mental nature is by way of self-generated masked personality-aspects of you that consist of many storied lifetimes where your soul cloths them with a physical body.

This process allows your soul to journey through time and space in many different lifetimes creating stories for you to learn and understand life, responsibility, and how to overcome the forces of duality. Once this is understood from the human level then the chaos and confusion that you are experiencing today is finally removed. Hence, no more suffering, just great miracles.

Why no more suffering? It is because your consciousness can move faster than the speed of light, which then allows you to bring into expressions those potentials of joy, health, and abundance. All that it takes is trusting in yourself as a divine being and a true creator God in your own right, leaving behind all of what you have been taught by your parents, your religious leaders, and your government.

Since us humans have collectively agreed that everything around us is real and solid, including a God that created us, the belief in it causes it to feel real even though it is all an illusion, a hologram that we take as being solid and real. The illusion of us feeling separated from our soul has allowed the soul to gain overwhelming wisdom through the experiencing of many lifetimes playing with the belief of positive and negative as being real.

Because we chose separation and duality over our divine state long ago (illustrated by Adam and Eve), we, as in all humans, created our world in a way that defines us today. Thus everything we see in this world, together with good, bad, sin, religion, and our governmental societies, we have helped participate in their creation, even though we may not be conscious of it from the human level. Even the battles of many wars throughout history, the human ego of today helped create them.

For Instance: When we chose to separate our soul's divine nature, the Christ self, to a human belief in duality, we changed our energy frequency signature into what is called today light and dark, and then on to good and evil. Once we began to experiment with the dark side of this dual energy, we began to fear it. (Adam and Eve's eating of the apple is the metaphorical example of it). This fear was so great that we wanted to move back into our divine state again.

However, it was too late! Our belief in this dualistic energy at the time was too strong for us to return home to our "I AM Divine State." So, we had to move forward. Hence, our "soul's consciousness of a divine state" and our creation of a "consciousness of a mental state" became integrated into a mental perception of us having a rational mind that now carries the forces of positive and negative. And now, both our "divine state and our mental perception of positive and negative," has become the essence of our total being – for they are now as "one consciousness."

It took your soul (icon for Christ), your part in universal mind (icon for God), and self-awareness to move you outside of your "soul consciousness of a divine state" and into an outer superficial mental consciousness (human) that held a belief in duality as the means to understand life, good and bad, right and wrong, and to answer the question, "Who am I?" It was the masked human ego, represented by the serpent in the Garden, that has made it possible for you to move beyond your divine state and into a two and three-dimensional body and on a three-dimensional planet for the testing of positive and negative (the eating of the apple).

My dear friends, it was perfect because it gave your soul, by way of the human ego, an avenue to explore all the unknown principles of duality because it brings to you the understanding of responsibility, the wisdom of understanding your choices, and it helps to identify you as a true Christ in your own right. The old saying that "God knows all things" cannot ring true enough without the masked human ego participating in choosing duality and physical earth as a means to appreciate and understand all things, including joy, pain, and suffering.

You see, in the beginning of our earthly life a long time ago, when we feared the forces of the wind, fire, cold, rain, the sun, and the air we breathed, especially when those elements of nature became harmful and damaging, it reflected back to us our dark creations because we, in our mental and emotional state, had no way to control any of them. So, in order to appease these wild and uncontrollable forces, we began to call them gods.

From that point we, all humans, began to offer these gods sacrifices, believing that we would be saved from their fury and the intense viciousness that they brought. However, as time passed, we learned that our sacrifices did not work, for our dark creations kept on haunting us thereby evoking those dark and fearful creations to come to us again but in a much stronger force than before, especially our emotions of guilt, shame, unworthiness, and that we are prone to do bad and evil things.

The more we pushed our dark creations out of our head, especially the darker ones, the more the dark forces pushed back at us, eventually becoming our human beastly nature, which religions happen to call the devil. Because of seeing ourselves as a victim, we began to deny these dark emotions within ourselves to the point of projecting them onto others, blaming them for our failures and the way we felt. This blaming game created a force of responsibility and accountability (sowing and reaping in the Bible), where in the end, the hurt inside of us began to be expressed within our light creations, thereby distorting even our light creations as well.

For Instance: Love, trust, and that we are the creator of our experiences, became confusing and difficult to understand as it led to the distortion of our light creations. Thus ushering into our life experiences, where love, trust, power, and our ability to create, became very limited. Therefore, not only did we avoid our dark creations at all cost, we reluctantly moved toward our light creations with even greater caution thus seeking counsel because we feared them as much as our dark creations.

This all led to where we began to deny half of who we were, creating such a strong emotion of sin it led to the perception that we were small, powerless, limited, and unworthy, a sinner that is in need of a savior. So, soon thereafter, we, all humans acting as one, created religion as our counsel to give us advice and support. Religion then became our next belief system in attempting to explain where we came from, who created us, and why do we create bad things.

That is when we concluded that we were imperfect thus calling our dark creations evil thereby banning them as sins against God, which religion said was our creator. This meant that we literally banned half of who we truly are, which caused us to become out of balance. Then we began to hide our dark creations (sins) and did everything within our power to control them because we wanted to be accepted by society, our family, and that we belonged somewhere, like to some religion that held the same beliefs, values, and concerns.

It was religion that told us that these dark creations would send us into a hell of fire forever, creating such a fear approach to our belief systems, we soon became locked into a consciousness that good is something that comes from God, and all that is bad and evil comes from the Devil. That is when religion realized they could join up with kings, rulers, and governments to control us, using fear and punishment as the foundation for their power.

Because of our soul's divine state of persistence, and its resolution to remember, we, the group collective consciousness of the mass, unconsciously agreed that we desired another chance to remember our true "I AM" identity. Hence, deep within our soul, our desire to remember remained, thus allowing Jesus to appear on earth to tell us who we were.

However, because of Jesus being killed, it meant that his presence on earth and his message was not accepted by mankind. And yet, Jesus' presence on earth had planted the Christ seed deep within our soul's consciousness, telling us that we are more than what we think, which took more than two thousand years before its germination took hold within our outer superficial human mental consciousness.

My fellow searchers, you are the master artist of your life – for you are the mystery and the secret behind God and her world of miracles, and these miracles exists only through you and not Jesus, which is why you are the only one that can bring them into your life. Your human experiences are truly a work of art and now, it is time to allow your soul to unlock the secrets deep within your consciousness.

However, to become a true master, like Jesus, in your own right and a bringer of many miracles to experience, you must remember "who you truly are," "where you truly came from," and "let go of your human belief that you are only human," and that you only came from your parents – for this is your soul's untold story as much as it is mine. Once you awaken to the masked human ego, to your Spirit, to your Soul, to your connection to Universal Divine Mind, and to your human personality-aspects from past lifetimes, and integrate them as "one body of consciousness," you will become a true master in your own right just like Jesus did.

Your soul has been waiting for the human ego for a long time to evolve in consciousness to where you, while in the flesh, understand that the truth about who you truly are lies in understanding that you have no mind because all thoughts come from a mental disposition, including from your past lifetimes. It is just that you are missing from being conscious of "who you truly are" because of being too busy worshipping your mental perception of a mind and a God that is not real.

The chaos we see around the world today is a sign that the human aspect wants a change because religion, the bible, our family, the media, and the governments of the world cannot offer us anything more – for they are all broken and outdated. Even the measurement of how we look at time is outdated. No longer can they take away our responsibilities (sins) because the human aspect and our soul is the mystery behind the real identity of Christ.

When you learn how to invite your soul back into your life, and leave behind the God of perception, that is when the miracles will begin to happen for you – for indeed, your soul is the Christ that is missing in your life. All that is required is the human ego to move beyond what the perceptional mind is telling you – for you are all of your experiences from the past and yet, none of them are the total you.

So, how long will you wait until you begin to sense your own soul, the Christ you are, and allow it to be fully present in your life? Remember, the human aspect that you are today only represents about three to five percent of "all that you are." However, you cannot discover the other ninety-two or ninety-five percent unless you come to terms with who you are not.

My dear seekers, the ending of this strong dualistic energy cycle is fast approaching and we can celebrate it by allowing the year 2012 to come to pass without looking at it as if Jesus is coming to save us. However, there are many of us that are not willing to let go of the old dualistic ways in seeing oneself as a sinner because they have not yet have had the deep calling of one being more than just a human.

Therefore, these people will remain in their old ways in experiencing their pain, and they will do it by playing more with the drama energy and how they want to experience it. But, as for those that have the calling to move beyond this old dualistic energy, they will prosperous beyond their own expectations.

So, if you are ready, let's make this journey together, and while you are at it, invite in your soul to participate in helping you understand what you are about to read – for it is truly your "untold story" as well.

Now, I ask you, do you have the courage to come face-to-face with who you truly are or would you rather stay in the frame of thought that feels more comfortable to you? If you are indeed ready, then the best way for me to tell you the story is convey it to you the way my soul conveyed it to me about "my beginning as a child of God a long time ago when I was in the first creation, and then right on up to my ascension of today."

Once you understand this, you too will see that my journey through time and space as a child of God is indeed similar to yours, with the exception of your human stories (lifetimes) and how you chose to play them out.

Chapter 2

The Challenge

Have you ever asked why one is born into a family that is rich and educated while another is born into a family that is poor and uneducated? Or, why is one born into a family that was ill-treated, physically, mentally, or both? How about being born physically challenged or as an orphan? How about born in the most repressive regimes? Or, how about those born ugly while another beautiful? What sin did they all commit to be born into this world that way?

It does appear like there are a lot of things that one seems to be battling with in life today because of where one was born. As you can see, some are still suffering because of it. Just look at the African nations where people are literally starving. What sin did they commit to merit such suffering? Can you answer the why of it all without bringing God, or the phrase, "that's the way it is," or judgment into the subject?

Even if you mention God it still comes hard to answer the question without using logic, emotions, or reasoning. Of course, due to our emotional ties to our belief systems, most people will always try to answer the questions intellectually. Why? It is due to our perception of life and who we think we are compared to God.

Many of you at one time or another has perhaps felt like giving up on life just because of all the bad things not letting up. After all, it does seem like things are getting worse as far as the economy, the politicians, terrorists, earthquakes, tornados, fires, and those nasty and ruthless storms that don't even show mercy for anyone, not even for the poor, the handicap, or even those who are starving in Africa.

Many of you are saying right now that you don't feel safe anymore. Some are even asking where God is in all of this chaos, especially those who are suffering with such emotional anguish. How about you? Do you feel that you are trapped in a world of chaos and confusion and don't know what to do, where to go, or who to talk to?

Religions say to move toward God for your answers, admit that you are a sinner, ask for forgiveness, and then take up the Bible and go to church – for that is where you will find your answers and your salvation. Do you really believe by telling those in Africa who are literally starving to death, seemingly without end, that they can find their salvation in the Bible, and in a church that tells them never to sin?

Religions maintain that the Bible spells it out unequivocally that we suffer because of sin. Well! What sin did those babies in Africa commit to deserve starvation and the illnesses they suffer? Or, babies that are born in other countries, even America, without fault of their own, starting life off as being addictive to drugs or other ghastly things? How about babies born with no arms, legs, and without eyes? What sin did they commit?

Can you answer these questions without trying to get too intellectual and righteous with your answers? After all, what makes you so special to be born healthy, and in a country that serves you well?

My fellow seekers, what we are seeing and experiencing today has nothing to do with God's laws, sin, the end days, or about Jesus returning to earth to collect those that feel they are blameless. The real truth is that religion, man, and government have always made everything complex, puzzling, and mysteries when it comes to God, Satan, one's Soul, one's intellect, and how we all should be managed, but largely sin and suffering. Of course, the best way to hide the real truth is for you to remain obsessed with fear, punishment, and guilt.

By religion, with the help of governments, around the world keeping you locked into the conventional belief about God, family, sin, karma, and how you need them, those in authority preserve their power in setting up the ground rules to control your belief systems, thus manipulating your reality in what you will experience. With the conditioning of the rational mind, through religion, education, science, and government, the probability of you experiencing confusion, anxiety, drama, and lack of miracles is actualized by nearly one hundred percent just because of the way you will measure your belief systems and self-worth.

Therefore, to step into the consciousness of "mastering your own life," is to understand "who you truly are, where you truly come from, and then realize that you gave up free choice a long time ago" because you have tied it to your thoughts of duality, to your church, to your family beliefs, friends, and to the government. You see, the soul you, does not belong to this world and therefore, it does not belong to a church, religion, or your family beliefs. In fact, the soul you don't care what you should do today or tomorrow. All that your soul cares about is the experience.

Your rational mind knows how you believe and think, which then sets up who you believe you are – for you are what you think and believe in. If you believe with all your heart in the forces of duality and in a God of punishment, then that is what you will experience in life. It's that simple!

For instance: My human story starts off in 1948 where, for a brief moment, my human identity was not known to my parents, my brothers, or to the world. Then a few minutes later, my parents celebrated my birth by giving me a name. With this name I was then introduced to my family, myself, and to the world. However, what was unknown to me and to my family at the time, other than my human name, was what my story was going to consist off for this lifetime.

Now, the church would say that my life story began somewhere after my baptism – for my baptism, by all accounts, set my story up to become a Catholic and a believer of Jesus as my Lord and Savior, thus setting me up as a sinner already before I even uttered my first words. This means, unconsciously, and as a child of God, I agreed to a belief system and a reality that my suffering had already began before I made my first choice as a human. Thereby, through this act by my parents, and that of religion, it became the first step in me giving away my "free will."

Through baptism, not only did I become a supporter of my parent's belief systems, I also became a personality limited to following the rules that were established by the Catholic Church – for it was to be my ticket to heaven when my story (life) ended.

Now, other than my story starting off as a sinner, and the family lacking money, I was born and raised in a tiny house that managed to squeeze in seven people. Moreover, as I grew older in the belief of being poor my future for further education was in doubt thereby, I was already preconditioned to fail. However, once I graduated from high school, and with a few years working as a laborer, I began to believe that maybe I could make it in the business world as an entrepreneur.

Of course, I asked myself at the time, "Where am I going to get the money to launch a business because my family has no money and I know of no one that would loan it to me? Nevertheless, even though I was young and naïve, and took on the belief of being poor and uneducated, it did not mean that I lacked the skills to start a business over someone that was born into money and had a business degree. It came down to believing in myself more than where I was born, or if I had a business degree, or if I had access to money.

Anyway, the year was 1971 and I was in my early twenties before money finally found me. It found me by me taking on three partners in addition to myself, and since I was the one with the experience and the one with a plan, I became the president of the company. However, the business lasted three and half years before it went belly-up in April 1975, which led to bankruptcy, not just for the company, but I had to file on a personal note as well.

It was devastating to me at the time but my passion to be in business prevailed, which is why eight short months later (December 1975) I went back into business for the second time. However, this time it was with one partner, and it lasted from December 1975 to spring of 1993 before my world once again was turned upside down – for I was thrown out of my own company because of an unsigned agreement with my partner. It was a time when I believed God really had forsaken me because it hurt.

At first, my thoughts went to God and how I threw him out of my life at a very young age. And because of it, I justified to myself the lack of God's miracles in my life. It was a time (spring 1993) when I actually began to fear God on a level of such anxiety and dismay that I thought I was literally doomed. I even had thoughts about attending church again, wondering if maybe I could save myself and my family from God's wrath and my stupidity.

However, even though I was feeling and thinking this, something was still eating at me. I began to feel that my failures had nothing to do with my former partners, where I was born, my education, me believing in God, or even my stupidity. You see, following several months of prayer, despair, blaming, and allowing my mind putting me down, I began to sit still and take a few deep breaths. At first, it was only a few minutes a day, and then I finally worked up to about thirty minutes a day.

Now, while I was doing this deep breathing, unconsciously knowing of their latter effects, I still felt my mind for several more months putting me down as a failure before I began to notice that my mind was beginning to slow down as far as downcasting me. Even my thoughts of blame and betrayal began to slow down. That was the time when I really felt my emotions on a conscious level and how out of balance I had become.

Yes, failing twice in business and losing my income hurt. Not only because of feeling betrayed by the person that I had always considered my friend and spiritual advisor. It hurt because I felt angry, clumsy, foolish, stupid, and frustrated at myself for being the laughing target for him and others. Yes, many people had a good laugh on my account. However, what hurt the most was that I believed that I let my family down.

So, instead of trying to be positive and force those feelings out of my mind I allowed those emotional hurt feelings to come into my heart. I remember saying to myself, "Yes, it hurts, and I am angry, but I and my family are okay.

Then one day, while sitting still doing some deep breathing, I began to feel someone talking to me. When I first felt this vibrational forum around me, I thought that maybe my mind had fallen into the mode of making things up. And yet, in spite of what my mind was judging it to be, I could feel the sincerity of my soul because somehow I knew it was not coming from my rational mind – for I felt it deep within my heart.

It was then that I felt my soul intuitively conveying to me: *"I am you at a higher level – for I am your soul and I have come forward to help you learn of who you truly are. I am here at this time for your awakening, and to reveal to you the true nature of how to create miracles, and the why of it all being a mystery to you. It is not about your business, education, where you were born, your intelligence, your intellect, your failures, or about God. It is about the wisdom that you have learned from every experience and encounter that you have had with yourself, with your past lifetimes, and with others."*

It was from that point I decided to let God, and all ties to religion, go, and to trust only in what I was feeling coming from my own soul. Once I let everything go, including what religion and government wanted for me, as well as what I was taught by my parents, and others, as far as my beliefs, it was in that moment when I felt my soul cradling me. And before I knew it, my soul conveyed to me again:

"Along your path of many lifetimes contains the wisdom of your experiences, and when you place "all that you are" as in this lifetime only because of your beliefs, upbringing, and who you think you are, then I, your soul, cannot bring forth the wisdom of those experiences to you. And, because of it, you and I have been separated. Being aware of "who you truly are," is more important than all the treasures, education, and power in the world."

It was from my deep breathing that finally reconnected me to my soul, and my soul did not care about my intelligence, money, success, fame, God, religion, or wanting me to be smart. All that my soul wanted was for me to become "aware" of "who I truly am" – for I am not only human, I am a divine being, a Christ also, and so are you. Once I understood this, then miracles came to me automatically with no effort.

It was right after I received these messages, my soul indicated to me again that, *"Once you understand this, then all of those things and more will come to you automatically anyway because you would be "aware" of who you are, therefore drawing toward you all that comes with the knowing of who you truly are."* That my dear friends is when I realized there was nothing to fix about me, perhaps other than a little love and care for myself.

It was in that moment when I decided to open up another business for the third time and become a competitor to my former partner. So, in the fall of 1993 I incorporated my new company and worked out of my home until the spring of 1994, which I then made enough money to move into a leased building. From April 1994 to December 1994, my sales were about $94,000 dollars. Today (2012), my business annual sales are in the millions, I have written two books, and the third book, you are reading it now.

My friends, if you believe in destiny, that you are a sinner, that you have to belong to a religion, or go to church, or that you are unworthy of miracles because of where you were born, or that you are not educated enough, then you are processing who you truly are in an intellectual way, through the rational mind and not through your soul.

Intellectual energy coming from the rational mind will always teach that you must make a choice according to who you believe you are and what you have been taught by others, like your parents, religion, and the educational system, as well as what constitutes your human identity in this lifetime.

Throughout this whole ordeal from the time I was born to my mid fifties, I have learned the hard way before I found the secret behind God's miracles. The secret! True miracles don't come from God, or others, or your religion, or your education, or government, they come from you because the real God is indeed universal (no persona). It is your soul that is the Christ that you have been waiting for.

So, stop and look at your issues and see why you struggle through life. Sit back, do some deep breathing, and allow your soul to come in and join you, showing you the patterns of your dogmatic beliefs and how you have been following them because of tradition.

Believe me! When you learn to move beyond your rational mind and its dogmatic beliefs, your soul essence will make its appearance. It will not care if you are a king, a queen, a president of a country, or that you are a pauper, a drunk, a drug addict, or a non-believer of God, or just an ugly sinner, because all that your soul wants is to join you and show you how divine you are no matter what you did.

There are many among us that try to reason with this icon of God, his Bible, and his mysterious ways, and what we seem to overlook is the rational mind and how it follows to the letter the rules that were set down by man, religion, science, governments (kings), our educational system, and our family history of beliefs a long time ago. What is not thought about is the rational mind obeys what we think we are and what we have already decided to believe as our reality.

Therefore, the rational mind will automatically see chaos and disorder as something that needs to be organized and fixed. The best way that was found by the rational mind to organize it was to invent a God like person with supernatural power in order to understand it and yet, all that man was trying to do is understand his own mind.

Because of how the deceptive and rational mind works, which is metaphoric for the anti-christ in Revelations, you have been overlooking the real truth about God and your soul. God is not a supreme white male being unto himself or even a Hebrew God but is a result of pure universal mind. Your soul consciousness is waiting for the human ego to open up and become aware of it.

My fellow seekers, to master your own life and bring in the miracles you seek I suggest that you take a good look and see why you confine yourself to a prison like mentality. I did, and I was greatly surprised by learning that my prison was that I was hiding from my own soul (Christ). Yes indeed, I actually found that I held a belief in a God that came from a mental perception of what I thought He should be, and therefore what I should be.

I used a belief in fear, unworthiness, where I was born, not intellectual or educated enough to be heard, or successful, as well as a belief in sin, and I allowed my emotions get the best of me when it came to family and friends. However, once I was enlightened by my soul, I then proclaimed my authentic identity and my "Sovereignty," and began to create multitudes of miracles for myself. And yes, your soul will certainly take you out of your comfort zone.

So, believe me, when I say this! Even if you are a devoted follower of this icon of God found in the Bible, that you attend church regularly or belong to a special religion, and that you are devoted to your political party, you too, will one day (either in this lifetime or another) come to a point where you will want a change, because you, like me, will too finally give up and let this God, his laws of duality, sin, and your affiliation to your political party go.

To discover your soul's story and the real you, you must learn to move beyond the intellectual emotional formulas of the mental mind (brain), that of science, who you think you are, the educational institutions, government, religion, family history, your dogmatic beliefs, and then move beyond the idea of Jesus coming for your salvation. You could say it is about letting everything you know or have been taught, go, even the dissolving of yourself because that is where you will find the greatest truths.

Like me, your soul too has a story to tell and mine, like yours, is twofold, because all humans have two stories to tell. You have a story that is tied to this lifetime and your soul has a story about "your personal journey through time and space."

My dear friends, we, as humans, have always looked at ourselves as not being equal to God, and to top it off, we are told that we are helpless sinners that are in need of a savior. As a result of this belief, what is being misunderstood is that our human consciousness is only being fed just enough energy by our soul to keep our three-dimensional human identity alive. Thus, keeping our awareness of who we truly are so limited that we end up becoming locked in it because of our belief that some God created us, and that our physical reality is all that there is.

Come to trust in your soul and awaken to who you truly are and let go of who you are not. You are not a sinner and you never were. It's all been a big lie! But a lie that was necessary in order for your soul to gain the wisdom of your choices and experiences. So, don't ever think that you've had such a difficult life that there is no possible way for your soul to come into your life and help you, for your soul is the Christ and your spirit is who you truly are, and they both want to come into your life to work with you as one.

In my years of living, I have learned that the distress and worry I experienced have indeed been the cause of not knowing "who I am." So, take stock of your soul and forgive yourself. Make a choice, take deep breaths, and feel your beliefs in each choice you make, and when you do, the results may surprise you.

I tell you my story to illustrate how most of us put all of our faith in a God of duality that lives outside of us and in a book where He will come and save us, someday. A someday that will never come because the rational mind will always move toward the belief in a name that is higher than self. When we compromise our true nature for a God that lives in a book, and is outside of us, we become a slave to our rational mind, and to others, in offering reason and logic as the means to what we think is right and wrong, and what we deserve in life. The results are nothing but pain and suffering.

The more you act from fear, worry, emotions, and doubt, the more you become disconnected from your soul – for it is the soul, not some God or religion, government, educational system, family, friend, or business that brings you health, joy, safety, abundance, and all the miracles you can stand.

Allow your soul to take away your thoughts of fear, distress and limitations, and replace them with thoughts of focus, awareness, compassion, intuition, and imagination, and the process of remembering who you truly are. By taking deep breaths and inviting in your soul, and not some God that lives in a book, you will no longer need to tell your story about why you are hurting. You are the source (God) of your miracles. It is you, and only you that can heal the pain and suffering you are experiencing and no one else, not even Jesus.

When you finally let go of your mental prison of beliefs and allow your soul to move into your human temple, you will move beyond the mind of intellectual energy. That is when all your tears of hurt and suffering will end. You will find that it is not your education, government, or your belief in God that brings you wealth, health, or joy. It is your soul – for the soul is your wisdom in hiding.

You see, ever since the beginning, when we first left the garden and became a consciousness of two, we have been searching for God and our share of the divine. However, what has not been realized is that we have been searching for ourselves because of the question we asked a long time ago, "Who Am I?" This search for God, and our share of the divine, has led us into some excessive and overstated life experiences that became very challenging to our soul.

This challenge has caused us to create many games that were played in the astral realms first where we tried to take over another soul in order to increase our energy, wisdom, and the understanding of spirit and our divine nature. This action caused a deep belief that God's divine energy somehow could be brought into us through force, thus we became overly aggressive in taking over another soul's energy. Well, it did not work because no one can imprison or kill another souled being for the sake of stealing one's divineness, at least in the long run.

So, when the game of battling each other became old in the astral realms, we, all souled beings, started to come to earth to play the games out all over again. But this time, we did it in physical form so we could feel and understand our choices. Our quest at the time was to find God (the source of our power) however we could, which then led to the philosophers in those days to proclaim that the mystery of God lies within the rational mind.

This belief continues today, which is why our mind of reason has become our God thus limiting us on the physical level and yet, something deep within us is telling us that we are more than what we are seeing, smelling, touching, tasting, and hearing. We are more than our physical senses, because indeed, we are all a divine being. It is just that we have forgotten.

My fellow seekers, with the help of the angelic realm and the art of me correlating with my own soul, which you can do too, I will answer the question of "who you truly are" by taking you through an exceptional journey that will not only help you find the true meaning of God and his divine nature. I will help you discover how creative and masterful you are in creating your own life story here and now.

From this journey that you are about to partake in, you will not only discover your soul and how it desires to be part of your human life. You will also discover the "art of mastering your life" is indeed about learning who God is, who you are, the purpose of your existence, the divine plan, and how creative you are. So, take several deep breaths and let's begin this journey together. You have tried to figure God out using your rational mind, and now the time has come for you to take a different approach.

Chapter 3

The Beginning

(Where Did I Truly Come From?)

Where did I truly come from? Where was my beginning? What a great questions to ask your soul. I did, and the answers I received wasn't quite what I expected – for my soul conveyed to me that my true beginning was not with my parents but began a very long time ago when I was first awakened (born) from out of myself in a place called the First Creation. Most of us call it the Garden of Eden.

Now of course, that answer puzzled me a bit because I was under the idea that I came from my human parents, and that it was my ancestors that came from the Garden of Eden, not me. Next, as I sat quietly in my chair taking deep breaths over what I just received from my soul. I intuitively felt my soul expressing to me again:

"You have been programmed for hundreds of centuries to come from a rational persuasive and susceptible mind when it comes to understanding God, your human self, where you come from, why you are here on earth, and who created you. And now, you are ready to unlock your consciousness memories to who you truly are, where you truly come from, and who truly

created you." It was from that point my soul began to inform me of my beginning, and it was long before I was born into this lifetime.

My soul began by taking me all the way back to the very beginning of my first awakening as a souled being – for I, in fact, as well as you, was part of the First Creation, known to many as the Garden of Eden. This means I was around long before earth, the physical universe, before my physical parents, and even before the name God or my religion was part of my consciousness.

However, before my soul took me back to where I made my first appearance in the first creation (garden), my soul conveyed to me these words: "*My human aspect, (referring to my human identity in this lifetime) you do not realize that you were personally part of the story of creation foretold by the prophets in Genesis. It is just that you have forgotten because of your many lifetimes on Earth. So, allow your human ego to open up to me about what you have been taught on the subject. Allow me, your soul, to introduce myself to you – for "I AM" of no name that will assist you in unlocking your consciousness to who you truly are.*"

Now, instead of me speaking in third party expressions – for it can get rather confusing, I will instead convey to you what my soul conveyed to me as if your soul is speaking to you directly also. This will allow me to be very clear and more precise with my presentation to you in what my soul revealed to me.

However, before I begin, I like to ask you to take a moment (ten to fifteen minutes) and do some very important deep breathing. Take a deep breath through your nose, take it all the way down into your stomach, and then release it through your mouth. This will help bring in your soul (higher Christ self) by raising the vibrations of your human ego so you can feel the energy in what is being said here.

So, assuming you did this deep breathing, let's begin! Throughout history religion, with the help of kings, rulers, and governments, has shaped, molded, and defined God, Jesus, and the Spirit of One as a way to control and influence the process of keeping mankind asleep to the real truth, all because of power. Since most people are familiar with the text in Genesis and its historical account concerning man, earth, and how we were conceived and formed, then the story of creation foretold by the prophets plays an essential part in what we all believe about ourselves, God, Satan, Earth, good and evil, and our beginning.

Man has always pondered over his origin, his soul, his purpose, why he's here on earth, his suffering, and if he is good enough to make it to heaven when he dies. Religion has always taught that the Bible is God's word entrusted to them in handing down the written word that was taught by the prophets. Religion states, and I paraphrase here, whatever was written in scripture has been written for man's instructions, how he should act, worship, pray, and follow to the letter the word of God.

So, I ask you! Is it meant for you to never understand the Bible, God, Satan, Earth, or why you are even here on earth unless it is studied and presented to you only from an intellectual and conceptional point of view? Don't you think you are being taken for granted here? Why would you want to limit yourself to only abstract thinking and reasoning, and only to religious views?

What man and religions have overlooked and ignored for centuries is the true nature of God is absolute, divine, compassionate, unchangeable, as in unconditional, and is in the form of Spirit Consciousness first and foremost, and that God is but Universal Divine Mind. Thus, the remnants of what man describes as God is nothing more than man-made, including man's idea of God's laws, sin, and the physical universe.

This means God's true "composition," which is very important here to understand, is that God is a Goddess or Spirit Consciousness only, and that her makeup consists of all souled beings (you and me) that are infinite and divine in nature, and that we transform this pure unadulterated universal energy into a molded composition. Be it a star, a planet, an animal, a physical body, the air breathed, and even a car, a table – for all things manifested, physical and non-physical, comes from all souled beings in transforming this pure unadulterated universal energy into a variety of manifestations.

Therefore, the God that you understand as a white male supreme being who created you and all things is not an individual personality unto himself but is the makeup of all souled beings because you, I, and all angels and humans alike, are souled beings first and foremost. Therefore, you, I, and all angels and humans alike, are infinite, unchangeable, and divine in nature. Otherwise, there would be no you, me, life, or earth.

Religions has been describing God, since his inception of long ago, from a dualistic and psychological manner, existing only in the rational mind, without having any physical evidence, that God is an actual person unto himself and the one that created all of us and all things. Of course, Christian believers have proclaimed Jesus as the physical evidence of God in the flesh and yet, Jesus has always expressed himself as pre-existing those who he spoke with while he was on earth.

John the apostle, who walked with Jesus, wrote that Jesus was with God in the very beginning, even before earth and man (John 1:1-5). In John 17:5, he writes *"and now, father, glorify me in your presence with the glory I had with you before the world began."*

As you know, man has always looked upon God and Jesus as *one* and the same personality. Perhaps it comes from the idea when Jesus proclaimed in John 10:30 that *"he and the father are one."* If this is true, then let me ask you this! Where do you think man, earth, the fish of the sea, the birds of the air, the animals, trees, water, the air you breathe, and what you see as stars, planets, galaxies, and universes come from?

What constitutes the "composition" of these things? Is it energy or are these things and man animated by some magical force or power that only comes from Jesus? If God, and or Jesus, is/was the original expression of creation, the divine spark, then God would have to be also the pause between the desire to create and the beginning itself. Do you agree?

So, because creation exists, then Universal Mind (God) has to be the explosion and the Spirit of One (Goddess) has to be the implosion, the movement and the motivating spark because it takes awareness, imagination, expression, compassion, and focus, not withstanding sacred geometry, to bring anything and everything into existence, including your human identity, mankind as a whole, even Jesus and the Kingdom of One.

If you look at God as representing universal divine mind, and as the out-breath that brings forth this pure unadulterated neutral energy that the son (all souled beings) delivers, like planting a seed, to the Goddess side of himself for expression, then the Goddess side of you, or your spirit, is the in-breath that is never-ending, and that you have no mind other than your connection to universal divine mind (God).

Therefore, since you are in the image of God and the Goddess, then the in-breath of your spirit (the Goddess) is the divine mother and the womb of all your creations awaiting the awareness of your "I AMness of no name" to trigger the God side of you (your connection to universal divine mind) in manifesting your choices.

Since you are in the direct image of the Goddess, then your choices must consist of you having compassion, unity, focus (power) and that your expressions and creations must consists of pure unadulterated neutral energy, which then causes the out-breath of form to appear (something of structure, like earth or the physical body).

My dear friends, the mother-father God that you understand as a single solitary white male Hebrew God that created everything and everyone is not a personality unto himself but is a Goddess acting as the "Spirit of One" in encompassing everything – for nothing is left out, not even energy.

More plainly, God is not a person, deity, or a being of supernatural abilities. God is a Goddess that has a composition of an infinite spirit, a soul consciousness, and is part of a universal divine mind that transforms universal pure unadulterated energy into a molded form, a form that can be anything, even earth and a physical body.

It is the Spirit of One (Goddess) that maintains the link between all souled beings, also known to religion as the children of God, and the oneness of consciousness of all that exists in form and non-form. The out-breath of God (which is universal divine mind) occurs simultaneously with the in-breath of the Goddess (your divine spirit), and with you having no beginning and no end. The in-breath of your spirit (Goddess) becomes the final and absolute return of the form and formless back to the out-breath of your connection to universal divine mind (God) for manifestation.

For instance, the children of the Mother-Father God are the prime example of the in-breath and out-breath of the Spirit of One (Goddess) in action playing with universal divine mind (God). Therefore, the expression or the phrase that communicates the idea of the word God and Goddess is just a way the reasoning mind can convey to the human ego the thought of something being more powerful than itself or your human self.

This means that with each eternal moment of the Spirit of One, the mother-father Goddess, you, as it is for all souled beings, were expressed and created (formed) into existence at the same time and with equal authority and divineness. Hence, no soul is older, younger, has more power, or is better than another soul no matter if one is in spirit, or in human form, or is black, white, yellow, red or brown, male or female.

You, like all souled beings, are a continuous (eternal) consciousness spirit that uses the in-breath of your own spirit (mother) and the out-breath of universal divine mind (God) in triggering this pure unadulterated universal energy in unendingly birthing from the abyss of darkness and nothingness (the womb), conditions of things into manifestation.

In other words, all that is seen around us today, physical and non-physical, good and bad is the in-breath and out-breath of our (us souled beings) divine spirit and our connection to universal divine mind. Nothing is left out because without our divine spirit and our connection to universal mind (mother-father God), there would be nothingness, and according to the angelic realm and the [1]Crimson Circle, we can even find our spirit in that too because nothingness is something even if it is absent of life.

Let me refer to Albert Einstein and how he proved that everything is energy, and at the same time, is not truly energy, including your physical body. According to Einstein, all that is matter is, in fact, nothing more than rapidly moving particles of energy. And today, science is finding that those particles are in fact energy lines. We experience this energy as our unchanging essence and yet, the physical dimension was formulated with very slow vibrational energy thus creating a more solid energy in order for us, as souled beings, to feel our experiences in the things we choose to express.

---

1   The Crimson Circle is a global affiliation of New Energy spiritual teachers and facilitators. The purpose of the Crimson Circle is to inspire human and spiritual consciousness around the world. Crimson Circle affiliates are experienced metaphysicians, healers and spiritual counselors coming from all walks of life, a wide variety of spiritual backgrounds, and from more than 100 countries around the world. The Crimson Circle started in the living room of the Hoppe's home in the Rocky Mountains outside of Golden, Colorado. At the time, Geoffrey was an executive and co-founder of AirCell, Inc., an aviation telecommunications company. Linda was owner/manager of Sundance Group, Inc., a marketing consulting company. Geoffrey had been privately communicating with an angelic being known as Tobias for several years. As word about the Tobias Materials began to spread the meetings quickly grew beyond their living room. You can learn more about Crimson Circle by dialing in on their website at www.crimsoncircle.com.

In other words, very slowed down energy allowed all of us souled beings to touch, hear, see, smell, and taste everything that we desired to experience. Therefore, everything that we created, as an individual or as a group consciousness, comes from the in-breath of our own spirit (mother) and the out-breath of the father, which is not a solitary white male personality unto himself but is in the framework of universal divine mind transforming its make-up of pure neutral energy into a field of potentialities for all of us to experience.

For instance: We, as souled beings, asked a long time ago to know the real truth about God, and without having mystery tied to it. So, our soul committed itself to bring about the potential for us to learn this while we are still in human form. This is why we have many lifetimes. It is just up to us, as humans, to reconnect to our own soul and remember. Yet, the remembrance and the reconnection do come when we are ready to receive it.

Behind all things manifested, with and without form or matter, is our own spirit giving it birth and life at some level. All things, including our human self, Jesus, all souled beings, and all the potentials and experiences we chose to manifest into form, even the house we live in and the car we drive, comes from us spirits and our connection to universal divine mind and not from some God outside of us.

Why, because everything is pure neutralized energy transformed in to a potential that can be seen, felt, and experienced. The exception is consciousness, which is the state of being aware of who you truly are. It is just that everyone, in their ignorance, call this energy, God.

What has happened is that we have forgotten that the Spirit of One projects itself into everything, including good and bad, a car, a home, and even our description of Satan, because nothing is manifested into form unless it was an expression (using universal energy) of the Spirit of One first. Nothing is left out, which is why Jesus said, "God and I are one." It is the same for you, me, and all mankind.

Now, for the record, the words of Jesus has been changed a little since he walked the earth over two thousand years ago because Jesus himself has made it known to his disciples of today, that when he uttered those words, he actually said, "God and I are one, and so it is with you." However, because of control and power, the "so it is with you" was removed from the Bible by the authorities of the times.

For example: In Romans 13:1-7, "Let every person be subordinate to the higher authorities, for there is no authority except from God, and those that exist have been established by God. Therefore, whoever resists authority opposes what God has appointed, and those who oppose it will bring judgment upon themselves. For rulers are not a cause of fear to good conduct, but to evil."

"Do you wish to have no fear of authority? Then do what is good and you will receive approval from it, for it is a servant of God for your good. But if you do evil, be afraid, for it does not bear the sword without purpose; it is the servant of God to inflict wrath on the evildoer. Therefore, it is necessary to be subject not only because of the wrath but also because of conscience. This is why you also pay taxes, for the authorities are ministers of God, devoting themselves to this very thing. Pay to all their dues, taxes to whom taxes are due, toll to whom toll is due, respect to whom respect is due, honor to whom honor is due."

Now, you tell me! Were these verses in Romans 13:1-7 set up by a true and loving Jesus/God or was it the authorities of the times re-writing scripture to fit their need for control and organization? In fact, do these verses even sound like what Jesus would say?

To make a bold statement that the "*higher authorities should never be resisted or opposed,*" and then make it sound like it is coming from God himself seems to me as nothing but propaganda that was written by man. How is it, in Romans, if Jesus is God, depicts his genuineness and unchanging ways by stating that it is his servants *(the ruling authorities)* to make judgment upon you, me, and those who oppose them and not God? To top it off, the ruling authorities are entrusted by God to inflict punishment on those that do not follow God's appointed powers that be. Now, you know why there are wars.

In other words, according to Scripture, it is not God or Jesus that judges what is right and wrong because that is *reserved* for those that are in higher authority than the common man and yet, still man, to make the call of judgment against you. Wow! If God is actually the author of Romans 13:1-7, and if Jesus is God, then I believe Jesus is very inconsistent with his love and how he spoke to his prophets and followers when he was with them on earth by saying, "*Love thy neighbor as thyself*" (Mathew 22:39). I thought that the Bible teaches that we have to go through Jesus if we want eternal life and not his servants!

You can find throughout the Bible all kinds of inconsistent verses and teachings telling you to follow those that are of a higher authority, which tells me that the Bible today has been re-written by man many times for the purpose of control, organization, and power, therefore should not be trusted as God's (Jesus) true words.

Here is another example: In Leviticus 19:18 *"Take no revenge and cherish no grudge against your fellow countrymen. You shall love your neighbor as yourself. I am the LORD."* And then, in Leviticus 20:27 *"A man or a woman who acts as a medium or fortune-teller shall be put to death by stoning; they have no one but themselves to blame for their death."* As you can see, we just don't go far enough with our study of the Bible when it comes to truth or understanding God. We just allow the authorities of our time to dictate to us what God wants for us to do.

You can see this in the verse of Leviticus 20:27 above. As you can see, it is in the best interest of the authorities (governments and religion) to keep you from looking within yourself to reconnect to your own soul. It is better for the powers that be to keep your search for God outside of you, and then scare you into believing that what you will find within, is Satan's army of fallen angels. They overlook the fact that Jesus himself was a medium and fortune-teller, and so were God's prophets from the past.

Then we wonder why we have wars, as most all wars are caused by religious misinterpretations and their twisted ideas about God's words. Because of the misinterpretation of God's composition as being of everything and everyone, including nothingness, as well as energy, and universal divine mind, then we, as humans, overlook the obvious fact that the Spirit of One is always creating itself anew. Constantly expanding her consciousness, her truths, and her awareness through each souled being, you and me – for we are the children of God, and also God himself.

We have forgotten that our core essence has the same composition of the Spirit of One (Goddess), which is absolute, unchangeable, is in the form of spirit, and that we have a soul that is connected to universal divine mind that is infinite, unadulterated, pure, and neutral, thus we are a spirit of one (a Goddess-God) in our own right.

So, stop looking for perfection, for you are perfect already. Therefore, God and you, as in all humans, are one and the same just as much as Jesus and God are "one" and the same, which is why you are perfect already, and why you look at Jesus as God. My friends, you are a God and a Christ also! You have no sins because sin is nothing more than the misunderstanding of "who you truly are." How can you sin if you are a Christ just as much as Jesus?

Remember, religion portrayed Jesus in his days as a sinner and therefore, can't have it both ways. If they portray God's absoluteness as being perfect, pure, supreme, incorruptible (without sin), everlasting, and indisputably the source from which you came into being, then you, at your core level, have the same divine essence as the Spirit of One, and that of Jesus too.

This means, we, as souled beings, are divine and complete already. Our spirit is untouchable, everlasting, incorruptible, and pure (without sin), and that we all are the source and authority for what we are experiencing right now. It is just that we refuse to take full responsibility for what we are creating as a Goddess and instead, we prefer to hand our responsibilities over to an imaginary mental idea of a God that consists of duality that lives in a book.

Religion depicts God's "compassion" as man having sympathy, love, kindness, and to respect his fellow man. However, according to my soul, the Angelic Realm, and to the Spirit of One, "compassion" means more than what religion describes it. The true meaning of compassion is togetherness, harmony, and unity, or as in agreement with "all that is," including the concept of the Spirit of One (Goddess-God), your soul, your connection to universal divine mind, and to all that you created, as One.

We, as mankind, seem to carry this image in our head that God somehow looks like man. If we search our heart and get out of our head for a moment, we would find that God was not created in the image of man. It was the other way around because religions, without realizing it, portray God as being created in man's image. Why is that? It is because they look at God from the seat of reasoning, and therefore they interpret all things from a dualistic mentality.

Read the Bible – for it states that God hates, God is jealous, God is revengeful, and God is the first to cast man into hell if he doesn't follow his rules. Doesn't it sound like man has given God all the attributes of himself, including the image of God being a male persona? We have forgotten that we were shaped and formed in the divine image of the

Spirit of One. Therefore, collectively, we (male and female), and all angels alike, including the fallen angels of Satan's army, and all that surrounds us, are unique and absolutely as *one* in Spirit's image.

This means, the composition of the Spirit of One is everything because nothing is left out, not our human self, or all souled beings, or even the car we drive, or the house we live in, or the insect on the ground, nor is Satan's army of angels, including Jesus. We, and all soul groups alike, work together as one unit, for we are all the Godhead.

Compassion is the divine sensitivity that gives us the wisdom of understanding that we all are part of the Spirit of One. We all have a divine consciousness. We all are connected to the Kingdom of Universal Divine Mind, as with Jesus, and all that is material, including the earth and everything in it. And yes, even those that do evil! By understanding the true meaning of the word "compassion" it allows us, as humans, to see the Spirit of One (Goddess) and Universal Divine Mind (God) in everything. For nothing is left out.

The birds of the air, the fish of the sea, the animals of the land, even the insects that crawl on the land, including what our brothers and sisters choose to manifest, good and bad – for all is *one*, nothing is left out. This is why Jesus said to love thy neighbor as thyself because we, our neighbor, and all that live are one, connected by the "compassion" of the Spirit of One, and that of Universal Divine Mind.

The word "compassion" not only connects us to our fellow man, to mother earth, every animal, plant, birds of the air, and fish of the sea, it also unifies the human ego to the Goddess part of each of us (our own spirit-soul), to Jesus, and to the Kingdom of Universal Divine Mind (heaven) forever and ever no matter how far we choose to journey into the dark energy of forgetfulness.

Maybe you have noticed in your teachings, religion portray God's "unchangeable" ways as *God knowing all things* and that he is *incapable of changing his mind* about those that fall into the darkest of creations. This includes his jealousies and judgmental ways when it comes to following his rules.

For instance, religion's explanation of parables and prophecies in the Bible come from the idea that God and Satan are two different personalities, and that they are a force unto themselves. One is positive and good while the other is negative and evil, giving us the impression of God's composition is that of duality. Hence, final and unchangeable, justifying the interpretation of God's words to fit religions need to control.

Religion has overlooked another observation of high importance when it comes to the true nature of God's unchangeable ways. It is that God is a Goddess that consists of a "spirit" first and foremost. God is symbolic for the in-breath and out-breath of all creation and that God's true "composition" is of an infinite spirit that stimulates its connection to universal divine mind, thus causing pure energy to transform into something, be it dualism or neutral. (Genesis 1:27).

This is why your core essence is also unchangeable, it is in the form of spirit, and you have an inner consciousness that is infinite, pure, neutral and unadulterated, and you, at your core essence, are without sin. The story of Genesis reveals that every component of creation, including God, humans, all souls alike, the air we breathe, the ground we walk on, and all that has life and non-life is all part of this endless pure universal energy that keeps everything and everyone as one unit and alive.

Thus it is not that God is a white male solitary personality that holds a personality unto himself, for everything dwells within this unchangeable Spirit of One whom we happen to call God. This means, you are also incorporated to all that exist because nothing can exist without spirit, consciousness, and this infinite unadulterated pure universal divine energy, not even Jesus or mother earth can exist.

The universe is filled with this pure unprocessed and undefined energy that needs focus in bringing it into your mental and rational mind and applying it to the level of your consciousness, or your understanding of who you are and your belief systems before it can be transmuted or formed. This is why it is so important to look at your beliefs before you make judgment on what is truth.

If you are a deep believer that you are a sinner, because of Adam and Eve or what you have been taught by religion, then that is how you will formulate this unprocessed and undefined energy that you call God in relating it to your creations, experiences, and your reality.

This is why people never see miracles come into their lives. All they see are their illnesses, financial problems, bad relationships, and how things never go right. That is what they are creating for themselves over and over, all because of the belief that they are not the creator of their experiences or even their suffering.

Because of religion's explanation of God's composition as being dualistic (opposing energies), a personality unto himself, and separate from you, mankind has been tricked into believing that they are sinners. When in fact, all that they (children of God) are doing is expressing and playing with the in-breath and out-breath of their own spirit's unbiased and unrefined energy that they have labeled as positive and negative.

However, man is experiencing exactly what the Spirit of One intended for him to do, even if it is good and bad, for that is where the Spirit of One gets its wisdom. The Spirit of One, and all that dwells within it, including Jesus, you, me, and all souled beings, were set in place before any beginning of earth, before physical man (male and female), before the concept of positive and negative, or good and bad, and even before the idea of God and Satan, which is why you have never sinned.

In and from the beginning, your spirit was patterned (and still is) in a divine unrestricted love state where it held no form (physical body), no positive, no negative, no light, no dark, no judgment, no guilt, no sin, no fear, and no name. However, once you were introduced to the mind of a mental nature, and the perception of having a split consciousness that consists of two parts, you took on a consciousness of separation. This developed into what is called today positive and negative. The Bible calls it "the Tree of Knowledge of Good and Evil."

Said more simply, if your "I AM" essence (spirit consciousness of no name) is in the direct image of the Spirit of One, then you too, before leaving the First Creation, which is your divine state (Garden), could only express what was constructive and in alignment with the law of divine love because that was the core essence and oneness of the Spirit of One and the Kingdom of Universal Divine Mind.

This means, when you, all souled beings, first played in your divine state of non-duality eons ago, there was no avenue for you to express good and bad. Because of it, you had no means to experience your creations other than from a state of absolute divineness, oneness, and in accord with the Spirit of One because you were in the same harmonious pattern of the essence of the Spirit of One. In other words, there is no need to seek heaven because heaven is where you came from thus making heaven already part of you.

It was only when you left your divine state of consciousness (first creation-heaven) that you developed your sense of awareness or the "I AM Sovereignty" part of you as being your own spirit identity. Each souled being is a Goddess-God (spirit of one) in their own right. It is just that you have forgotten.

You have been taught for centuries to believe that the beginning was God, that "all that was," was God, a Spirit or Source from which we, and all that exists, had come into existence. Thus we look upon this Supreme Being solely from a solitary white male authoric personality, existing unto himself in a faraway kingdom, and as a super-personality that has special and magical powers that no one can match.

However, there is an expanded truth coming out of the angelic realm and from your own soul if you have the courage to listen, and it is starting to spread around the world where people are beginning to awaken to the excessive practices of religion and how they portray God and Jesus.

Religions fail to see that the Spirit of One as a life force that is infinite in nature, pure and unadulterated neutral energy that has zero biasness (not dualistic) against her children no matter what they do. If you are not conscious of who you truly are and how to relate to your soul, then your experiences in life will always consists of pain and suffering, no exceptions.

My dear friends, to routinely trigger miracles of awe and amazement without even asking for them, it involves opening up to the greatest covert action ever instituted. It was done by the Spirit of One herself. The purpose was to intentionally fool your own spirit, not because of discontent for you but out of love for you.

So, if you are ready to move past the old dualistic energy of the Bible and hear the New Expanded truth about God, Jesus, your soul, universal divine mind, and the true story of creation, then I am here by the grace of my own soul, and by those of the angelic realm, to pass it on to you.

Chapter 4

The Spirit Of One

To improve on what is being written here and to awaken you to "who you truly are," along with your connection to the Spirit of One and that of Universal Divine Mind, I will do my best to narrate it from what I have learned from my own soul, and what I learned from [2]Tobias' [3]Journey of the Angels. My soul has described to me in

---

2   Tobias is an angelic being who has lived many lifetimes on Earth. He is most noted for his lifetime as Tobit (also known as Tobias), one of the main characters in the apocryphal Book of Tobit. According to Tobias, his last lifetime on Earth ended in about 50 BC, and he came back to earth from the angelic realms for what he called the "biggest evolution of consciousness humanity has ever experienced." Tobias helped assists those who were going through spiritual transformations, seeking to integrate their divinity with their human self, and to rediscover the God within themselves. His spiritual and inspirational messages were delivered through Geoffrey Hoppe of the Crimson Circle, Golden, Colorado.

3   Journey of the Angels is a personal study course published by the Shaumbra Institute, a subsidiary of Crimson Circle Energy company, Inc. Golden, Colorado. The study was given by Tobias in late June 2009, channeled and presented by Geoffrey Hoppe of the Crimson Circle. It is a study where Tobias takes you back to the "beginning," what he calls "All That Was," so one can actually remember and experience the original state of Oneness. From there

great detail my beginning in the First Creation (Garden), right on up to my first encounter with my soul in this lifetime.

My soul's presentation to "who you truly are, where you truly came from, and your connection to the Spirit of One" will be in a new and uplifting study than what religions have forever described as your physical beginning.

Therefore, I am in hope that my soul can help you learn how to "unlock the consciousness of your own soul." Thereby, answering the questions about why earth was created, why you came into physical form, and how it was on a request that actually came from you, and not that you were kicked out of the Garden or you being randomly born to your physical parents – for it all becomes clear and without mystery.

Man has always looked upon the male and his rational mind as holding supreme authority over the female because man looks upon God as a white male deity unto himself. You know this to be true just by the structuring of the world system and how all holy books have been interpreted that way because of Eve. The female and her soul, in all religion, are looked upon as beneath the male and his soul when it comes to the order of things, which is not true.

The male looks at the female soul as beneath his own because he sees the soul as the "I" in self that inhabits the body and acts through it. Not only does the male see his soul as supreme over the female soul. Religion too looks at the soul as the "I" in self, but after death, they say the soul no longer performs. Thus the soul waits in a place of nothingness until it is once again reunited with the physical body in a new world in which death will be removed forever. Of course, with this type of thinking, then what happens to the soul if you cremate the body?

Some religions say that the soul can be destroyed by God because of it not being immortal. Mathew 10:28, "*And do not be afraid of those who kill the body but cannot kill the soul; rather, be afraid of the one (God) who can destroy both soul and body.*" You can also find in Ezekiel 18:4, "*For all*

Tobias reminds us of how and why we left home on purpose and takes us into the experience of the "wall of fire." This is how Tobias refers to the moment when we were shattered into billions of pieces and the potentials of everything we would ever experience. Tobias also continues the study into the development of 144,000 spiritual families of the Order of the Arc. And finally, Tobias reminds one what it was like to leave the angelic realm to come to earth. In fact, my soul's story correlates with Tobias' story.

lives are mine; the life of the father is like the life of the son, both are mine; only the one (soul) who sins shall die." As you can see man struggles over the definition of what a soul is more than the physical body housing it.

When you look at Ezekiel 18:4, the verse is describing you as a God unto yourself because all lifetimes that you have created are indeed yours. "*The life of the father is like the life of the son*" because the father-mother Goddess that you are, is as one with the mind of the mental (son) that is used to create your illusions. "*Only the one (soul) who sins shall die,*" is nothing more than the many personality-aspects of yourself that loses sight of one's own soul and all the lifetimes that it has created in order to understand life, and who you truly are.

When you look at God's essence as only masculine, you overlook God's most important part, the feminine side because this is the real side of you that not only gives life but it is also the side of you that is your spirit consciousness. Therefore, when you fail to see God's feminine side as your spirit (male or female), you overlook your own divinity, because without your spirit consciousness, the masculine side of God (universal mind) becomes nothing.

This means, without God's feminine side, there would be no use for universal divine mind (the real God) because there would be no you, no physical universe, and no soul consciousness (male or female) for you to develop wisdom, and then expand. In other words, how can you have an out-breath (universal mind) if you don't have an in-breath (spirit) first?

What gives God's masculine side (universal mind) life is the infinite in-breath of your own spirit consciousness, the "I AM," for that is the only part of you that is the source that exists as being real. Everything else about you is just an illusion, for you and your illusions are "*both yours (mine)*". It is Spirit, the Goddess, that is the real you. For it takes the feminine, mother, and the wife part of you (your soul) to arouse the husband's-masculine-father-God part of you (universal mind) to form or transmute the out-breath of life so as to experience it.

My fellow searchers, we, as souled beings, are the example because that is how the Spirit of One experiences life. She (Goddess) experiences it through her children. We, all souled beings (male and female), act together as one unit, or if you like "One Universal Mind (God)." Yes, we, all souls and humans together, are the Godhead. This means there is no single solitary white male God entity outside of you or separate from you. It is just you!

Therefore, God is male, female, black, brown, yellow, red, and white, and not only those things. God is everything that has form and non-form because nothing is left out. From the beginning it has been your spirit, the feminine side, which has set into motion the splitting of your consciousness into two parts. One side of you as being a mental perception of having a rational mind that contains the belief in positive, negative, and sin , and the other side of you is your spirit and soul consciousness, which is the real you.

From your mental state (the deceptive you), the positive side became symbolic of the outer masculine you (Adam-Son) while the negative became symbolic of the inner feminine side of your mental consciousness (Eve). The Goddess part, the real you, became symbolic of the in-breath for your spirit, and the Christ part of you, that gives life to the out-breath of the God part of you in what you, as a souled being, chooses, is what you manifest into form or non-form to experience.

So, if Adam is symbolic of your outer masculine mind of a mental nature that carries a positive twist to it and Eve is as your inner feminine soul side of that same mental nature that carries the negative twist. Then the serpent in Genesis is symbolic of your deceptive personality that became famous in identifying your human self as being separate from the other two parts of you. Together, they all became one unit, you, as a three-dimensional being – mind, body, and spirit.

It is you in what your rational mind accepts as the human personality that sees itself as real and yet, the only thing that is real is your spirit and what belongs to the "I AMness" of a Universal Mind. It is the inner soul side of your mental consciousness (Eve) that records what your outer masculine side (Adam-Son) thinks, feels, and expresses to your spirit, and that part of you that holds a "universal mind" (God), to be manifested or given life too. Thus sin, in its truest formula, does not exist for your spirit or soul. Sin is only associated with your mental perception of a rational level and, since your mental consciousness is not real anyway, then sin is not real either.

It is the feminine soul side of you that gives your outer masculine rational mind many thought patterns and desires to be played out in the physical, and it is up to the masculine rational side of you to make the choice on which thought pattern or desire you want to express, manifest, and experience. This is why the male feels that it is the dominate force over the female and yet, all that the male is feeling is its own power within to choose.

Therefore, it is the oneness of your spirit first, the in-breath of the Goddess, along with Universal Divine Mind, the outburst of God, that has birthed the desire to know itself (you). Your spirit did it by creating the mental you (a false you that is looked at as a God) that is nothing more than the human brain, or what man understands as his rational mind. Thus, the God that you understand as your creator, and to whom you give worship, is not about a white male personality unto himself but is a false God.

The real God is that of "Universal Divine Mind" and how it carries within it the out-breath (husband) of the Goddess to serve your spirit (wife), the in-breath, in giving life to your expressions and belief patterns. Woman giving birth in the physical sense is the prime example that it requires spirit (the feminine, the in-breath) to bring God's (the masculine, the out-breath) creations into physical manifestation.

In other words, it is your spirit that is in the direct image of the Spirit of One, and you, as an "I AM" unto yourself, cannot create anything, not even belief systems, without your connection to Universal Divine Mind (known as a Universal God). Once you became aware of your sovereignty as an "I AM" unto yourself a long time ago, you created a son. Again, who is that son?

It is the outer masculine mental side of your rational consciousness (symbolic of Adam) working together with the feminine aspect of your soul consciousness (symbolic of Eve) in manifesting a false personality (symbolic of the serpent) that defines outwardly your assumed identity (the name you hold in this lifetime). This is why Jesus stated that he sits at the right hand of God, for Jesus represents the sonship within all of us working together with our own soul and spirit in taking action, which is why we can do the same thing as what Jesus did, if not more.

Since it is the soul side (Eve-feminine side) that gives birth to your ideas, beliefs, and expressions, which in essence come from your outer posturing ego personality, it then takes your spirit to breathe life into what your masculine mental and rational side (Adam) chooses to experience.

This is overlooked by your outer masculine side, and why it seems like the masculine side is doing all the work.

Since your posturing ego personality comes from the masculine mental and rational side of the deceptive mind (the false God), and not directly from your spirit (the real God), then this ego personality (serpent) will always come between your soul (Eve-wife) and your outer masculine side of your mental consciousness (Adam-husband). This is why your soul (Eve-wife) takes on the burden of responsibility. Remember, everything here is still just you!

Now, since your soul has to take on the burden of responsibility for everything that you choose to experience. Your soul then creates many physical and non-physical aspects of you to be played out so that you can experience what is chosen. This is why your spirit (Goddess), soul (Eve), divinity (Christ), and your posturing ego personality (the serpent-beast), became part of your "I AM Essence," or "Universal Divine Mind," while you were still part of the first creation or you in your divine state.

Also, this is why your soul (Eve) and divinity (Christ-Spirit) had to take on the negative role while the outer masculine Adam mental side of you (the brain) took on the positive, and that your posturing human personality took on the role of reckoning or accountability (sowing and reaping).

Your Spirit is smarter than you think, for she (you) created it all in order to create a friction between your "I AMness or Spirit," your soul or the "Christ you," your deceptive mind (the false you), and your celebrated human personality (the opposing you) in order to feel both sides of herself (or yourself).

The whole concept of a solitary white male Hebrew God who lives in a book and proclaims himself as the sole creator of you, and all that surrounds you, has put a tremendous burden on you because, your spirit and soul, became impossible to define, describe, study, and prove. How can you study God, your spirit and soul, or prove of their existence, if they are inconsistent in dealing with your own creations, and that of a God being a mystery to you until you die and go to heaven or hell?

Therefore, it took the splitting of your consciousness into two parts, one part of you taking on the mental image of a masculine (the positive or out-breath-false God) and the other part of you taking on the image of your soul, the feminine side (negative or the in-breath of the soul or

Christ, the real you). By your spirit splitting your consciousness into two parts it created a vibrational energy force that rotated the masculine-feminine energy within you to act in an opposite pattern. You know, Christ and the Anti-Christ, and yet, still you!

Hence, your consciousness took on an inner and outer manifestation where it addressed itself as a masculine-feminine energy that began to rotate in a circular movement that caused both sides of you (the real you and the deceptive you) to vibrate in opposite directions. Thus you, as a God also, created duality, and that is why you feel separated from your own spirit and soul, which is why the masculine (male) feels dominate and alone.

You see, the masculine, or the male deceptive side of you, and your superficial human ego personality, took on a positive spin while the feminine or inner female soul real side of you took on the negative spin. This is why negative and sin is not really bad or evil. It is just part of the same force that positive comes from. It is the same for light and dark. It is not that dark is evil either because it comes from the same source as light. It is the same with man and woman, for both man and woman can be a male in one lifetime and a female in another, which is why both man and woman are equal when it comes to the authenticity of their spirit, and that of a God of oneness.

When you finally move beyond thoughts, beliefs, and the idea of your spirit taking part in any duality, such as good or bad, religion, or that you are a sinner, then you will transcend your state of two parts (masculine-feminine) from vibrational rotating energy patterns to a new energy pattern of unity, harmony, and balance that aligns with your spirit and the "I AM Essence of a universal divine mind."

This is where you will experience the Christ that you are. (Meaning, you move from out of the tree of knowledge of good and evil and back to the tree of life). It is equivalent of the Christ part of you coming into the depths of your physical existence (like the center of earth) and pulling you out of the fires of hell.

Your spirit and soul is the Christ that is the real you just like it is for Jesus. It is timeless, infinite, unchangeable, and full of wisdom, and it brings healing, calming, and pure soothing comforting expansional energies to everything you choose to experience. If you just allow it in. When you begin to recognize and understand that your journey home is not about dying or going to heaven but is about you becoming aware of your own spirit, and to the real truth that you have really never left, then you know that you are already home (in heaven).

Interestingly, it is about becoming a sovereign self-ruling God in your own right where your spirit places the crown of freedom (Gold) on the head of her son, the false you, or the deceptive part of the human aspect, which is your rational mind. This means, the son or your masculine side of the deceptive mind (false God), your soul (the feminine side), and all the deceptive parts and pieces of you that you have created (lifetimes, or your many personality-aspects), come together as one body of consciousness. It is about you becoming a king and queen (God-Goddess) unto yourself.

Theologians who teach that God is a male God unto himself and must be worshipped are still asleep because they fail to see the "composition" of the real God as your own Spirit/Soul that is unconditional, unchangeable, and non-dualistic. For the real you is the "I AM of no name," and your connection to "universal divine mind," is everlastingly and constant.

This also means that you have been asleep because you have not yet truly moved beyond the thought of duality, sin, and separation. It is just that you are under the perception that duality and sin are real because of how the deceptive mind (brain) interprets its thoughts and beliefs. Even in the Bible, God maintained that his name is simply "I AM" (Ehyeh), for the real God, has no name and no definition that suggest duality – for you too are in the image of the Spirit of One, thus a God also.

Your spirit, like the Spirit of One, is unchangeable, absolute, infinite, and you have a consciousness that is forever in a divine heavenly state. Thus, you have never sinned. How can you sin if your spirit has no thoughts – for your thoughts come from the mental part of you, the false you? Your spirit, without fail, always acts on awareness, imagination, intuitiveness, compassion, and it meets itself through the rational mind (the son), along with all of its thoughts. It is just that you have been deceived into believing that the rational mind and your physicality is all that you are, including the belief that you have sinned.

The real you is nothing but spirit consciousness, and the components (parts and pieces) of what you have created are constantly expanding your soul through your many personalities (physical and non-physical lifetimes). This means the real you has no form and no name because you are just spirit consciousness, and that you use the deceptive mind of a rational attitude (the son) to create your world of illusions, including the idea of Satan, good and bad, and that one is either male or female. Again, this is what is meant by Jesus (the son) sitting at the right hand of God – for your spirit, your mind of mentalness, and your physical personality aspect of today, is God.

So, by giving yourself freedom from your dogmatic beliefs for awhile, you too will feel your soul speaking to you. Not separately as from your spirit, mind, body, and the many personality-aspects of you, but in one voice. Allow yourself to feel that you are more than just this human lifetime. You are the make-up of your spirit, soul, physical body, and many lifetimes, or that of many personality aspects of good and bad.

Remember, the Bible says that we were created in the divine image of God. This means God was not human nor was He part of a dualistic force. God and the Bible text are metaphors (not real) to demonstrate that it is only the deceptive you, the rational mind, and your human personality (serpent), playing with the forces of positive (light) and negative (dark) in order for the real you to grow in wisdom, understanding, and learn responsibility for the choices made.

If you are experiencing ups and downs (duality) in your life then you are following a false version of God and yourself, which is why you suffer because you are looking at God as if He is separate from you. The "I AM that you are" is above duality, and therefore sin is not sin at all, as you are not as you think you are either. However, all that you see is your human personality as being real, thus you believe you sin, all because you see positive and negative as real, which is why again you suffer.

If you believe within your heart that there are two different forces, positive (good-God) and negative (evil-Satan), as if they are real, and that they are part of your makeup, then you are working from a deceptive part of you. It is always the deceptive you (the rational mind) that believes in sin, good and evil, right and wrong, heaven and hell, duality at its best. So, be aware that your spirit only understands things as experiences and not as sin – for that is the grace aspect of you coming into your life to free you from your suffering.

We, as souled beings, are patterns of light and wisdom, manifested into a human form. As light and wisdom, we all have direct access to all parts and pieces of ourselves that are scattered throughout the omniverse, which is illustrative in the Bible as God's Kingdom. In spirit terms, it is illustrative as many dimensions or multi-consciousnesses.

Even the Bible addresses Adam and Eve as being part of the Spirit of One long before they became intrigued by the "tree of duality." This is nothing more than a metaphor in demonstrating to you that, in the beginning, before you moved into the role of duality and forgetfulness, your core essence was, and still is, divine in nature, and that you are *one* with "all that is" (universal divine mind) and always have been.

My fellow searchers, the real God is not part of a force of duality nor is God an individual unto himself. The real God is consistent with its unchangeable ways and with its infinite, pure, and perfect application of a real you that only holds the heart of unconditional love and compassion without end. Since you are in the divine image, then you are already perfect, unconditional, and you are without sin. It is just that you believe you are not these things, which is why you experience sin and karma. After all, you are the God creating every bit of it.

Adam and Eve were not real people, they represent a symbolic message telling you how you transformed your conscious focus from your divine essence (the higher you) eons ago to a consciousness of a dualistic belief system (the lower you) that holds the concept that you are either a male or a female, and that you are good or bad. This led to believing that positive and negative are derived from two different forces and yet, in reality, all things are as *one*, including God and Satan.

We, as souled beings, have vested many lifetimes playing a role that consists of either male or female, and yet we are neither, for we are, in our truest essence, both. We are an "I AM" to our own Spirit as much as God and Jesus are an "I AM," therefore equal.

As you can see in the story of creation in Genesis there is a new expanded truth that goes far beyond the literal interpretation. Not that I am saying the original story was wrong or false, it is just that the original story was interpreted from a materialistic and rational viewpoint. By giving you the real story without the literal twist of religious and scientific views, it helps you understand in a more concise way who you truly are, why you are here on earth, and why you volunteered to leave the First Creation (the garden-divine state) to come into physical form.

My dear friends, all that is required to chat with your own soul is the willingness to open your heart and mind and feel your "I AM Presence" knocking on the door of your human consciousness. So, if you are ready to open up your human consciousness then I am ready to present to you a new expanded version of where you actually came from, who you truly are, and why you came to earth. I also promise that I will not get to deep in to the scientific attempt to refute or prove that there is a solitary white male God that holds all power unto himself.

Instead, I will offer you a snapshot of your own divineness where you hold within an expanding thought pattern that doesn't need to be imposed on by the falseness of the physical mind. When you learn to allow the collapse of old dualistic patterns into infinite possibilities, what you will experience is a consciousness of freedom that will end up altering your reality of suffering to multitudes of realities that hold no suffering.

Remember, God, Allah, Jehovah, Eternal One, Creator, Great Spirit, Jesus, YHWH, Ehyeh, Source, Ishvara, and there are many more I am sure, are just words, icons that the human mind wraps itself around on an emotional level in order to understand himself and the environment that surrounds him. That's why there is no heaven and no supreme being who is a white male deity, with long white hair and a beard, sitting on a golden chair waiting for his servants, the priests, the evangelists, and/or those higher authorities to give him the list of names that deserve heaven or hell.

My dear friends, it is just you! You are a Christ also! When you finally let go of the idea that a single solitary white male God created you and the environment around you, and stop trying to define God as something out of a science-fiction movie, then you will discover the real God, *you*.

It is through the churches and their standing with a false God that we look upon them in hopes that religion and their false God will forgive us for our sins. It is because of this, we fear this false God more than we fear Satan, which is why we overlook our divine purpose and why we exist in the first place.

Look, have you ever asked yourself why the Spirit of One created you? Was it for recreation or was it for you to become a free and sovereign "spirit of one" in your own right. Meaning, you take full responsibility for every thought, choice, and deed. If religions counter this by saying that you exist for a purpose, then whose purpose?

Are you to become a slave to a God of rules and punishment, to Jesus, a slave to religion, or how about a slave to your beliefs, family, friends, government, the media, or how about your political party? What about a slave to your human ego, your intellect, or your intelligence? Remember, the meaning of a slave is someone who accepts another's set of rules, even their own rules as well as their family.

Listen, if God, in the beginning (beyond time, space, and physicality), was "one" or was "all that was," complete unto himself, then "who are you?" Here is something to consider. A true and loving God would never allow himself to be a mystery. He would never judge what is right or wrong. He would never force you to follow rules of any kind and he would never have others condemn or denounce you or any of his creations, no matter how evil one is.

Now, why would God not denounce you or give others the authority to condemn you, even if you were completely evil? Because, if a single, all-knowing, all-powerful God created you, then don't you think he should take responsibility for his own limitations? A God that creates imperfections is not a true and loving God. To say otherwise is like saying a person is not at fault for his own limitations. After all, God expects you to take full responsibility for your limitations. Why is God any different? Are you not in the divine image of God?

My fellow searchers, to do otherwise would make God inconsistent, therefore unreliable and changeable, which is why in my opinion, as well as from many of the angelic realm, the Bible is nothing more than old energy that is filled with text that has come from man more so than from any God.

Once you awakened to the wisdom that you are a divine being and that your core essence is of spirit first, before time, space, and physicality ever was, then understand that the first thing spirit would have bestowed upon you would be "awareness." Otherwise, you would not be conscious of your existence.

You see, it is the divine sense of "awareness" that we, as souls, decided to develop first once we became an "I AMness" unto ourselves when we first separated from the Spirit of One, which of course, was in mind and consciousness only.

For instance: When we were part of the Spirit of One, we really did not have an awareness of who we were. It took focusing our consciousness to awaken our awareness to create a belief system about leaving that portion of ourselves that is divine in nature to discover our real identity, which is why we had the blessings of the Spirit of One. We were not kicked out of any garden because of some tree that bared forbidden fruit.

You know as well as I do, the tree, the serpent, and the fruit are all symbolic. It is just that you will not admit to it because of your religious beliefs. You have been taught to believe that the beginning was God, that "all that was," was God. However, according to Genesis 1:27, man and women were indeed created in the divine image of God. If this is true, then God and "all that was" (us souled beings) were Etheric first, and then we became physical.

Religion say that Adam and Eve were created first, as well as being physical first, however according to Genesis: 1:27, it was the Spirit of One (the Goddess), and then all of us souled beings (the children of God) that came first, before Adam and all that is physical. You see, if God was "all that was," the "original oneness of consciousness complete unto Himself in the beginning," as religions say, then that means God knew nothing other than him being aware of himself.

So, if God knew nothing but his awareness in the beginning, then God, in truth, did not know what was good and evil, or even what love was. The reason why God didn't know these things was because none of it was created as of yet! Remember, it took the in-breath of Spirit and the out-breath of all souled beings (the children of God), to introduce good, evil, and love to the world, as Adam and Eve's biting of the apple are symbolic of the act.

In fact, it took the in-breath of the Spirit of One in a passion of desiring to know herself that led to the question, "Who am I?" From that question, the Spirit of One sparked the out-breath of God (universal mind) to instantly manifest countless images of "herself" in order to see and understand "herself." Well! My fellow searchers, we, as souled beings, are the out-breath (explosion) of that act.

Every one of us is a Goddess (Spirit) unto ourselves. We, all of us together, are the Spirit of One, the Goddess, and yet, we are taught to say God because of religion wanting to push the male soul as a supreme being over the female soul, which is completely a lie.

Therefore, the first explosion was not the creation of the universe or earth like science believes. It was the implosion (in-breath) and explosion (out-breath), the movement (passion) and the arousing (spark) of the Spirit of One, the Goddess, breaking up into gazillions upon gazillions of pieces of herself, and each piece was a souled being that was born (awakened) in the same divine image of the Spirit of One. That my fellow searchers, is when we, as souled beings (the children of God), became a conscious living being and a "spirit of one" in our own right.

So again, God is not a single, solitary white male personality unto himself that created everything. God is a composite of the Goddess, or us, as souled beings, where "all that was," is now the Spirit of One becoming "all that is today," which is us souled beings. Therefore, within each soul (you and me) contains the divine spark or essence of the oneness of Spirit and a pure and unchangeable you, because you, me, and all humans alike, are a divine being that is God like.

For instance: Look at the sun's light as symbolizing the Spirit of One, and the energy generated from the sun symbolizing universal divine mind (God if you will) and yet, look at them both as "one unit" that represents "all that was." This would mean nothing existed other than the Spirit of One, or in this example the sun. Look at it as there was no earth, no physicality, no universe, not even time or space, or even darkness, just the sun and its radiant light (the Goddess) sitting there in an empty abyss of non-awareness.

In this example, if you look at the sun's core essence as nothing but light and pure neutral energy as representing the Spirit of One, then in truth, God never existed. Why, because it took the Goddess (Spirit) in giving life to God (universal mind), not as a single unit unto himself but as something part of her that directs, influences, and controls this pure universal divine energy to serve her.

Therefore, the composition of the Spirit of One was at first nothing but Spirit (female), and then she took this infinite unrefined unadulterated pure universal divine energy and transformed it as part of her, which is why your core essence has the same composition as the Spirit of One. This means your core essence too is nothing but spirit (Goddess), and that you are part of a universal divine mind (God) that draws on pure energy to serve you in what you desire to manifest.

So, there you have it! Your physical body and physical reality was created by you, which is why you, and only, you are responsible for it. God is not a real person unto himself here but is symbolic of every souled being (you, me, and all angels) transforming pure raw neutral energy into manifested form that has been sparked by the desires of your own spirit. It was magical, divine, and perfect because the Spirit of One knew that her children could do more than just be aware of themselves if they were with understanding and wisdom.

Through the breaking-up of the "original mother-father Goddess (Spirit of One)" into what is now the children of God (us, as souled beings), the second creation was formed into existence through the mental activity of her children. You see, because of having the same authority and power as the Spirit of One, we, as souled beings, mimicked the Spirit of One and manifested a deceptive and misleading psychological consciousness of an exaggerated ego personality that led to inflated thoughts about self and others, which is symbolized by the serpent in the garden.

However, the serpent in the Garden is symbolic as being the human ego personality and the psychological consciousness is part of our mental nature. We did this so we could learn, feel, expand, and get to know all things rather than just be in a state of incompleteness. That my fellow searchers was the beginning of a new day or what is now our mental and rational consciousness today. We, all souled beings together, became the creator and experiencer for the Spirit of One, which correlates with Genesis.

In fact, the story of Genesis is nothing more than the Spirit of One creating and manifesting many personality aspects of herself (children of God or we, as souls) in order to learn the wisdom behind what is known as positive and negative (the "Tree of Knowledge of Good and Evil," duality). It was the only way for the "spirit of one" within each "souled being" (you and I) to learn who we are, to learn our uniqueness, and to become a complete sovereign "spirit of one" in our own right.

In other words, before our deceptive or rational mind (Adam), our soul (Eve), and individual deceptive nature (the serpent), everything was all based on the Divine Kingdom of the Spirit of One's consciousness without the children of the Goddess (you and I) having any understanding of life, wisdom, and what it meant to be alive and making choices. All that we souled beings were in the beginning was a consciousness that had a non-active awareness and a non-activate spirit. We lived within the womb of the Spirit of One (mother-Goddess), like a baby lives in its mother, alive in spirit but not aware of our own spirit, consciousness, and divineness at the time.

However, once the Spirit of One allowed her children (us, as souled beings) to be born, which is nothing more than us, as spirits, becoming aware of ourselves at the time. We took action on forming a soul consciousness, a deceptive mental and rational level, and an individuality (ego) that held the forces of positive and negative as being real. We then took on a belief of being separate from that portion of us that made us a "spirit of one" also.

Now, that you have an idea of who you truly are, let's begin this new expanded version of creation where we, as souled beings, lived in the first creation, before earth, time, space, and any physicality ever existed. Let us call this first creation, not only heaven, home, or as the Spirit of One, but look at it as representing the original oneness of our own spirit from which we, as souled beings, became aware of ourselves. This was truly "all that was" in the beginning.

According to my soul, in the first creation, nothing existed outside of it, not even the Spirit of One or us souls. We were all within the kingdom of the first creation, or metaphorically speaking, inside of the womb of the mother-Goddess as a divine being but not yet awakened to our own spirit consciousness. Again, there was no earth, man, plants, animals, stars, or even the universe at the time. These things came much later.

When we were birthed (symbolically speaking of becoming aware of our existence) in the first creation (Garden) from the womb of "all that was" (Spirit of One) in the beginning of our consciousness, we, as souled beings, were given everything that the Spirit of One had, including individuality and total freedom to express, love, experience, and choose our own fate. This means that the Spirit of One, as a single consciousness, was no longer because now she resided within her children as a universal consciousness.

We even had the choice to turn our back on our own spirit because we always knew (from a higher consciousness) that we would return to our divinity (Christ self) one day. After all, we are together, the Goddess or God that manifested a deceptive mental and rational side of ourselves, called it our son, the prince of harmony (peace), and then placed within it a consciousness of duality so we could leave our divine state (home) on purpose to go out and discover "who we are."

At first, we were given no rules, no laws, and we were not told what to do because every soul had divine free will. Every souled being was given the essence, purity, depth, and as being the source for whatever was created, no exceptions. Because of how the Spirit of One, in the beginning, broke herself up into us souled beings, the Spirit of One could not control the expressions of her children. Why? It was because the Spirit of One was no longer, because now, she is (became) her children in expression.

You see, once we, as souled being, were born (awakened) out of the Spirit of One (mother-Goddess) that is when we became aware of our own uniqueness as a "divine being." That is when we, as spirits, became aware of "all that was" in the beginning, which was, just us souled beings. There were no universes, earth, or physical form. We, as souls, did not even have a form as of yet because we were just consciousness. It was just us souled beings and our connection to universal divine mind sitting there in awe.

This awareness created such an excitement within us, we, as divine beings, filled our oneness of consciousness with wonderful concepts to consider for the understanding of oneself that were very pleasing and, in fact, beyond words to describe. As we know now, the Bible describes our divine state as a beautiful garden, whereas my soul calls it the first creation.

Nevertheless, we, as a child of the Spirit of One, explored our divine state (first creation) with irresistible excitement every time that we felt our awareness bubbling-up within our own spirit consciousness. We, while in our soul state of consciousness, and in our excitement to discover who we were, we, all souls, took our divine state of consciousness and manifested a consciousness of duality. This gave us a feeling of being aware of what was around us.

Because of this awareness feeling, we then felt a strong affection of warmth and tenderness, opposed to reason and logic, coming from deep within our divine state that we now interpret as unconditional love running through us as well as through our deceptive dualistic mind. It was magical and it was with perfection, for we did not have any need or desire other than to just be one with our divine state and all that surrounded us in the first creation (Garden-divine oneness of all).

In the first creation we could feel our divine state of consciousness hugging and loving us unconditionally, even though we were feeling it through our deceptive and dualistic rational mind (Adam-son) and our individualized ego consciousness at the time. However, a new awareness of exploring beyond what was known only as us, as souled beings, being in a divine state was beginning to come up over the arising, and we again felt excited about going off to discover more of our divine state.

So, as we left the comfort of our divine state of consciousness to explore our divine uniqueness (symbolic of the first creation), we finally came upon its limitations for the very first time From feeling the limits of our divine state (first creation) for the very first time, it sparked our interest and awareness to the point where we began to recognize our divine state as being part of a dualistic consciousness (tree of knowledge of good and bad). Because of it, we experienced something that we did not understand.

In fact, we felt something that we never felt before. It was fear! Fear was not an issue with us souled beings before because we did not know what fear was. However, because of playing around with the awareness of our deceptive and mental consciousness for the very first time, we noticed that we had a dualistic sense of ourselves that we had never felt before. This feeling triggered within us an uncertainty about what we were feeling and experiencing as we became exposed to this fear. This would be symbolically speaking of Adam and Eve noticing that they were naked in the Garden.

Then all of a sudden we felt an emotional response to what we were experiencing that seemed to have no reference point to what we were feeling. It confused us because it was never there before. We thought that we uncovered everything tied to our divine state of consciousness, which is why we said to ourselves, where did this creation of duality and the emotional feeling of fear come from?

As we looked upon our divine state (the Garden's or the first creation's limitations) and this deceptive mental dual sense of ourselves, we, all souled beings, felt unfulfilled and distant whereas before we always felt filled and warm. We felt detached and removed from our divine nature, and from the divine oneness of all souled beings in a way that we never felt before. The feeling we were experiencing became difficult to describe and yet, somehow we had a deep feeling that we would like to go out and discover what was beyond our divine state and that of universal mind.

As we looked and contemplated about wondering further out into what we were feeling and experiencing as duality and limitation, along with our mental perception of feeling separated, we still could feel the love of our own divine state. Thereby, making us feel warm and comfortable.

It wasn't until our own divine state challenged the deceptive dualistic side of our rational and mental side of us to leave the "kingdom of one" (life of limitations) to learn how far we could journey out into this cold and dark emptiness feeling of our new divided consciousness (positive and negative) to see if we can answer the challenge. Religion interprets it as Adam and Eve leaving the Garden under protest!

You see, the question of duality, individuality, and experiencing some type of dual consciousness, were unknown to us at the time. Therefore, I ask you to put all fear aside about being kicked out of the garden because the garden is nothing more than we, as souls, taking on a role of discovering this split consciousness of a dualistic and mental framework. How can we be kicked out of some garden if the garden is nothing more than our divine state of consciousness challenging our mental state of consciousness to forget about our divine state for awhile for the purpose of expanding our consciousness and learning wisdom?

The same is true for Adam and Eve, for they are just a myth and are symbolic in helping you to understand that your core composition is of a masculine-feminine energy that has a consciousness, a soul, a spirit, a mental constitution that you describe as a mind and a human body. Together, they are as "one body of consciousness" unto yourself. It is not that you, as a souled being, were kicked out of the first creation (garden, or more accurately your divine state). It is that you left voluntarily.

My dear friends, we, all souls, left the fist creation on a voluntary challenge that actually came from our own spirit, which is that portion of us that is the mother-Goddess. Because of what we were feeling at the time, we took the challenge and we were excited about what duality would bring to us and to our soul as a whole.

You see, in the first creation, or better said, in the beginning stages of our divine state of consciousness, when we were only exposed to the uniqueness of knowing that we are a "spirit of one" in our own right, we never felt anything like fear and uncertainty before, or even that we had a soul. Not even our spirit knew what fear, limitations, and uncertainty was at the time. All that we knew was that by going out into the discovering of a split consciousness, positive and negative, our state of understanding who we are, as being divine, would expand into something of great value.

However, in doing so, we exposed ourselves to vast experiences that we have never felt before, pushing us far beyond our limitations, thus gaining great wisdom and understanding from these experiences.

So, on that day of long, long ago, before earth, the stars, the astral realms, and before our physical body was ever created, we said farewell to our spirit and to our divine mind of a universal nature, and to "all that was" (just us souled beings). Then we moved (became focused) into a consciousness belief, even though it was just an illusion, that supported a dualistic consciousness of positive and negative, and a mental constitution that we depicted as a mind, where we, as souled beings, never experienced before.

You see, the first circle of creation was about you, me, and all souled beings, and not about a solitary white male God living in some heaven unto himself. It was you, I, and every souled being (all angels), having the awareness that we were a divine being that was somehow individualized. Because of our knowing that we were a divine being, and that we were in the same patterned of the Spirit of One, we, as souled beings, created our perfection of things where in the end we had little wisdom and no feelings of life or experiences.

We even had no desire to move forward in our understanding, other than to just be part of each other. This is why, my fellow searchers, we all chose to take on the challenge and move outside of that portion of us that makes us as a Goddess also. Yes, all souled beings, moved from "all that was" in the first creation (one's own divine oneness of consciousness), and into a new place (a deceptive dualistic mental consciousness that consisted of positive and negative) where we could learn more about who we really are as a Goddess.

Chapter 5

Leaving Your Divine State

(The First Creation)

So, there we were, all souled beings, in our divine state, and before the challenge was made with our own spirit to leave the first creation, exploring and developing our soul, playing with universal mind, and our individuality. Then, after some time, not like time as we understand it today, but rather time marked by our experiences in what we were choosing and expressing in our divine state, we souls created physicality and all of the astral realms.

In fact, time in the material world came from the offshoot of our experiences in the first creation because of how one experience followed another, and that is how time became marked in the physical dimension.

Once we, as souled beings, were birthed from the womb of the Spirit of One (symbolically speaking), we were awakened to the fact that we became the in-breath (source) for the mother-Goddess. Which means, we, all souled beings, were and still are, the source for all that is seen today – for we are the ones that stimulated the out-breath of universal mind (father-God) and transformed the infinite field of pure neutral energy into whatever likeness we chose to reflect outside of us as appearing real, like form for example.

Case in point: We, as souled beings, are the ones responsible for creating our own physical bodies and stories (lifetimes) to be played out as being real and yet, they are just illusions that feel real to us, even our physical bodies are not solid or real. In other words, all that we are, believe it or not, are just a hologram that our spirit created in order to feel and understand life. Thus how can a hologram sin? If there is no such thing as sin then there is no such thing as karma. It's only the belief in it.

The symbology of Adam and Eve in Genesis was needed in order for your spirit to create a soul, signified by Eve, which then would personify your freedom to expand your conscious focus outward beyond your divine state in order to accumulate wisdom (symbolic of the "tree of knowledge of good and bad)."

However, when you did, as all souls did, you were left with a feeling of being separate from that portion of you that is your spirit. Whom today religion and man describes as God, for the word God is just an icon that signifies you as being the "I AM" and the source for what you create.

To really understand the challenge that was placed before you in the "first creation" was for you to learn the real truth about "who you truly are and what your purpose was as a child of your own spirit." However, in order to meet that challenge, you needed something that would help you forget that you are a divine being and a composite of the Spirit of One.

So, my dear friends, your spirit helped you forget by introducing you to a personality of a deceptive mental nature that held your focus in and around your individual ego persona, thus producing a feeling deep within you about being separate from your own spirit, your soul, divinity, and from all other souls (angels). In the end, creating a consciousness of forgetting, where you ended up getting lost in that ego persona.

Not only did your spirit give you the sensation of individuality and self rule, your spirit also gave you a deceptive personality where you sensed immense power and authority that ended up producing a personality of control, judgment, planning, and to confirm what you were actually feeling was in fact real. You can actually say the deceptive personality that you developed and created a long time ago actually came from you, and it became recognized as the ego personality part of you. The Bible identifies it as the "serpent in the garden."

And so, the beginning of a new day was created (a deceptive mental and rational consciousness that caused friction between the masculine-feminine and the ego personality within yourself), which correlates with Genesis in the Bible as Adam, Eve, and the Serpent. It was the only way for your spirit, and that portion of you that is divine and universal, in answering the question, "Who am I?" It was the perfect solution for all souled beings in becoming a complete "Sovereign God" in their own right.

This is equivalent of the Spirit of One passing down the throne to herself – for the Spirit of One is no longer because she is now her children. In other words, we, the children of God together, are the Spirit of One. Therefore, there is no God unto himself – for all that is, is just us souled beings acting together as the creator of everything you see and don't see.

This means us, as in all souls and angels alike, were in the beginning, before time, space, earth, and all that is physical, had a functioning spirit. We had a soul, a deceptive mind of a mental nature, and we had an individualized ego persona about us while we were still in the knowing that we were a divine being. Yes, we souls were in the knowing that we had all of these parts of us while we were part of the first creation. This is symbolized by Adam, Eve, and the Serpent being in the Garden of Eden before being thrown out.

The throne is just symbolic of each and every souled being (you, I, and everyone else) having the same power, rank, and privileges as the Spirit of One, because together, we are the Spirit of One, and therefore equal to whom we call God. This is why we, all souled beings, like Jesus, were there in heaven (first creation - Garden) already before time, space, and physicality.

In other words, we were all there in the first creation in the beginning before the second creation was ever shaped and formed. The second creation is the make-up of physical and non-physical dimensions, and therefore not real because all that is real is your spirit. The second creation is only of deceptive images of things that are not real, like a hologram. We just think they are real because of our focus is coming from a deceptive mental and physical state that uses the human rational mind to figure things out.

You see, it took our spirit, our soul, our mental perception of a rational mind, and our individual self-awareness to move all of us souled beings outside of our own divine state (the first creation) and into the abyss of a mental state that was void of any beliefs, choices, and creations. From this mental state that we called the second creation, we, as souls, then created an illusion of a physical nature that consisted of duality (positive and negative, good and bad) in order for us souls to know and understand life, and to answer the question, "Who am I?"

Therefore, it was your spirit (divinity), along with your soul (Eve), the deceptive side of you (Anti-Christ), the rational mind (Adam), and your individualized ego personality (serpent) that made it possible for you to expand beyond your divine state (first creation), and into a three-dimensional physical body and onto a three-dimensional planet (second creation) for the testing of positive and negative (the Tree of Knowledge of Good and Evil).

Even though the Bible states that Eve was led astray before Adam, the story is to help you understand that it took your own deceptive masculine mental side of the rational mind (Adam), and your outer posturing ego personality (the serpent), to create the illusion of being separate from your soul (Eve). This allowed the lower you (the mind of deception) to take on thoughts and beliefs of separation, positive and negative, and good and bad, duality.

It was the only way for us souls to journey out on our own and change all that was known at the time as our divine state and into a whole new creation of duality even though it was deceptive, hologramic, and illusionary. It was perfect because it gave our spirit a way to explore the unknown principles of mental imaging, playing with opposites, and the experiencing of physicality or slowed down energy.

It was also the perfect way for us (as souled beings) to learn and know all things, including responsibility, accountability, and how far we could go into a deceptive dualistic consciousness in understanding our choices, and then becoming a God of wisdom, compassion, and a God of sovereignty.

As the Bible portrays Eve as passing the apple to her husband Adam to eat, it simply means that Eve, symbolic of our soul, became the holder, like a woman carrying a baby seeded by her husband, in what the outer deceptive Adam side of our rational mind (a mind that has a false sense of self) desired to learn and experience (taste) about positive and negative, or good and bad, opposites.

In other words, Adam was the first to bite the symbolic apple because, in truth, the thought process and desires come from the deceptive side of our mental state, or the Adam principle first. It takes the outer rational mind to begin the thought process and not our soul. Our soul (symbolic of Eve) was created to record all thoughts, ideas, and desires that come from the deceptive side of our mental mind, and then our soul passes those thoughts, and or beliefs, right back to our rational mind (Adam) to make a choice. That is where religion begins their account of how Adam was misled by Eve, which of course is false.

Once your spirit and soul had everything in order for you to go out and explore beyond your divine state (the first creation), your spirit moved all of its authority as being the source and the giver of life to the deceptive masculine part of you (symbolic of Adam) as being the decision maker, the creator, and the power behind the throne. This is why you have this strong belief of the mind being the power and source behind what you get in life and yet, it is far from the truth.

As you can see there is no sin here! It is just your spirit (Goddess) and soul (feminine side, or Eve) passing all authority to your outer deceptive divided rational mind, the son (Adam/Jesus), to make choices in order for you to know and understand life. For instance: Jesus' spirit, the Goddess, passed all authority to the "son of man," which is symbolic for his outer physical mind, to become the standard for all of us. Thus, we, all humans, are a "son of man" just as much as Jesus. This means, we are all equal to God and not less than because together, we are God.

This is why man (male and female), the masculine within, looks upon his Spirit, the Goddess, as being a male solitary personality even though technically, the God of the Bible is only a mental version of himself, which is why religion and man look at God as being dualistic like himself.

This has caused the male gender to feel superior to the female gender, which of course, is false. It just feels that way because mankind (male and female) only works from out of his rational mind, the masculine. You see, the deceptive side of the mind sees itself as the power, the intelligence, and the creator behind the throne.

To help you even more on this point, your soul, the feminine side of you, allowed your rational mind, the masculine, and the ego personality, the superficial side of you (serpent), come between your soul (Eve) and your perceptional mental mind (Adam) in order for you to believe that you are indeed separate from your divine and Christ like state. This is why the Bible states that Eve took the bite of the fruit first, which of course again, is false.

Note: Please excuse some repetitiveness! I repeat some things in order for you to understand "who you truly are" and "where you have truly come from." This is very important to understand because it actually controls the ageing of the physical body. Your physical body ages according to your beliefs and to the wisdom you display externally on the subject of "knowing who you are."

Because of the question, "Who am I?," and the challenge your spirit put on the illusionary side of the masculine mental side of you and your soul, the feminine, it allowed you, in mind only, and again is not real, to venture out beyond the consciousness of your divine state (first creation) and into a mental version of you that was built on separateness, deceptiveness, lies, and duality or opposites (second creation). This means everything outside of you is just an illusion.

Remember, Einstein, and other physicists, knew that there wasn't really any such thing as physical reality because it is all made up of atoms. According to many physicists, atoms are not even real because atoms are thought of as more of a possibility than something solid.

In other words, if you stood inside of an atom you would experience enormous amount of empty space with very little electric charge buzzing around the far edges of the atom, as well as in the center. Then you would see a tiny nucleus composed of protons and neutrons. Therefore, according to physicists, anything as small as a proton behaves more like a wave measurement than a basic unit of matter, which means it is not as a wave matter or a wave of energy, but a probability wave. If this is so, then matter as we know it evaporates!

Now, since we, as humans, gather our information from our belief systems and our five physical senses we then reconstruct those patterns of energy waves and reassemble them into what we picture as our reality to experience. From this action we, as souled beings, use our deceptive mental side of the mind in reassembling what we call atoms of matter, which then provides for us the sensation of what we expect to see and encounter as being real and yet, none of it is real.

Thus our spirit made it possible for us to create a whole new world of playing opposites, like being a male or female, experience up and down, good and bad, as well as physicality and non-physicality. This process allowed us, as souls, for the very first time, to experience something completely different then what we were experiencing before in our divine state.

This gave us souls a chance to play the deceptive masculine mental side of self against the feminine soul side of self, contrary to our divine state, which is why, even in the eyes of our spirit, there are no wrong choices that we could make, good or bad. Because in the end, it all makes no difference to our spirit what we chose to experience. All that our spirit was looking for is the experience and the wisdom that comes from the experience. This is why there is no judgment, sin, or karmic retribution coming from our divine state. It comes from our belief that we did something wrong even though we did nothing wrong.

This also means, we can heal ourselves and bring into our life all the miracles we wish. All that is holding our miracles back is our belief that everything is solid and real, including sin and retribution. So, if you are experiencing karma, then it is coming from believing that you are a sinner and that you are only a physical being in need of healing. This belief not only brings in shame and guilt for what you have done, either in this lifetime or some past lifetime, it also brings in your emotional ties to what you have done in your past.

For instance: You have emotional ties to many past lifetimes that deal with family members, your enemies, your phobias, your religion, and many more emotional ties that you are unconscious off. The only way to relieve you of these emotional ties to your past is for you to meet yourself in other people, including your family members. It also helps you to learn that you have forgotten that there are no wrong choices here, and that you have never sinned.

I will talk more about karma and retribution and what it means later in the book. But for now, understand that there is no such thing. Again, how can you sin if everything is a hologram and an illusion, with the exception of your spirit and divinity? What you are feeling is only the experiences of duality, your mental perception of things, and the challenges you chose to put on yourself in order to learn who you truly are, and to become a sovereign being in your own right. It is from the wisdom of many dualistic experiences that will, in the end, carry you into your sovereignty as a true Goddess (God) in your own right.

You see, as said before, the word negative became associated with the feminine part of you as well as with bad, and the word positive became associated with the masculine part of you as well as with good. Yet, the negative-bad in its truest context of the word only means darkness, ignorance, or what was unknown to you at the time. The word positive-good in its truest text means to move forward as far as soul growth, and you do it, as all souled being, using your deceptive mental consciousness and your connection to universal mind in creating the things you desire to experience.

Of course it was terrifying for us, as souls, to leave our divine state (first creation). However, our desire to go out and express on behalf of our own spirit overrode any fear that we were feeling. This is why our spirit does not interfere in the affairs of us being human, even when we are choosing and creating appalling and tragic circumstances for ourselves and for others. Our spirit and soul (mother-wife) has immense compassion, unconditional love, and holiness for her deceptive masculine mental side (husband), even though he (the deceptive self) has taken her (soul) for granted.

Now that we have cleared-up some of the confusion about the story of creation that the Bible speaks of, and about who you truly are and where you have come from, I ask your permission to begin a new story of creation because the time is right in bringing in this message. Of course, instead of starting with the creation of man and earth, I will begin this new story of creation where you, as for all souled beings, were there in your divine state of consciousness or what I have been calling the first creation. So, if you are ready then let us begin!

My dear co-creators, after playing and absorbing everything that your divine state offered in the first creation, you, as all souled beings, got to know every inch, depth, and width of your divineness (garden). This led to a feeling of being empty and unfulfilled, which is why your spirit invited you to embark on a new adventure that would take you far beyond your divine state and into a deceptive mental state that would relate only to rational thoughts, beliefs of duality, mental impressions, sensitivity, imaging, physicality, and memory.

However, what came with this challenge was a warning about moving beyond your divine state, for no one knew at the time, not even your spirit, what you would find beyond the margins of your divineness. Therefore, you had no idea what you were going to experience. In fact, you did not even know if this was going to be the end of you or the beginning of a whole new you. You see, at the time, who knew what rational thought, or that the feeling of something consisting of two parts, and the sensation of emotions and imaging would bring to you to experience.

Nevertheless, feeling very excited about leaving the edges of your divine state of consciousness, you, for the very first time, noticed a disruption coming from what you understood as your comfort zone. Then, as you turned to say good-by to your spirit and to the kingdom of divine oneness you cheered in this feeling of going out on a new adventure in spite of it.

So we all, as souled beings, took the challenge and moved outside the limitations of our divine state (first creation) and into a new thought process that came under the guidance of a consciousness of a mental and rational state that consisted of duality. As we began to move past the limitations of our divine state of consciousness at the time, we, for the very first time, felt depressed because it was, after all, the very first time we really felt the love of our spirit running through us.

In fact, this love of spirit felt unusual as it made us feel unfilled and alone where before we always felt connected, warm, and comfortable. Even though feeling this disruption of our comfort zone being challenged, we felt something deep within our being that was strong and influential. It was a knowing that the divine spark, our true essence, was part of our mental state as well, for it was the divine spark within that made us feel and know that we were a divine being out exploring.

So, there we were at the edge of what we always knew to be our divine state (first creation). As we, all souled beings, faded into this abyss of rational thought, emotions, imagining, and the illusion of duality, we moved into a consciousness where we felt nothing but endless ignorance (symbolized by the abyss in the Bible). That is when suddenly everything shifted! As it shifted, we tried to pull ourselves out of this feeling of endless ignorance because it produced nothing but deceptive behavior on our part. However, it did not work.

To our surprise, this boundless feeling of being ignorant to this mental rational thought process seemed immeasurably deep as the pull of duality became stronger and stronger. It was more than anything that we had felt before. In fact, our awareness of knowing that we were a divine being began to lessen and fade to the point where our focus on our divine state suddenly became very unstable. It felt like we were being ripped away from the awareness of being a divine being.

Then the next thing we felt was the feeling of falling, a falling that pulled us more and more into this boundless abyss of ignorance, endless deceptive mental expressions, and a vibrational energy of duality so strong, we actually felt it was against our will. From this feeling of falling into the unknown vibrational forces of duality and into the unknown deceptive mental consciousness at the time, we all asked ourselves (symbolically speaking), what was it that we just experienced? At first we thought it felt like it was a dream but then we said to ourselves that it couldn't have been a dream because it felt so real.

However, we, as souled beings, shrugged the feeling off and made a note to ask our own spirit (the divine you) about it when we returned back to the knowing that we were our own spirit in expression. However, to our surprise, just after we decided to make a note of the experience, we felt something deep within our soul telling us that we'd better return back to the knowing of being a divine being before it was too late.

So, we, all souled beings, put out a distressed call to our spirit to help us return back to the "kingdom of knowing" that we were a divine being (heaven) just out expressing our desires to learn more about who we were. However, we were surprised again as we found ourselves not returning back to our divine state. Instead, we found ourselves getting deeper and deeper into this endless pit of a deceptive mental consciousness that consisted of a very strong vibrational energy of duality. The Bible calls it the abyss as well as good and evil.

In fact, this endless deceptiveness consciousness was so dark we called it nothingness because we did not understand or see (feel) anything, not even ourselves. At first, we thought maybe our spirit didn't understand our desire to return back to our divine state of knowing. Yet again, we experienced something that we did not experience before. We all felt a strong negative wave of energy passing through our deceptive and rational consciousness to where we, for the very first time, felt fear.

This emotion of fear scared us to where we all began to command ourselves (in thought not words) to return to the comfort of our divine state again. However, as we continued to command (pray) ourselves to return to our divine state (first creation- Garden), we found ourselves moving closer to something that felt heated, intense, and angry.

Then, out of this endless deceptive mental state (abyss), a heated, intense, and angry energy wave of a flaming wall was coming toward us, actually rising up from out of nowhere, and it didn't feel good to us at all. That is when we, all souls, took a deep breath and called out to our spirit once again as we had never done before and said, dear spirit bring us back home to the first creation where I know I am one with my divine state.

As you can see, you, as all souled beings, pleaded and pleaded with your spirit to bring you back home to your divine state, telling your spirit that you had no experience with fear and this deceptive and rational part of you – for you did not know how to deal with it. However, your plea to move back into your divine state of knowing still did not work.

So, you again said (metaphorically) in a very loud thought, you are the offspring of the Spirit of One and therefore demand to return home, back to the first creation (Divine State). Since nothing happened, this led to you thinking to yourself that you will leave it in the hands of your soul to bring you back home where you always felt your connection to your spirit and universal mind. And yet, again nothing happened!

Then, symbolically speaking, a cold chill came over you. It was a feeling that you did not like and a feeling that felt extremely upsetting. This feeling was guilt and shame, which came conscious to you at the time because of you moving beyond your divine state. It was right at that moment where you thought to yourself that you should have listened to that deep voice within because you were warned about venturing out beyond the "kingdom of knowing" that you are a divine being.

It was at that point where you felt overwhelming guilt and shame for moving your focus from your divine state to a deceptive mental state of reasoning that housed an energy force of positive and negative. This was the very first time where you, as all souled beings, experienced duality, because from out of this feeling of guilt and shame, your very first belief system was formed from the seat of your being.

Yes, this was the time where we, as souled beings, actually created a thought process where we came to believe that we are indeed separate from our spirit. It was because of the activity of rational thought and our emotion of fear is where we manifested a belief that became known to us as our fall into sin. This feeling of guilt, shame, sin, and separation caused us to beg our spirit for forgiveness because of leaving our state of knowing that we are indeed divine in nature.

You said (thought) to your spirit! I now realize that I did something bad and wrong, and that I have sinned against my spirit and I am sorry for it. You even said to your spirit. "If my spirit would bring me back to my divine state of consciousness again (first creation), where I know that I am safe, I would dedicate myself to worshiping my spirit." Note: Now you know where the belief in worshipping came from.

Yet again, nothing happened, other than this energy wave of a flaming wall of dualistic vibrational energy (sometimes called the wall of duality) getting closer and closer to us. (Now, the angelic realm and Tobias's Journey of the angels calls this "wall of duality" the "wall of fire." Yet, for this presentation, my soul calls it the "wall of duality or the wall of dualistic vibrational energy" because it holds within it powerful violent and uncontrollable flames of hell and suffering).

Now, as we souls sensed a lot of fear, which caused us all to call out to our spirit one more time, we all bowed down to the extreme cruel and devilish power of our ignorance to this rational thought process and what we were experiencing with this "wall of duality" – for we hoped that our spirit would see us in a desperate need for help. We even gave our solemn oath to never go against our spirit again. We prayed and said, "Hear me oh spirit, if you love me, remember me and bring me back home, back to my divine state (the first creation) where I know that I am save and a divine being."

Note: Maybe now, you understand why we misinterpret the Bible and its texts, for they are talking about your spirit and not about some God kicking you out of some garden. It is you that is the God, the Adam, the Eve, and the Serpent in creating your own world to experience. Therefore, it was you, from a mental and rational state of consciousness, who kicked yourself out of the Garden and not some God outside of you.

However, religion proclaims this God of the Bible, Adam, Eve, and the Serpent as something that is separate from you, which is not true. Why, because you are all of those parts and more. This is also why you seem to worship a God and yet, in reality, you are worshipping and giving tribute to a false God, a God that is outside of you and is mental.

Remember, all that happened here is that you moved your conscious focus from your divine state to a deceptive mental and reasoning state. Because of it, your thought process of a mental state manifested your belief systems so fast that those beliefs began to obscure you from your divine state. It was because of your fear, lucid thoughts, and beliefs is where you ended up designing a course of action that led you into a field of consciousness that produced nothing but duality and a false God as being your reality, which is in truth just an illusion.

However, don't feel bad because of it, for it was the greatest blessing and gift that you ever gave yourself because it became the vehicle to learn everything there is about life, love, and who you truly are. However, let us talk about that later in the book. Right now, let me get back to my soul's story!

As we, all souled beings, gazed at this uncontrollable and violent wall of duality moving toward us more and more, we knew at that moment, it was going to swallow us up in its blazing inferno if our spirit didn't act. We felt fear that was beyond our understanding which caused us to scream out one final time asking our spirit to save us.

It was, in that moment, just before the destructive flames of the wall of duality reached us, we, all souled beings, heard a voice deep within our consciousness. It was a voice from our spirit (divine state) saying that we will never be alone. With that my dear friends is when we, as souled beings, were drawn deeper and deeper into this violent wall of vibrational energy with such brute force it slashed our consciousness into millions and millions of pieces to where we felt powerless and inferior to it.

The fear and tormenting we were experiencing at the time bewildered us to the deepest levels of our being. And yet, we still felt our consciousness being ripped apart but this time into billions and billions of pieces. There seemed to be no way for us to get out of this chaos and fiery flames of torment that was surrounding us and ripping our consciousness apart.

We tried and tried to get out of this vibrational energy shredder but to no avail. We even tried to get ourselves rebalanced by calling once again to our spirit for help. However, as each of us was being shredded apart more and more, what we were experiencing seemed to be endless thought patterns that were based on judgment, attitude, emotions, and beliefs that were connected to this deceptive dualistic vibrational energy. Each time we called out to our spirit, this opposing wall of inferno ripped our energy and consciousness even more.

All that we had felt and experienced were waves and waves of positive and negative energy potentials pulling at our core essence in such a fashion, we all began to change our attitude to who we thought we were. It was that this deceptive dualistic force was very brutal and destructive on the core of our soul. We even began to believe and take the attitude of our spirit deserting us because of feeling guilt, shame, being separate from spirit, and that we somehow had sinned. This is when our spirit revealed to us the secret of our divine state, for we all felt the vibrations of our spirit conveying to us.

"Now that you have focused your consciousness to go out and experience the theory of rational thought, being separate from your divine state, and to feel and use the forces of a vibrational energy, known as positive and negative, as well as, to find out who you truly are, then the very nature of "all that you were" in the first creation is no longer a oneness because now, you are a consciousness of two (divine and mental)."

Therefore, no matter where the journey of duality takes you or what thoughts or possibilities you choose to express and experience (good or bad), you will, in the end, get where you are going and become a sovereign "I AM" unto yourself. In other words, this was the time where your spirit was no more a oneness unto itself, for she, or your divine state (first creation) and your deceptive mental state of a reasoning consciousness (the second creation), became incorporated into the forces of duality, where both are now the core essence of you. It is the same for all souls.

This means, you cannot go back home (heaven) to your divine state (first creation) like it was before because you have created a confusing deceptive mental version of yourself that took on a belief that rational thought and dualistic energy is real. And now, together with your divine state, you have become one with "all that you are" today. Therefore, the only thing that you can do is to integrate "all that you are" as one.

You see, "all that was in the beginning," before your mental and dualistic state was created, was you in your divine state, or what was called the Garden in the Bible, and now "all that you are today" is what you have learned and experienced since the time you left your divine state (first creation). However, "all that you are now" is also part of your divine state, your soul, your deceptive mental and reasoning state, and your physical state as well.

This is why you, in the end, become a God unto yourself that "knows all things" because heaven and hell are not out there. Heaven and hell are now part of you and every souled being. So, stop looking for heaven and a God that lives beyond the sky! Heaven, and the God that you seek, is you.

In other words, you, a child of God (symbolically speaking), are more than just part of the Spirit of One, you also have a deceptive consciousness that holds a belief in positive and negative, a consciousness of rational thought, and that you have a soul, a spirit, and a divinity (Christ like being) that makes you, and all souls alike, as one body of consciousness and yet, individualized.

We, all souled beings, are the one God that made everything appear in the second creation (abyss) and not some solitary persona of a God unto himself that is all powerful and all-knowing, for that is the illusion and a lie.

So now we know about the wisdom of creation, as it was hidden from us until we evolved enough in consciousness to discover that God is not a solitary personality sitting on a throne waiting to place judgment upon us. God is an icon and not real, and therefore false.

The real God is the make-up of all souled beings (you and me) acting together as one unit. This is why "all that is today" and "all what has been created," for nothing can exists without the Spirit of One and you being part of it, not even Satan, darkness and light, was all created by us souled beings. Thus, no single while male God here, it is just us souled beings playing with universal energy.

Chapter 6

Moving Into A Divided Consciousness

Once you chose to move outside of your divine state (first creation or garden) and into a "deceptive divided consciousness state," you, as all souls, created a false version of yourself, a mirror likeness that became your main focal point. From this deceptive mental likeness, you faithfully devoted your total beingness creating multitudes of potentials for you to experience, good and bad. You even joined together with the mass group consciousness in creating a false god and a false devil outside of you in order to explain your existence and to deny responsibility for your creations.

It was from these massive potentials and possibilities, as the number is so great it is impossible to comprehend, where each souled being, including you and me, manifested what is known today as the "second creation." The Bible calls it the "abyss" and Science calls it the big "bang theory."

Now, as my soul moves forward with this presentation, I do ask you to always keep in mind that the core essence of your real identity is that you are a divine being first and foremost and therefore, infinite, unchangeable, and you are without sin. You are a soul that is made up of the same qualities of the Spirit of One. You have a spirit that incorporates a consciousness of a divine state, a divine imagination, being very intuitive, compassionate, and you are aware of who you truly are at the soul level, even though you have forgotten from the conscious level.

Therefore, the choice to "split your consciousness of one," as it was for all of us souled beings, into a deceptive mental likeness of yourself that held a belief in duality is what triggered you into creating multiple lifetimes and multiple potentials, both good and bad, for you to experience. It was the only way to learn who you truly are and your connection to your own divine state.

You can say the "second creation" is indeed the make-up of all souled beings working together as the Godhead bringing in the "in-breath and out-breath of spirit and universal mind to what has been manifested ever since we souled beings left the first creation (divine state).

The angelic realm, and my soul, calls the second creation the etheric-astral and physical realms put together as one creation and yet, this one creation consists of many dimensions, potentials, and possibilities to great to count, including earth. You know it by, *"In my father's house there are many mansions* (John 14:2).

Through science, the Big Bang theory is the prevailing scientific study of the origin and structure of the universe, including earth and yet, this is not true. Science use the term Big Bang theory to refer to the idea that the universe was originally extremely hot and dense at some thirteen billion years ago and has since cooled down by expanding to the present adulterated energy of duality, and it continues to expand today.

This theory is supported by the most comprehensive and accurate explanations from current scientific evidence and observation. Detailed notes of the study of form, the structure of organisms, the distribution of galaxies, and the huge amounts of energy that sometime equal to the energy output of an entire galaxy provide strong evidence for the Big Bang theory.

A combination of analysis and theory suggest that the first huge amount of energy output and galaxies were formed about a billion years after the Big Bang. Since then larger structures have been forming, such as galaxy clusters and superclusters that appear to be close together.

However, here is what has been forgotten. The Big Bang theory was not about the structure of living organisms, such as plants, animals, man, or the distribution of galaxies or planets, not in its entirety anyway. There was more to it than just the structuring of living organisms.

It was the "Spirit of One" breaking up into gazillions upon gazillions of pieces of herself, and within each piece, the image of the "Spirit of One" came into a state of existence as us souled beings. We, all souls, and what we have created, are the evidence of it. Yet, science can only explain it from an intellectual manner and therefore, overlooks the universe as being a hologram created by us souled beings. This is why science has a hard time moving past the concept of dualistic vibrational energy.

However, science is beginning to learn that the universe could be multi-dimensional, and that when vibrational energy such as anti-matter and matter are smashed together the results is neutralized energy. Of course, this suggestion by science scares religion.

You see, your spirit knew that in order to become a sovereign "I AM" in your own right, and to know "who you are," you had to lose your memory and awareness of being part of something bigger than just your deceptive mental and human likeness. Otherwise, you would have ignored moving into the wisdom of the "Tree of Knowledge of Good and Evil," which is nothing more than you, all souled beings, taking on a mental state of intellectual thinking that only believes in a force of positive, negative, and physicality as being real in order to learn about live.

You see, as soon as we, all souls, felt separated from our own spirit a very long time ago, we mimicked the Spirit of One and, having the same defining features, we gained the ability to create many, many personality-aspects or likenesses of ourselves, called lifetimes, in order to see our collective self explore as many dualistic potentials and possibilities as possible. It was from our very own soul where we found that by creating false deceptive mental images of ourselves and placing them into many physical bodies, we could play opposite roles from what we did before in some other lifetime, thus the question "who am I" would then be answered.

Therefore, the biggest lie ever told that was introduced to you a long time ago was the idea that you are not, and have never been God, even though the word "God" is only a distinguishing emblematic celebrity, an icon, because you do exist as a divine being in your own right. It is just that you have forgotten.

My fellow searchers, we are all gods, and we are gods that chose to take the plunge into the flaming fire of dualistic vibrational energy and into rational thought patterns to explore as many potentials and possibilities as we could, even if the action defied our divine nature. And now, the challenge is for us to find the courage to question the status quo. Jesus was such a man, and it cost him his life, which symbolically means we die for our own sins.

In effect, we will remain dead until we recognize that we are not sinning, we are only experiencing what is not known to us, as an individual soul and as a group. Therefore, with this type of knowledge, this can be the day for our awakening (ascension), and all that we have to do is allow ourselves to invite in our soul as the Christ that we have been waiting for. The Christ consciousness is not about one man. It is about all of us souled beings having a consciousness that is filled with wisdom, understanding, and clarity about who we truly are.

My dear friends, there is no heaven or hell that separates you from your Christ roots. There are no religions, beliefs, faith, or spiritual leaders that you have to follow. It is only you, for the savior is not about Jesus coming to save you. It is about tapping into your own divine consciousness and rescuing the false deceptive likenesses of your many human aspects from the chains of rational thought, duality, and their (yours) emotions of suffering.

It is up to you if you are ready to welcome in your soul (Christ) identity, which is filled with wisdom, and let go of the idea that someone outside of you is going to save you from your conditions. Know that you are more than just human. You are a Christ also that is filled with understanding, wisdom, and clarity because of your many lifetimes, and all that is happened is that you have forgotten that you created them.

All the choices you have made from the beginning of your awakening in spirit as a divine being to your present now moment have come from the memories of your yesterdays (past lifetimes), which is why the angelic realm always say, the future is the past healed. All that you have to do to heal yourself is to let go of the old and remember who you truly are.

Therefore, I ask you to set aside the deceptive mind and its rational thinking patterns about your dogmatic beliefs, your definition of Christ, and the idea of sin for awhile and allow your spirit, and the expression of your soul nature (wisdom), to come forward and help you remember "who you truly are."

However, if you are still uncertain about "who you are," then allow me to continue with what my soul revealed to me. Let me begin where I left off in the last chapter about the violent and uncontrollable energy moving upon us, as souled beings, because of our choice to leave the oneness of our own divine state (first creation).

You see, as this violent and uncontrollable wall of duality (vibrational energy) moved upon us with such brute force it not only ripped us into thousands and millions of pieces, it ripped us into billions and billions of pieces. It was in fact right after we were slashed apart by this violent deceptive dualistic vibrational force repeatedly that we, along with the pain and terror that we all were feeling and experiencing at the time, saw something we had never seen before.

Because of self-awareness, we instantly connected with our soul, and from that point we all began to see our shame, guilt, fears, and all of what we did at the deepest level. In fact, the moment we saw our soul, we tried to run from it and hide. This caused us all to cry out to our spirit once again, asking not to judge or condemn us for what we did. Thus, without realizing it, we all created another belief system, which was, the belief that good and bad are somehow the defining energies of a force outside of us that brings to us judgment and punishment.

This vibrational force later became what we now call God and his wrath, which is why there is no need to pray to this false God, because in reality, he is really not there. Oh, we can speak to our own spirit. But to a God outside of us, no! Because of our many lifetimes playing with rational thought patterns, logic, and vibrational energy, we now have a belief system that we must pray to a God to save us. Where in fact, the only one that can save us, is oneself, for one is God and the Christ and yet, we keep running from ourselves.

From the belief in good and bad, that of judgment, our lucid thought patterns, and our belief in sin, this uncontrollable and violent wall of duality once again started to rip us apart, over and over. Because of the slashing and ripping of our consciousness, we again screamed out to our spirit for help and yet, nothing, no sound, no feelings, nothing was coming back to us from our own spirit.

In effect, the more we screamed and hid from what we were feeling and experiencing, the more this violent and uncontrollable wall of dualistic vibrational energy would find us and drag us right back into ripping us into even more pieces. And yes, we all felt abandoned and alone.

What this ripping and tearing of our consciousness was, was nothing more than we, as souled beings, continuously expressing more and more of deceptive thought patterns of duality, and we, at the time, did not even realize we were doing it. This slashing and ripping apart of our energy and consciousness took away any hope that our spirit would ever bring us back to feeling safe again.

Because of those feelings, we, all souls, finally gave up on our own spirit in taking us back home to the peaceful and quiet first creation where our divine "I AMness" resides today. We even got to the point where we did not want to remember our divine "I AMness," because every time we did, it brought nothing but pain, sadness, and suffering. This is why most of us fear our divine state and our soul (Christ) today because it feels dark and scary, which is why we turned to a God of make-believe.

So, when hope was lost, which was a very long time ago, we finally let go of the desire to go back home to our divine state. We even allowed ourselves to let go of trying to maintain any sense of ourselves, which of course, brought on the thought of being doomed. Then in one more last effort to bring us back home to our divine state, we all mustered up an inner strength to find the memory of home and our soul, and to reconnect with it.

However, once we did reconnect, this violent wall of vibrational energy again grabbed our consciousness, slashing it into even more pieces, where in the end, produced nothing but more deceptive and emotional expressions of duality. It was at that point we finally had enough. So, we, all souls, surrendered, for we had no more strength to remember who we were. It was from that point we lost all recollection of who we were, where home was, or that we were even a divine being that had a soul.

That is when we allowed ourselves to fall deeply into this deceptive violent flame of dualistic vibrational energy, which then caused us to see nothing but endless nothingness (abyss) as our reality. In fact, it all felt like death, complete isolation, and darkness. It was from that point we, since all that we felt and experienced was nothing but isolation, darkness, and pieces of ourselves, we all began to observe ourselves as nothingness too, not even a souled being.

You can actually say it was like we were completely dead and cold and yet, we were all still alive because we felt our awareness. Remember, at the time, we had no form to us. It also felt like we were in a nightmare because everything seemed as nothing but continuous pieces of nothingness, death, and void. It even felt like we were as much part of the void as the void was part of us.

In fact, according to Tobias's "Journey of the Angels," you can feel this deceptive vacuum of nothingness inside of you today. Why? Because this was perhaps the most difficult time and dramatic experience that you have ever experienced because it created your largest fear that you could ever know. This fear was death or that you can go out of existence! As you know, most people are afraid of death because they just don't know what's next.

This endless nothingness that we all fell into after leaving our divine state (the first creation) a long time ago, and what the Bible calls the abyss, had no external parts or form to it. It did not even have any sort of activity, life, or impulse. There was absolutely nothing around us but endless darkness and vacuums of void, which is why our spirit is still part of nothingness. After all, according to Tobias, nothingness is still part of something.

According to my soul, and that of the angelic realm, we, as humans, tried to escape this nothingness feeling by creating drama because it helps us feel alive. As we all know, drama is a type of energy that can twist us inside out for a long time. Most drama comes from family because of our karmic ties to them, which is why family will fight and argue with each other over the littlest things, especially when one wants to move beyond the family belief patterns.

Now, as we fell into this cold dark endless pit of nothingness trying to feel something to build on, all that came up was more dark, more fear, and more nothingness, which again made us feel hopeless and dejected. We actually felt dead because we couldn't feel our identity, presence, and our soul because we (at the time) were only of a consciousness without form that believed we were nothing.

However, something happened where we suddenly felt our existence on a conscious level. Of course, what we were actually feeling was our own soul (Christ self) that we had seen way back during the time when we were moving through the violent wall of dual vibrational energy and into the second creation. From what we were feeling coming from our soul caused us to feel renewed. It made us feel that we did in fact exist, and that we had to come from somewhere.

Even though we were surrounded by this vacuum of nothingness and our rational thought patterns of duality, darkness, and ignorance, we still could feel our existence at a conscious level, even though we had no form to us at the time. This feeling caused us to become even more aware of our soul consciousness. That is when we came to the conclusion that all of this feeling of not existing, or that we are nothing, and that everything around us was nothing, was in fact caused by a dark force so terrifying we labeled it evil and bad. This is why most people are afraid of the dark.

The Bible calls this force Lucifer, Satan, Serpent, or the Devil. Yes, we, as souled beings, came to this conclusion because that was the time where we began to hear our thoughts, feel our emotions, and feel our individualized consciousness as if we were alive even though we couldn't observe, or witness, or touch ourselves at the time, for we were all formless.

After all, we were a mirror likeness of our divine state, which means there was no physical body or even a deceptive mental body that we could actually see with our eyes or touch because at the time we had no eyes or any feeling of touch. Our "wholeness of being" was that we were nothing but spirit, consciousness, thought and expression, even though our thought patterns were coming from a deceptive mental version of ourselves.

Though we were nothing but these things, having no form to us, we somehow knew that we could think, feel, and that we were aware of our being. So, because of being aware of ourselves at the time, we then realized that we must be alive because, if we weren't, then we would not be aware of our thoughts.

It was a time when we really felt, for the very first time, that we wanted to experience something, anything actually, no matter if it was right or wrong because it made no difference to us. That my dear friends, is when we all began to express our thoughts, ideas, beliefs, and images of things outwardly and into what the Bible calls the abyss. My soul calls it the second creation.

Allow me to move away from my soul's story a bit! You see, once you became aware of being conscious in your divine state in the first creation, you moved beyond the consciousness of your divine nature and left the first creation on purpose because of the challenge coming from your own spirit. However, once you left, you forgot that challenge, and instead labeled it as something you did wrong or bad, which then brought you shame and guilt for doing it.

Even today we, as humans, have forgotten that our spirit has never ventured out beyond the gates of our divine oneness. It is only a mental perception on our part that we did, which is why we have this belief that we've sinned. That, my fellow searchers, is the gift and the love that came from our spirit because in the second creation nothing existed since we, as souled beings, had never been there before.

The gift we received from our spirit was, "How could we ever come to know ourselves if we had stayed within our divine state of oneness?" The answer was found that we couldn't, which is why we, all souls, chose to move beyond the gates of our divine state in order to understand duality, the playing of opposites, feel the emotions of fear, and to create our own path in finding our own "I AM Sovereignty." It had nothing to do with Adam and Eve disobeying God.

From out of the love for our spirit, we, in our deceptive mental and physical state, would then share those experiences with our spirit and with our soul brothers and sisters. So again, there is no such thing as sin. Sin is just a word that is not understood from the standpoint of the rational mind as of yet.

Now, moving on with my soul's story! As we, all souled beings, were beginning to get our awareness back into focus from this nothingness feeling, we began to feel other souls around us. You see, when we were in the first creation, we had no concept of other souls. We were all part of the Spirit of One. However, once we moved into this nothingness (second creation), we began to feel and become aware of other souls around us. In fact, it felt different than before when we were in our divine state.

Actually, it took us, as souled beings, feeling and becoming aware of each other before we personally felt the energy of other souls around us for the very first time. Never before did we have or feel this experience. This feeling of each other's energy really surprised us, and not only that, it confused us because without realizing it, we thought that we were alone in this vacuum of nothingness.

Now, at the time, the idea of feeling the energy of another soul brought to us overwhelming excitement. Because of it, we thought to ourselves that we could work together in trying to establish who we were and where we had come from. However, because of the excitement of not being alone in this dark nothingness, we all gave way to joy, which then caused us to presume that there might be many souls like us.

Of course, after you, as did all souls, made your introductions, symbolically speaking, you asked, not in words of course because you had no form or language at the time, if anyone knew who they were and where did they come from? Interestingly, their reply to you surprised you – for they said that they had no idea. The souls, in fact, that you asked turned around and asked the same question to you. (Now, it was not as if everyone was speaking in words here or that we had a physical body. It was all done telepathically using thought patterns, and with using energy to serve us).

Then, from out of the blue, just about everyone at the same time, including you, thought that perhaps someone knew the answer but were unwilling to disclose the information. So, because of this feeling that someone had this information but was unwilling to disclose it is when all souls, including you, decided to attack each other and try to force the information out about everyone's existence, and where everyone had come from.

Even though everyone, you included, found themselves battling with each other, everyone concluded that they must have been created, therefore having a home somewhere. Again remember, you did not have a physical body at the time or any type of language. Never-the-less, you fought with and against your souled brothers and sisters with brutal tactics, even though you may not remember that you did. It was like you, and everyone around you, were trying to devour everyone's energy. Everyone tried to seize each other's energy and consciousness in an effort to destroy it or own it.

For instance: In the beginning of our physical adventure it didn't take long for us humans to come up with slavery. This is a prime example of what we did in spirit first before any physicality. We tried to own other souls. So yes, we all fought hard and long, trying to overcome another soul.

Then again something happened that you did not feel before. It felt like you were beginning to defeat the souled being that you were fighting against because that souled being just laid there as if it was dead. That is when you, the one standing, thought to yourself, "Wow," what a feeling, for that felt good! Then right after that comment, or I should say thought, you felt energy being redistributed to you that seemed to be coming from the souled being you just defeated.

Note: When I talk in terms of a soul standing over another soul looking as if he or she is dead, I am symbolically speaking as if one had a physical body. It is not that one had a physical body. It is that one held a weightless type of consciousness that radiated some type of light. I speak this way as if it is a physical body to help you understand in symbolic terms in what my soul was conveying to me.

Now, let me get back to my soul's story. This caused a feeling of a surge of energy moving right through your being. That is where the misinterpretation of power comes from because this was the very first time you, as all souls did from fighting each other, felt power, and you liked it. We all liked it! However, as soon as you felt this power, the souled being that you just defeated seemed to come back to life. When that souled being came back to life it jumped up and attacked you with such fury that it traumatized you, causing you to surrender to that same souled being that was supposedly dead.

That is when the souled being that was once dead felt what you just felt a moment ago about the surge of energy (power) moving through its being. So, as this souled being was standing next to you as if you were dead, like it was a moment ago, you also came back to life just like the other souled being did when it looked dead. That is when you jumped up and attacked that souled being once again but this time with greater force than before.

So, there you were, along with who you were battling with, dying and coming back to life over and over again. Coming back to life beating, thrashing, fighting, and struggling with one another, both of you trying to subdue each other into believing you could destroy one another to the effect of stealing one another's energy (power). This battling seemed to gone on forever, long enough to where you, along with all souls, were getting tired of slaughtering one another, feeling that one was dead, and then out of the blue come back to life again to fight again.

Note: A good example of this is when one person puts another person down because of their way of life or because of looks and how it makes that person feel more superior and, the person that was put down less superior. This happens all the time, and we all do it unconsciously to our family, our kids, our friends and neighbors, and we also do it by putting down others belief systems because of how we feel we are right. That my dear friends, is stealing energy!

Of course, in the beginning of our mental adventures this felt very strange and bizarre to us because at one moment we were dead, and then the next moment we were alive and well again!

All souled beings fought and fought, killed and destroyed each other, at least we thought so, and yet, everyone felt their existence over and over. All of this was leading to everyone becoming very exhausted and done in because no one was able to overcome or kill another soul. That was when we, all souled beings, finally realized that it was pointless and futile to continue with this energy stealing and fighting.

You see, everyone forgot that they have the same divine quality and proportion of power as the Spirit of One within each of us. We are all a souled being (Goddess) first and foremost before any mental or physicality. So, how can we take over or kill another souled being if we all are infinite and have the same power as the Spirit of One? In other words, we cannot steal, kill, or take over another's consciousness, for it is all a deception.

However, it felt like we did because we would feel a surge of power move through our beingness when we did subdue someone, and then again that feeling soon disappeared once they came conscious of themselves again in what one was doing. That is when we, all souls, came to realize that one souled being can never destroy or take over another. At least, in the long run!

Everyone, including you, realized how pointless this fighting each other was. So, eventually everyone grew to be very good friends. This is when you, as did all souls that you noticed around you, decided to form into a soul group, calling your soul group a family. Now, the soul count in your group could have been in the hundreds, thousands, or millions, though the number is irrelevant.

However, from that point, the souls that you once fought became now your family. Then each soul in your family group took an oath not to ever again fight each other. Your family group proclaimed that they would work together in an effort to find the answer to the questions, "Who am I, who created me, and where did everyone come from?" You could say as a good example of this, it would be like the battles we Americans had during the Civil War, and then everyone joining together to become one family, one country, America.

However, out of nowhere, your family group of souls suddenly came across other family groups of souls. For example: America coming across other countries that just had the same encounter as you and your soul group did. To your surprise, every one of them seemed to feel outside of you and to your soul family group as it did for them, causing once again the addictiveness of power within oneself and within each group.

Because of them feeling outside you and your soul family, everyone began to fight each other like you fought each other earlier, attacking, devouring, killing and energy stealing. To the point where you found yourself fighting your own soul group members all over again, even though you, and them, just made a pledge not to do that. Then, like before, everyone became tired and had gotten nowhere, for the results were the same as before.

Now, this battling and fighting went on and on forever, or it seemed that way, until all souls finally broke up into 144,000 different soul groups, with each family group having numbers in the hundreds, thousands, millions, or perhaps billions. Again, the number count in each family soul group is irrelevant for this narrative purpose.

However, the original group that you first battled with developed into a stronger bond than before, because from out of the first group of souls you battled, you really felt their energy, divineness and their uniqueness, as it helped you understand your own individuality and divineness.

Because of this, even though you did not remember at the time, you placed your divine state deep within your consciousness as if it did not exists, similar to disguising it from yourself and others. Your goal was to go out and experience duality without the fear of your creations taking over your divine "I AMness." This way you believed that your "I AM essence" or your spirit would always remain pure.

Now, after all of our battles, and getting nowhere with them, we, as souled beings, did become aware of two major things that we could do.

First, we could create an illusion for a brief period and second, we cannot enslave or possess the consciousness and energy of another souled being. We also came to the conclusion that we were a conscious being in a place where there was nothing but souls because there were no signs of creation anywhere. There were no stars, planets, galaxies, universes, and no physical earth, not even plants, animals, vegetation, or humans. It was all dark endless nothingness. Even you felt that way because you had no form to you either.

Now, after realizing that we, as all soul groups did, can create illusions and images of things because of our deceptive mental nature, the desire for more power became very addictive. However, before going into more battles over power, all 144,000 different family soul groups melded their energies together, and filled that endless vacuum of nothingness into billions and billions of potentials and realities that gave birth to a massive amount of dimensions, including a physical dimension to play out some of these potentials, as an individual and as a group. This would be the big bang theory coming into manifestation.

My fellow searchers, it was from these 144,000 different soul groups that we, all souls, joined together, first as individuals, and then as a group, that created everything seen and unseen, and not some single solitary white male God in some heaven. It was us, as souled beings, that had the desire to express our illusions about how to answer the questions of who are we, who created us, where did we come from, what is duality, and how do we get back home to our divine state (first creation).

From there, we, all soul groups, extended our illusions to include light and dark to help us learn the wisdom of duality and that of our choices. Now, because of taken on the belief in light and dark, the desire of each family group to answer the questions mentioned became unclear and distorted. Why, it was because of it becoming a search for power and control more so than trying to find the answer to the questions.

You could say the battles between each soul family group intensified greatly because of the utmost desire to feel and have power and control over one another or soul group. It became very difficult for us souls to let go of this feeling of power and control, which seemed to always lead each of us right back into fighting over something that is not real anyway.

You see, when we, all souls, felt our individual identity a long time ago, we started to have feelings of power and a feeling that we could create anything we desired because we learned fast that we could create something out of nothingness. This is why it is easy for us to imagine how everyone, all gazillions upon gazillions of us, as souled beings, grouped together with other souls and formed an army of 144,000 different soul family groups, ranging in the hundreds, thousands, millions, and perhaps billions, all trying to control each other as well as each other's soul group with as much force as possible with our creations.

Just stop for a moment and imagine this. See how possible this is because it explains today the whys of religions, governments, nations, as well as race fighting each other, all trying to maintain the control and power they think they have over another. In fact, all that we are doing today, as humans, are replaying what we did a long time in the etheric realms. Until we learn that we cannot kill another or take over another soul, even though we are human, peace on earth will not be possible.

In recap! We, as souled beings, in the beginning, learned about power by encountering each other through the feeling one's energy around us, then using our perceptive mental consciousness in trying to figure who we were, and then battling each other to see who was stronger or more powerful. That is when we learned that we had the power to create and destroy. This power felt exhilarating to us and we wanted more and more of it.

Not only did we want to feel powerful, we desperately wanted to use it in order to define ourselves. However we used our power, we forgot that we were really transforming energy from one state to another, which is why we chose death in the physical. We needed to come back over and over again in a new physical body to pick up where we left off in an effort to resolve our issues with our illusion of power, control, and death.

Chapter 7

The Structuring Of The Second Creation

(Outside of Your Divine State)

After the birth of power we, as souled beings, claimed this power as a true and reliable force to be reckoned with. Then later, as we moved upon the earth surface in a perceptual mental and physical state, we misunderstood this power to be a single solitary white male God that created everything, including mankind. We looked at this false God as "all knowing" and all "powerful," and to the point that he can, at will, destroy, protect, as well as defend. Yet, this false God is just an illusion put in place because of the belief in power.

My fellow searchers, it was because of power, we tried to understand the external factors of life and our environment a long time ago. For example: Where did the universe, the stars, the sun, the planets, earth, and the plants and trees get their life? Why do we have air to breath, water to drink, food to eat, and many other things we enjoy and need for our physical existence? Since we did not understand the whys of these things, we adopted an illusionary single solitary white male God as the creator of it all.

Yes, most of you accredit your intelligence, appearance, skills, talents, and all that you benefit from in life coming from this illusionary single solitary white male God. Many of you even give your thanks and worship to him for your food, your possessions, your kinship, and much more to this God of a perceptual mental nature. A God that has nothing to do in bringing about the food you eat or the wealth you accumulate, for all of it actually comes from you and group consciousness.

It is for that reason you have defined your reality and shaped your world based upon this illusionary white male Hebrew or non-Hebrew God, and every time you have a problem, as an individual or as a group, you pray to this false God for peace, help, protection, and miracles. However, what do you get? You get more problems, more wars, less protection, and no miracles, all because you don't understand that those things actually come from within you, for you are the creator of it all.

What has been forgotten is that when we left the first creation (separating ourselves from our own divineness) and moved into the second creation (a perceptual mental state of consciousness), and after battling with our soul brothers and sisters over power and control, we, without realizing it, created multiple dimensions of an etheric nature that has now become so intertwined with each other that we ended up creating a solid universe and a sensory perceptual mental image of a God like being that created it all, which his further from the truth.

At first, these ethereal or unearthly like dimensions were filled with expressions of feelings and thought forms until we finally found ourselves in a place of consciousness where we, as souled beings, created the illusion of light and dark. Now, this was not the light that corresponds to everything good and warm or the dark that means evil and sinful. It was a type of light and dark that came from our dualistic consciousness and yet, we somehow knew that this light and dark were not coming from our spirit or soul, all because we found ourselves fascinated with it after leaving our divine state.

The experiencing of light and dark amazed us to the point that we realized we could make things happen very fast, like magic, because of the illusion of power and how we imaged things as fast as a lightning bolt moving across the sky. We became overwhelmed with how we could separate this light and dark into whatever perceptional result we wanted it to be. It was amazing and very noticeable to us, that as fast as we could express a thought-form, light or dark, it would appear before us as fast as we thought it possible.

You see, once we, as souled beings, passed through the wall of duality, which is nothing more than us souls moving from our divine state of focusing to a rational state of perceptual type of focusing that locked us into a belief that light and dark was really real, we, without realizing it, brought with us, from our divine state, a limited and yet, a very large amount of pure neutral energy to play with.

It was from this limited, even though overwhelming, amount of neutral energy is what we used to form our delusions as truth and as authentic in order to make what we were creating appear to exist as real, when in fact, what we were creating was not real. However, it all felt real to us.

Ever since then all 144,000 soul groups (families) have been playing with this limited, and yet vast amount of energy, without knowing we were even doing it. Being blinded by the illusion of power, we have been shifting and transforming this pure energy and converting it from one form to another, filling this vacuum of nothingness into multiple dimensions, as one of them is indeed physical and yet, all of it is illusionary.

With the persistence of creating false beliefs due to linking everything to our perceptual and rational nature, and the action of carrying them out, and with every experience we could imagine, no matter if it was good and bad, we carried them out as if they were real. Once this was done by us souls, we then filled those dimensions with every possible potential, question, and occurrence, along with every possible answer and outcome to them. We even did the same for every choice, as we created every possible solution to those choices.

In fact, for every possible illness, sadness, relationship, war, worry, financial problem, and more, for it is endless, there is a solution to everything because we, all souls, created it and stored it away in all those dimensions. Yes, we even created a path to find our way back to our own divineness. It is just that we have forgotten the path because of our layered lifetimes (consciousnesses) of many fabricated beliefs that we have taken as our truths. Now, we suffer for it!

Also, let us not forget, because of the ripping apart of our energy and consciousness when we first went through the wall of duality, we placed a piece of our energy and consciousness into every dimension that we created, into every belief, into every potential, good and bad, and into every solution to any problem, including the truth of us being a divine being. All that is left to do is for us to wake-up and tap into those many layered consciousnesses (lifetimes) and get the answer we need in solving any challenge that we have placed upon ourselves, including the healing of any disease.

My dear friends, this is where miracles comes from, for that was what the ripping of our energy and consciousness was all about when we went through the "wall of dualistic vibrational energy." We, all souls, have already experienced every possible scenario; nothing was left out, including every disease, knowing lack, having good and bad relationships, and many, many other things.

All that is left now is for us to remember that we are multi-dimensional, thus having the authority to reconnected to every fragmented piece of our consciousness that was shattered when we went through the "wall of duality." However, since most of us cannot remember going through the "wall of duality," our soul became part of the dark, for we all placed it there because of not wanting to take responsibility for our choices and actions.

We, as humans, without realizing it, have been following our soul's divine plan in the manifesting of many lifetimes that it takes to become awakened to our false beliefs (lies) and the truth that we, as all souls, are the Godhead that created it all, even the ripping away of our consciousness. Actually, the second creation has become the playing field for us to play out those many scenarios as potentials and a gift of love from our own spirit so as to experience every possible situation. In doing so, we, as souls, will eventually discover the answer to the questions, "Who am I, who created me, and why am I here on earth?"

According to my soul's interactions with my outer ego personality (the name I hold in this lifetime), there is no such thing as mistakes, no such thing as sin, no wrong choices, no guilt, no shame, and there are no judgment put on us. This means that we should not be judging ourselves or others because all that we choose and experience here on earth have been blessed by our own spirit.

The choice you made a long time ago to move forward and go beyond your own divineness (first creation) to create and experience as many dualistic and non-dualistic potentials as possible has indeed been a gift to your spirit from you as much as it was a gift from your spirit to you. This is why you will never receive judgment from your soul (the Christ you) no matter what you have done or do in the future.

In spite of what religions and the world say about you being wrong and that you have sinned against God. The facts remain! You have never sinned or made a poor choice because, in the end, there is no such thing. You are simply "choosing" and "experiencing" with energy to know what life is on behalf of your spirit. And now, you contain, within your soul, a knowing that the divine (real) you are, in truth, the "I AMness" of Christ.

This means that you have the ability to free yourself from all the illusions and false beliefs that you have ever created, including the illusion of power, sin, and that you are only human. It is you that puts limitations on yourself, for you have always been connected to your "I AM Essence" from the beginning, and no one can take that away from you, not even if it takes you to eternity to become aware of it.

You have taken on the belief that your reality was created for you, that you were placed in it by some God when, in truth, you have created every minuscule part of it. And now, because of it, you cry out and pray to what is real, what is truth, and where is God when you need him the most?

My fellow searcher, everything you see and experience is nothing but an illusion, a three-dimensional hologram, even the pain and joy you feel is an illusion because everything you experience in life, you created it all in the mind first and no one else, not some God or even a Devil. This is why Jesus (Yeshua) could heal others. He made it clear to them that they could heal themselves because of it being just an illusion.

The second creation has become our playground to test and play with as many potentials of duality as we can, and we did this in order to learn who we are in the scheme of things. How could we have ever known who we truly are if we would have stayed in our "I AM Essence" of non-duality? It took us, all souls, to move outside of our divine essence (first creation) and into a consciousness of a perceptional mental and physical state (second creation) in order to find out who we truly are.

Yes, I know it was terrifying to leave that part of us that is divine, especially thinking that we may never return to the understanding of being a divine being again. However, it had to be done or else we would have never known the wisdom of all souled beings as the "Christ." You see, our spirit couldn't have done this by herself like our soul could do it by way of our deceptive and perceptive nature.

It took the love of your spirit to give you complete freedom and self-rule to move into a deceptive and perceptual mental state and discover all that there is to know about duality, good and bad, light, and dark, positive and negative. It was from this dualistic energy that you, all souls, created that everything began to take shape because of all those expressions that you birthed into manifestation, from a perceptual mental level, that gave part in creating earth and all that you experience in the flesh.

Yes you, together with the 144,000 angelic souled families, created dimensions after dimensions and with every fantasy that could possibly be imagined. Every one of them was tied to good and bad, a heaven and a hell, and even potentials where you could one day bring in new energy that would expand beyond duality.

All souls working together made things happen at a tremendous amount of speed because of the hundreds, thousands, millions, and perhaps billions of souls in each of the 144,000 angelic families giving life to their thought-forms. Of course, speed is also an illusion because it just happened as fast as we souls thought about it. As fast as everyone perceived something, it was manifested for everyone to play.

Maybe you can imagine how these groups of angels, as you were part of one of them, while interacting with each other, were moving and bringing things to life with great speed.

You can actually define what we did just by taking a moment to think about it as if one day a long time ago man came upon the earth's moon, and then decided to explore it, not because of being disobedient to our spirit or to find ourselves lost, but because man wanted to experience the moon and the act of being captivated That, my dear friends, is what many of us did a very long time ago.

Yes, we are the off-spring of the Spirit of One out exploring and experiencing what it is like to create, and then leaving that creation to move onto another. However, during the movement of energy that we were creating in the beginning stages of forming and structuring our mental consciousness, we all began to notice everything that we were creating was beginning to slow down. At first, we welcomed it in because it gave us a little time to reflect on what we were doing. Then we realized we were not manifesting things as fast as we did before!

Of course, understand that this was also something new that we all did not experience or knew before. And because of it, it scared us! We said to ourselves and to fellow souls, if this slowdown of energy continues than what is going to happen to us? Will we create ourselves out of existence? This thought frightened us to our very core. Therefore, out of the blue, and not knowing what to do, all soul groups once again decided to attack each other to gain power and control.

Yes you, and your soul group, again began to steal and have war with each other one more time in order to claim another's energy. You, and all souled beings, came to believe that by stealing another's energy it would keep you from going out of existence.

Remember my fellow searchers, at the time, everything we, as souled beings, decided to do as a group consciousness was never done before. Because of not knowing what the outcome was going to be with this slowing down of energy, everyone feared everything. That, my dear friends, is why we still have war today in the physical. We all believe that we just don't have enough energy (power) to survive so we try to steal it or take it by force.

Most people are so frightened that they are going to go out of existence when they die because of the uncertainty about who God is and who they are, it makes them afraid. We all have forgotten that life is nothing but hypnosis and perception, for ideas and false belief systems have been part of our reality ever since we took on the belief in power a long time ago.

You can say, because of energy stealing coming from the illusion of power, it became so bad in the non-physical dimensions that even you could not stop yourself from participating in it. That is when you, and all souled beings, once again formed into groups one more time, and then attacked other soul groups as hard as you could. They in return attacked your group as hard as they could.

Once again, everything went into chaos because of the fear of going out of existence. Each family group formed hierarchies, assigning a soul to do a certain job to be carried out. Examples are: a ranked system, combatants, planners, and of course prophets. And yes, this was done in the non-physical dimensions first.

However, this time around we, as souls, took a greater vow then we did before, and with such extreme intensity, not to some God, but to our angelic family group that we created a pact with. Even to the point, where in the end, we would give our life in support of anything the group declared as truth no matter if it was truth or not. In fact, to facilitate this pact, we souls vowed to a certain belief system and hierarchy, like a religious conviction or political party for example, and it locked us into a consciousness of inflexibility, which then became the very means of our being.

You can see this today, for all wars are really based on religion and belief systems and yet, these beliefs and religions that everyone adopted are nothing but false idols we worship, all because of our vows to them a long time ago. It was due to our vows and our strong misleading beliefs that our energy level began to slow down to such a degree that we, all souled beings, ended up creating a physical reality. What is interesting here is that we were not even conscious of this happening at the time.

Now, as one group of souls thought they were better than another, it created an energy around all of us that became quite distorted and misused. What everyone first thought was their quest to go back home to their "I AM Essence," now became a fight for power and control of all dimensional territory. Actually, the desire to move back to one's divine state was forgotten, because now, the only desire we had was gaining as much dimensional territory, power, energy, and control as possible, and today, we humans use religion and government as the means to do it.

You see, the wars and energy stealing became very intense. So intense that we, as souls, again tried to steal, kill, and injure another soul. We even tried to cast another soul into other dimensional realms just so we could feel that the soul was somehow dead.

My fellow searcher, no matter how hard someone tries, they cannot destroy or kill another soul because eventually that soul will awaken to itself. Oh, one can control another soul by having a soul feel less important than another for awhile or feeding them a belief where they lose themselves, like to a religious belief. However, in the end, that soul's divine spark will someday awaken to the real truth of it being a divine being, thus, leaving behind all beliefs that contain any judgment what-so-ever. So, I guess it comes down to how many lifetimes will it take before you understand this?

Because of these very intense battles and energy stealing that we were participating in, everything around us, including all those dimensions we all created, continued to slow down to the point that we became overwhelmingly anxious about everything collapsing on us. Even to the point that all 144,000 diverse angelic soul groups began to feel that we may go too far. Yes, even far enough where we were even thinking that we too could work ourselves out of existence by everything falling into itself or back to the void.

Even today, we have some humans that do think about the void and how it may swallow everything up. It would be like all of creation collapsing into itself. This was, and still is, a frightening thought today!

Chapter 8

The Divine Plan

I decided to title this chapter "the divine plan" because from the human perspective, our spirit, soul, and divinity, all in one body of consciousness, has been a great mystery to us for a long time. Because of human nature, and that physicality can be emotionally overpowering, we have forgotten that the divine plan is in essence veiled by our own soul. Veiled because of how the soul, the Christ we are, carries out the completion of who we think we are as humans compared to an awareness of understanding who we truly are.

My dear friends, the soul's plan has always been, from the beginning of you leaving your divine state eons ago, is to become aware of "who you truly are," which is, you are a full-fledged Christ in your own right. However, because of being exposed to choice, you, all souled beings, moved away from your divine plan through the desire to understand your existence, and to answer the question, "Who am I?" This led to another question: "How do you become a creator and a sovereign being in your own right?"

However, because of these questions, we, as souled beings, became entangled with power and control, and because of it, we all became stuck in a mental world wind of deception, perception, judgment, and a false impression of who we truly are. Therefore, before coming to earth, and after we moved beyond our consciousness of a divine state, a divine plan was drawn up from an idea where a number of souled beings from each angelic family decided it was time for everyone to take full responsibility for their creations.

Thus, a very long time ago, before we humans came to earth, a very intense learning program was developed and formulated to achieve the ultimate purpose of freeing ourselves from the stuck energy that each of us caused as an individual soul and as a group consciousness. This program consisted of a few voluntary souls who would shift their energy into a physical dimension in order to find the answers to what was happening to us because of how energy was slowing down at a fast rate.

However, when we souls, as I was one of them, and maybe some of you were too, entered earth a long time ago, we got confused about this divine plan and instead became caught up with our human plan. Because of this, we souls, and now as a human expression, have forgotten about the passion of our soul desiring to learn, to discover, to grow in wisdom, to have good and bad experiences, and then finally mature enough in consciousness to become a sovereign being.

Therefore, the divine plan and our human plan are not the same. The divine plan is not built on our human goals to have money, have a great home, be illness free, or about winning a lottery. It is not even about having power or control of anything. All humans are a divine being, therefore, we can have all those things and more anyway just by learning the real truth about who we are, and to understand how energy and universal mind works.

You see, once we moved outside of our divine state of consciousness (first creation), we took on certain attributes of duality. Mainly, the belief in rational thought and how it gave us the ability to understand life, which then led to "I am alive, I believe in sin, I am either good or I am evil, and then taking on the veil of forgetfulness." Of course, the most important thing that it did was that it all felt real to us on an emotional level.

Well, this feeling of everything around us appearing real caused the divine plan to become a shadow that eventually became unavailable to us at the conscious level. Because of the illusion of power coming to represent our survival and strength, we, once we moved onto earth, took on many false beliefs and lifetimes that ended up creating a human plan instead of following our soul's plan. After all, our soul's plan is for us to learn our real identity and become a sovereign being in our own right. A Christ unto self just as Jesus did!

Of course, our divine plan can change if we allow it to integrate with our human plan from a conscious level. The divine plan can consist of our material wishes while still fulfilling the passion of our soul's desire to learn about life and our true identity. However, to integrate both plans is to become aware of our soul's plan and then learn to open the door of our outer consciousness and allow our soul to be present in our life at all levels of our consciousness.

In other words, you still can have fun, be healthy, and have everything you desire while on earth. It is just that it comes down to recognizing who you truly are first, and then you taking full responsibility for what you create.

Just look around and you can see that everything is in turmoil today, for the human plan doesn't seem to be working. History will always tell you that the human plan has been nothing but failure because everything you understand about life is based on the principle of power, perception, duality, rational thought, materialism, and literal interpretation.

For instance: Look at our elected officials and our religious leaders, and you can see that the only thing that they are looking out for is their own interest. They have no interest in your divine plan let alone your human plan. Their interest is to keep everyone in fear, because through fear, they keep their power and control over you.

Fear allows governments, religions, businesses, the media, and even our families, to control everything about our life including how much money we need to make, how much to give to the church, how much to save, spend, what we should eat, how we should dress, and many other things to keep us asleep to the real Christ, you. Yes, it is easy to spot those individuals and groups, even our family members, for they love to control everything around them, including how crazy and mixed up we are by leaving the family beliefs.

Of course, they do it by having you become dependent on them, like they are smarter because of their degrees, or because of their intellectual abilities, or their religious teachings, or maybe they just somehow feel that they know better than you for what is in your best interest. They also do it by keeping you focused in a perception of what you see, taste, smell, touch, and hear are actually real. In other words, everything is taught, observed, and understood only from a human point of view.

For example: Governments from all over the world seduce the general populous in favoring changes where wealth should be more evenly distributed among those that are in need. They do it by telling their lies about the rich and how wrong it is for them not to give more to the poor. Then again, if one is equal with God then one has the same authority as God, which means, the poor can be as greedy as the rich just by allowing others and the rich to support them, including government.

In other words, since all souled beings have free will and our equal in authority as God then the poor is choosing to be poor just as much as the rich is choosing to be rich, and they are choosing it to experience it from a soul level. It's the same with our diseases. We, as humans, overlook this because of how our structured society is based on power, and therefore judges it wrong if the rich don't help the poor. It can also mean that a soul was very rich in one lifetime and now in this lifetime, the soul wants to choose what it feels like to be poor.

A lot of us spend countless hours on our knees, and some of us with our rosary beads, in prayer, asking God for guidance, understanding, health, and forgiveness. A God that, in reality, we don't even know! My dear friends, and I say this with sincerity, one of the biggest and most effective lie was that, a long time ago, the rulers of the world got the churches to work with them in developing a book that says we are a sinner, and we believed them.

We have been taught by the church that God gave us the free will to choose and yet, we cannot see the forest from the trees. How can religion say that God gave us the free will to choose, and at the same time, tell us if we do not follow His rules, then we will be condemned to a hell of fire forever and ever? That is not free will! Forever, my dear friends, is a long time!

You see, we do have free will, but without realizing it, we gave it away a long time ago to the religions of the world, to the ruling governments of the world, to our family history, and to our lifetimes past. If we all have no choice but to follow God's rules and those of others that believe what is best for us and our salvation, then what we are being taught by the church, and told by our governments, is false.

Free will is something that comes from the divine Christ part of each of us where the Spirit of One has equally proportioned itself among all souled beings (her children) to do as we please, no matter if we create nothing but good, evil, or that we wish to be rich or experience poorness.

You see, it is not that the rich has to help the poor. It is about one choosing, from the soul level, and fulfilling their own divine plan to follow in order to become awakened to their real identity. If one chooses to experience poorness, limitations, cancer, bad relationships, or even the ghettoes, then who are these groups, or even you, to dictate to them how money should be redistributed, or if one should have their inoculations, or if one should have chemo, or even if one is wrong because of their religion, education, race, gender, or position in life?

Yes, most of us pray and pray to God all the time, asking Him what is it that we should be doing, and without realizing it, our own soul hears us by responding to us to do whatever we choose. It does not matter to our soul what we choose as long as we are choosing something. However, when this happens, we get confused and don't understand this reply because it does not match with our family history and our own dogmatic belief systems.

What you don't realize is that your soul is responding to what you chose a long time ago in becoming aware of your own "I AM Essence," and to become a sovereign being in your own right. My dear friends, there is no lack of anything, not even money or health. There are no illnesses, and God is not withholding anything from you, because it is only your perception in "who you think and believe you are."

If you believe that you are only a human that lacks the means to make money and heal your situation, then your own soul response to your request to be a human in need. It's that simple!

Look! Whatever snapshot that you have taken about life, your body, and your lack thereof, no matter what that lack is, then so is your life, your body, and your lack of healing. Whatever you believe about food then so is your body. Whatever you believe about genetics then so is the body. Whatever you believe about medicines and drugs then so is the body, and whatever you believe about a God that judges and punishes because of sin then so are your experiences.

How can religion say that God gave us the free will to choose if it comes with a set of rules to follow? We have been tricked and misled because we are diffidently following the will of those in power, not counting following our past personality-aspects of other lifetimes. We have been hypnotized using the icon of a God that lives in a book as the basis for our successes and an icon of Satan and the rich as the escape-goat for our failures and shortages in life.

You, each of you, are your own God in choosing what you want to experience. Therefore, if you feel alone, poor, and rejected then you are choosing it. In order to keep you in fear, those in power will always tell you not to look within yourself to find God because they want to keep you looking for God (Jesus) outside of you, using the mind of rational thought and the church as the primary source for your information.

My dear friends, those in power know that the rational mind and the church is the key to keeping you separated from "who you truly are," thus your miracles come with a price because you have to look for those in power to receive it. If you don't think this is true, then why do you pray to a God outside of you for a miracle, or that you depend on the government, or someone to heal your situation?

By those in power telling you that you are only human, a sinner, weak, powerless, and vulnerable to Satan and his army of angels, it makes it easier for them to steal your energy and keep you in a hypnotic sleep state that robs you from receiving miracles. Thus, those in power stay in power.

Most of us believe that we make choices every day. And of course, that again, is a big lie. In truth, we think we are making choices for ourselves. However, without even realizing it, our lives have been set up by external events that have nothing to do with our inner divine choices. And to maintain this lie, the church, the media, our family, and the government asked us for our loyalty, our vote, and our allegiance.

By the church asking you to seek God using the mind of reason, the church actually can close down any thought or belief of you moving into a consciousness where you will find your own soul's agenda. For instance: Allow me to demonstrate how much you are lied to on a daily basis by the government, religion, family, friends, and the media.

Right now you actually believe that you are either a male or a female, or that you are rich, poor, or somewhere in-between, because that is what you see in the mirror and in your bank account from the physical aspect. However, there is more to you than just your physical body and what you have in your bank account. Most of you know this to be true just by taking the time to feel it.

It is not about you being either a male or a female, or that you believe that you are rich or poor, or that you believe in some God that created you. It is about becoming aware and feeling the masculine and the feminine parts of yourself, and the sovereignty of your own spirit within to draw toward you your heart's desire. It is all there! However because you are the greatest recipient of deception in the cosmos, it helps you to avoid responsibility.

The external words that we express as prayers mean very little to a God that we don't even know, and is not really there to hear it. Why, because we fail to understand that all we are doing is experiencing, using pure energy, and interacting with everyone and everything for soul growth. We have forgotten that our soul is not interested in our human plan to be rich, healthy, or have a great relationship, or even our belief in God. Our soul only understands our experiences, good and bad, as wisdom, and not that we are a sinner because of our acts, for that is the illusion and the lie.

The soul's responsibility is to get you to "know" who you truly are as a sovereign "I AM" in your own right and not help you get things for you to feel good. You can waste a lot of money and time trying to get out of your conditions because you want to feel good or fit into some God's plan, or your own human plan. However, the more you follow the beliefs of others, the more you will drift down the river of duality and suffering. A reality that seems real because of you feeling it as such, for energy, positive, negative, or neutrality wants to serve you, and it will no matter what you believe or choose to experience.

If you are an unconscious creator then the energy you bring into yourself will serve you that way. If you believe the forces of positive and negative are all that there is then the forces of opposite will serve that belief. If you are a conscious creator that understands neutralized energy then this energy will serve you in a more expanded way. So, it is up to you what you want to experience in life because that authority was passed down to your deceptive mental and human consciousness a long time ago.

Look, pain, sadness, poverty, or even happiness, riches, or having no pain, are not really felt by your soul or spirit because they (your spirit and soul) know already that every experience you have now, or had in the past, lies in its wisdom and not in what is right or wrong, good or bad, or with some God or Devil. My dear friends allow the seed within, the seed that contains the crystalline white energy of the Christ consciousness to germinate, for you are indeed one of the "Lost Children of Christ."

Now that I have gotten this out of the way, my soul desires to continue with the story of our journey where we, as souled beings, were battling and interacting with each other in the beginning stages to form our spiritual families. According to my soul, this was the time where we began to mature in such a way that we, without realizing it, prepared ourselves to take a long, long journey of discovery.

You see, we, as souled beings, have forgotten that this endless vacuum of nothingness is about our deceptive mental thought forms and the patterning of the dualistic energy that we all fell into a long time ago, and how it turned out to be a delightful and wonderful creation for us after all. Of course, religion and science explains it as the void. In fact, this void allowed us, as souled beings, to come together and create many, many dimensions, including the physical dimension, where we could come together and form a divine plan that would help us return back to our Christ consciousness.

Even though the memory of our divine state seems to have been buried deep within our consciousness, our spirit (the, I AM) can still feel us on the human level through our thoughts, emotions, and all that we choose to experience, good and bad. Our spirit loves us for it because we, on the human level, bring back to our spirit, the wisdom of our experiences. This is how we, the God that we are, comes to know all things.

All the prayers you pray to your spirit are felt by your spirit, and because of your spirit's love and compassion for your human identity, your spirit will not interfere or hold back your human creations. Your spirit will support you no matter what you choose to experience, good and bad, because your spirit and soul already knows that you will one day find the answer to who you truly are and where you have truly come from.

Your spirit knows that the human part of you will someday come to know the "I AMness" within yourself because you are a Christ in the making. Therefore, nothing can destroy your soul or take away what you have experienced, like being poor, rich, ill, healthy, famous or just being the hired help, because within each experience that you have had lies the wisdom of your choices that you have made throughout your journey.

This is why your souls knows that you, in physical form, are all about time, space, light, dark, consciousness, and learning, and how they all come together as one body of consciousness, you in your wisdom. If you are stuck in a belief that these things are separate, then what you will experience in life becomes very limited until you learn to let go of this single solitary white male God that looks upon itself as the creator of "all that is."

This explains why we unconsciously choose poverty, starvation, hardships, illnesses, dejection, grief, bad relationships, depression, or the opposite of these things. Everything that we have been doing from the beginning with our battles, the stealing of energy, killing one another, no matter what we have done, has been for soul growth, and has nothing to do with sin, karma or doing something bad, or some God forgiving or condemning us.

My dear friends, sin is a lie, a big lie because the choices you make, good and bad, is about preparing you to become a mature and sovereign "I AM Christ" in your own right. You, as a human, are a Christ and a God; learning how to create, use energy, and how your spirit works. Through your angelic family and your human family, and also through your many lifetimes past, you are learning how to be a Christ of compassion, unconditional love, understanding, accountability, and of wisdom and responsibility.

It took the children of the Spirit of One in knowing itself because the Spirit of One knew it could not do it alone. How could the Spirit of One learn and understand who it was unless it was through the gazillions upon gazillions, and more, pieces of herself, known as us souled beings, for we are the "Lost Children of Christ."

We, the children of the Spirit of One, learn from each other on how to become a sovereign "spirit of one" in our own right. We do it by sharing our experiences, corporation, insights, and our wisdom with all humans, including all angelic families, and with our own "I AM Spirit." In fact, it is through our human brothers and sisters, metaphorically speaking, that we can see and recognize ourselves, like a mirror image of ourselves.

Every souled being has committed to their individual journey through time and space even though everyone was awakened (born) at the same time, thus once again, leaving no soul older, younger, or even wiser than anyone else. In fact, there is no such thing as a soul mate because of everyone being sovereign. Everyone grows in wisdom at their own pace and according to their own path that they choose, which is why here on earth one soul can become awaken to their sovereignty before another.

This is where the expressions of "this is an old soul" or a "young soul" comes from. It is just that an "old soul" is someone that chose to commit to more experiences (incarnations) than another.

There is no measurement (time) of where you are at in your evolution, ahead or behind, because eventually, you will find your sovereign place in consciousness anyway by overcoming your beliefs that the answers are with religion, government, family, friends, businesses, and the media.

You see, eventually, everyone, even the diehard Bible thumpers, will discover that they indeed have all the answers and solutions within themselves. It is just that they cannot become a sovereign "spirit of one" in their own right unless they take full responsibility for their creations because there is no God or Jesus that can save them or do it for them, only oneself.

Everyone is allowed to discover their own divine path and how they want to execute it, which is why it is important not to judge another person just because of how one appears or how one chooses to work out their experiences on earth, positive or negative. One may want to experience being black, red, yellow, brown, or white, or want to just experience suffering, being a drunk, a killer of man, woman, and children, or being a rapist, or whatever means they choose, even poor and rich. Their spirit, the divineness that they are, will support them without judgment or condemnation.

Also, keep in mind here, the person receiving the suffering, being killed, or raped, or that one is black, red, yellow, brown, or white is not about being a weak individual. It is about one choosing to experience these acts and race in order to learn the wisdom behind the act of choosing. It can also be karma.

Now, let us go back to my soul's story about the great battles in the etheric realms when we, as souled beings, first became part of the endless vacuum of nothingness, and before earth ever was.

Once again, when we souls moved into this nothingness, and without any type of form, it caused us, after many great battles, to split into 144,000 spiritual families. The angelic realm calls these angelic families as part of the 144,000 members of the order of the Arc.

Of course, religion calls them the *"number of which was sealed of all the tribes of Israel (Rev. 7:4),"* thus overlooking the "Children of Israel" as metaphorically speaking of all 144,000 angelic families. This also explains the metaphor of the Jews being the chosen people – for all souled beings and humans alike are the "chosen people."

Each angelic family was headed up with names such as, the Order of Michael, the Order of Amael, the Order of Metatron, the Order of Gabriel, the Order of Sanunda, the Order of Uriel, the Order of Raphael, the Order of Luceffa (Lucifer), as the names go on and on until you reach 144,000 – for that is the total of how many angelic families they are. As said, you can have hundreds, thousands, millions, or perhaps billions in each angelic family.

Now, the Order of the Arc, according to Tobias's Journey of the Angels," became the doorway to enter the physical earth, as each family member of the 144,000 angelic families has a voice that carry its own geometric pattern in presenting their unique attributes in sharing with us what everyone has learned in their journey of discovery.

This is where the 144,000 Arc Angels were introduced as the voice in co-operating with each angelic family to hold our energy until such a time where we are awakened to it. You see, underneath all this forgetfulness was the desire to return back to our divine state and yet, it was also the desire to learn about ourselves, our "I AM Christ" consciousness, our angelic family, and to learn about creation, physical and non-physical.

For example: I am from the angelic family of Sanunda and I have worked with other angelic families in an effort to go out into the physical many times, not only for me to experience, but also to help mankind open up to the memory of who they truly are. I have been, and still are, a correspondent, like a reporter, that recorded and put to writing the words of the prophets in what is called the Bible today, which by the way, have been changed by mankind because of his hunger for power and control.

However, I have returned in this lifetime to correct what has been altered in the Bible, not to restore it back to its original form, but to open the minds and hearts of those that are ready to move past the old dogmatic consciousness of the Bible. You can say that it is time now for you, like Jesus, to reconnect with the Christ seed deep within yourself and break ground in becoming, the "tree of life" and the way for others to observe.

Note: From what my soul has narrated to me, it confirms to me of what I was told about this from the angelic realm as being a recorder of words from what the prophets spoke of in the Bible. And now, you can find what the prophets really spoke off in my two books titled, Genesis: Your Journey Home, 2nd Edition and the Book of Revelation: A New Beginning – for these books bring out the hidden message behind what was written in these stories. Call up www.terrynewbegin.com and see for yourself that you are the leading director of your life.

Now, back to the narration of my soul! To help me explain these 144,000 soul groups I will include some of what Tobias, of the Crimson Circle, said about them and how it affected the energy slowdown:

We are always surrounded by our soul and our angelic family group. They are there to support us in our choices and to serve us in this lifetime. We also have many angelic friends that specialize in many different things, and we can call upon them at anytime. In fact, while we are on earth we are a representative of our own angelic family in bringing back to them the wisdom of our choices and what we have learned by those choices, which is another reason why there is no such thing as sin, or karma for that matter. There is only the belief in it what makes it feel real.

Because of the worries coming from all 144,000 angelic families about the energy slow down coming to a point of crisis, there was a concern about all of creation coming to a complete halt. There were even concerns that consciousness would stop expanding and that everything could collapse in on itself. This would mean that everything outside of the oneness of our own divine state (first creation) would then go out of existence, or at least we thought.

This thought caused great fear and concern within the ranks of all angelic families. In fact, the worrying was so intense it caused all 144,000 soul families to come together and stop their battling with each other to find an answer to what was happening. This would be equivalent to all the nations on earth stopping their battles with each other because of the possibility of the earth going out of existence, including themselves.

To make a long story short! Tobias mentions of a measuring that took place, a spiritual measuring that involved spiritual geometric mathematics. At first, there was this working with scientific development about how to rebalance, rejuvenate, and return energy back to its original state. Anyway, at the time, there were many things that all 144,000 soul groups tried to come up with to solve the problem, and nothing seemed to work.

Once the energy level of every souled being started to slowdown to a critical level, the leaders of each angelic soul family began to connect with each other and put out a distress call to all angelic families to come together for the benefit of all soul families in what was created. Once the leaders of each family group understood the energetic situation, they all agreed it was essential to join together their energies for the common good or find the probability of falling into non-existence.

From that point all battling stopped, then representatives of each family group came together to set out a plan to stop the energetic slowdown before it was too late. In fact, this later became known as the "divine plan" because all angelic families came together to come up with a plan to bring stuck energy back into its pure neutral state again. You can say it was an overwhelming task of coming up with an idea of how to transform stuck energy back into its pure state again.

According to Tobias, the gathering of all these soul families became known as the "Order of the Arc" because each spiritual family had developed an archetypical energy (something that serves as the model for the collective consciousness) that was unique to them.

For instance, and I will only mention a few: The order of Raphael became the angel of fear; the order of Michael became the angel of courage, strength, protection, and most of all, truth; the order of Amael became the angel of hope; the order of Gabriel became the messenger; the order of Zadkiel became the angel of mercy; the order of Gaia became the angel of physical manifestation, the Order of Luceffa (Lucifer) became the angel of balance, and the Order of Metatron became the angel to help all souls connect to their divine state, for all 144,000 Arc Angels represent some type of archetypical energy that we all can connect to.

From this gathering of all angelic family representatives there was a lot of exchange of ideas about the possibility of moving out of existence because of the slowdown energy that was happening around us. Now, even though the emotions were high and that anger broke out in the assembling of the order of the Arc, everyone knew that some resolution had to be developed. (Note: This all took place while in spirit form first).

Now for some good news! Remember earlier in the book where I mentioned about us, as souled beings, were one with Spirit, and that we all decided to leave our divine state to learn about who we are? Well, as you know, it just means that we souls moved into a mental state of consciousness that was based only on ignorance, thought forms, perception, and obscurity, which then caused us to move into a deceptive composition that carried out the belief that we were separate and alone.

Well, because of this strong belief in being separate and alone, it caused us souls to believe that we only had so much energy to form our creations. This caused a belief in power, and once power was born or became part of the consciousness of us souled beings, that is when everything became confused. It was from these beliefs of long ago the battling between us souls for one's energy (power) took place. As you can see, even today, we are still battling each other for power and control.

Nevertheless, the good news is, deep within your beliefs, or I should say the lies you took on as your truths, even the belief in power, your spirit knew of this gathering of angels. This means that your spirit is beyond your deceptive and misleading mind and how it believes in positive and negative thought forms, as well as your spirit being beyond the human personality- aspect that you created as the means to experience those thought forms.

This also means you can now take great joy in knowing that your spirit has been watching your many human personality-aspects (lifetimes) learn responsibility journeying through time and space over and over.

Yes, your spirit and soul, which can also be called your Christ spirit, have seen the human you for many lifetimes working together with other souled beings and their false selves too for the common good in working toward releasing stuck energy. In other words, the day has come, if you so choose, that the human you (the false or lower you) can assist now and cooperate with the "Christ" you – for you should know now that you are an "I AM that carries only one name", "I Am That I AM.

Now can you see why religions, family traditions (dogmatic views), friends, activists, governments, as well as big businesses and the media prefer to keep you locked into the belief about positive and negative as being real? By having you and the human mass believe in duality, and sin as being real, their hold on you is certain that you will rely on them for support. Thus, they guarantee their power and control over you.

For instance: Look at the activists out there yelling for government help in supporting those that cannot take care of themselves or mother earth. These activists, without realizing it, continue to fall into the trap of their own intellectual understanding of God, and how they perceive themselves as a helper to God and Mother Earth in achieving the idea of taking-care of our fellow man and the environment around us. You also see beggars on the streets with their signs asking for food or money.

You hear our politicians preaching fairness to those that don't have anything, all because they have the false belief that we cannot take care of ourselves. All of this yelling, haggling, and asking government for help leads to nowhere, because in the end, all that we are doing is putting off self-responsibility, which just leads to nothing but more lifetimes before becoming awaken to who the real creator is. Each and every one of us is the creator of our miracles and our misery.

Anyway, according to Tobias' Journey of the angels, published by Shaumbra Institute of Colorado, channeled by Geoffrey Hoppe, July 2009, and I paraphrase here. As all representatives from each angelic family were there, many ideas and theories were put forth in resolving the issue of our energy coming to an impasse. However, one idea was brought forth that shocked the core of every soul. The idea was perhaps one of uniqueness because it was the riskiest of all and yet, it held the highest of hopes in providing us with balance energy and the wisdom of knowing who we truly are.

My fellow searchers, the idea was to call in the order of Archangel Gaia, the angel of physical manifestation. The call was for Gaia to lead a band of angels (souls) from all families to scour the dimension of physicality to find a place where we, as souls, could place a piece of our energy and consciousness into a physical body. It was a perfect idea because the physical dimension had not been subjected to any of the energy battles that went on in the other dimensions at that time.

Thus Archangel Gaia feeling very honored, as she represented her angelic family, took a group of angels (souls), as I was one of them, and maybe you too, went forth searching the physical dimension. As you know, Gaia found a place far off in the corner of the galaxy where she embedded the seed of life (seed of consciousness) on this small rock that is now called Earth. Gaia breathed life into this rock and then took up residence as the mother of the planet, for earth became her physical body.

Then Gaia eventually created the atmosphere, the air, the waters, the plants, and then to test her creation she, and many other souls together, created many different types of animals that would move upon the earth's surface to see if they could sustain a certain type of physical life form. If they could, then we too, as souls, could also.

Remember, at the time no one knew what type of body would work in the physical dimension. The plan was for earth to become a unique physical place where the energetic attributes of the planet could not be interfered with by other souls if one decided not to honor the covenant of physicality and attack it. In fact, because of the energetic attributes and energy patterns that were set up in the beginning, it became nearly impossible to attack or interfere with earth because it would draw those souls that wanted to interfere into a physical form.

You can say that earth became a magnificent physical planet for resolving the issue of energy slowdown and the rejuvenation of it back to its original neutral state. Now, according to Tobias, from out of this gathering of all 144,000 angelic families there were other ideas and plans brought forth other than the earth idea. However these plans were introduced, each of these plans were also used. Nevertheless, it was the earth plan that seemed to appeal to many souls because it required a large group of angels (souls) from each angelic family to descend their energy vibration so as to enter into a physical form.

That is when the attributes of the physical earth became a component of time and space, and a physical body that would feel pain, a mental makeup that was tied to positive and negative, light and dark (duality) that would allow us souls to discover the wisdom of opposites, and tie us to a reality of slowed-down energy vibrations where our creations would manifest at a very, very slow pace. All of this would then allow us souls to go back and forth in a physical body and re-experience what we did in the non-physical dimensions. We, as souls, could then reenact them out but this time in physical form so we could feel the pain as well as the joy of our creations, and then allowing us to release the stuck energy.

From this point Archangel Gaia set the stage where souls from all 144,000 angelic families could come to earth and feel these re-enactments of what we did in the non-physical realms but now in a very solid form and with real far-reaching implications, influences, and effects. Of course, the big question was who was going to be the first to go?

That is when the order of Gabriel was called in to echo the call for those brave souls that would take the plunge (fall) into physicality and answer the call to be the first to go to earth. Because of the uniqueness of physicality, there were just a handful of souls from each angelic family that volunteered, for I was one of them, thus having a very small amount of souls who were the first to come to earth.

Now, according to Tobias' "Journey of the Angels," he mentions the initial count was just under two million souls that decided to come to earth for the very first time because the order of the Arc could not guarantee anyone's return once these souls placed their consciousness into a physical body. In other words, it took a great deal of courage to be part of the first soul group to enter earth because of the complexity of the idea and the fear of not returning to the knowing that you volunteered.

Because of the strong energetic pull of duality and how it deals with the way in which the forces produce positive and negative motion in the physical, the Arc Angels just did not know if we volunteered souls would get so embedded in physical reality that we may never get out of it.

For instance: Because of forgetting once you are in the physical body, you could become totally lost in a place that only knows physicality as its reality. This is why the volunteer count of souled beings coming into the physical at first was so small because the risk was so high, which is why many angels did not want anything to do with it. Of course, as you can see with the current population of the Earth, many souls have changed their mind since then.

However, those that did volunteer first dedicated themselves to the expansion of consciousness and to the releasing of old stuck energy no matter what it took to achieve it. Also, that is when we found ourselves falling into a much more slowed down energy than what we expected because we began to feel our choices and creations first hand.

Now, those souls that were part of the first wave, as I again, and maybe many of you, was one of them that volunteered, knew the divine plan and the risk in getting lost in physical matter due to forgetting. However, the potential for liberating our soul, as well as our brothers and sisters, felt very exciting to us. Oh, we felt a lot of fear in doing this however, the excitement about moving into a physical body was more overwhelming than the fear of getting lost.

So, those of us that volunteered said goodbye to our angelic family, and when we did, our soul brothers and sisters were simply overwhelmed and in awe with our decision. Even today, after many of us have had about fourteen hundred plus lifetimes, our angelic family is still in awe over our decision to come to earth over and over.

This is why we should never dismiss our importance to the world. Of course we can, if we would just turn off our rational mind for awhile and feel our angelic family watching over us — for they are eager to learn the wisdom in what we are learning right now in the flesh.

My dear friends, there are an overwhelming number of souls that have never come to earth because they are still waiting to see if we can re-balance our energy using physical form and forgetfulness as the vehicle to achieve this divine plan of the Order of the Arc. They are in hope that flesh is the answer to rebalancing energy.

Of course, it has already been done by many souls as well as the man named Yeshua Ben Joseph (Jesus), which is why people today look at him, and many like him, as a God. Now, our angelic family is waiting to see if we can do the same and become an "I AM" sovereign being in our own right just like Jesus did. This takes an amazing amount of courage, strength, responsibility, and trust to become a sovereign "I AM Christ" in our own right.

Now, of course, if you happen to be one of those souls that have been on earth for many lifetimes, then please release any pressure that you might be feeling because of feeling responsible for your angelic family as well as feeling responsible for your human family.

For example: Do not take on the burdens of others, especially your human family because you feel obligated to them or because of your beliefs are not like theirs. You have these feelings of obligations because down deep within your being you are very emotional toward them because of your many lifetimes with them working out karma. Because of the warning you got from spirit on how seductive duality can be in the flesh, and how it can keep you on earth for a very long time, you took on the feeling of guilt. Spirit warned you that you would lose your memory of your divine state, of your angelic family, and that you would come to a point of just looking at yourself as just a human. So, just know that your spirit and angelic family are aware of your experiences, good and bad.

But also know that they know that they cannot rescue you because of your choices. After all, the divine plan is to see if you, as all humans, can overcome the flesh, integrate all that you have created, and become one again with your divine state. However, this time around a consciousness that is filled with a vast amount of wisdom, understanding, and a knowing that you are divine and a God also. Of course, your angelic family cannot rescue you anyhow because if they got to close to the physical earth they too would be sucked right into physicality.

So, there you have it! However, before we move onto the next chapter about coming to earth there is one thing you should know. According to the angelic realm, aliens cannot invade Earth. Why? It is because earth is very well hidden from all of the other parts of the physical universe. Also, since the energies of earth are so compelling it would suck the aliens onto earth where they too would take on human qualities, thus having to experience lifetimes of many just like we do. In fact, some aliens have already tried to invade Earth, and now they are part of the human race.

Therefore, the idea of aliens taking over earth becomes irrelevant and without bearing any fear or thought to it. Hence, it is us humans that we should fear the most because we are the most advance species in the universe. After all, we are the aliens that decided to explore the flesh.

CHAPTER 9

EARTH BOUND

Since I am not an expert when it comes to the earth, the sun, the universe, and or the solar system, I will rely on science, what I have been told by the angelic realm, and what my own soul conveyed to me on the subject. We all know that earth is the third planet from the sun, and according to science, the densest and yet, we, as humans, are evolving in consciousness even though we may not think so.

Scientists say the planet earth is the fifth largest of the planets in our solar system. It is the largest of the four terrestrial planets (Mercury, Venus, Earth, and Mars) and home to millions of species, including us humans. Scientists have also claimed that earth, the moon, other planets, stars, star clusters, and galaxies, houses an interconnected number of things that are bound together by gravity.

Science says that the universe can be viewed as having a hierarchical structure, and that earth was formed about 4.5 billion years ago and having life appear on it about one billion years ago. However, the consensus of Tobias' "Journey of the Angels," and I paraphrase here, life appeared upon the earth somewhere in the vicinity of 2.5 to 3 billion years ago, which is a big difference from the scientific table of measure, and that of religion.

Interestingly, the angelic realm does not measure time the same way science measures time. To the angelic realm time is not linear and consistent, time is measured by a sequence of events, or better stated, the evolution of consciousness. The angelic realm also say that time can be very compressed and sometimes stretched out because time can wrap around itself, looping in and out.

For example: We humans believe time exists because it seems obvious to us. However, according to the angelic realm, time does not truly exist. Time has to be attached to something of a structured nature, like the physical body, the rational mind, and that of earth, in order for us to experience life in a decelerated energy that feels real to us. Otherwise, we would not stay around in the physical body long enough to learn the wisdom of our choices.

If time existed as something real and fixed or unbending, like some of our beliefs, then we, as souls, would not be an infinite being having a consciousness that could accelerate, decelerate, and then expand again beyond our imagination. It is through our imagination and breath where we can expand our consciousness beyond what we see as something fixed, like truth, our belief systems, and how we look at ourselves as only human.

Another example is Gaia – for she is a spirit like you and me, and yet her expanded physical body and consciousness is the Earth. We, as humans, have forgotten that consciousness is not just about being alive and in human form or it being a small speck of light. It is about having the awareness to understand that consciousness is in everything, and it can expand infinitely, beyond our human senses and body, and beyond all dimensions.

For instance: We can give ourselves the freedom to grow in wisdom and in consciousness at an accelerating rate and create more potentials and possibilities for ourselves that can bring more abundance, health, and opportunities to experience. All that we have to do to bring it into our life is to look beyond what we believe to be time, space, physicality, good and bad, and that consciousness is limited only to humans.

Animals, trees, fish of the sea, and many other species do not look at time or their consciousness as being limited. All they sense is that they are connected to everything, all consciousness, and they don't care if today is Sunday, Monday, or Friday. It is only man that measures time and consciousness.

My dear friends, it comes down to this! The more we are stuck in the belief that we are not a divine being of an infinite nature, the more we will experience the physics of a long-lasting energy that produces intense and dominant gravitational variations between two extremes, like positive and negative or good and bad, physical and non-physical, health and non-health.

It is these extremes that move your energy in a decelerated way that will form denser molecules within your body. Thus your DNA is affected and you live out a linear time element experiencing nothing but opposites (ups and downs) one lifetime after another, and which you are your ancestors incarnated. This is why it is important to learn to open your rational mind and heart to a new consciousness where truth and time are not fixed or limited. It is just the belief in them that makes them fixed and limited.

Therefore, if you find it necessary to put a time frame on earth, then the age, according to Tobias and the angelic realm, is about 4.5 billion years and that we souls first appeared upon it around 2.5 to 3 billion years ago. However, Tobias did point out that the beginning of mankind coming to earth is more or less irrelevant because in a spiritual sense it was only a breath away.

My fellow searchers, time is not real. Time has been created for many things, especially for measuring our experiences, our consciousness, and to keep us in a belief system where the elements of earth (air, water, form, and fire) control our thoughts, views, and reality. Thereby, holding us, as a human group consciousness, in an agreement that truth and time are fixed so that we can carry out our choices in a linear way in order to learn the wisdom of our acts.

When we look at space we define it as a large area of physical property that includes solar systems, galaxies in the billions, and planets that seem to orbit around stars that are over many thousands of light-years away. Scientist measures these systems by their depth, length, and how they are all held together by gravitational forces. However, according to Tobias, and again I paraphrase here, space is nothing more than a physical dimension that is among many other non-physical dimensions that allows us, as spirits, to play.

Tobias also says space is not space at all just as much as time is not real. Space looks large and yet, it is small. Why, because it spirals and keeps on coming back on itself, which is why space, like time, cannot be measured. What we see as the farthest star from earth is actually the closest. Science overlooks this truth because of how it spirals back to itself using a series of curves that look flat.

For instance: If you were in space where there are no gravity and you began to walk in a huge circular built spaceship where the ending was the beginning and the beginning was the ending, it would feel like as if you were walking on a flat straight surface and yet, all that you would be doing is walking back to yourself.

Earth, in its beginning stages, was nothing but a large ball of flaming rock with a large cloud that covered the whole of it. Then gradually, in the course of millions of years, the surface burned itself out leaving a thin layer of rock. (Again time is irrelevant when measured against eternity and how it bends in on itself because of consciousness).

Anyway, once the rain began to fall upon the rocky planet, the rain finally wore out the hard cover surface of the rocks and carried the small dust particles to the lower lying areas that lay between the towering mountains of the earth. That is when the earth was ready for the order of Gaia to come in and breathe life into what we call earth today.

Today, you still have Gaia and the 144,000 Arc Angels with earth in its protection and balancing. They actually keep everything together from a consciousness standpoint. They will continue with that protection until all humans evolve enough in consciousness to keep the balance of earth with our consciousness.

The 144,000 Arc Angels, sometimes called the pillars of the universe, that come from all angelic families collectively stick together in harmony because of the singular most important cause, which is, the expansion of consciousness. Of course, today most of the forming and structuring of earth comes from us humans, which is why we are so limited when it comes to understanding the concept where we can actually have a good and healthy life.

The main reason for our journey to earth was to slow down our energy so we could take on physical form in order to experience our choices, thus giving us a great deal of understanding, awareness, and wisdom about who we truly are. You see, in the spirit realm our energy moved fast and we could create things with a click of a finger (metaphorically speaking). After all, there is no such thing as time, or truth, or space that limits us from creating what we desire, as humans. It is only our outer rational mind (brain) and beliefs that limit us.

However, with the testing of the earth's physical structure, along with the human body, and with the slowed down energy, we souls that moved into the physical could feel our choices and it took time for our choices to manifest. Once our choices were manifested, it then took more time before we moved through the experience. This is when time became known to us as a distinguishing belief system to measure our choices and actions into a period of sequences or cycles in order to learn the wisdom behind our choices.

By experiencing our choices, and the action we take, and because of our false belief in a divided consciousness, we do sooner or later come to understand that power, duality, and physicality are not real but are illusions that feel real. The belief in time and space created a time element of limiting our creations only to a physical reality until we expanded enough in consciousness to learn the wisdom behind our thoughts, choices, and the actions we take because of the misunderstanding of power, and that positive and negative.

Because of this agreement among all soul families, these 144,000 Arc Angels are now here to support all humans on earth, and each one of us can draw upon any of them for help at anytime. The reason the angelic realm calls these leaders Arc Angels is because of their make-up – for they are of an archetypical energy that represents all angelic families.

In other words, these 144,000 Arc Angels serve as the standard or model for all of us souls, for they hold within them the collective energy and wisdom of all 144,000 souled groups. Thus, each Arc Angel contains certain strengths, excellence, authority, and superiority that each of us souls possess within ourselves.

For example: Arc Angel Michael represents the angel of truth, which means you can find the real truth within yourself. This also means deep within your memory you know the truth about who you truly are and where you truly come from. It is just that you have forgotten. Also, it is not that you originated from your parents or from a single white male

God that holds all power to himself. It is that you originated from yourself.

Arc Angel Raphael represents the angel of fear, as this means deep within your memory you know fear is only something that is tied to what is unknown and mysterious. That is why you are afraid of the dark and of this God of the Bible because you are afraid of what this God might do to you if you stopped worshipping Him and started to worship yourself as a God. We, as humans, continue to convince ourselves everyday to stick to the status-quo just in case our preachers are right.

Now, as you can see, I cannot mention all 144,000 Arc Angels but I am sure you get the meaning here. It was us souls that named these Arc Angels after what is called the Order of Arc because they are like a light that connects all the soul families together as one. And we, all humans, can tap into this oneness at anytime just by choosing to and discover the attributes of each family that we hold within ourselves.

This is why intelligence is universal because in reality the human mind is not really real, for it is based on rational thought. Your real mind is universal and divine, and therefore does not belong to one soul or family, spiritually or humanly. This also means that you have no mind other than your "I AM" connection to universal divine mind. What you do have is a deceptive and misleading emotional mind filled with thought patterns and memories of all that you have done since the beginning of your awakening in the first circle.

Then again, to keep everything in perspective here, I do want to point out that when we, all souled beings, were in our divine state, we were in one thought, one action, and one movement with the Spirit of One. It would be like the cells in our physical body working together as one unit for the benefit of the whole body, as our consciousness together would represent the Spirit of One. However, when we souls went through the wall of duality it would be like each cell in the body taking on its own individualized personality as a souled being and our divine individualized consciousness becoming the mother (spirit of one) and how each of us souled beings are now connected to universal divine mind.

This is why our human aspect cannot go back to our divine state of consciousness (first creation-heaven) like it was before, for it does not exist. Can we go back into our mother's womb? No! We can never ever go back into a singleness of consciousness again like before, because now we are all multi-dimensional.

The only thing we can do now is that every souled being must move forward in discovering their own connection to universal divine mind, to their physicality, to their uniqueness, and to their own consciousness (spirit of one) and purpose as a sovereign God in their own right.

When we, all souled beings, begin to discover that our oneness of consciousness (our own spirit of one) can expand infinitely, we then can begin to understand and realize the qualities we possess are also part of the 144,000 angelic families, and their numbers of souls in each family, and vice-versa. In other words, we are all separate and yet connected just like our cells in the body are separate and yet connected.

Once this is understood from the human level we are then ready to become a sovereign Christ in our own right. This is why we, all humans, are part of the 144,000 mentioned in Revelation 7:4 – for no one is left out. It is our ignorance that one believes the Jews are only God's chosen people.

The Spirit of One has given us all a gift and that is the gift of our own oneness and consciousnesses, and our connection to universal divine mind, for we, as humans, are a "Christ like being" in our own right. It was Archangel Gaia who gave us the gift of a beautiful earth by her breathing in the energies that created the pathway from the Order of the Arc down to earth. Of course, today, because of the expansion of consciousness, there are now many different pathways and vortexes that leads us souls from the non-physical realms to the physical earth.

Gaia was responsible for breathing in the elements of water, fire, air, and the beauty we see upon the earth. Gaia also breathed in the energies needed to provide the rejuvenation for all that lives upon earth, including our human body. Not only did Gaia breathe in the waters of the earth, she breathed in all of the creatures that are in the waters, and the oceans of salt water to help absorb the negative energies that come from the human mass consciousness. As you can see here, there is no single while male God that created earth. It was just Gaia doing what she enjoys doing.

As you know earth's oceans encase two-thirds of the earth while the land cover is one-third. We need the two-thirds salt water to filter out the negative energies of the human mass to help maintain the balance of earth and its other occupants. Also, the two-thirds ocean waters represent our subconsciousness while the one-third land is representative of our outer limited human conscious. Together, they become one massive consciousness and yet, we only see and play with the outer limited consciousness, for only a few dare to explore the other two thirds.

Gaia also helped provide and breathed in what we see as the animal kingdom. It was from the animal kingdom that all souls have come up with the template for the human body of today. Everything we see here on earth has come from Gaia and her army of angels (souls). You could be one of Gaia's co-angels, which is maybe why you get emotional when it comes to protecting earth and its inhabitants. As Gaia breathes life into earth and everything on it, including giving birth to the human body, so can't we breathe life and consciousness into our own creations?

For instance: With the purity of purpose and with the focus of my own consciousness, I breathe life into this book to the point where it takes on a life of its own once it leaves my hand. Actually, it becomes an aspect of me, and therefore a dimension of its own, and when you read this book, it becomes part of you just as Gaia and the Christ spirit have become part of all of us.

Here is something else Gaia breathed life into that was very important in our early days on earth. She breathed in the crystalline energy deep within the earth. Not only were these crystalline energies used to help maintain balance between the physical and non-physical world, these energies were used to allow the process of our angelic consciousness to take on or change from one physical form to another.

For example: In the beginning stages on earth many of us took up residence as birds, whales, dolphins, animals that crawl on the ground, even insects and trees, and then later, when standardization came about, we took up residence in the human body as we know it today. This is an example of how the crystalline energies in the beginning allowed for transmutation of our angelic consciousness into the physical earth to take place.

Once Gaia set up the energies required for the birth of mankind upon the earth, the call went out again about who was going to go first. That is when only a handful of souls from each angelic family came forward to surrender to the densest and most compressed energy ever known. This means that earth actually became a test site for all spirits to come into a solid form and experience dense energy.

Now, as for those volunteers that came in with the first wave, we spirits had no form, and that we found ourselves having no knowledge of what was going to happen to us. All that we volunteers could feel deep within was a sense of the physical realm that was going to be the highest potential for consciousness expansion.

We also felt and sensed that the journey to earth was going to be a great challenge and yet, deep within, we seemed to know that it was going to somehow become an avenue for us to awaken to something that was going to celebrate our ultimate freedom. So, in our anxiety about coming to earth, we first volunteers, took a deep breath and made the leap into a physical creation.

Then of course, once we took the leap, we felt ourselves spinning and spinning, not like before when our consciousness was shattered into billions of pieces. This time we felt a new experience, as it felt like we were being compressed and squeezed into an enclosed container. This squeezing of our consciousness seemed to become denser and tighter until we wanted to break free but it was not going to happen because our consciousness and energy continued to become denser and stronger.

Oh, at first, we resisted and tried to fight our way out of what we were feeling but the more we resisted the tighter and denser our energy and consciousness became. It was like we were being squeezed into a bottle with someone placing a cap on top of it to seal us in so that we couldn't get out. Actually, it finally reached a point where we, for the very first time, felt physical pain. As our energy and consciousness tightened even more, we tried to remember our angelic family and what we volunteered for. However, the memory was beginning to be squeezed out of us.

We even felt our soul being overshadowed like it was being destroyed as we drew closer to the planet earth. Not only was this the first time we felt pain, we felt the fear of losing control of what was happening to us.

Note: Just imagine for a moment that you are over six feet tall and weigh about a hundred and fifty pounds being squeezed into an enclosed eight ounce bottle, and then having the cap sealed onto it, and you will get the idea of how you, in spirit form, felt when you first came to earth.

As we plunged into a dense darkness that was very restricted and limited. It felt like an endless journey as we went through a one way tunnel until suddenly everything began to open up to us, for it was light once again. However, this time the light was coming from the sun. This looking up at the sun amazed us as we stood there, even though at first, we had felt and had seen it from a more of a transparent body or a non-physical body than from a solid physical body.

You see, with our first appearance on earth, we did not have a dense physical body as we do today. However, we could sense the light of the physical sun beating down on us and on earth. Not only could we sense the sun shining down on the earth, we could sense the ocean, the land and its greenery, and most of all, we could sense the density of the air. That was also the first time we experienced gravity. You can imagine how amazing that was!

You see, earth became a kingdom where we could come to play in the physical, for we eventually descended our consciousness and energy closer and closer to earth where we finally took up a dense physical body. However, when we first came to earth, we weren't aware of the other volunteers even though they were right next to us. Why? Because we were so occupied and engaged in what we were seeing and experiencing that we never noticed anyone around us.

We had never visually observed plants, trees, rocks, animals, green grass, or even the blueness of the sky or the ocean waters. After all, this was never done before, and it took billions of years to create. You can say earth developed into a true Garden of Eden.

Now, once we first wavers came to earth for the very first time, we never had any type of emotion about fighting each other. We just allowed ourselves to breathe, feel, and absorb everything that surrounded us. It was beautiful, and we were at awe of what Gaia created for us to discover. Note: The time frame in human perspective took a very long time in creating the energies needed before we could begin our journey on earth.

Now, not to be misunderstood here, I will say this again. When we first came to earth, we had a very transparent type of physical body. In fact, our body was so transparent we could allow ourselves to flow right into a tree and feel what it was like to be a tree, or we could flow into a plant, animal, bird, fish, insect, or whatever was on earth at the time, even a rock. We could flow into all of them and feel what it was like to be them. In fact, you know this to be true just by taking deep breaths and then feel it within.

It was not that these things, like the tree or rock, were not conscious or alive, they were conscious and aware, and they allowed us to become part of them so we could feel their essence.

Note: I did mention this earlier! That everything is energy with the exception of your spirit and consciousness. Your spirit uses energy and consciousness to serve you. However, everything that contains energy has a consciousness to it. For example: Rock has no creative spirit to it but it has a consciousness. The rock has the breath of Gaia giving it consciousness, which is why when you create something, like a book, you too place a piece of your consciousness in it and give it live.

It took us, as souled beings, a long time to know the different forms upon the earth in its early stages and yet, there was no fear and no resistance coming from them. We just allowed ourselves to become part of earth and everything on it. We became part of the consciousness of the ocean, the land, the air, the clouds, even the rain that came from the clouds. By experiencing all of these things, and more, we have learned how physicality (biological life) rejuvenates and cleanses itself.

We spent millions of years just working with the physical kingdom and everything on it until eventually we, all souls, got so close to the animal kingdom that we actually birthed ourselves into a biological body that looked like an animal. Yes, I know this may freak you out. However, at first it did not matter what animal we appeared to look like because all that mattered was that we had begun to be born in a more solid physical form.

This was progress because previously our body was so transparent that we just rode along with the consciousness of the physical kingdom. However, now we were actually birthed into a physical form. It was amazing to us, and at the same time, we were very frightened by the idea that we could be born in a physical form.

Consequently, for the very first time, we were no longer a free spirit jumping from one living creature to another because we felt very connected to what we were taking on as a physical body. We actually became very committed to physical form, no longer just an observer, because now, we became part of earth itself, not just consciousness but physical too.

Here we are today, still committed to the physical earth and the physical body. In fact, today most of us are so afraid to leave the physical body, which is interesting because in the beginning stages we looked forward to leaving it. Nonetheless, this is when we actually took on more of forgetting where we came from. We even began forgetting our angelic family, the Order of the Arc, and most of all, our divineness and the oneness of our own spirit, as well as our connection to universal mind.

Yes, we became so intertwined with mother earth, and all that was on it, that we today see ourselves only as human. You could say that coming to earth was a miracle because we, as souled beings, took spirit energy and birthed it into a physical body. And let me tell you, my first lifetime on earth in physical form was an absolute thrill and yet, it became very challenging to me as it was for you.

For example: Here is something Tobias mentions in the "Journey of the Angels," and again I paraphrase here: There were a few of us souls, once we took on physical form, who did not understand life or death because some of us fell to our death just by walking off a cliff. Many of us did not know the effects of walking off a cliff. Most of us, at the time, did not know or understand that by walking off a cliff we would kill the physical form. This created a whole new experience for us souls. However, everyone eventually learned not to walk off a cliff or otherwise the body would die.

Now, let us talk about Lemuria, as most of us have heard of Lemuria. Lemuria was the first era where we, as souls, came to earth in a more dense physical form. The Lemurian era lasted for millions and millions of years, which is contrary to science saying it was a few hundred thousand. When we took on a physical form, the life span could have been up to one thousand years or less. It all depended on what we chose for a form to experience.

Because of our lack of understanding the physical form, it was, at first, hard for us to hold onto a physical life because of knowing little about the environment. We were like a small child of a few months old playing around the edges of cliffs, around water, not knowing what fire was, and many other things that could instantly take our life. Because of the lack of wisdom when it came to staying alive in the physical, we came close in not reincarnating again in physical form.

Now of course, during our time journeying through Lemuria there wasn't any fighting or wars because we were too busy getting familiar with our environment and physical body. It was that we were just too busy experimenting and playing with different incarnations. We would incarnate as a winged bird, an animal that walked, crawled, and even an animal compared to a dinosaur.

Yes, believe it or not, we took on many different forms, as in huge, small, even as small as an insect and as large as a great giant. In death, we would go between lifetimes sharing our experiences and wisdom with other souls so that we could learn to stabilize our lifetimes. We know this to be true because it is in the Bible. It's all there for us to read for ourselves. In fact, I believe that if we would take a moment and feel our energy we could feel what it would be like being an insect, a tiger, or a bird, and even a dinosaur.

Now, as we can see here, there was not very much brain structure or power in those types of bodies because in those lifetimes it was mostly about the physical senses. In fact, it was more about experiencing and feeling our senses than about having brain power. It was like we were too busy learning how to adjust to our biology.

For example: There were some of us souls who came to earth and did nothing but eat, as Tobias was one of them. They would eat until they died, and then they would come back to earth and do it all over again. It took awhile for the first timers in physical bodies to learn the wisdom of their choices. Also, during the Lemurian era, there was no such thing as sex because everyone was of dual sex. At the time we all had the ability to create our own offspring.

However, eventually, we souls decided to split our masculine-feminine energy and incarnate as either a male or a female. Remember here, this took place over millions of years. It was not over night. That is when we souls began to experiment with sex, even to the point of it taking control of our human self.

Maybe some of you have heard the old stories in the Bible about the ancient myths of Satyrs (half human and goat), Minotaur (upper body as a bull and lower body as human), Cyclops (race of giants having one eye in the middle of the forehead), and many other kind of animals, large and small that looked half human and half animal like.

However, after taking many, many notes between different lifetimes, we souls evolved enough in consciousness to come up with perfecting the physical form a bit better. We, as humans, at first were very ignorant when it came to living in a physical body, which is why, after so many lifetimes, playing with it, we came to realize that we needed some type of physical form that would basically improve our purpose for coming to earth, to learn, and hold to memory what we have learned, and a physical body that would carry our spirit energy.

We also found that certain species of the animal kingdom were better adapted for us to enhance our physical senses. So, we began to develop prototypes of a few biological bodies in order to gain experiences, and then we began to improve and upgrade the body cells, the organs, the brain, and the DNA of these prototypes.

Chapter 10

Uniformty Of The Physical Body

Up until we reached the Atlantean period, we only could look at ourselves as a soul that occupied many different types of species or biological bodies that were not in uniform with each other. Oh, we could recognize a fellow souled being from other animal species by the aura that emanated from them, no matter what form was taken, animal like, bird like, or whatever, we all had a certain aura about ourselves that made it clear that we were a souled being.

We could also discover another souled being in physical form from the native species just because we, as humans, seemed to roam around together in clusters, just like we do today. Now of course, we did not begin to communicate with each other on a verbal scale until we were thousands and thousands of years into the Atlantean era.

Now, just for your information, according to the Tobias material, channeled by Geoffrey Hoppe of the Crimson Circle, and again I paraphrase here, the physical body that we humans play around on earth today came from an angelic family called the Hapiru. The Hapiru family was a very highly refined spiritual family, for they were the ones that first developed their own community type system before any other angelic family. Once the Hapiru family settled into community living, their first objective was to standardize the human body.

Remember, during the Lemurian era we, as souled beings, took on many sizes, shapes, and species, as well as many different brain and cell structures. However, because of the angelic family of the Hapiru, they standardized the human body as we know it today. Of course, at first, the human body that the Hapiru family developed over millions of years ago looked more apelike than what it is today, which is why we theorize that man evolved from an ape. Of course, this is not true!

All that came to earth in the beginning were us souled beings looking for the right physical body which to play in the flesh. Remember, there were no prototypes before us to follow, for we, as souls, were learning as we were going. Anyway, thanks to the angelic Hapiru family, we have today the masculine and feminine physical bodies looking similar to one another with only a small difference.

As you can understand, these bodies that we are in today are much better than the many varieties of species that we were running around in during the early stages of earth over a billion years ago. Of course, after some time, we then decided to incarnate into these new physical forms of the Atlanteans, which means the territory of Lemuria, and its inhabitants of diverse physical bodies, eventually became extinct.

This is why we, as humans, should allow other species of the earth come to their extinction also instead of trying to control their evolution. We do it out of ignorance. In fact, that was the ending of what we heard as ancient Greek mythology about half man and half animal. This also means, through time, perhaps a million years or so, we, as mankind, finally came up with standardizing the physical body as we know it today through height, width, bone, brain, cell structure, the organs, and all of what the medical field understands today as the human body.

This was accomplished energetically using crystals that Gaia placed within the earth as well as with the crystalline energies. It was also done through surgical means as well as using electromagnetic energy. Of course, the hardest part was to standardize the mind, or should I say the brain, because most of us that were on earth at the time had different mental capabilities. After all, no one wanted their heads to be too small or too large. Everyone wanted their heads to be just about the same size.

Also, this was the very first time where we, as souled beings, came together to begin to take ownership of our physical body and our outer mental mind. As we can see, this was a very amazing time for all of us.

My dear friends, this is also a good time to point out that during the Atlantean era, while developing our human body and brain, there was no concept or a belief in a God. Now, at the time, we were looking for the source because on a mental thought, we knew that the source (energy) had to come from somewhere.

At first, we thought it was coming from mother earth (Gaia) and the crystals that were part of earth. However, we found that Gaia placed those crystals and the crystalline energies in the earth to serve us in developing the human body. In fact, we, as mankind, learned long ago how to manipulate these crystalline energies to where we could focus our consciousness on things that enabled us to lift heavy objects without physically touching them.

Actually, the great pyramids were built this way, which means the answer is no to the hundreds of slaves lifting rocks and placing them in a decisive pattern. It was all done electromagnetically using crystalline energies.

Once we acquired our human body and had the outer deceptive mind under control, including everyone having about the same size brain with similar capabilities. There were some of us who wanted more. Sometimes we humans are just not content with ourselves, for we will always find that we always want more.

For instance: A desire for a better looking body, a more intelligent brain, a better car, a more desirable home, and much more. Of course, this can also be a good thing as well as a bad thing. However, in this case, it was when we all began to create some imbalances of energy upon the earth.

You see, before we came to earth, Gaia had the planet in perfect energy balance. Then, after the angelic family of Hapiru founded the uniformed prototype for the human body, they decided to claim ownership of it. You can say that they felt deserving of a more glamorous body and mind than the rest of us that were not part of the Hapiru family.

The Hapiru family wanted to develop a body that would attain more brainpower, capability, talent, and looks than the other angelic families, which is fine if it was developed for the benefit of the whole. However, in this case, the Hapiru family, since they saw themselves more intelligent and astute than the rest of us, saw nothing wrong with having slaves and having the controlling interest of human life on earth.

Because of the Hapiru's intelligence and clever nature, they produced an extreme arrogance about themselves where they believed they were doing good for mankind. Sound familiar? They did not realize that they were bringing a kind of imbalance energy to themselves and to the planet that eventually became earth's destiny as well as the Hapiru's destiny as representing the Jews today. Yes, you read it correctly, the Jews!

You see, just after the standardizing of the human body (thousands and thousands of years ago), the Hapiru family, known today as the Jews, became the slave owners to over ninety-five percent of the world population at that time.

However, before talking about the Jews and the Hapiru family, let me mention that once the Lemurian race was extinct, the Atlanteans then settled into a communal type of culture where everyone took on the same human biology and a society that mutually shared their possessions and responsibilities with everyone else. There was no such thing as working from an individual state for advancement, or even the idea of capitalism – for everything was set up as a communal society as a whole.

At this time Atlantis was kind of broken up into four centers with each center having a ruling body. In the beginning, it was a ruling body that was not forceful in such a way to harm or enslave people and the earth. Meantime, and in the midst of all of this, there was a factious group from the Hapiru family that was led by a cruel and unstable leader who wanted to control all the lands of Atlantis, and the people that lived on it.

This was the very first time in Earth's history where an army was put in place, for it was this ruler and his army that brought in great conflicts and suffering to earth and to the people at the time. This Hapiru ruler and his army killed, stole, raped, and tortured the citizens of the world with such ruthlessness and relentlessness, and he did it without showing any mercy or compassion what-so-ever.

In fact, you can say, he and his army of destruction were the main cause of the downfall of Atlantis and the destruction of earth long ago. It was he and this factious group from the Hapiru family that brought in the imbalance energy that caused enormous earthquakes and hurricanes with such a magnitude it wiped out everything in its path. Even the rain and the wind storms had such a force to them that it caused great floods until one day the Earth's axles turned where, from the surface, it completely wiped out and destroyed everything.

However, before the destruction of earth, this ruthless ruler and his army enslaved everyone on earth, and then later earth was so out of balance that it destroyed the surface of the earth, which then just about killed everyone on it for the exception of those that moved deep into the earth. Because of the action of what this factious group took upon the earth, the Hapiru family picked up some incredible group karma, and many of them (the Jews) are still suffering today because of it.

The Hapiru family, which are the Jews mentioned in the Bible, even today feel that they are a special breed because of the idea of them being God's chosen people. Some of them still will not accept that all 144,000 angelic families are special because each and every souled being, no matter what angelic family one belongs to, is a child of the Spirit of One. No one individual, soul, or group, or family, is left out or better than another. We, all souled beings, are indeed equal to the highest of authority or what man calls today God.

It does not matter if one is white, black, brown, red, yellow, male, female, or that one is Catholic, Baptist, Christian, Hindu, Buddha, Judaism, Islam, or Sikhism, Atheist, or whoever, or even if one is good or bad – for all humans, even those souls that have never experienced earth as of yet, are unique and special. Why? It is because we, as souled beings and as humans, are Gods in the making. All that it takes to end all wars is for us to recognize and appreciate each other's divine abilities.

Now, my dear friends, this is a good time to mention here that the Palestinians, the Arabs, and the Jews are all part of this Hapiru family. They fight each other as well as everyone else because some of them still feel they are better than others. The holocaust, concerning the Jews during World War II, which was brought on by Hitler and the German army, was a direct result of those souls that participated in the Atlantean army of destruction.

Maybe now you can understand why the Jews were severely persecuted for centuries, including being slaves during others periods because it is all tied to family group karma to work out. The Jews, at one time, were the army of destruction, for they were the cause of the Earth's destruction. However, the Jews, the Arabs, and the Palestinians do not have to suffer and fight each other or anyone else any longer because of what happened in the Atlantean times, for they have suffered enough throughout history.

They continue to suffer because of the emotional guilt and shame they have put on their angelic family, which is why they fight each other, even though they are from the same angelic family. They actually suffer more than any other soul group on earth, all because most members of the Hapiru family feel that they haven't suffered enough and yet, a great majority of them are beginning to awaken to the idea that they do not need to suffer anymore.

Of course, now is also a good time for those of us souls that do not belong to the angelic Hapiru family to learn to forgive because of the Hapiru family having suffered long enough for what they have done. As we all know, we don't need another holocaust or the earth's destruction. What is needed is forgiveness, friendship, understanding, non-judgment, and unconditional love toward all things, human and non-human.

Now, even thought you still have Jews, Arabs, and Palestinians today still fighting each other and other angelic families, this fighting will soon come to an end. One can see this by the younger groups wanting freedom from the type of government that limits them. They don't want any more dictatorship governments or a religion that is so rigid and inflexible that they come very limited. Therefore, the suffering of the Hapiru family and other angelic families will come to an end soon. It is just a matter of time.

Now, not to lose sight of this one God theory and what my own soul narrated to me, let's go back a moment and discuss again where we, during the Atlantean era, wanted to know and learn about where energy came from.

As the search for the source continued, for God was not a concept back then, we first believed it came from the crystals, the sky, and the stars. When we, as mankind, realized it was not found there, we thought it may have come from the human body. So, once the body died, we then cut the body open to look for the source. Of course, we did not find it there either.

However, because of our ignorance and lack of understanding of the source, for we, as souls, are still learning, we began to think that the source must be coming from the physical body while alive, which then led to cutting open the body while it was still alive. Yes, we became a little removed emotionally and underhanded with our fellow man and yet, we again found no source. One could say we became very hungry to learn where the source was coming from.

You see, back then, we thought that if we could find where the source was coming from, or how energy was made, we could get more for ourselves. We thought that by adding more energy to ourselves we could live longer, become more efficient, and be more comfortable. Hmm, that still goes on today, doesn't it? Anyway, since we could not find the source outside of ourselves, we decided to go back to the brain and see if the brain was the founder of energy because, after all, the brain, or our outer deceptive mind, gave us the emotional feeling of power.

Because of taking on the belief of power while in spirit form first, and how we carried that belief into the physical, the leaders of the Hapiru family (since they were the masters of over ninety-five percent of the populous at the time) decided to come up with a headband that the ninety-five percent of the world population would wear, telling us, even though it was a lie, that it would improve our intelligence, our standard of living, and our understanding of things.

Now, even though we humans do not wear a headband in this lifetime, those in power still do this today by them telling us, the populous, what is best for us so they pass laws forcing us to go along with it, using the false belief that it is for our own good.

My dear friends, the headbands were all a lie because the lie led the authorities of the time to tune into the mental frequencies of our rational mind. Then once the authorities were tuned in, they manipulated the mind into controlling the mass through fear and false belief systems. Even today, the authorities control us, not with headbands, but with fear, obligation, and punishment, which creates the same results.

Once the authorities of those days gained mind control over the mass population of the land, the more we, as a human group, separated ourselves from our own spirit, soul, universal divine mind, and body. And today, those in power, even your motivational speakers, now look at the rational mind as the king and the source of what is gained in life. Because of the hypnosis of the mind, using fear, belief systems, motivational workshops, and intelligence as the foundation, we now look at who is smarter, stronger, makes more money, and who has the right religion and education as the basis for a blissful life.

Look, we all have been tricked into believing that God is always on the side of good, which is why we believe that one is predestined to go to heaven if one is good while those that are bad are bound to hell forever and ever. We believe this because the Bible says so, not realizing the Bible was written and rewritten over time to fit the ruling authorities of the time. Yes, even in our time of today, government and religion are now conspiring to re-write the Bible once again to fit the new world (new technology), for the old God has to be updated.

As you can see all of this bickering over the source (God) once again caused a belief within us which took us back to our games of fighting each other just like we did when we first entered into the second creation. Just like we did eons ago in the Etheric realms, we, as humans, today are still trying to steal energy by battling one another for it. We all are trying to attain as much power and control as possible.

It is not that we are trying to devour another soul like before but we are using fear, religion, belief systems, and the rational mind to control one another in order to steal energy to gain more power. However, and I ask you to allow me to say this! This was no mistake or sin on our part here, for we, the human race, and the Order of the Arc, designed it that way, which is why there is no such thing as a mistake.

You see, it was very important to come to Earth to relive the experiences that we had when we first entered the second creation (mental and physical state) in a very physical way so that we could gain the wisdom and understanding of the choices we have made in our journey of life. This way we would eventually learn that battling one another for more energy, power, and control, like we did before in the Etheric realm, is not going to work in the long run. For we, as souls, are in the direct image of the Spirit of One, the mother-father Goddess, and therefore have the same authority as the Spirit of One.

It is that we must learn to awaken from our sleep state and come to terms with ourselves that we are all a Christ in the making, and that our power is equally distributed among us. We all have the power to create any miracle we wish to create, be it rich, poor, having bad or good health, or having a great relationship. In fact, the truth of the matter is that there is no such thing as power. It is just an illusion! How can power exist if every souled being holds the same authority as the Spirit of One?

Anyway, back to how to unlock your consciousness memories. Once the battling began to occur but this time in the flesh, the earth became very volatile and unstable during the end days of Atlantis. This caused some small human tribes to set off on their own trying to find some calmer places. They did find those places by moving from the surface of the earth to where they went underground. This was possible because the tribes found caves that were built in the times of the Atlantis and they just extended the caves deep into the earth.

Some of us that are on the earth today, without realizing it, have lived in those caves in some past lifetimes – for we did exists then, as we were scattered in caves all around the world for thousands of years while the surface of the earth was being healed or rebalanced by Gaia. Those of us that did go beneath the surface of the earth during those times relied heavily on the crystals and the crystalline energies that were planted there by Gaia. We actually got our light, energy, food, and our oxygen from these crystals.

However, after a few thousand years living deep within the earth, we began to revert back to more of a primitive way of life. I know this because when I communicated with Master [4]Melchizedek in a channeling session with him about prehistoric man, he told me prehistoric man came after the destruction of Atlantis, not before.

Now, for those that died during the time of Atlantis shifting, they found themselves near the earth realms in a non-physical body. This is when we, as souled beings, finally took a hard look at what happened when we were in the flesh. That is when we realized the harm and destruction we caused upon ourselves and to the planet earth. One could say, we finally understood and realized that we were like children playing without thinking, and because of it, we did not take responsibility for what we did.

---

4   Melchizedek was the king who helped Abraham in Sodom and Gomorrah (Gen. 14:18).

It was through our lessons of the past, as humans, that we, as many of us do today, come to realize that by Atlantis becoming a communal state, we forgot about individual self responsibility, which is why we became lost in a belief system of power, domination, and the concept of distribution being controlled. This is when we began to take another look at ourselves and what our purpose was, which was, to find the answer to the questions, "Who am I, and why am I here on earth?"

This is also why it is very important that we need to be careful of not moving back to this "communal type system of distribution" where we only rely on government and religion for our needs, because in doing so, we will again lose our individuality and creativity. Fortunately, many of us today, even though it could be unconsciously, have come to realize the nature of our spirit and why we were born in the flesh, and what life is all about.

Note: It took losing our freedom of choice a long time ago and becoming a puppet on a string for those that love power and control. Today, most of us still give away our power and our free will to those that love to control us through fear, promises, religions, and belief systems. Of course, I am in hopes that this book will help cut those strings a little from those that want to control us through these organized systems.

Now, let us get back to the story of "who you truly are" and "where you truly come from."

It has now been about 25,000 years ago since we, as humans, began to resurface from beneath the earth, and once we moved upon the earth's surface, we noticed that Gaia had cleansed the earth of the fires, the earthquakes, and the violent storms, for the planet once again was balanced. The animals, trees, birds, and even the insects were once again plentiful. Even the sky was blue again and the valleys showing their greenery, for mother earth found that she was very resilient and durable, which means we too, as humans, are very resilient and durable.

Because of fear and false beliefs, it is important to look at our past experiences, not from a point of sadness or that we can sometimes be cruel, but to understand it as being part of our experiences in order to learn wisdom and responsibility as a group and as an individual. When we look at our past and what we are experiencing today as chosen experiences instead of someone doing something to us, and seeing it without judgment, or if right or wrong, we actually become a sovereign

"I AM" in our own right that is filled with the wisdom of all that we have experienced.

It is when we learn that there are no victims here, without judgment or resentment, for that is when we can heal our past, which then sets the stage for our future. As you know, most religious people do not believe in reincarnation, and because of this, they misunderstand that over ninety-seven percent of their beliefs come from their past lifetimes.

Therefore, their future in what they will experience in life will always be predetermined by their past lifetimes without even realizing that they have given up their "freedom of choice" (free will) to their past beliefs and to their past aspects that now control them. They don't understand that until they become open-minded when it comes to reincarnation and its implications, and that they are a Christ too just like Jesus, they will always follow a path of destiny (sin), which is nothing more than working out karma because of fear and belief systems.

By embracing and accepting what comes before you, with nothing but unconditional love, compassion, and non-judgment, and seeing the wisdom of what you are experiencing, the path of your reality will change in a most magnificent and rewarding way.

Chapter 11

The Search For God

Once we humans came from out beneath the Earth after the fall of Atlantis with a more primitive attitude and outlook on life then when we first entered the earth and made our home on the surface again, we began to think about the source, for we thought, at the time, that there had to be something, like a deity, that made everything right again.

From what we know through the study of our planet's history and of mankind, when we, as man, first appeared upon earth, which man seems to calculate as being around prehistoric times, and after about 20,000 to 25,000 years of evolving to more reasoning thought, we didn't know how to define what we were seeing around us. Because of the complexity of density and how energy works, we labeled the sun, stars, moon, water, air, the trees, the mountains, the ocean, and just about everything imaginable a God.

Because of misunderstanding spirit, together with our ignorance of the environment, we, as mankind, assigned gods to everything. I can actually say that we, as mankind, went god crazy, worshipping just about anything that came along, all because we had no understanding of where the source comes from. However, as scripture came known to us through religion, we learned of a Hebrew chap named Abraham that changed this "many" gods idea into a "single" Hebrew white male god idea.

Abraham was the son of a man that sold carven images of many gods for a living, which is why Abraham became very indifferent when it came to these carven images of many gods. You can conclude that Abraham had a difficult time keeping up with all those gods, which is why he decided to promote the "one God model." Therefore, it was Abraham who said, "Let there be one God and let this God be a Hebrew God that lives beyond the stars in some heaven."

It was Abraham that taught the people of his day a new belief in a single solitary white male God that created all things, including mankind. Because of man's ignorance it did not take long before all humans finally took up the idea of Abraham's "one God theory," for it made sense to everyone at the time. The only difference today, most religion has put this "one God theory" as representing their own group.

Actually, this was the first time when the word "pagan" became the means for those that did not acknowledge this single deity as the creator of all things. In fact, it was due to this belief in a single white male Hebrew God that created all things that actually separated us humans even more from our own "I AM Essence."

It was a time where we forgot that consciousness is in everything, including ourselves, as well as the stars, the sea, the ocean, the forest, the animals, and even the rocks placed under our feet, for everything has consciousness. However, other than us, as mankind, the rest of these things do not hold a soul, for the stars, the sun, the sea, ocean, forest, rocks, and animals are here to serve us. We, as a mass consciousness, is the Godhead that gives these things consciousness.

Because of ignorance, fear, and mind control, we finally became stuck in a network of false beliefs where we ended up separating ourselves from the Source of Life even more. Through ignorance, fear, and mind control, those in power at the time created the perfect set-up in creating the grandest lie ever conceived by mankind, which is, a single solitary persona of a Hebrew white male God unto himself, who has all knowledge, is very powerful, and has the wisdom to know all things – for this lie still remains today.

As time moved forward once again we began to become indifferent to the idea of this "one white male God" being a Hebrew. Therefore, in the attempt to find the ultimate truth and return to our true nature, we began to fight each other over the very truth we were seeking. Because of this, earth became the home for many different belief systems and religions, each proclaiming they have the exclusive path back to this "one God."

This "all white male Hebrew God" of Abraham's began to take shape as many different gods, names, and meanings, such as, Great Spirit, Jehovah, Supreme Being, Elohim, Alpha, Immanuel, Holy One, Allah, and many, many more. Thus, we, as mankind, once again, in our ignorance, have made God a confusing deity.

However, as time moved on, the consciousness of mankind began to open up to a new thought that birthed a "deliverer" (Messiah) to help us remember our true essence once again.

Since we became lost in so much energy of doubt, ignorance, fear, and the many naming of Gods, we became inflexible with our belief systems to such a stubborn nature that it held a potential for us to become lost forever or for many lifetimes. In fact, because of our stubborn nature, we did become lost to being the creator of our own world, our experiences, and our own karma. All of this happened because of how we looked upon religion and our "one male God" as being the only truth to the question of how the world and our environment had come about in the first place.

Some of us actually created a belief system (lie) so strong that there is a very real danger of becoming lost in the physical for a very long time. One could even say that the potential is so great that it has the possibility to last forever, which is why the Bible calls this belief the "unpardonable sin." You see, without the avenue of reincarnation to remember again, one could be forever lost in one's own consciousness.

My fellow searchers, the "unpardonable sin" is nothing more than you keeping to your stubborn nature of believing in sin and in a single solitary male God that created all things. Sin is nothing more than you believing in good and bad, and a God outside of you as "all that there is." Once you learn to let go of this belief (lie), along with the belief in this single solitary white male Hebrew God that created you, that is when the Christ (your soul) within you will manifest and set you free.

Of course, to help prevent us humans from being stuck in this energy consciousness of sin and hell forever, the angelic angels from all 144,000 spiritual families formulated a plan to help awaken us from our self induced sleep. In fact, the plan was actually simple!

First, the angelic realm would write a book in such a way that it would contain within it three different levels of understanding. Once each level was mastered and understood by an individual, while in human form, then that individual would move on to the next level where they would come to a knowing that they are a Christ too just as much as Jesus.

To implement this plan however, it took those souls that have already awakened and mastered the flesh a few lifetimes ago to come back to earth as prophets. This plan would then allow these prophets to take on many new lifetimes working with the angelic realm in creating a book. A book (scriptures) that applies to any religion on earth that would be introduced to mankind as something that was written by this single white male God. Then finally, have this book of several religions become accepted as something larger than themselves, for this book eventually became known as "holy."

Because of how we, as humans, got caught up with our spirit, universal divine mind, and our physical body over millions of years, this holy book (scriptures) of any religion would be written in a three-dimensional format, giving us, as man, a narrative account of how we became lost in the first place.

In other words, each dimensional level in this "holy" book of several religions contain a message of wisdom in the words written for those that are ready to move forward in their understanding of spirit, and then evolve to the next dimensional level. For instance: The first metaphoric dimensional meaning written in this holy book of any religion was to help us, as mankind, evolve to an understanding where we needed something to help us maintain order in our lives.

The second metaphoric dimensional meaning written in this holy book of several religions, using the same wording and language as was written in the first level, will help us, as mankind, evolve in consciousness to the point where we begin to understand and rationalize our thoughts as we learn to deal with our fellow brothers and sisters.

The third metaphor dimensional meaning found in this holy book of several religions is about a deliverer that would be born among us to bring in a new message of joy and the wisdom of the "day of the harvest." (In the Christian Bible it is found in Mark 4:26-29).

My fellow searchers, the "day of the harvest" is actually symbolic of the day you come to a true understanding and realize that you are a divine being in a human form that needs no leaders, no religion, and no outside white male God to show you the way, for you are the God showing you the way.

It is interesting to note here the correlation between the three levels of your human nature: spirit, mind, and body and how it relates to the three narrative accounts of the holy book. You see, the wisdom contained in the holy book is designed to first guide mankind through his physical life and physical reality. Then when man's material concerns are in order, then man would move into the realm of thought, reasoning, and intellectual understanding, which happens to be where most of the population and religions are today.

The holy book, as written by the prophets of all religion, demonstrates the true wisdom behind the written words that was actually implanted deep within our soul's memory a long time ago when we first moved away from our divine state (first creation).

You see, within this three-dimensional holy book there are three major sub-books: the first sub-book is called the book of Genesis, for it records the origin of God and Man, and it also holds the wisdom of our journey as mankind and our true identity as a Christ also.

The second sub-book is made up of the four Gospels that can be found in the New Testament, for this sub-book is about the earthly life of the Deliverer. His message was that we are indeed a true Master, a Christ, and a Goddess also, making each of us, as an individual soul, the Deliverer and Savior of ourselves. It was the Messiah named Yeshua Ben Joseph, known as Jesus, that came in the physical world over two thousand years ago to remind us of who we truly are.

Now, the third sub-book is called the book of Revelation, as this book is not about the end days nor is it about Jesus coming to save us. It's a book that reveals the end of our suffering and the awakening to "A New Beginning," for it reveals to us that we are indeed a divine being and a Christ like being in our own right, and while we are still part of the flesh. It is actually a book that describes our own ascension from a three-dimensional dualistic consciousness to a new energy consciousness.

In their divine foresight, the Arc Angels placed the wisdom of the "harvest" not only in the end of this "book" (Revelation) but also in the beginning (Genesis). This way, those of us who are ready for the "harvest" (ascension-awakening) will recognize the "beginning" was not so much about Adam and Eve falling out of grace but was based on our own journey through time and space incarnating in the physical. In the end, we learn the answer to the question, "Who are we?" For those who believe the "end" is about being lifted up into some heaven because of their religious beliefs, they will be doomed to remain in their suffering (sin) until another time.

It has been about two thousand years since Jesus came to Earth to help us open up to our divine self. Jesus did not come to earth to save us but to seed the Christ consciousness within us. It is oneself that can save oneself. Interestingly, there are many among us who are here today that were actually on earth with Jesus at the time. As for me, I was here on earth with Jesus to help Him plant the Christ seed that took over two thousand years to germinate.

Yes, the Christ seed of Jesus is what opened a spiritual corridor for mankind that would eventually become the pathway for man in joining with his divine consciousness here on earth.

Now, Jesus, and those of us on earth today that walked with him, was not trying to start churches or any movement in those days. All that we were doing was attempting to bring in the Christ seed so that later, maybe many of us could bring in our divine nature here on earth in this lifetime. However, because of the misunderstanding of Jesus and his mission back then, those that loved power and control worked very hard to maintain the status quo, which still goes on today by our religious leaders.

Even though it does go on, many of us that lived during Jesus' time have re-incarnated on earth over and over as priests, rabbis, monks, and even as nuns. Many of us came into these lifetimes over and over in the past two thousand years to play the role of spiritual teachers. The reason for us coming to earth again and again was that we finally became tired of getting down on our knees and attending religious ceremonies to listen to the rhetoric about God's rules.

So, as a result, there were many of us that left the churches a few lifetimes ago, as I was one of them. And today, most of us stay away from religion and those that preach the words of "having to go through Jesus as being the only way to salvation." Yes, there are many of us today that can recognize those that have let go of religion and their dogmatic views just by the way we have remained quiet and shy in our youthful years. Even today, some of us are still shy to come out and declare themselves as a God also.

There are some of us that spoke to spiritual angels from the other side of the veil when we were children, even to the point where we thought it was natural. Some of us did not understand why others could not see or speak to these angels as well. We also might have heard of someone that could move objects without touching them, or someone that could read minds, or could leave their physical body to view the past, present, and future.

At first, and from a subconscious level, when some of us made our appearance upon the earth in this lifetime, we thought that we would be accepted as prophets like we did before. Instead, we were called misguided people that somehow got caught up with the devil. Many of us were, and still are today, viewed as not normal because of the beliefs we hold about spirit.

So, in our youthful days it caused some of us to withdraw, and because of it, we easily became intimidated by those in power. Most of all, some of us have lost our confidence in trusting ourselves to be who we truly are. Instead, we continue to hide from the truth all because of family and mistrusting the God that we are.

Even though many of us became married, had children, and busied ourselves with day-to-day jobs, we somehow knew that we were different for a reason. After the struggles with our differences with others, as well as with our own spirit, soul, mind, and human identity, we knew the time had come for us to learn why we were here and what our purpose was.

Therefore, after the questioning of our failures, the whys of being different from other family members, and the whys of people making us feel guilty, ashamed, and intimidated because of our beliefs, something happened. This happening started after the year 1999 and going into 2000 where something occurred that sparked a memory deep within our heart center that caused us to rise up from our panic-stricken life to an understanding about "why we are here on earth."

It was a reminder that was put in place by our very selves a long time ago, and it is called the Christ Consciousness. However, my soul call's it, opening up to our divinity. It was from this awakening within that has allowed my soul to come forth to unlock my consciousness memories of my past to the present, right to the time where I was part of the Spirit of One, to who I am in my now moment. Now, not only do I remember "all that I am," I remember that there is no need to search for Christ, my Soul, or God any longer, for I have always been enlightened, and so are you. It was just that I have forgotten.

Now, speaking for myself, I have been awakened to a lot of things, thanks to my soul. My soul awakened me to the time when I played in Lemuria taking on the form of a tree, a bird, and even roaming the land as a big animal like creature. During the Atlantean age, I was awakened to the fact I worked in the temple of Tien as a scientist who worked with energy. Then after the Atlantean age, I incarnated as a warrior many times. However, the one that changed my life forever was when I incarnated as the disciple Peter.

Yes, the very same Peter that walked with Yeshua (Jesus) over two thousand years ago. From there, I incarnated many times as a priest, a rabbi, an Arab sheik, a monk, and even a politician. I have also lived in the ancient times of Egypt, Greece, and in China. I was even around during the American Civil War, as I was a Tennessean that lived and worked in Washington, DC. I actually visited Gettysburg a few days after the great battle between Lee's army and the union, and here I am today a businessman living in Northeast Tennessee and a bringer of New Energy Consciousness.

Not only did I work with Yeshua (Jesus) when he walked the earth. I have also worked with Melchizedek, the angel that worked with Abraham, for I too was with Abraham during his time on earth. I have also worked with Tobias of the Old Testament, with Adamus Saint-Germain, known as Samuel in the Old Testament, who later became known as the incarnation of Mark Twain or Samuel Clemens, who was an American writer from 1835 to 1910.

In other lifetimes, I have worked with Kuthumi Lal Singh, who was Balthazar in the time of Jesus, as he was one of the wise men who came to honor the birth of Jesus. Kuthumi was the King who delivered the gifts of gold, frankincense, and myrrh. Kuthumi was also an incarnation of

St. Francis of Assisi. Yes, I have worked with many masters, including the archetypical energy of Archangel Michael.

Of course, this may sound far out there to some of you but you too would be surprised to learn who you were and who you were associated with in the past. However, the main thing to remember here, which is also very important to understand, is that no one is any better than another, for you too are a Christ just as much as I am, as Adamus Saint Germain is, as Melchizedek, Kuthumi Lal Singh, Tobias, and many other grand Masters, even Jesus (Yeshua) himself. Always remember there are no souls that are higher or lower than you, for all souls are God, and therefore equal.

Here is another thing to remember, which is also very, very important, the lifetimes that you have lived in the past, no matter if you were a king or a pauper, or even the disciple Peter, you are not them today. So, get the idea out of your head if you believe that you were someone of importants in your past lifetime. It all doesn't matter because who you are today is all that counts. For example: Even though I was the apostle Peter during the time of Jesus. I am not him today, for I am the integration of Peter's experiences and the wisdom of "all that he was and what I am today."

In other words, I am not any of my past lifetimes. It is that my soul holds the wisdom of all those experiences that I played out." So, I ask you to never put anyone above you, not even Jesus, for Jesus would be the first to tell you this. Actually, Jesus would be the first to tell you that it is time to free him from your religious rhetoric. Jesus has moved on, working with the Order of Sananda.

Yes, Jesus loved his work on Earth and he loved being with us at the time, however it is time for him, me, and you to move on. It is time for all of us to be the Christed one now, for we, as humans, are a God as much as God is a God, and more. Always remember, it is not about who we were, or are, or how important we were, or are, or whether we know some master from the other side, or that we are in the flesh. It is about "knowing" who we are today.

So, my fellow searchers, the Bible, as we know it, and its message that came from the messenger (Yeshua), has come full circle. The only thing left now is for us to let the Bible and this God of duality go, because now, it does not fit our new understanding of who God is anymore. Not only does Jesus tell us to move on, the energies of Buddha, Mohammed, and

Moses also tell us the time has come for us to move on, and to carry the Christ consciousness even further than they did.

Yes, they too have helped plant and spread the Christ seed but now these wonderful masters say it is up to us to display the authority of the Christ within ourselves. We have known the message behind the words written in the holy books of religion for many lifetimes. It is just that it has not entered our heart yet.

The whole purpose for us playing around with vibrational energy and duality is to feel and experience our creations, good and bad, through physicality. We, as a God and a Christ also, gain wisdom by living out our chosen experiences as if they are real, though in truth, they are nothing but illusions put there by our own soul.

The "I AM" within, the mother-father Goddess portion of you, can only experience life through you, which is why your spirit has always held you in the highest esteem, and has always accepted your creations, never suggesting that you did something wrong or that you have ever sinned. Why, because your spirit would have never experienced life if it wasn't for you playing around with the forces of duality (taking the bite of the symbolic apple).

By understanding the reason of duality, vibrational energy, and your creations, you can then pass this wisdom on to your spiritual brothers and sisters, as well as to your own angelic family, who have never experienced flesh before. This way, when your angelic family decides to come to earth, they will not choose the same road as you did, thus making it easier for them to ascend faster than you. This is why there is no such thing as sin, for you have become a savior to them and to all parts and pieces of yourself as well.

My dear friends, it is time to get the concept of sin out of your dualistic mind and heart, and replace it with the concept that "you are a God and a Christ also" experiencing and learning for the benefit of becoming a sovereign being in your own right. While you're at it, get heaven and hell out of your head too for there are no such places other than Earth to experience your hell and heaven. Remember, it's all about choices and experiences in order to learn wisdom, understanding, and responsibility.

We are all dreamers and we create our own illusions through the measuring (time) of our understanding (space) of Spirit (I AM). We build our own reality and our own concept of that reality because of the way we use our belief systems and our energy. We have brought Satan to life by misinterpreting our energy and experiences, thereby creating an attitude based on external emotional factors, which affects our beliefs and our choices. It is our emotional choices that create the ability to deceive our senses into believing something exists when in reality it doesn't.

It is not that the preoccupation with sin and guilt is a mistake because it was a very important step towards where we are and where we are going. It is why we took on physical lifetimes again and again through reincarnation, working out our shortcomings and beliefs (lies). If we tried to do it all in one lifetime, it would be much more difficult to recognize our illusions and lies.

You see, the rational mind has a funny way to trick us into believing that we are not worthy of being a divine and Christ like being in our own right. The rational mind has the tendency to give us a title, like how intellectual and intelligent we are because of our education and our place in life.

We are here on earth to expand our consciousness, and our soul does it through the cries of our miseries and human conditions. Of course, as we grow in wisdom we can also experience joy, strength, and vitality. Therefore, the only way, we can change our conditions, if we don't like what we are experiencing, is by changing our belief systems, and then make choices from the heart center instead of our head.

Look, when we, as humans, go back to the non-physical realm after each incarnation, it gives us a break, a breather, a timeout, and a chance to review how we are doing in our quest toward sovereignty. When our stubborn and rebellious nature allows the "Christ" within to become the master teacher over our rational mind's expressions of duality, one will bring harmony to oneself, to our current life, and therefore to the world.

When your spirit has experienced all things, then your soul will truly have dominion over all forms and structures. Yes, you will literally recognize yourself as a God in the making instead of you looking for God. Jesus displayed himself as being fully balanced and integrated, thereby becoming a Christ in the flesh. You can do the same.

We have trained our mind to do the same things over and over, and because of it, we expect change. How can there be change if we are to stubborn to open up our consciousness to other possibilities? It is our human personality that allows us to look into our physical conditions and see what beliefs we are reflecting. When we learn to trust only in our own divinity (Christ) and understand that we have a human ego personality that needs training, we will immediately remedy imbalanced situations for ourselves and for the world.

My dear friends, the time has come to take Jesus and yourself off the cross, for the cross is just symbolic of your suffering. It is time to let go of this old energy of the Bible as it teaches nothing but fear, guilt, suffering, and judgment. It is time to receive and understand the Bible in a new energy of expansion and joy, instead of using it to generate more fear of God, Satan, feeling guilty because of others, and feeling shame because you don't have the heart to tell others and your family, "no."

Once you learn to move beyond judging what is good and bad, and why you suffer, you will find harmony in all things, including your own creations. You will begin to expand your awareness in ways that you never thought was possible. You will also begin to free yourself from the limited human thought process that duality offers, which will enable you to learn even more about your past lifetimes.

When you come to realize that your focusing and creating have always come from such a small and limited part of your total consciousness, you will begin to open up to a whole new energy of expansion that is designed as the final segment of your journey through many lifetimes. This new energy is not like the dualistic vibrational energy of positive and negative. It is expansional energy, for this new energy coexists with vibrational energy in allowing you to create something that is beyond positive and negative.

As you know, dualistic vibrational energy has been around since you passed through the "wall of duality" and onto the physical realm. What you have been doing with this vibrational energy for eons of time was reusing it over and over without realizing it. You, as all humans, have been transmuting this vibrational energy of two and putting it into many different forms, like lifetimes, to create your experiences and your reality on earth.

Actually, you can say that when we, as souled beings, left the first circle, our spirit gave us a certain amount of energy to go forth and see what w could do with it. This is why we, all humans, build and destroy things, and why we try to steal energy from one another because all that we see and understand is limitations.

However, some of us may be discovering something new that was not expected after playing with this vibrational energy of positive and negative for many lifetimes. New energy is suddenly popping up out of nowhere. In the book of Revelation it is called the "New Earth."

Now, this New Earth is not about seeing heaven on Earth, even though it can be, it is about New Energy of Expansion coming to Earth to replace the Old Energy of positive and negative as the primary source for our creations. This New Energy is something very important that happens to those that finally let go of their old dogmatic theological principles of good and bad, right and wrong, and the idea of Satan versus God.

This New Energy comes in through transforming dualistic energy into a "new energy of four," which is completeness and expansion, for they are:

1. Your Positive Consciousness (outer male self)
2. Your Negative Consciousness (inner female self)
3. Your Consciousness of no force, as it moves back and forth to light and dark; and
4. Your Christ-Soul Consciousness, as it can also be called your gnost or solution consciousness (an answer to any question no matter what that question is)

Instead of having the resistance of positive and negative managing your life, you can begin to work with *positive* and *negative* in a *neutralized* means. Through this neutralizing, it opens the door for your long lost *Gnost* (Christ) consciousness of no force to come into your life as a solution maker to all of what you desire to be and do. This is what creates your miracles in an unlimited way, including healing.

In Revelation 11:11-12, we can find how it speaks directly of an energy shift by using the words, "three and a half days" (3½). This, in effect, is a metaphor to imply a leap in consciousness for humanity from an energy frequency of a 3-D level to a New Energy level of 5-D that causes a shift in consciousness to a reality that is higher than the current 2-D and 3-D levels. It is referred to as "three and a half" rather than "four" or some other number because we will still be living here on earth in a 3-D body. However, everything changes.

How we connect to our Christ (gnost) consciousness is what the half day (½) is all about. It represents our leap (ascension) into a new consciousness of four, as it is about who we truly are while we are still part of physical earth. The number "one" over the number "two" indicates how we moved, in the beginning, from an "oneness of consciousness" to a "consciousness of two" a long time ago.

Now, through transforming our energy of "two" to an energy of "four," we can now begin to expand our mental state of consciousness of opposing forces to a new expanded mental consciousness that harbors no duality, only completeness and expansion. This is why the word "day" here is symbolized by using the word "understanding" in its place. (This is explained in my new book: "The Book of Revelation: A New Beginning.")

To clarify on this missing Gnost consciousness just for a bit, since I did not mention it before this time, it is a consciousness that we, as souls, always have had within us but we have chosen to hide it due to the idea of learning responsibility. However, once we become aware of this lost consciousness, two things will happen. First, we come into the wisdom and understanding that we are a Christ also, that we are a God unto ourselves, and that we are the Creator of our experiences, thus responsible for everything that we are experiencing today.

Second, we bring into our life a divine energy of four that helps us find the creative solutions to what we see as problems. These solutions flow freely to us instead of the results being bound and limited to only positive and negative. Our Gnost consciousness is the fourth component of our being, along with the body, universal divine mind, and spirit. It is the part of us that has never forgotten that we are indeed a Christ also. It is our divine creative solution to every situation.

However, before we can bring Gnost back into our life, we must first get out of our rational mind of duality thinking. Our Gnost consciousness is the bridge between the nonphysical, physical, and the Christ realms. This means we cannot use our Gnost consciousness with a mind that still beliefs in duality because the mind of a 2-D nature cannot function in the Christ realms, which by the way, are the realms of solutions and miracles.

Gnost can only be used through the Christ consciousness, which we bring into our earthly consciousness when we realize that we are a Christ unto ourselves. How our Gnost consciousness works is something very hard to explain. This is because words always engage our 2-D mind as seeing things as right and wrong, good and bad, and our Gnost consciousness is beyond the capacity of the 2-D mind to comprehend. However, with the help of the angelic realm I will do my best.

First, I would like to ask you, how many times have you prayed to God to help bring healing to you and others with having no results? How about the prayers where you asked for miracles, love, money, relationships, and many other things? When you engage in prayer for help, you are asking a God of fiction and the angels to do these things for you instead of taking the responsibility to create them for yourself. You are a Christ and a God also that has the authority to create miracles for yourself, including your healing.

Look, when our prayers do not seem to be answered we usually move right into our 2-D mind to try and figure out some way to make it happen, which is why they don't happen. Doing this can wear us out – for I know because I have done it myself many times.

You get frustrated which causes you to go back to your old ways of doing things, back to the old beliefs (lies) that say: God is not responding because it is not meant for me to be healed, have money, or have love at this time, or my life has already been planned out by God. Thus, I must not be worthy of health, abundance, or love while I am in the flesh, or that maybe God is reserving this for me in heaven.

When you learn to uncover the truth that you can shift your 3-D consciousness to a 5-D physical consciousness while on earth, you will come into a *knowing* that you are the *source* and the *creator* of your life, your miracles, and your creations. Your Gnost consciousness of no force is the core passion within that is activated by your total trust in you as the source, the Lord of Lords, the Christ, and the master of your fate.

When we discarded our Gnost (Christ) consciousness long ago it was when we handed all authority over to our 2-D mental level. That is when we began using positive and negative, as well as reason, to control our reality. Eventually, we stopped our exploring of positive and negative and became a follower of others because of logic and rational thinking.

We all fell asleep or died to the knowingness that we are the source, the Christ, and the creator of our reality.

You have all the resources within you to become a sovereign being in fulfilling your own miracles. It is just that you have forgotten. Religions, governments, businesses, even your families, help keep you in this sleep state because they will judge everything you do from a 2-D level, especially the consideration of you claiming to be equal to God, let alone that you have the authority of a Christ in creating miracles for yourself. It comes difficult for them to understand that there is no power or higher authority than you. Not even God or Jesus is higher than you.

Religions most likely don't even know what Gnost is but you can be sure they don't want you to know about it because it gives you back your "I AM" identity, power, and divine creatorship abilities in creating all the miracles you can stand. They don't want you to bring Gnost back because it would literally take away their power and control over your life and give it back to you, which is where it belongs!

Just remember, your Gnost (Christ) consciousness can only be used with having a mind that expands beyond the traditional 2-D core belief in positive and negative.

Now, according to the Tobias Material, channeled by Geoffrey Hoppe of the Crimson Circle, it will take awhile before scientists understand what this "new energy of expansion" is and how it works because when they measure it against the old vibrational energy of positive and negative, it is going to be difficult for them to analyze. You see, they're going to find that it doesn't respond like the old vibrational energy of two.

Even today scientists that study the physical forces of positive and negative, and how it relates to each other, are beginning to see this New Expansional Energy but they do not understand it because, to them, it looks like chaos. What they are missing is that this New Energy (New Earth) is always in chaotic measure because it is raw pure neutral energy that has not been called in by the creator (you) to bring it into order so it can continue to expand.

You see, this New Energy of Expansion is real for those that have learned to accept everything that they are experiencing in life because in truth they are the ones that created it. We all fail to see the God that we are before separating ourselves from our divine state that happened a long time ago. We have forgotten that the image of God is not of a duality form or a human form. God, like you, is of a no form, and with having no force to it.

Now, according to Tobias and the angelic realm, this "new energy of expansion" has come into our physical universe in September of the year 2007, all because of the divine plan we took on billions of years ago. The angelic realm is saying this because they can see the physical dimension and our consciousness is beginning to expand. How fast it will expand is up to us as a collective human group. They also say that this new energy is going to cause many changes to mother earth, good changes.

They say the changes will affect the way we use old energy, like oil for instance. Oil will be something of the past in the coming years – for scientists will discover a new energy that will come from water. We will know this new energy of expansion coming in by the changes in our technology. Scientists will find new methods to heal the physical body without abrasive medicines or having to cut the body open. All of this will be the results of new energy.

All this chaos that we are seeing with our financial markets today and the politics around the world is going to continue for awhile because of this expansional energy coming to earth – for it brings out truths. Oh, we will have some of the old energy institutions that won't like the changes, for they will try as hard as they can to battle it and keep it from coming in.

However, it will not work! Even the churches will fight hard to keep this new energy out, for they will preach as hard as they can to keep the God of the Bible alive by telling us we need to go back to our ideals when it comes to following and worshipping God. Nevertheless, through time, the churches will have to change because more people on earth are going to begin to understand that the source is within and not outside of them, or in a church, or in a white male God.

People are even going to understand that it is not God or Jesus that is going to save them. It is themselves that is going to save them, for we are going to learn that there is no God in heaven directing our life or our destiny. We are even going to learn to embrace the concept that "we are a God and a Christ also" and that our "I AM" is a divine human that opened up the pathway for our own Gnost consciousness to come in.

Remember, the difference between truth and a lie is about becoming aware that you are the true creator, and that it is not some God that lives in a book that is going to save you. The reason you cannot remember past lifetimes is because you have been living through the rationalized mind, which has been layered with lies upon lies (beliefs upon beliefs).

It was the creating of your human ego personality that deceived you into believing that you were separate from your spirit and soul. In fact, despite the exterior appearance of separation from God, there is no such thing. It is only the separated human you that believes that you are separated. You have forgotten that you have the authority of the Spirit of One, even though you keep giving something that feels like your power and energy away to others.

My dear friends, it is not power or energy that we are giving away to others, it is only a reflection of how we give away our own authority to others such as governments, religion, family, friends, and businesses without even realizing we are doing it. We give our power and energy away because we fail to understand that it is our beliefs that keep us trapped. Thus, we choose to suffer on a subconscious level over something that is false, a lie, and illusionary.

The reason you feel like you have sinned is because deep within your being you feel guilty for the mismanagement of your energy in what you did since the time you left your divine state. As long as you feel guilty about the mismanagement of your energy, this feeling of sinning will remain. It's that simple! Therefore, it is up to you, and not Jesus or any religious sect, when it comes to the forgiveness of your sins.

Remember, Jesus did not forgive sins during his time here on earth. Rather, Jesus opened the minds and hearts of those that were ready to forgive themselves and take full responsibility for their creations, which is why they were healed. When you choose to accept responsibility for everything that you are experiencing in life, and stop blaming others for your unhappiness and illnesses, you will realize the conditions that you think of as sins are actually illusions and lies that were created by you, the real creator.

This means, once you integrate the wisdom of "all that you are" into your own "I AM Christ-Gnost Consciousness," then sin will no longer be part of your thinking, and therefore your experiences, because now you will not look at your creations as something right and wrong, or good and bad. Instead, you will begin to produce joy, health, abundance, good relationships, and many healings.

My fellow searchers, it is about releasing the belief in sin and your emotional connection to family, friends, government, religious beliefs, or to whatever keeps you from your own "I AM Essence." You have come to believe that there is such a thing as power, but in reality, it is just the desire to experience life. Power is an illusion to the human identity, a lie that was created to help you experience your choices.

What has been forgotten is that your energy, in its natural state, is pure, unprocessed and neutral, which means it has no actual power and yet, it possesses the authority of the creator, you. Power is something outside of you, and because nothing outside of you is real, then power is also a lie and an illusion. The power you think you have is actually coming from belief systems that are based on lifetimes of being hypnotized by your emotional connection to your family, friends, governments, religions, and businesses of all kinds.

If you use your creative will to think you have power to help others because of your connection to them, you will always experience the forces of drama and duality, as this creates more experiences of ups and downs in your life. You will not be able to escape these ups and downs until you open your heart and recognize that it is your beliefs of old and your emotional connection to them that keep you there.

You see, it is not for us to judge another's purpose, or why one dies, or how one misbehaves, or how one chooses to live. It is only for us to love them unconditionally without judgment of any kind. By doing this, we take a great deal of weight off our own shoulders and theirs.

Remember, you are not responsible for your brothers and sisters in what they choose or experience because each and every one of them is a God and a Christ unto themselves that chose what they are experiencing, either consciously or unconsciously. When you allow the emotional forces of drama to pass through you, instead of having your emotions part of what you believe to be true, they will die from lack of your creator energy and a new joyful harmonized habit will be formed within you.

It is important to remember that your belief systems are lies, no matter what you believe. Why, because all beliefs are derived from the memories of your past lifetimes. It is because of your strongly held belief systems (such as in Satan), that these lies have the ability to take over your reality, your truths, and become the ruler of your experiences on earth.

Belief systems also have the ability to mask the basic truth of who you truly are. You agreed to come to earth and experience many false beliefs, but none of them are being inflicted on you by some outside force. You brought them into your life for a variety of reasons, and the major one is for soul growth.

The lie of a God that created you, and that you must worship, is part of your own divine plan. Hence, this lie distorts your perceptions and your choices, and therefore your reality. Religions, governments, friends, and families keep you in this hypnotic state because of your emotions and how you hold onto them.

What you are learning here on earth is that you cannot be a sovereign "I AM" being in your own right until you realize that power, family, religion, and government are only an illusion. The same applies to every person and every nation that tries to dominate another. This is obvious because every time anyone tries to dominate another soul or nation, by force, it ends up in failure. There are many today that are finally coming to this awakening, even nations.

Many of us are in the process of bringing all aspects of ourselves into harmony by no longer seeing the world and ourselves through the eyes of a false God. It is time to see our soul brothers and sisters who are playing the game of duality in a new way, as fellow Gods who are simply acting out what they have already done in the astral realms so they too can become awakened. The choice to see through the eyes of compassion and honor, rather than dogmatic views, is exactly what will at long last bring harmony and peace within you and to all nations.

What is important to remember is that ignorance is acceptable for a time and we have spent many lifetimes in ignorance because of our emotions. But also remember that our divinity (soul) will give us many opportunities to turn our ignorance into a "knowing" that we are a God and a Christ also, which means ignorance eventually turns into wisdom.

We, as humans, tend to believe that by making idols of whom or what we think God looks like, we can draw closer to the divine that we feel so separated from. We tend to believe that, by focusing on these images and being good enough, we will somehow receive the Holy Spirit of God. What we have failed to realize is that the Holy Spirit of God is already very much alive within us now, even if one is a killer.

We are greater than any form, name, image, icon or concept of God that we might worship, or that is hanging on our wall. These idols and images, even our physical body, are made of matter. We are more than a material form. Therefore, we should not worship an idol, a body, or a name, any name, including Jesus, as being holy and separate from us, for we, all souled beings, are again a God and a Christ also.

As a true disciple of Christ, we do not need to pay attention to the influence that our acts will have upon others but only to the influence our acts will have on our own evolution towards higher understanding of Spirit. When we are always doing things for our church, family, friends, and government, and the effects they have on our life, we soon merge our individuality into their belief systems and lose sight of our own identity. Remember, there is nothing in this material world, or anywhere else outside of us, that is worthy of our worship.

There are no temples, churches, deities, prayer beads, or crosses that need be our places or objects of worship. There are no priests, ministers, rabbis, or other persons who may act as representatives between us and our own divinity. We do not need any representative to teach us about an invisible God who needs to be worshiped. Each and every human carries within them the temple of God, as we are our own church and we are the body of Christ.

My fellow searchers, the divine plan was simple. It was to allow us humans to experience the joy of life and the wisdom of creativity as a God. However, most of us have chosen to suffer through the lessons of our beliefs, our attachments to them, and our emotional connection to "all that is." It is amazing, and it shows how we, as Gods, have manifested our playground of suffering in order to experience life and learn responsibility.

It has been described throughout this book how groups, such as religions and governments, offer their solutions to the problems we have created, saying they can guide us through life into an "effortless" Garden. But, this is a denial of who we truly are. Entrance into heaven only comes when we exchange our beliefs and faith in some external leader, doctrine, or some God of judgment. If we accept these beliefs, we are offered the ultimate "reward" of escaping individual responsibility.

However, the price of that "reward" is rejection of your own Christ Consciousness. Therefore, it is up to you to decide if it is worth the cost.

Chapter 12

You Are A Divinine Being

What makes you a divine being? Your divinity is a gift that has come from the Spirit of One, where you, like all souled beings, have an equal portion (share) that can never be stolen or taken away. Therefore, your divinity is what makes you equal to God and as a Christ also.

As mentioned in Chapter One, the Spirit of One was a consciousness that held the in-breath of the feminine and the out-breath of the masculine essence of itself, for that was "all that was." When the Spirit of One asked the question, "Who Am I," she became the implosion and explosion that sparked the awakening (birth) of all souled beings (Children of God) as being unchangeable, absolute, infinite, and that we all have a spirit that has a consciousness that holds a masculine side that is connected to "universal divine mind."

Yes, we, all humans and angels-souls alike, are the Godhead that created the etheric/astral dimensional realms, including the earth realm, the animals, the fish of the sea, the birds of the air, for nothing was left out, not even our human body or that of nothingness. It is "all that was" (Spirit of One) becoming "all that is" in what is seen now as us souled beings. We contain within us the divine creative essence and sovereign energy of the Spirit of One in a unique and personal way that is now our true identity, for we are a divine being in disguise.

Now, we may see ourselves only as a human but be assured, we are a "souled being" that has within us the divine spark and the creative essence of the Spirit of One to set in motion billions upon billions of potentials, good, bad, and balanced, for us to experience. Our divinity is the essence of our Soul and our Gnost consciousness in expression reminding us that we are a Christ also, before we were ever a human.

This is why Jesus said we could move mountains because we are the divine creator that can bring forth any miracle we desire to experience, even a new planet.

When we, as souled beings, first became aware of our own identity in the beginning, all that we knew and understood was that we could only express what was constructive and in alignment with the divine law of unconditional love because that was the true essence of the Spirit of One. When we first played in the first creation – as the Bible calls the Garden of Eden – there was no avenue for us to express good and bad because it did not exist at the time.

You see, because we cannot have an out-breath without having an in-breath first, then we, like the Spirit of One, are more of a Goddess (feminine) than we are a God (masculine-mind). Why? It is because the in-breath of the Goddess is our spirit and soul, for we are the divine mother (spirit) and the womb (soul) of all that we desire to create that causes the out-breath of God (universal divine mind) to appear in some type of form.

This means God, the masculine, and our connection to universal divine mind, is not a personality unto itself but uses pure energy and transforms it from its neutral state to taking on some type of form that was chosen and expressed by our soul, the feminine, in giving that form life. Since we are a Goddess, what we choose to create and bring into form, like a physical body, or illnesses, or hard times, is in fact our own making, and therefore our responsibility for creating it.

So, if you don't like what you are experiencing right now, then by all means, change it. After all, you are the creator of your experiences. It was your spirit, the feminine side (Goddess), which set into motion the splitting of your consciousness of "one" into positive and negative that now appears as your deceptive mental mind. Now, you embrace the belief that the rational mind is what holds the power of God.

The rational mind that you embrace as holding all power has forgotten that it takes the soul (feminine part of you) to birth the desire to experience life and to know itself, which is why women in the physical sense give birth. Thus, the human female is a metaphor for the goddess and the soul side of you in giving life to what your outer rational deceptive mind chooses to create. Yet, man looks at the female as beneath him.

The female is symbolic of the truth that it requires the in-breath of your soul consciousness to bring life into manifested form, like your physical body. However, "she, your soul consciousness," cannot do it without the outer masculine side of the deceptive mind. Therefore, since it is your feminine side (soul) that gives birth to your ideas, desires, and choices, then it is the feminine side or your divinity that must take on the burden of what your outer masculine or deceptive mind side of you chooses to manifest.

This is why the male blames the female for the original sin and not himself, for Eve is symbolic of our soul consciousness accepting with great love all that the outer masculine deceptive side (Adam-mind) chooses to take action on no matter if one is male or female. Since our feminine side is the divine essence of the Spirit of One, which makes us a Goddess and a Christ also, our feminine side is the "I AM" and the divine side of us (Christ) who took on what our outer deceptive and rational mind chose to manifest, good and bad.

Therefore, it is your soul, the divine side, that holds the negative (dark-sin) and positive (light) roles that the outer masculine deceptive side chooses to experience. As all life comes from consciousness (the in-breath of the feminine) then life itself cannot be manifested, unless the outer masculine deceptive side of the mind (the out-breath) gives it some type of form for you to experience.

You can understand this with the example of a photographic print made from a negative. The negative (feminine-soul) is used to cause (create) the positive (masculine-god) image to appear or become visible (manifested form). This is why man believes that God created everything without realizing that nothing can be created or manifested without the Goddess and its connection to universal divine mind.

This also means, whatever you think, express, and manifest in life has to be stored somewhere. It cannot be stored within your masculine side (the rational mind) because that is the part of you that makes choices and then acts them out in a form like state. Therefore, whatever you think, express, and act on in the physical sense must be held or stored by your feminine side (the soul) to be played back later when the outer positive-masculine side (mind) is ready to accept the choice to experience them.

Every time a choice is made, good or bad, your feminine side, which is the divine and Christ soul side, which is also the negative and the dark side of you, then holds the memory of that choice within your soul until, at some point in time during your journey of many lifetimes, your outer positive-masculine deceptive side takes full responsibility for the choice.

(Eve giving Adam the apple is symbolic of this act as well as the Christ side of you taking on your so called sins – for the Christ side of you holds those dark thoughts and the actions you took until the human ego (the beast) and your outer rational deceptive mind takes responsibility for them).

So, my fellow searchers, we, all souled beings, were the ones that gave the word "negative" a meaning of it being bad and yet, in this context, the word "negative" is just part of our divinity and soul, which is why it also holds the meaning of darkness, ignorance, and what is unknown. For that reason, I say unto you, never be afraid of the dark because the "negative" and the "dark side" is your divinity and soul at work helping you feel and understand your choices that were made in past lifetimes and the choices you made in this lifetime by bringing them to your awareness to examine and experience.

This is why there is no such thing as sin – for how can it be sin, evil, or bad, if you are gaining overwhelming wisdom and understanding from the choices you make. The "Book of Life," and what is called the "Akashic Records," are all about your Christ consciousness (divinity) holding your stories of many past lifetimes where you played with your light and dark creations, for neither of them are about a real book.

Everything you did in the past, in the present, as well as what you thought and felt, has been registered and held within your soul/divinity until you are ready to face them as a sovereign being in your own right. Everything from the beginning was and is forever recorded within your soul memory and you cannot escape from what you have done (good and evil) from the time you left your divine state (first creation) up until this now moment.

However, you can heal what you have done just by recognizing and accepting your past lifetimes as well as taking full responsibility for them and everything that you did, past and present. As a result, your divinity (Christ) comes in by accepting everything that crosses your path, good experiences or not, and whether or not you feel it is your fault. However, it is not only about what you see or understand from a conscious level. It is also about what is at the subconscious level.

For example: How many of you are afraid of the dark? Afraid enough to stay up all night sitting or lying in a bed or chair with a light next to you? How about never going out in the night time darkness? The reason you are so afraid of the dark is because of your past, either in this lifetime or from your past lifetimes.

You see, all of us, at one time or another, have had some past lifetime experiences where we lost hope and trust in ourselves and in others. Why? Because, believe it or not, many of us created for ourselves experiences where we were an abuser, and in another lifetime, we played a victim of an abuser. So now, from a subconscious level, we feel guilty and ashamed for what we have done, even though we played the part of being the victim.

Because of this shame and guilt, we buried those dark experiences of being the abuser deep within our soul, which happens to be part of the dark side, thus we become afraid of the dark.

Once we made the choice to move beyond our divine state (leaving the first creation) and move into the deceptive mind field of duality and thought forms, the part where we understand that we are a Christ also seemed to become clouded because of what we were creating in the astral and physical realms. Not only did we create many lifetimes playing with the forces of good, we also played intensely with the forces of bad and evil.

That is when we began to curse ourselves for what we created, which is why we took on a belief system of destiny. Once we took on a destiny role, we also took on the belief in sin and karma, for they have become part of our experiences. Because of this strong belief in sin and in karma, we began to hide our dark creations deep within our soul. Yes, we forgot that our soul is part of our divinity and Christ consciousness.

By choosing to shape a lifetime around some evil acts, either this lifetime or lifetime past, we created a consciousness of regret. This caused us to take our bad creations and dump them into our soul as lost memories, or one could say lost aspects of self. Well, after awhile, we began to look at our divinity (Christ), since it is part of our soul, as something dark, bad, and negative, even as a demon because when we feel something around us that cannot be seen or explained, we become overwhelmed with fear, and that fear is caused by our shame and guilt.

Why? Because every time we feel that divine energy around us, it seems to have a suffering energy effect to it, which is why it can become hard to accept our Christ consciousness. We ignore it because we feel ashamed of what we did in some past, and now we are scared of it. Now, don't confuse Satan, the devil, or the beast, as being your divinity, because these personalities are not real anyway. It is just that our divinity became the dumping ground for all our bad and evil creations throughout our journey of lifetimes.

After all, the energy of those dark creations had to go somewhere because they just don't disappear. In fact, this is the true meaning of Christ taking on the sins of the world. The Christ is really you taking on the sins of all aspects of you and your world of creations, good and bad, until you learn to face them as your own creations.

For instance: It is like a child being physically and mentally abused, and because of the ordeal, the child holds itself as the blame. Thus the child creates, deep within its consciousness, a feeling of shame and guilt that finally leads to the child becoming afraid of everything, including the dark, and all those that reminds the child of the ordeal.

My fellow searchers, there are many of you that are afraid of the dark, which is why your divinity (Christ self) must come to the rescue by holding your shame and guilt within your soul memories until you are ready to face them for what they really are, just experiences that you have chosen throughout your journey of lifetimes so as to become a sovereign "I AM" in your own right.

This is why there is no such thing as sin. For everything you did, good, bad, and the evil things that you did in some past lifetime(s) have been held by your divinity, the soul, until you were ready to take responsibility for them. Of course, what you have forgotten, even though you can feel it deep within, is that you have paid the karmic price for everything that you did (past and present). However, what some of you are feeling now is the shame and guilt for creating them in the first place.

You see, what you are forgetting is that your soul held these creations lovingly and without judgment so you could learn the wisdom of the act, along with your choices. Sometimes, without realizing it, you do quiet your rational mind and that is when those thoughts of rape, torture, killing, stealing, being abused or being the abuser, come through to your conscious level. When it does, it scares you almost to death.

That is when we fall to our knees in prayer, saying to ourselves. Why is it that I think about these terrible things? Why can't I have only good thoughts? Wow! How right my preacher is about the devil and how he is constantly testing me, which is why I must keep guard of him at all times.

One may have fear and guilt so deeply embedded within their soul (divinity) because of something they did in another lifetime, or maybe in this lifetime, they continuously, without realizing it, punish themselves over and over. The amazing thing is, they probably don't even know they are doing it. It is not that they have done something wrong by having those thoughts, or that they think that they have sinned, or that some devil is testing them. It is about feeling ashamed and guilty for the harm they believe they caused others many lifetimes ago.

For that reason! It is time to take Satan, the Beast, and the Anti-Christ out of the equation because truthfully there are no such personalities. Satan is nothing more than your rebellious and defiant nature of past lifetime aspects trying to come through to your present lifetime to be recognized by you. The Beast is nothing more than your ego moving into a physical personality that becomes unfaithful to your own soul. The Anti-Christ is nothing more than your outer deceptive mind taking on the role as being your God, which is why God, the one that most of us believe in, have the same attributes as man, therefore a false God.

This is nothing more than the outer deceptive mind (Anti-Christ) being afraid of the real God (the Christ) all because we feel guilty and ashamed for the misappropriating of our godlike energy. We have cursed our divinity (I AM Christ) and have run from it for many lifetimes simply because we have misinterpreted the dark as being connected to Satan.

You see, it is our soul that takes us through endless cycles of lifetimes because our divinity (Christ self) loves us so much. We have forgotten that our divinity and soul memories are there to remind us that spirit has given us freedom and expression to go out and experience whatever we choose, good and bad. The soul will hold our guilt, shame, and all that we have done lovingly without judgment until we have the courage to confront them, which is why we have reincarnation and nothing to feel guilty or ashamed about.

This is the true meaning of Christ "taken on the sins of the world." Because it is your world that you have created for yourself to experience, your divinity (Christ-soul) now holds those memories of your past aspects, good and bad, until the time comes when you are ready to face them. When you do learn to face them, then understand what you did has nothing to do with sin but only experiences that you chose in order to become a wise sovereign "I AM" being in your own right.

Your journey through the physical realm is to help awaken you to the understanding that each character you meet in life has a meaning to your own evolution. They become the trigger to setting off your soul memories of your past personality-aspects. Therefore, whoever you meet in life, like your father, mother, brother, sister, spouse, your children, uncles, aunts, friends, neighbors, as well as your enemies, are all put in your path of life by your own soul in order to trigger your memory in forgiving yourself, them that harmed you, and to forgive all past aspects of yourself.

By being introduced to many personality-aspects (lifetimes) of your past in any given lifetime it brings in the opportunity for you to heal, resolve, and then release these aspects (lifetimes) of you with great love, for you are their creator. You created them to play a part, good and bad, in order to experience life and now, the wisdom of those experiences are part of your wholeness. When you accept these light and dark creations with love it then helps you to remember or reawaken to your soul, thus healing begins.

You see, when you first became clouded with your multiple light and dark creations, as you journeyed throughout time and space experiencing them, you went on automatic pilot, or into a sleep state, where your human personality became the dominant level of your experiencing and focus.

Remember, your spirit wanted to experience itself and yet, at the same time, you had no agenda to follow so the mental and human part of you became the motivating force behind your desires to experience thought forms in a dualistic materialized manner.

Because of this desire, you, as all souled beings, imagined (created) the illusion of having a consciousness consisting of opposing forces, positive and negative, that soon became layered into a structured form that consists of you having a:

1. Spirit body
2. Soul body
3. Intuitive body
4. Mental body – Rational Deceptive Thought Forms
5. Emotional body
6. Etheric/Astral body, and
7. Physical body.

Of course, embedded within each layer there are many belief patterns or, as Tobias calls them, networks. This way, with spirit, soul, and divinity as your hidden companions, and the source for your creations, you, the human self, the one that had a great desire to learn about life, could feel and experience good and bad. With the help of your human ego consciousness (the beast), you then gain the wisdom of your experiences.

The seed you planted within your deceptive and rational mind, as well as your human personality (Adam self) eons ago about God kicking you out of the Garden, now defines your reality, although it is not true. Every suggestion, idea, and thought that you have accepted about God, Satan, the serpent, the anti-Christ, and the Garden, is nothing but a hypnotic state that maintains the credibility of the reality that you perceive as yours, which is why you suffer.

Of course, this was your plan all along and not some white male Hebrew God that created you. It was you who caused it to happen! You see, once you found yourself playing with a belief system of good and bad, light and dark, it soon led to the birthing process on Earth where you lost trust in your soul and placed it with your rational mind and human personality. This act caused a deep feeling of separation between your soul and your new found belief system of good and bad, light and dark, and your human ego personality.

This then led you through endless cycles of lifetimes repeating the same experiences over and over until you eventually learn to take responsibility for what you are creating. Because of your belief in light and dark, meaning good and bad, as well as there being a God and Satan separate from you, and your emotional ties to it all, you ended up putting more and more distance between your divinity, your spirit, your soul, your rational mind, and your human ego, all because of being afraid of your dark side, which is nothing more than your divinity.

The trust you lost with your divinity that you happened to cherish, but somehow feared, is the distance measured in terms of where you are in consciousness, where you are today in your beliefs, and where you are with your spirit and divinity.

Because our thinking is more tied to our belief in light and dark (God and Satan), then our trust in our own Christ-divinity has become forgotten on a human scale. The human ego, and the mental and physical part of us, now became the place where we could escape from having to deal with what we did, good and bad, until we evolve enough in consciousness to address what we did. This allowed our rational mind and human ego personality to surrender to a belief system that we are not a divine being but only a human being that needs a savior.

However, there are some of you that are ready once again to trust in your soul. After all, it is your divinity and your soul that took on all the attributes of your so called bad creations. It was your soul that allowed you to separate your good and loving creations from your dark and negative creations because of having so much love and honor for you.

Now, your dark side holds your enlightenment and wisdom to the extent of allowing you to ascend into a "new expansional energy" where you will not be afraid of your dark side. Why, because the light and dark are nothing more than you coming into a knowing that you are a Christ also and an oneness unto yourself.

Instead of seeing your dark side as something evil and powerful, and your human personality weak, consider letting your dark and light side come back together where you, in human form, will experience a whole new and safe energy. When you can learn to trust in your dark side as much as your light side, and then integrate both by inviting in your soul here on earth into your human personality, that is when ascension begins. That is what Jesus talked about over two thousand years ago, and what you have been waiting for all this time.

When we can invite our soul-divinity (the dark side of us that was wrapped away in a belief of it being evil) into our reality of today without our human ego-personality and our rational mind resisting it, we come to a place in our heart where we will find peace and freedom from all that is happening around us.

When you come into the wisdom of absolute love and trust in yourself as being a Christ and a God also, and that you have gone through your trials and tribulations of lifetimes on Earth, that is when you move into the third circle of creation. It is in this third circle where you become a sovereign divine being in your own right.

Look, those of you who are ready for ascension (harvest) it doesn't mean that you have to vanish from the earth like our predecessors did during the biblical days, because now, there is a new type of birthing taking place on earth. It is New Expansional Energy. This New Energy (New Earth) is coming to earth in a very fast way, and all that you have to do is allow it to flow into your heart without trying to fight it.

So, learn to follow your heart without hesitation because your "I AM" identity is within your heart center and not your head. It is god, with a small "g," that is in your head, a god that is made up of duality, and thought forms of a mental nature. Remember, no one knows the mother-father Goddess as well as the Son, and no one knows better than you, the son, what the father-mother needs.

Why? It is because you are the *father*, the *mother*, and the *son* in action. Jesus understood this principle as the method of communicating with his Christ self, and then integrating it with his human ego personality. Now it is up to you to do the same.

My dear friends, Jesus, the physical man, symbolizes the Son of Man within all of us while we are on the Earth plane, and Jesus, the Christ, symbolizes the Son of God in all of us because his divinity, like our own, became part of his inner consciousness, thereby making him not only the mother-father Goddess unto himself but also the Son.

It is the same with you and me! This is why it is said "the only way to the Father is through the Son" (John 14:6), for you are both. By merging your outer rational mind (anti-Christ), your human ego personality (the beast) with the father-mother-Goddess (Christ), you come to understand your relationship to your outer human self (son principle). In so doing, you become the standard of how you must harmonize the masculine-feminine energies within yourself and become a Christ unto yourself.

Jesus was called Lord because he followed his sovereign divine will (the, I AM within himself), mastered the law of cause and effect (sowing and reaping), and had come to know the Christ principle within himself by integrating his outer rational and deceptive mind (anti-Christ), his spirit (Christ), and his fallen ego personality (the beast) as "one body of consciousness."

Through this mastery, Jesus had come to know that blissful state of a harmonious consciousness, otherwise known as the Kingdom of Heaven within himself, which is nothing but higher understanding because of the wisdom learned journeying through many lifetimes.

Jesus demonstrated this in order for you and me to realize that our divinity and our dark side is the I AM Christ within, and that our outer positive-masculine deceptive aspect of self (Adam principle) needs to become balanced with our inner feminine side (Soul-Eve). This balancing is how we awaken to our divinity or sovereign Christ self. This is done through our dark side that we eventually awaken to as our divinity.

When you no longer place blame on others for what you are experiencing, you will integrate all that you hold as your characteristics, understanding, and the wisdom (including dark and light creations) of your many lifetimes into the fullness of your own spirit. When you learn to integrate the wisdom of "all that you are," you can finally move into a fuller awareness of the Christ, because that is who you truly are already.

Your human ego personality is the eye through which you perceive or view your physical reality, and it can cut you off from the real you (Christ) if you get carried away with judging and interpreting things as good and bad. It is this very judgment that prevents you from integrating your "I AM Christ" identity to come into your human life.

Once you embrace everything with love and see everything as a gift, even a deadly disease, then your human ego personality (the beast) will release the energy with which you are manifesting these things. This will then allow you to come into harmony with both sides of yourself.

Remember, it is from out of your human ego personality where your Christ self comes out from behind your ignorance (clouds), that actually becomes the healing force that integrates the wisdom of "all that you are."

Chapter 13

The Creation Of Many Personalty-Aspects

(Physical and Non-Physical)

The meaning of the word "personality" in the dictionary calls forth the "totality of a person's characteristics, such as attitude, interest, behavioral patterns, emotional responses, as well as other traits." However, the soul looks at a "personality" as a lifetime aspect where you take on a behavior pattern that defines only one of many parts and pieces of you to go out and experience a lifetime story to express certain thoughts, beliefs, and feelings to serve you in learning "who you truly are."

When the Spirit of One, in the beginning, became the implosion and explosion, the movement and the motivating spark for the in-breath and out-breath that delivered the composition of us souled beings as absolute, unlimited, and in the form of an infinite spirit that uses pure energy, then the in-breath of our own spirit is the divine mother and the womb waiting for our soul to cause the out-breath in outlining a lifetime story in the physical as an narrative account to serve us in our journey of learning wisdom, understanding and taking responsibility for our creations.

You see, since we souls were shaped and formed in the divine image of the Spirit of One, and having the same authority (power), then we souls did at one time come to a conscious awakening where we asked ourselves "who we were?" This question that we souls asked ourselves, like it did for the Spirit of One, also became the implosion and explosion, the movement and the motivating spark for the in-breath and out-breath that delivered to us, as souled beings, the composition of many personality-aspects of self (physical and non-physical) to serve in bringing to us wisdom and understanding.

Now, the difference between what the Spirit of One brought forth and what we, as souled beings, created as a personality-aspects (lifetimes) is that we have a soul that contains the same creative essence and sovereign energy as the Spirit of One in a unique and personal way.

For instance: We, as an individual soul, are equal to the Spirit of One and not less than, whereas our human personality-aspects of many, after death of the physical body, do not have the same creative divine essence as our soul. Thus our soul, the real self, is the source and the authority behind what we, as humans, bring into manifestation to serve us, be it good or bad makes no difference to the soul.

In other words, the many personality-aspects (lifetimes) that you, as a souled being, have created to serve you in your quest to know who you truly are do not have creatorship abilities as you do because you are the soul that created them. Your soul can set up a series of lifetimes, like three, six, ten, or less, where you take up a physical body, a name, and a story to work out many sequential lifetime experiences, good and bad, so as to learn the wisdom behind your choices.

Once you learn the wisdom behind your choices and how dualistic vibrational energy works, your soul then creates a "super personality-aspect" that comes into a physical lifetime where you, in human form, integrate your soul and all of your personality-aspects into one body of consciousness.

You see, your soul, or higher self, creates personality-aspects of you (physical and non-physical) because it is the natural way for you to learn about all things without getting caught up into the mental and physical activity of how energy works.

All that your spirit knew in the beginning once it became aware of itself is that if found itself focusing in a consciousness of a mental nature that could generate visible images. Because of this attribute, your soul then instituted a pathway in answering the question of "who am I" by creating many personality-aspects (physical lifetimes) to serve you in a unique and special way. Then allowing, sooner or later, the human part of you to come back to your soul, carrying within it, not so much of what you did, but the wisdom of your choices and how you experienced them.

By your soul activating many personality-aspects of itself in this way, you eventually learn how the forces of opposites work as well as learning who you truly are. Because of this wisdom and understanding, you begin to accept that you have done nothing wrong. Thus leaving behind what appears as sin and the emotional wounds that causes imbalances to your body. Keep in mind here that it is only the wisdom of the experiences that comes back to the soul, which is why your soul still remains pure and without sin.

Your soul is eternal and maintains the link between the unadulterated universal divine mind that your many, many personality-aspects, physical and non-physical, uses to manifest the memories of all that you have experienced throughout the spirit, astral, and physical realms, including your current and future lifetimes. These personality-aspects of your soul (physical and non-physical) reside in multiple dimensions (known as God's Kingdom) that you can tap into when you are ready to release the old ways of looking at who they are and who you are.

Remember the old proverb, "All life comes from the sea." This actually represents your subconsciousness or the inner self, for the soul is part of your subconsciousness. Your soul is the place that holds the memories of all that you have ever been, done, and have experienced. This even includes memories where you have sent an aspect of yourself into the future to investigate potentials for you to experience.

Now, do not confuse this method with the idea that your future is already created or chosen because it is not. The future aspect that your soul creates is to investigate and seek out possible potentials for the "you of today" to make a choice – for your soul is always with the latest personality-aspect that is playing in the physical realm, which is *you*. This is why, in a way, you in this lifetime, is not you in some past lifetime, for your soul has moved on to learn more about itself in a new personality-aspect that is the present you.

Never forget that you are playing with the energy of opposites when you are here on earth or at least until you ascend those forces into a no force, neutrality. Once the human you overcomes these energies of opposites, your soul will then stop creating personality-aspects (lifetimes) to play out dualistic potentials to experience because the human you would have experienced enough of duality to understand its purpose.

My dear friends that is when the human you will move into a new expanded consciousness and begin to create nothing but happiness, abundance, and joy, and many other great and wonderful things, because now, you know who you are.

As we all know, there are a number of people that do not believe in reincarnation, and maybe you are one of them. However, if you do not believe in reincarnation then you could be overlooking the obvious fact that your spirit is always creating itself in a new way all the time that is unlike a previous encounter of itself.

You see, the soul, the real you, constantly expands its consciousness through each personality-aspect (lifetime) that it creates. Hence, if you, from the human level, are not aware of what your soul can do, then the probability of your soul creating a future aspect to investigate outstanding potentials for you to experience, or even to bring in a potential for healing in what you are experiencing today, can become very difficult, if not impossible.

By not knowing what your soul can do makes your future experiences become more for creating destinies (sin and karma, or ups and downs in your life) instead of future lifetimes dealing with joy, abundance, and harmony. You see, your multiple lifetimes are attached to you in the same way that you are attached to your soul, by threads of energy.

Therefore, we all have available to us, through our experiences in many lifetimes, all the wisdom of those experiences to serve us today, even the wisdom to heal ourselves, for we are a God also. This is why it is said that we, as humans, only use a small part of our mind.

Of course, it is not so much of the mind being used in a small way. It is that we fail to investigate why we still hold onto our old dogmatic beliefs about a God that says we are sinners instead of listening to our own soul and what it can do for us if it is not held back by such resistance to change.

For Instance, Genesis 1:22, *"God blessed them, saying, "Be fertile, multiply, and fill the water of the seas; and let the birds multiply on the earth."* As you should know by now from what has been written in this book. God is just an icon and only a metaphor for your own spirit in giving birth to multiple personality-aspects of yourself. Thus setting into motion all kinds of natural growth patterns (be fertile, multiply) for you to play out in the flesh, which will then have an effect on your total consciousness.

The verse is not so much written for humans to be fertile and multiply, even though we do that anyway as a group consciousness, creating it that way. It is about us souls creating many personality-aspects or lifetime stories to be played out on earth in a sequential manner. When we die in a particular lifetime, we, for we are a souled being, move on, either to another lifetime or to the angelic realm.

However, the mental aspect of you, the deceptive part of you, that is now non-physical moves on into a dimensional realm that matches with your belief systems that you had held, and still do, while your soul moves on in creating a new lifetime on earth.

As long as you hold true to your belief systems about a particular lifetime then that "personality-aspect" is still part of your total body of consciousness, even if you choose to come back to earth to play out another lifetime. This is why one could have many evil and mischievous thoughts but never play those thoughts out in a current lifetime. All that is happening is that one is feeling those other aspects of itself in a lifetime where one did play them out, and now those aspects of the past just want to come home to their creator, *you*.

The wording of "filling the water of the seas," means nothing more than your subconsciousness is filled with many choices, expressions, and wisdom that were already chosen by your deceptive consciousness, and now your soul is flooding those choices, expressions, and the wisdom of what you have learned, mentally and physically, to your present human personality-aspect to bring into life for you to experience.

"Let the birds multiply on the earth," means allowing your deceptive state of a mental consciousness, to accept the influences of your divine plan, which will then mold your outer physical personality-aspect into the pattern of what you have chosen to believe as your truths. Remember, you, as a souled being, are spirit consciousness first and foremost, which means everything else is illusionary.

You are *not* your deceptive mind, your education, your beliefs, or your physical bodies. You are not even a male or female, or even your other aspects or lifetime stories. You are all and none of them at the same time. However, when the physical body dies, the mental version of you that believes is a male or female will move on into a dimensional realm (light or dark) that you have created for yourself when you were part of it and the earth.

If you believe only in a God of good and a Satan of evil, then that is the dimensional realm that you will create for yourself to experience when you die in the physical. Also remember, you can be stuck in that artificial dimensional realm for a long time because of beliefs, which is why you hear of lingering spirits that stick around their home or where they worked when they die.

However, when your soul is ready to create a new aspect for a new incarnation once the aspect that is lingering around moves on to a mental dimension, you come back to earth living out those same beliefs (lies) over and over until you have had enough incarnations to break through your stubbornness nature when it comes to your fixed beliefs.

My dear friends, you are a divine being that is equal to God, and I cannot say this enough, for your core essence is of the same eminence, ability, intelligence, and power as the Spirit of One. Hence, no one is above you or below you, for you are it. You have the talent and the authority to create anything you wish including healing, abundance, joy, and sorrow if you like.

Two thousand years ago some of our prophets listened to a great master and became enlighten by him, and then as time went on, religion has elevated this great master to a God that is above us all. My dear friends, Jesus is not above us because we are all equal masters otherwise, we would not have life. We have forgotten that we are the extension of the Spirit of One.

Therefore, exercise your authority wisely while you are in the physical. If it's hard to accept the idea of you being equal to God it is because you have been hypnotized by lifetimes of being told that you are a sinner, and that you are less than God. It is about allowing your divinity (Christ and or Soul self) to come in. It is actually waiting for your invitation and acceptance.

Remember, form is just something you created for yourself because in truth, it does not really exist. You are a spirit that is consciousness only therefore, the only way you can experience life is to create personality-aspects of yourself. These aspects will draw the energy needed to reflect your choices and beliefs that you wish to experience outward in a physical form.

However, in order to make this happen, your soul needed to create a consciousness to keep you playing with the energy of opposites, which is why the first thing that your soul created once you came into the second creation was a "belief system" that delivered to you the forces of positive and negative as the means to feel and experience your choices. Since they are your choices, you have to take full responsibility for everything you create, for you are the master that is responsible for them.

You see, since we, from the soul level, mimicked the Spirit of One and created many personality-aspects of ourselves, we too gave each of our personality-aspects unconditional love and the freedom (as in free will) to go forth and create beyond what was known without our soul's interference.

In other words, our soul not only creates many personality-aspects to play in duality, our soul gives them the freedom to make their choices in their own unique way in order for our soul, the higher self, to grow in wisdom, understanding, and responsibility.

So, if you still have thoughts about sin being real, it is because this belief in sin is not coming from the real you (the soul), it is coming from each of your personality-aspects that have lived before because each of them had the freedom to choose when they were part of a lifetime story. Therefore, all that is left for you to do in this lifetime is to learn how to integrate those many personality-aspects of the past. Once you integrate them, you become free to create all the miracles you can stand.

By the Spirit of One fragmenting itself in the beginning into gazillions upon gazillions of souled beings (you, me, and everyone else – for we are gods in the making), it has given itself the opportunity to learn and know all things. Hence, the Spirit of One, depicted as God by our religious leaders, does *not* know everything because the Spirit of One gets all of its wisdom and understanding from its children (you, me, and everyone else) because, we together, are the Spirit of One, and therefore equal to.

Once you became a fragmented piece of the Spirit of One, the first thing you did, as all souled beings, was create a feminine-masculine aspect of you. Ever since then, your soul has been creating aspects after aspects (physical and non-physical) in order to learn everything there is to know about yourself, about life, about duality, and about how energy works. Every aspect that your soul created, no matter how it was judged, good, bad, or evil, was an aspect that was created by you as a temporary personality to learn the wisdom behind the choice.

This provided you with experiences where each aspect of you would someday return home to you, for you are their creator. It is about you coming into a lifetime and integrating all the wisdom of those experiences with your current physical aspect, and then letting go of the act of what you chose. You only played it out to learn the wisdom behind the act.

It is from this integrating of all your personality-aspects, including your divine/soul self, where you become the super aspect to bring in all the parts and pieces of you that have served many different functions and identities (lifetimes), for they have now served their purpose.

So my dear friends, since you are the master and the Christ, are you now ready to bring in all these parts and pieces of you, all that wisdom, no matter what they (you) did, good, bad, or evil, back into the wholeness of being one body of consciousness again? You have only forgotten that you live in a reality that is not your true and natural reality. You have been hypnotized by your beliefs, your past personality-aspects, and those that want to control you and your energy.

My fellow searchers, it is your belief systems that keep you trapped in a consciousness of opposing energies, thus you continue to suffer. Of course, you agreed and accepted to buy into these opposing forces a long time ago, which is why there is no devil or bad spirits trying to inflict you with pain and suffering. You inflict yourself for a wide variety of reasons and the two biggest ones are that you will not accept your past personality-aspects (lifetimes) as your creations, and that you believe in sin.

Belief systems are very powerful and seductive because most are nothing but lies. They hold you firmly into an inflexible consciousness that believes you are not worthy of God, and therefore you need a savior or someone to heal you. The only savior you need is to allow your divinity (Christ self) to come into your physical life and integrate all the parts and pieces of you, thus healing occurs. This can't be done if you still believe in a God that punishes and calls you a sinner.

Because of the strong implant of there being two different forces (God and Satan), you work with group mass consciousness, creating many personality-aspects, good and bad, so you can explore everything there is to know about opposites. In fact, this is a major key to learning wisdom because with duality there is always a reverse energy that you put out there in order to find the wisdom of your choices, and for you to become balance once again.

For instance: If one is playing as an evil doer in this lifetime or did in a past lifetime then one will, at one time or another, play the opposite. This is how an individual will discover who he or she really is in the scheme of things. You see, one's spirit or soul has no agenda other than the desire to experience itself and learn who it is.

So, stop and think about it! You are nothing more than what you believe and desire to experience in life, no matter if it is good, bad, or evil, which is why you choose many lifetimes playing the opposite. You have created many light and dark personality aspects that have been a prevailing force in creating a mission of spiritual discovery. What you must realize now is that these personality-aspects are still out there trying to serve their master, *you*.

Now, these light and dark aspects have brought you immense wisdom and freedom. However, these aspects have also brought you many struggles that have led to much confusion.

For instance: You have created aspects in the past where they went out and experienced lifetimes where they did many bad and evil things, like stealing, raping, killing, and taking advantage of their fellow man. Then, when those aspects of you died in those lifetimes, that aspect of you, not your soul, moved into a dimensional realm where it lingered for awhile or until your soul was ready to create another lifetime in an effort to feel and understand the opposite of what that aspect of you did.

For example: There has been many in this lifetime, men, woman, and children, that have experienced what it feels like to be taken, killed, raped, being taken advantage of, and many other horrendous acts. For, they are now the victims of what they themselves have created when they were the victimizers in some past lifetime.

Once these victimized aspects who were once a victimizer in some past lifetime dies in this lifetime, those personality-aspects that were the victimizers, prior to them becoming a victim in this lifetime, are still out there in some dark dimension waiting for their soul to create a super aspect to incarnate in a "new lifetime" so as to accept and integrate both the past victimizer and the abuser aspects of themselves without having guilt, emotional pain, and the shame of sin.

Now of course, if you, in this new lifetime, do not believe in past lifetimes, then you open the door of your consciousness where those victimizing aspects of your past come into your current lifetime and influence you in the choices you make. This is why you sometimes ask yourself, "Why is it that when I seem to get ahead in life everything seems to go amok?" Well, the reason it goes amok is because many of your past personality-aspects (lifetimes) want to come back home to you, their creator. However, you don't allow it to happen.

By you unwilling to accept your personality-aspects of your past as your creations because of not believing in reincarnation, then you are only going to keep them and you in turmoil until you do. You see, these personality-aspects of your past that are floating around out there in other dimensions are getting tired of waiting for you to accept them as your creations.

Because of you, on a subconscious level, feeling guilty and ashamed of what they (your other aspects) did in a lifetime past, you, without thought, continually push away from any new ideas about reincarnation and your religion. Thus, miracles and healing come hard for you to bring into your life.

Since you are afraid to open your eyes, heart, and rational mind about the real God being you, all because of your emotional ties to your past personality-aspects and what they (you) did or didn't do. You, because of fear that is hidden deep within your soul, continuously are influenced by those past aspects of you. They are creating your hell in this lifetime.

This is why it is important to open up your heart and hypnotized mind, and allow your soul memories (the parts and pieces of you) to come through to your human level because it helps in integrating all of those light and dark personality-aspects. Remember, they are the cause of you not receiving your share of miracles and healing in this lifetime.

My dear friends, it is time to tear down the wall of inflexibility where you believe that one lifetime and one religion is all that you have had. How can you move forward to ascension and become a sovereign "I AM" in your own right if you keep on believing that you are only responsible for what you created in this lifetime, and then only see yourself as a human in need?

How many of you have had thoughts about killing people, stealing, raping, and many other revolting thoughts? And yes, how many of you have had thoughts about how nice you are, or how emotional you get when you see cruelty, or when one talks about a dead relative. How about thoughts of being born in the right or wrong family? How about thoughts of being a super person where you would like to protect the world from evil?

Oh yes, you have heard these voices in your head many times, and they have made you even argue with yourself sometimes. After all, these voices of do's and don'ts come in with overwhelming emotional feelings, and it not only scares you, it confuses you too. What would you say if I told you that over ninety-five percent of the time, when you have these thoughts coming into your head, they are not really yours from this lifetime? They are thoughts that are coming in from your past personality-aspects (lifetimes).

It is these personality-aspects from your past lifetimes that are clogging up the very natural flow of your energy and creativity of today, which is why you struggle through life. Because of not accepting and acknowledging these past personality-aspects as your creations, they will continue to confuse and torment you until you do.

These personality-aspects from your past lifetimes are looking for you to forgive them no matter what they have done, for they were *you* at one time or another. Of course, the forgiveness comes from your soul or Christ self once you awaken to it. By accepting your past aspects with unconditional love, and without judgment, you open yourself up to their wisdom, for it is your wisdom too. It is not that you have to accept their anger, lack of self worth, or their beliefs because that belongs to them or you in the past.

Just remember, you are not these personality aspects anymore! You are not even the victimizer or the victim from the past, which is why it is important for you to acknowledge and accept them as your creations. It is just that you today are the super aspect (the Christ) that your soul created to be the place of the homecoming for them. You, without realizing it, have paid the price and bared your cross for your past creations. So, forgive them and yourself, and know what you choose today is only yours.

However, if you are locked in a consciousness of fear, being afraid of the dark, and confining yourself to only seeing yourself as a human only waiting for Jesus to save you, then the choices you make today will always be made on the basis of your past aspects and their beliefs (yours at the time).

Can't you understand that these past aspects or lifetimes are getting tired of having low self-esteem? They are getting tired of wandering around in other dimensions looking for you to accept them when you come into a physical body. They are tired of being lost and homeless, which is why they are looking for you to welcome them home, their creator and savior.

Now, to help you understand these personality-aspects from your past lifetimes, I will use the analogy that Tobias has placed on these "personality-aspects" into three diverse colors categories, of which I will simplify, by using my own words, to make it easier for you to understand.

First, let us look at the color of white as representative of something mentally clear. Therefore, the first is how we, for example, create "clear" aspects to go out and serve us in performing routine tasks, like using a computer, cooking dinner, driving a car, working with others, and many other tasks to serve us, the creators. According to Tobias, some of these clear aspects could become a bit unbalanced. However, they have a natural way of coming back into balance with us very quickly.

These "clear" personality-aspects of you use very little of your energy because they know that they were created to serve you in your now moment, and they do it with ease and with the understanding that you are their creator. Clear aspects usually work well with other clear aspects. However, once in a while, a clear aspect can get pushed aside by a gray aspect.

For example, when you say to yourself or to someone else that "you are having a bad day," it indicates that a "gray" aspect just pushed aside a "clear" aspect. The angelic realm uses the color gray because of how you allow yourself to become clouded with your beliefs.

Here is an example of a gray aspect: Let's say you begin your new day by visiting a friend and when you entered your friend's home, the home was filled with strangers that you have never met before. Now, before you entered the home, you were feeling cheerful and confident. But now that you are in the home, you, all of a sudden, begin to feel nervous and agitated because your friend asked if you would like to have something to eat or drink while you were standing there among the crowd of strangers.

This usually indicates that a "gray" aspect just pushed aside a "clear" aspect that was feeling cheerful and confident before you entered the home. Fortunately, you have many clear aspects that serve you in a clear and beautiful way on many different levels. Without realizing it, you create multitudes of clear aspects that go out to serve you, the creator, and they come back to you, integrating into you the wonderful wisdom and the experience of the lessons they have just learned.

These many colored personality-aspects are extensions of your soul, and when you acknowledge and honor these diverse personalities as your creations, they will glow like a child when getting praises from their parents. When you understand this, they come in to serve you even greater than what you would expect.

As you become aware of how you have a personality-aspect for just about everything you do, like knowing how to cook, drive a car, mow the grass, and yes, even golf, you will find that the way they serve you enriches you to the point of feeling that heaven has found you on earth. How many times have you driven your car for miles, and then said to yourself or someone else, "I cannot even remember driving those miles?" Always keep in mind here; you are, after all, just a spirit having an experience.

Now, "gray personality-aspects" act differently than "clear personality-aspects." There are many gray personality-aspects that you have created throughout your many lifetimes, and they make up the vast majority of the issues and belief systems that you have in your life today. Of course, there are many shades of gray as there are many shades of beliefs that you experience. Most of the gray personality-aspects integrate with you once you leave the physical world in death. This is because you step back and look at what was really important and what was not.

For example: Let us say that you are terrified when you visit strangers to the point you become very agitated and nervous about being there. You fear that something is going to happen so anxiety takes over. Then all of a sudden, you are either looking for a pill or the door. Where do you think this comes from? It most probably comes from a past lifetime where you visited some strangers and a conditioned developed that turned into something that caused you a great deal of harm.

Now, because of that past life experience, you have created a deeper gray aspect of yourself that today still lingers around in other realms, waiting for you to come back to earth in a lifetime having a phobia of meeting new people, even if those people are kind and friendly and would never harm you.

Here is another example: Let us say that you are scared of high places in this lifetime because of an incident where you came so close to falling that you felt the angel of death pass right through you. Then, at the end of your life when you do an overview, you realize that it was just a bit of stuck energy. It became stuck, and you didn't do anything about it, so it remained out there slightly separate from you.

Therefore that gray personality-aspect integrates back into your soul without carrying forward to another lifetime, unless of course, you were killed by falling from a high place! In that case, you would have created a darker gray aspect that would linger in other realms, waiting for you to come back to earth in your next lifetime having a phobia about high places. These examples can relate to most phobias.

Look at babies and how some of them come into this world having some type of phobia. These babies already owned these conditions long before they ever had the life experiences to make them afraid. Gray aspects provide much resistance in your life, because these gray aspects constantly engage your rational mind into thinking you don't look good, or you are poor, or you are not smart enough to run a business, and many other things you don't believe you can do.

How many times do you say to yourself that you are not spiritual enough to have good things in life, or that you are not intellectual enough to attend parties? Gray aspects are the ones that really wear you out physically and mentally. When you say, "Why am I so tired all the time?"

It is more than likely that these gray aspects are occupying a large part of your consciousness, and therefore a large amount of energy without a lot of resolution.

Gray aspects are usually those that have lost hope and a sense of who they are, and you can feel their doubt on an emotional level. Actually, the dark aspects, which I will discuss next, consider your gray aspects to be your weakness. Therefore, a dark aspect will always try to get rid of your gray aspects, because your dark aspects are very strong-willed.

Gray aspects are like your children, which is why some of you have a hard time letting your children go when they move out of the home or die. Because of these gray personality-aspects acting through memory, you become very emotional when it comes to letting these gray aspects of yourself go, which is why it becomes almost impossible for some parents to let their children go, or for that matter, siblings letting go of each other.

You have forgotten that your children are really not your children, just like your siblings are not your siblings, because they are their own person, an "I AM" unto themselves. You are simply the person who agreed to be the channel in bringing them to earth and taking care of them until a certain age. Most parents accept the burden of caring for their children no matter what age they are without realizing that they need to find their own way in life. The reason you do this as a parent is because you look at your life as a spiritual one.

Therefore, the health and welfare of your children are viewed as your responsibility until you or they die, and maybe even beyond. When this happens it is due to creating gray personality-aspects in a belief that you must take care of your children long after they have grown, because you believe that is why God gave them to you.

My fellow parents, you don't own your children! They are not yours to own! When you let them go, including your siblings, when they become a certain age and give them the same compassion that your own "I AM" gave you long ago, then your gray aspects are free to integrate with you. By letting go of your children when it is time, as well as your siblings, you allow them to come back to you in a new divine way that allows you to love them unconditionally, no matter what they do or who they are.

So, if you are having financial issues, health issues, children issues, sibling issues, depression issues, anxiety issues, and/or accidents that seem to come suddenly and frequently, and if there is constant drama in your life, then you are creating unsafe space for your gray aspects to come home to you.

Most of you suffer dearly because you are not aware that you create many diverse personality-aspects. Some of these aspects even fall to their knees asking, "Where is God, and is Jesus coming to save me?" My fellow searchers, these gray aspects are stuck deep within you, and they are constantly trying to get your attention through your emotions.

You can feel these gray aspects all around you. Just try changing your beliefs for a moment to a new belief, like you are equal to God or that you believe in reincarnation, and you will see how fast these gray aspects will jump right into your head keeping you always tied to your old dogmatic beliefs. It is these gray aspects that you tend to carry with you over and over to your next lifetime just because you are not ready to let Jesus down off the cross and put yourself equal to him.

Now, let's talk about your "dark" personality-aspects. These aspects of you can be quite overpowering. You have dark aspects that linger over you all the time because they want your attention. Some people have dark aspects that actually take over their conscious level and they don't even realize it.

You can see this just by looking at the news about individuals killing, robbing, raping, and other horrendous acts, and then these individuals are confused because of what they just did, which is why some people regret it after or they kill themselves. Those that kill, rob, and rape without showing any mercy or emotions in the act are usually those that are doing it to experience the act, and therefore becomes a dark aspect of its own soul when he or she passes on.

Most of you do not realize that dark aspects have no reasoning or emotional level, because what they want is your soul. Yes, your soul is all what they are after. Dark aspects cannot even be loved in the way you usually interpret love, because they view love as a form of weakness. Most everyone has dark aspects of themselves, and these aspects can arise at any time when you are most vulnerable. You fear these dark aspects with such concern you end up running from them, which is why these dark aspects are called the devil or evil spirits.

Many of you today have already dealt with your most darkened ego personality-aspects where you, in some past lifetime, have committed some horrible acts. You know this to be true just by feeling it. You can feel deep within your soul some type of guilt and shame in what you did in those past lifetimes, even though you have already paid the price (karma) either in some past lifetime or this lifetime.

There are many attributes of the dark but the first and foremost is that they want what you have! They want your soul. Your dark personality-aspects are nothing more than parts and pieces of you that are angry, very frustrated, and they hate you because you have a soul. You see, your many clear, gray, and dark aspects do not have a soul like you do because they are your creations. How can they have a soul if it was your soul that created them? Remember, what I said earlier, your soul is always with the current lifetime, which is, you in the human form today.

These dark personality-aspects represent the things you oppose today in what you see as cruelty upon others – for they are your wounds of past lifetimes. You can say that these dark aspects of you hate all ethnic groups and color, even the ethnic group and color you have taken on in this lifetime.

For example, let us say that you are a white person in this lifetime and you believe that you hate all ethnic groups, even some of white color. Now, why would you believe that you hate these groups, including your fellow whites? It could be because you might have been a person that belonged to all of these ethnic groups in other lifetimes where you created much pain for others, as well as playing the opposite role where you were the receiver of pain. And now, you carry this pain of guilt and shame into this lifetime by hating all ethnic groups. This example can also take a reverse role for all ethnic groups and color.

However, let us continue with this example: Now when you see these different ethnic groups on television fighting each other over who is right, who is being terrorized and tortured, and who is doing the terrorizing and torturing, you get very frustrated with all these ethnic groups by saying to yourself that you hate them all, the ones being terrorized and tortured as well as the ones terrorizing and torturing.

Now, why would you hate the ones being terrorized and tortured? You would think that you might have some compassion for them. But you don't! So, why is that? Remember, this is just an example to show you how your dark aspects come in to find a way to destroy you.

You see, since you played the opposite or both parts and were part of every ethnic group, brown, black, yellow, red, and white, as well as what each ethnic group represents in some lifetime, you find it frustrating when you see these groups acting in a way that displeases you.

Now, why is that? It is due to feeling guilty and ashamed for what you did in some of those lifetimes of long ago even though you had paid the price for all of it in other past lifetimes. Therefore, you keep running away from those dark feelings instead of confronting them. This is just a small example of the dark personalities that you can carry within your soul memories.

You have some dark aspects that think you are a fool and that you don't deserve the power you have as a souled being. These dark aspects feel that you are not prepared or experienced enough to handle your life, so they want to take over. They want to be in charge of you in everything you do. They want to have the life you are living today, which is why they attack you in your vulnerable areas of the mind. They get you thinking in fear, doubt, and that you are not worthy to have a lifetime of joy, health, or abundance because they see you as a weak person, even though you sense some truth to what they are saying.

My dear friends, your dark personality-aspects are an accumulation of all the wounded hurt energies that you have experienced over long periods of time, which is why everyone has a variety of dark aspects. Also, your dark aspects do not like each other, because each one wants to be the boss of your soul, and therefore your life.

So, when you feel darkness come around you, like being afraid of the dark, then stay still, as you are in safe space. Just breathe in compassion, and not try to change them or pray to God for protection. Most of all do not run from them because it feels like the devil is after you; just be with them and allow them to pass through you. Take a deep breath and observe them from a still space, a place of compassion. Most of all do not be in fear, no matter what they throw at you, because nothing can truly hurt you. By having compassion for them, you are not trying to change them.

Remember what I said about compassion. It means accepting these dark personality-aspects of you as they are, and without judgment. By doing this, you will provide a pathway for them to return home to you, their creator. You can integrate all of your aspects (clear, gray, light, and dark) by making a conscious choice to do so. When you make a conscious choice to integrate them, even the most difficult ones, the process, at one time or another, allows itself to come to fulfillment.

You will know that you have succeeded, because you will not feel any more resistance, tension, or anxiety in your life. In fact, you begin to feel clear and complete. The tiredness of your body and mind will go away as you begin to feel a constant circulation of your blood (energy), which makes you feel renewed.

Once you become aware that you created many aspects where you lived upon the earth in other lifetimes, you actually begin to heal yourself. The majority of these aspects will come home and integrate with you, thus relieving you from the afflictions that they have put upon you. Also, by becoming aware of living in other lifetimes, you begin to understand how extremely creative you are. That, my fellow searchers, is what will trigger self-responsibility, which leads to healing, joy, and sovereignty.

Instead of looking to others to take care of you, like family, friends, governments, religion, and businesses, you begin to take responsibility for yourself and your life. The blame you put on others or some devil for your lack of happiness and success begin to disappear.

When you start to become aware of who you truly are, you begin to feel and see those clear, gray, and dark aspects of you that were traumatized, the ones that did not like you, the weak ones, the ones that wants to control you, as well as the strong, the intelligent ones, and the beautiful ones that can help you become very successful.

You also learn that every aspect of you has a counterpart or opposite, and when you integrate these aspects, you end up tapping into the wisdom of all of them. This is when you will find an answer to every question that you could possibly have because the energies that were used by your many personality-aspects contain within them a resolution to every question – for energy carries within it, its own balance.

Any phobia that you might have or be experiencing today, like fear of the dark, lacking confidence in making money, feeling low self-esteem, feeling anxiety when meeting people, contains within them, even if you cannot see it, its counterpart or reverse aspect that knows how to resolve the issue. If you open your heart and soul, you can tap into those aspects whenever you are bold enough to do so.

Let us not forget that every aspect that your soul created had a purpose, which is why there is no such thing as a mistake or sin. In fact, this is a good time right now for you to stop listening to those that call you a sinner. You are not sinner and you never have been! Oh yes, you have had past aspects (lifetimes) that lacked self-worth, lacked abundance, and you had some aspects that were monsters, but all of them had a purpose. Now, the only thing left to do is for you to accept these aspects from your past with total compassion and with unconditional love, for you are a Christ also.

By receiving these past aspects with great love and compassion, you actually create a safe space around you that becomes very important in balancing your energy. You will know when you are in a safe space when you are not concerned anymore about your illness, money, losing your job, home, or what people say about you because you seem different.

When you come into your passion for being a sovereign being in your own right, taking full responsibility, you will never have to balance your life again. The money, your health, and the joy of life will just flow in without you even making an effort.

When you feel that the dark is going to consume you, or that things are bigger than yourself, or you keep hiding, then you are not in your safe place. To be in a safe place is to understand that you are a God and a Christ also, and when you learn to do that, those dark aspects of you will then find their way to a place of no fear and total unconditional love.

So, are you ready to take responsibility for your life? Are you ready to open your heart and soul memories to who you truly are? Do you really want to believe that you are more than human? Like I said, you have many personality-aspects that are fragmented and alone out there wondering around in many dimensions where you have given up responsibility.

Even today you are taught that the devil is the one that brings you suffering. It is not the devil! It is those past lifetimes, and here you are today in a new lifetime still not accepting responsibility for what you (they) have created. There are many aspects of you right now that are looking to come back to you, their creator. However, many of you want to disown them by saying you only live once.

Can you imagine what this does to those hurt and wounded aspects that you give no attention or love to? They become very angry because you fail to see them as your creations. After awhile, these aspects become so angry they work hard to destroy you. They do it by setting you up where you get to sabotage yourself. My fellow searchers, this is what makes you the way you are, and you don't even see it – for others will see it first.

You see, your aspects will wait until you begin to accumulate money, have a good relationship, or what is called seeing a light at the end of the tunnel, and then they come in and begin to influence you in making bad decisions in such a way that you end up losing everything. When you do, and after a few years of depression and anxiety trying to find yourself again, you make a comeback and make something out of yourself once again. Then they once again come back into your life and do the same thing all over again.

You are the owner of your temple for the "I AM," and it requires you to be in human form, to learn and accept all that you are. It cannot be done any other way than you coming into the flesh and accepting responsibility for all of your creations, past, presence, and future. That is when you will finally move onto the third level where you finally meet your Gnost (Christ) Consciousness, a consciousness where you, your soul, will not create anymore aspects of you because now you are a sovereign "I AM" being.

Always keep in mind that aspects are the way of the soul when you work out of duality, for they reflect the very love that your spirit had for you in the beginning when the Spirit of One said, "Go forth," I give you complete freedom to do as you please. You did it by creating other aspects of yourself, and now the time has come to allow them to come back home to you, their creator, in a whole new way.

It is you that is the divine being, the Christ that has been promised to open the gates of your memories and welcome home your children of many personality-aspects. It is you, the Christ, that is the second coming and not Jesus. It is you, and only you, that can save your aspects from their sins, for you, in some past lifetime(s), are the one that created those sins. So, admit to them, forgive yourself, and then integrate your many personality-aspects with unconditional love. There is no judgment here! Neither on yourself nor on anyone else!

Chapter 14

Belief Systems, And How They Affect Your Reality

Now, let's talk about belief systems and how they actually create your reality. It was, and still is today, the use of belief systems that enabled you to take on form a long time ago in order to experience life. By accepting the process of using belief systems as the means to transform pure universal energy into something completely different than your divine core essence, it readily made it possible for you to create as many personality-aspects (lifetimes) as needed in order to feel and experience those belief systems, instead of just imagining what they would feel like.

However, it becomes very confusing to your current lifetime because your soul in creating these personality-aspects carries within each of them their own belief systems, agendas, and matters that need attention. Because of your strong established beliefs that come from your past lifetimes, and what you pickup in your current lifetime, it keeps you trapped in a consciousness that only portrays life as who you believe you are. Like being a male or female, and a sinner for example!

If you seem to make an effort to move past "who you believe you are," the initial reaction of your rational mind is to try to jam you right back into your old way of thinking because it seems to be unnatural to believe otherwise. One of the building blocks of not being aware of your past lifetimes is that it sets up a massive layering of your consciousness where you will find it almost impossible to make choices from your current lifetime.

Oh! You may say that you make choices all the time because of free will! Well, on the contrary, you only believe you are making choices using free will because ninety-five percent of them, believe it or not, are coming from your past lifetimes. They come from your past lifetimes where you had your own agenda to attend to at the time. This plays a big part in why many of you don't become financially secure, have a good relationship, rid yourself of an illness, or have other aspirations fulfilled in this lifetime.

So, how do you stop these past personality-aspects from serving themselves and start serving you in your current lifetime? Here is a key point to remember! Your spirit has no agenda or desire other than to experience itself through you. Therefore, if you belief in sin, hell, good and bad, or that you're not educated enough, or that you're unworthy of having things, or even you having the power to heal yourself, then that is the seed that your soul will nourish you in what you experience.

If someone tells you, day in and day out, that you are a sinner, not educated enough, and that you're not worthy of having things because of just being human, and you believe them, then that is the energy seed that your soul will create for you to experience. It's that simple! If you hope to have a great life and be rich someday then that hope can last for lifetimes just because you're sending the seed of hope as being the method of manifestation instead of choice being the method to make it come about.

As long as you believe in hope, which means nothing more than a wish, then your soul will create a reality that will match your hope as being someday. It's the same with believing you are a sinner. So, if you have had many past lifetimes holding these types of beliefs, then those past aspects or lifetimes will always choose your current reality under the disguise of hope and sin. The reason, you have created every part of it.

It is not about hoping to have things in your life. It is about you taking on the belief that hope is the vehicle in getting you what you want in life. Once you understand that you are the creator of your beliefs and reality. Then the only thing that will give you what you desire in this lifetime is the decision to make a "choice" in opening yourself up to "who you truly are."

For instance: Many of you pray to God and the angels to bring you out of sin and to help you find the real truth. However, there is no real truth just like there is no sin. If you want real truth, then earth is nothing more than a playground where you, like all souls, create belief systems so you can learn about life, who you truly are, and then eventually become a sovereign "I AM" in your own right, and therefore create what you want.

As said before, nothing is real about you other than your spirit and soul consciousness. You are not your mind, body, or even a male or female. What is forgotten is that you actually have the ability to feel your rational mind storing and retrieving information from the experiences you have had throughout your many lifetimes of the past.

You have forgotten that the rational mind has developed into a highly complex system where it has become susceptible to influences and suggestions routinely, especially those influences and suggestions that come from group consciousness and authority figures. Look, allow me to ask you a question. Who do you think the creator is? It is God or is it you? It is *you*, and the sooner you realize this the sooner you will begin to enjoy life in a more abundant way.

Now, you can believe anything you want, like sin or you being a male or female, and that God is responsible for your successes and the devil is the blame for your failures. However you choose to believe, the reason you do not create the things you want in life, like joy, happiness, no illness, great relationships, or having abundance, is because you have become so hypnotized by the mass consciousness. It is your belief systems of your past lifetimes, and by the beliefs in your current lifetime, that keep you from receiving your grace.

You have become so occupied with your belief systems and what is truth throughout time and space, you are now trapped in a world of deception, trickery, and delusions that you take as your truths, which of course creates your reality. Because of these deep seated beliefs you have about sin, God, the devil, and that Jesus is your salvation, you shape and define yourself, your world, and your reality as being real.

My dear friends, it was someone long ago telling you that if you could not touch, taste, smell, hear, or see the world around you, then it wasn't real. Therefore, since you can do these things then the world and what you understand as your belief systems must be real thus making sin and punishment just as real. However, the truth is! It is not real.

Because of your physical senses backing up your belief that all things are real, you have opened yourself up where your many past lifetimes have become so intertwined and interconnected with you in this lifetime, and with each other. With your mental and physical state of today, it has become impossible for you to understand who you truly are from the rational mind.

This means that you will never find the real truth by trying to analyze God from the human level. All that you will do is become frustrated, which many do, and that is why you will always fall back to your old ways. Why? It's because you cannot figure things out on a conscious level when it comes to your spirit, your soul, universal mind, the physical body, and that you are a God using the rational mind as the vehicle.

The only way you can open up to your spirit, your soul, universal mind, the physical body, and you being a Christ also, is by moving past your physical senses and your deceptive mind, and move into your Gnost or Christ Consciousness. It is about getting out of your head and move into your intuitive and imaginational consciousness if you want to discover who you really are.

You, a long time ago, agreed to this unnatural state of being in the flesh. You forgot that you took on the illusion of matter and that you are playing a wonderful game that ended up building networks and networks of complex belief systems (lies) where you got stuck in a world that feels real but is not. Because of these networks of belief systems that you and mankind have built up over time, they have become such an elaborate root system for you to understand. Like any root system, you only look for truth in what you see above and not below.

Understand that life on earth is nothing but hypnosis and belief systems, and when you allowed yourself to come to earth, you agreed to take on the attributes of forgetfulness. This gave you the avenue to create many lifetimes where you ended up creating many shades of clear, gray, and dark personality-aspects of yourself to serve the real you in discovering who you truly are. These personality-aspects of many are now extensions of you, and when you come to understand them as such, they will be your avenue to freedom and ascension.

Belief systems are like a magnet that draws in the energy you need to support your idea of who you think you are. Since you are always free to choose what you believe, then what you believe is who you are in totality because of those beliefs. For instance: If you hope to get to heaven someday than perhaps *someday* you will.

However, if you make a conscious choice to get to heaven today then be assured, you will get to heaven, today. Getting to heaven or becoming rich or healthy begins with you taking full and complete ownership over all parts and pieces of you that have been functioning and performing on separate levels of consciousness.

Take a look at how you actually divided your consciousness into an amazing tool where you have come to a crossroad where you can integrate the wholeness of "all that you are" into the oneness of a sovereign and free "I AM" in your own right. A crisis in your life might simply mean that a change is trying to take place within, and if you do not listen, then you will have to continue your crisis until you do listen.

Think on this! Nothing happens in your external world that does not happen first within your rational mind because of your beliefs. Your entire reality will always be based on your beliefs, either in this lifetime or lifetimes past. If you change or release your beliefs to a neutrality belief, without judgment of any kind, your world and reality will also change.

If you become conscious of how your beliefs are the controlling factor of your life, and then learn how to use your divine imagination, you could literally create magic in your life. Go the extra mile and learn about yourself instead of getting tied up with religious teachings, rituals (which always come from man), and why you hate or dislike someone. By finding out what makes you the way you are, you will begin to get more out of life than perhaps what you are getting right now.

Have you ever taken the time to find out why you believe what you believe and why you experience the things you experience without ever taking a look at how those beliefs got there in the first place? Many of you believe that you were put on earth by some higher power and yet, you don't know why. Is it just to obey certain rules that man laid down for you to follow or was it to appease some God that isn't real?

Remember, and I know you have heard this many times; "What you get out of life is derived from what you put into it." However, when you add the words "through your belief systems," then it becomes more profound. Whatever you are reaping today is the measure of what you have believed in the past and how you carry out those beliefs today.

If you want a different harvest in your todays and tomorrows, you must choose different belief systems about who you think you are. Your rewards and failures in life will always be in direct proportion to the consequences of your beliefs. It's that simple!

We are always given opportunities to see the potentials of positive and negative within our choices before taking action. The rules that we create with our belief systems are strict and we know deep within that these rules will remain until our 2-D rational mind and 3-D inflexible nature are exposed as the culprits of deceit, lies, and confusion. Our human personality loves to control the 3-D world we live in, and those of us who reject our own divinity for the sake of saving our belief systems can only experience the limited realities of a dualistic world.

Regardless of how much effort you put into something, if it is not backed by the "knowing of who you truly are," then your endeavors will be limited. Taking something as your own that someone else has declared as the only truth is living your life through the clouds of unawareness and falseness. The real truth is what is imparted to you from within your own being as you evolve, which then changes your truth as you evolve.

In other words, treating the Bible, or any holy book, as infallible truth is basing your whole life on statements that have come from its original writers in helping you to evolve from a child-like mind to an adult-like mind. The Bible is not meant to be taken in a literal sense forever, and truth itself is what you recognize between the lines as you evolve.

The study of any holy book is fruitless if you are only seeing the letter of it alone. It must be seen through spiritual and poetic soundness before any useful truth or wisdom can be gained from it. A person, who claims to be a preacher of God, and then claims they can take away your sins, knows not what they are talking about.

For generations, the world has tried to build God around the human mind in understanding good and evil as sin, and all that they have accomplished is limitation and suffering. Man has always looked at God and truth as unchanging and yet, God and truth evolves as man evolves.

For instance: You look at the gift of seeing with your eyes as something physical first. You believe with all your heart and soul that your physical eyes are the reason you can see things. This is far from the truth! The reason you can see is because the brain is hard wired with your physical senses, like touch, smell, taste, hear, and sight.

My dear friends, it takes the brain to see things first and then the brain instructs the eyes of the human body to see what you are looking at. If the brain doesn't see it then the physical eyes cannot see it, even if the object is right in front of you, which is why the mind is the culprit for pain not your physical body. It seems like the physical body is in pain but in truth it is only your rational mind and or brain instructing the body that it is in pain.

Because of the density of your physical body, you only see what the brain understands as something that appears solid, and therefore must be real and true. Therefore, if the brain only understands things as being solid, then the eyes has no choice to see what is understood by the brain as being solid, even though nothing is solid. So, if the brain is filled with beliefs that are hardwired with what you perceive as being truth, then how can you see beyond what you believe is truth?

Because of your beliefs are so hardwired with your brain, then what the brain doesn't see, the eyes cannot see either. It is the same with your truths. This is why the rational mind cannot comprehend what is beyond the physical realm unless you move into your imagination and intuitive consciousness. The rational mind can only pretend that it can imagine and feel what is beyond the flesh.

For instance: Your rational mind can dig up your belief patterns from past experiences or lifetimes, and then it can try to recreate them to give you some type of indication of what it would be like to move beyond your mind.

You see, when I say that the only way to move past the rational mind is by way of your imagination and intuitive consciousness, I am saying, your intuitive and imaginational consciousness is your spirit expressing itself with passion to feel beyond the rational mind and the physical. The imagination is that creative parts of you that can help you break through the physical barrier of the deceptive and rational mind, and your intuitive consciousness is the only thing that can take you to a knowing that you are a Christ and a God also. Your imagination and intuitive consciousness can also take you beyond the limitations of what your rational mind or brain sees as fact.

Every day you are exposed to hundreds of suggestions that somehow find their way into your consciousness. Some of those suggestions end up forming into your reality while others lie within your rational mind waiting for the day for you to see them as your truths. Understand that every suggestion or idea that has come from someone else has found itself as part of your consciousness, either unconsciously or consciously. Then through time and space those suggestions begin to create a portrait of you that become a network of belief systems to you later.

As you can see, by nature you have become very much unaware of your belief systems. You take for granted in what you see with your brain and hear with your ears are, in fact, truth and nothing but the truth and yet, it is far from the truth.

In order for you to evolve to the understanding of being a sovereign "I AM" in your own right, your belief systems, while in the flesh, need to get the most from every physical experience. This means, every time you experienced an incarnation you gave enormous attention to what your belief systems produced as your reality. Now, in this lifetime, you can come into some awareness in recognizing those beliefs as lies.

So, I ask you, be selective with your belief systems because it reflects on what you put into your new body when it is time to reincarnate again. You live and experience what you think and believe all day long. You place all your truths in what you perceive and see around you, and then you make a judgment about who you and others are. You look at yourself as either being rich, poor, middleclass, ugly, or beautiful, male or female, and yet, you can be so much more.

Oh! You try hard to figure things out. You study positive books that may help you gain some insights about becoming financially free, and all that happens is that you continue to get confused and broke. Because of this type of thinking you can get very mental, which makes you even more confused and stuck. That is when you can get frustrated and depressed, which then causes you to lose your passion to move forward.

Even more than that, look at someone who tries to create someone else's reality according to what they believe is right. Like making someone feel guilty because they don't go to church or they don't give thanks to God before every meal. What happens is that they will run straight into energetic conflicts within themselves, and with each other, where they will continually create for themselves many disappointing situations.

My dear friends, these disappointing situations can come in to their life in many different forms. Of course, the energy of stress, drama, and conflict will eventually tire them out so much that it can cause them poor health and bad choices.

The belief systems you have about God as well as with positive and negative are two of the most dangerous energies and most destructive beliefs known to man today. The whole concept about a single personality of a God that created you, and the idea of positive and negative being real because of your rational mind saying so, are more dangerous to man than your own emotional ties to family, friends, or even money and relationships.

You hold onto these beliefs because you are so afraid if you let go of the concept of God, and that of positive thoughts, you will be flooded with negative thoughts that would result in you living a depressed life that holds nothing but unhappiness. When you learn to let go of this concept of a single white male God as well as the concept of positive, negative and sin, you are going to realize that there is something far grander than what you are trying to hold unto.

You are going to realize that there is, "*you.*" Not the "*you*" that you see in the mirror, but the *real* you. The creator you! The, "*you*" that can transcend your human beliefs beyond what the brain understands only as positive and negative, good and bad, and even sin. It is the "*real you*" that knows how to bring everything into your life, like money, relationships, good health, food, and many more great things.

Here is something to consider. Most Christian religions teach that when Jesus comes back to earth, he will raise up from the graves all those that died before and they will be taken up to heaven to be with Him (John 6:39-54). Does this really sound possible to you or is it something the rational mind loves to rap itself around in order to feel like there is something beyond you that can save you?

Think about what this verse is saying! What about the people who died before the time of Christianity or what about those who displayed good in their heart ten million years ago? On a very practical and simplistic level, what about the bodies of those who have died which have long since been transformed into dirt (dust), trees, plants, and even food for animals and other humans? What about the bodies that were consumed in fire? This is just one of the problems with taking the words of the Bible literally.

Here is the real message to this mystery. When you have released all of your belief systems in a God of good and a Devil of evil, then your karma, called sowing and reaping in the Bible, has been fulfilled, which means that any karmic conditions that you hold within from other lifetimes past has now been released from mother Earth, and therefore you can integrate all that you are, including your soul and Christ like being in just a blink of the eye.

When you finally realize and accept who you really are, you are no longer bound to the rational mind or limited by your past. When you no longer have to work out any karma, it will be time for your past human personality aspects, the many lifetimes that you have had in a physical body that have died before and have been since buried, will be released from the earthly forces of positive and negative.

You see, the energy that you left behind in those buried bodies of other lifetimes now can leave mother earth (the grave) and move back to its creator, *you* – for you are the *Christ*. Your past lifetimes of many colors have been waiting for the day (incarnation) when your Christ energy returns to you, because each of them, no matter where you lived upon this earth, are now free to be released from their earthly bonds (grave) to integrate with your soul in this human lifetime.

Every time you lived and died, the body that you occupied was usually buried within the earth, therefore much of your energy remained trapped in the earth because of what you had for belief systems. This is especially true of the lifetimes where you were not very aware and identified solely with your physical form. Therefore, much of the energy of who you have been in the past has been held by Mother Earth (Gaia) until the time of resurrection (or your awakening) when you are reconnected once again to your Gnost (Christ-Soul) Consciousness.

This is the real meaning of Christ raising the dead from the graves. It is that you are the Christ raising your trapped energy from many lifetimes of stuck belief systems and integrating them with your total self of today. It all stems from the acceptance that you are a Christ also!

When the human personality aspect of you in this lifetime realizes that you are the chosen one, the super aspect, then you will be ready to release all of your clear, gray, and dark ego personality-aspects of the past.

Here is the main point! When you learn to let go of everything that you are attached to, either emotionally or just in the simple things like having to have a Starbucks coffee or a cigarette every morning to start your day, then who or what is going to control you? Nothing! When you let go of your attachment to money, health, relationships, businesses, family, friends, religious rituals, government, your job, even your life, and most of all your emotional belief systems, then the only thing left to control what you think and feel is *you*. So, I say unto you! It is time to claim who you truly are!

However, before you do, remember this! The rational mind is going to kick in because the mind is programmed to protect and defend you. You created it that way a long time ago! You gave up your "I AM" sovereignty to a deceptive mind in order to experience life, and now it is time to take back your "I AM" sovereignty and place your rational mind in the back seat.

Right now your rational mind has played the part well in keeping you tied to your belief systems and to your truths in order to feel alive. However, once you let go of the rational mind, the first thing it will ask you is, "What do you want me to do with what I have been taught since the beginning?" The rational mind will even ask you what shall it do to maintain your health, your job, intelligence, and most of all, how to protect you and your family.

In truth, the rational mind really doesn't know that much about the health of your body or how intelligent you are when it comes to protecting you and your family anyway. The rational mind only operates on a mental nature of logic and reasoning, and therefore it will be tied to only what is past and practical. Thus, the rational mind will only pretend to know what it is doing. In fact, your physical body has a higher intelligence than your rational mind when it comes to healing the body.

As far as your job or protecting you and your family, it takes the higher *you*, the, *you* that have a better understanding of your mental nature. So, when you say to yourself that you are going to let go of everything and only trust in yourself. The rational mind may get very distrustful and argue with you because it is tied to a belief in a God that will save you. This is why the real and profound you has to come out and tell the false you that you are serious about becoming a sovereign "I AM" being in your own right.

Therefore, always keep conscious of the fact that the rational mind is a generator of lies because of your past. Understand, energy loves to move and expand, and it can't if you keep it stuck in the form of belief systems that are tied to duality and your past.

Chapter 15

How Susceptibility, Vulnerability, and Belief Systems Led To Control And Death Of The Soul

We all know lies can perpetuate more lies. After all, we humans have been around for millions of years here on earth to perpetuate those lies. So, somewhere along our journey of many lifetimes, we became very susceptible to the suggestion that we don't choose how we are going to live our lives. My dear friends, we all took on the belief a long time ago that our destiny has been laid out for us by some higher power.

We, as a human group consciousness, have perpetuated this lie so much so that we are now stuck in a world of lies. Because of the rational mind being hardwired to our memories, the rational mind became a complex tool where we used it for a variety of different tasks and functions.

For instance: Judgment became a way to help us remember things, like not to jump off a high place or put our hand in a fire. The rational mind also became a good source for information, like remembering things to help us survive, or hold dearly to our heart what we feel is important, as well as helping us understand other individuals with certain qualities. Some of which we liked and others we did not like.

Now, this was a good thing until one day someone figured out that we can use the rational mind to inject many ideas, beliefs, and positions on any given subject matter. For instance: Projecting ideas like moving everyone toward traditional values, following certain rules or laws, and then everyone agreeing to submit and comply with what we believed would maintain some level of stability and normalcy.

However, as we all can attest too, this type of thinking opens up the door for those in power, like governments, religions, businesses, the media, and yes, even our parents and friends to come into our space and influence us on what they think is best for us. Of course, this thinking will always cause a big energetic collision with our soul because, beneath of it all, our soul holds a different agenda.

If we take away all that we have designed and built with our rational mind and belief systems, we are going to find nothing but our core essence. We, again, are a being of pure "I AM" consciousness that has a divine plan to become a sovereign being in our own right. So, when we look at who we believe we are, like being a sinner, or that we are a male or female, or that we are only human, it is nothing but a deception, lies, illusions, and mind control. It is mass consciousness hypnosis at its best, and a belief that we are not an "I AM" God unto ourselves.

Now, let me clarify what I am saying here. It is not that you and mass consciousness are doing something wrong. It is something that you, as all humans, agreed to do a long time ago. That is, to feel what it is like to experience control, deception, and commit to a distorted reality that is not real. How can it be real if you, at your core level, are only made up of an unadulterated "I AM" consciousness, and you have a spirit that is only of light that is connected to universal divine mind?

What happened along the way in our journey of life is, because of our reality being built on control and power, all of us learned to lie very quickly. You can say that lying became a way of life for us humans. Now, don't take this personally, for it was all on purpose. In fact, we humans became expert liars because it was the only way to cope with our twisted and corrupted realities of past lifetimes, and perhaps even this lifetime for some of us.

Now of course, from these lies of our current lifetime, and that of our twisted realities of past lifetimes, we turned those lies into the truths that we listen to today. These truths included how to protect ourselves, how to survive, and most of all, how to create many personality-aspects in order to discover who we truly are.

Not only do we lie to others all the time, we lie to ourselves because we do not want to admit that we are purposely being tricked by individuals that love to control everything, including our own family members. It is a combination of suggestion and susceptibility that has created most all of our beliefs, and now those beliefs have created our make-believe reality of today.

Because of our many lifetimes, we have populated our memories with such belief systems that we don't even know that they exist because they are like the root system of a group of trees that toil from beneath our inner consciousness. Don't forget! A tree has two elements to it like our consciousness, one is above and the other below or deep within.

Our consciousness and sub-consciousness, the visible and invisible, are very active from within and outside of us. This is why we follow many belief systems of others and the beliefs that are tied to our past personality-aspects (lifetimes). We pretend we are not acting on a lie or some past belief because all that we see is that we are following our truths from this lifetime only.

So this means we have been following an energetic trail of lies for many lifetimes, and now we are caught up in a tangle of lies that are so deep within our consciousness that we cannot see our way out other than to keep the lies and hope for the best. Because of these deep seated lies that we hold within that we take now as our truths, and that we would die for, we now believe today that there is a higher power than what we perceive ourselves to be to come and save us.

Remember, there is only this pure divine "I AM" consciousness that is the essence of you being a Christ also. Therefore, it is *you*, not someone outside of you, that is the real higher power here, and it is buried deep within your soul memories all because of vulnerability.

Because of our built up lies over many lifetimes, we humans continue to ignore our higher self because we are afraid to go deeper into ourselves because of how we look at our religion or our rational mind. Without realizing it, we, as mankind, have learned to perfect the art of guarding against anything new that might come along and destroy our idea of God or how intelligent we are.

It is like we don't want anyone to take away what we have confidently believed about God, our religion, and our intelligence. We have even conveniently overlooked how consciousness has evolved over the last ten thousand years. Instead, we stick to our old ways without even giving it a second thought.

People lie to themselves all the time by saying that there is no such thing as other lifetimes. They do it because they are so afraid to see beyond the veil of physicality and what might happen to them. They don't want to admit to being the creator of their world and their suffering. They would rather blame what they are experiencing on other people in order to feel secure about who they are and what they believe. This way, they can keep denying responsibility for what they create.

My dear friends, when we stopped choosing a long time ago in some past lifetime, on a conscious level, we stopped being a true creator. When we stopped creating from a knowing consciousness, our soul became dead to us. Now, I am not talking about a literal death! It is just that we began to follow other people as if they knew God on a personal note. That is when our soul and or Gnost (Christ) Consciousness went into a deep sleep (death), waiting for the time when we have had enough of the lies.

It was a death that feels like death because we stopped choosing from a sovereign "I AM" perspective. Oh! We may say that we are choosing what we want in life but that is not entirely true because we are choosing from the bunch of lies that we have adopted as our truths. When we stopped *choosing* a long time ago from the soul level that is when other people began to choose for us.

When we stopped trusting ourselves as an "I AMness," we lost our connection with our own soul and or Christ (Gnost) consciousness. You can actually say that we pushed our soul aside in favor of following the currents of life in the way our rational and lucid mind understands it.

My dear friends, if you truly believe that you are your rational mind and physical body, as well as your religion, and that your human name is who you truly are, then your soul just goes into a state of nothingness. Like a sleep state, where it allows the false you (the lucid mind-anti-christ) to claim itself as being the decision maker (king) until you are ready to face the truth. This is what is called, the "death of the soul."

This is why when you read this material, and if you decide to think about implementing some of it because of it feeling right to you, that is when your rational mind will move quickly in a judgment role to see if it can discredit it. The reason! It is again because of you being vulnerable and susceptible to the power of persuasion.

Now of course, you, at some level, made a conscious choice to be here on earth at this time. You also made the choice to experience what you are experiencing today. You created the trap a long time ago that you needed to create lifetimes of repeating the same belief patterns over and over. Especially about some God or savior that is coming in to save you.

Look, you also have created the means to read this book. You are looking for something that will move you beyond this trap of repeating the same old beliefs and the life you are living over and over. Just remember, no one can save you but you. Nobody can uncreate what you created for yourself to experience, except you. Yes, I know it is easy to say it is someone else's fault, and yet difficult to say that you are the blame for what you are experiencing.

When I first began to channel the ascended masters from beyond the physical veil, I found that my rational mind did not have the capability or the understanding to be a sensitive instrument to supernatural forces. In fact, in the beginning stages of experiencing psychic sensitivity to non-physical forces, I had a hard time understanding what was being expressed to me. You see, the rational mind always pretends to sense and perceive things as if it knew the common denominator between my soul and my human self, not realizing that my "I AM Essence" is the true psychic here.

What the rational mind does is that it has the tendency to ask questions like, "Who are you?" "Who do you think you are?" Do you really believe that God has chosen you to speak for him? Anyway, what comes from the rational mind is something like this: "Whoever you think you are, there is one thing that you are not, and that is, there is no way that you are equal to God."

You see, the only thing that the rational mind can come up with is that you are a child of God, you are a sinner, and you are a human being that was created by God. Therefore, you will never be equal to God. Why? Because you were born of your physical parents and you possess a certain truth about God that holds true to you and your relationship to him that feels real.

You have forgotten that the rational mind is a creation that came from you a long, long time ago. It is about understanding that the rational mind can only determine what is logical and what makes sense because everything that comes from the rational mind comes from the seat of thought and memory. You have played the mental game over and over, and all that it does is strengthen the belief that the mind has power. The mind has no power other than to serve your soul.

Look, the real truth is, you are your soul! You are not your rational mind because the rational mind loves to struggle and weigh things out (like judging things as right or wrong) before making a decision. Your rational mind will take in what it knows about you from the present, and then presents it to the world what you believe about yourself.

The rational mind completely overlooks all of the parts and components of you, all those personality-aspects of you that lived before, prior to your lifetime of today. The rational mind just cannot understand the "wholeness of you in your oneness of being" or "all that you are" like your soul can, because all that the rational mind can understand is that truth is a consequent that follows as a result of something known to be real. Thus truth is based on the perception of what the rational mind sees as a principle of fact, otherwise the rational mind will reject it.

For instance: The process of using the mind and physical senses is the accepted principle in acquiring information about who you are and what you believe to be true. Therefore, it is your consciousness that is the real psychic here because consciousness can expand beyond the rational mind and your physical senses.

Look at your pure "I AM Soul" consciousness as the in-breath and your rational mind as the out-breath, and if you stop taking in-breaths, then the rational mind and your physical body would stop living. This is why you suffer because you have stopped your soul consciousness from flowing through your rational mind and physical body in a natural way.

You, as all humans, act out your truths in a very real way, so real that your personality-aspects (other lifetimes) tend to take over without you even knowing it. Just one aspect from your past can come into your present lifetime and completely influence the rational mind and take over all of your truths and yet, every aspect of you is just you. Therefore, all parts and pieces of you are your truths as much as they are your lies.

You have truths and lies about you that only want security, happiness, and comfort while other parts of you are afraid of the bigger you, the real divine you, which is why you are afraid of God. You are afraid to look at God in any other way except as God being your creator and protector.

You see, the real God, the "I AM" within you, holds all the parts and pieces of you, and the human you believes this as truth, which is why the human you in this lifetime struggles to accommodate the victim you.

Remember, a 'victim you' will never look beyond the 'deeper you' that holds the 'divine you' that doesn't need security, comfort, or happiness because the 'victim you' would rather marvel over becoming a victim. You see, if one becomes a victim then one becomes absorbed in a belief that God would favor them because of what happened to them.

Because of the many belief systems that you hold onto as only being one truth, then happiness and comfort become conditional, and therefore your heart is closed off to other possibilities. You know! "I will be happy when I get a raise," or "I will be happy when I get married," or "I will be happy if I could just buy a car, a boat, or home." Or, how about, "I will be happy if my spouse or children would just listen to me and do as I say. After all, I am the educated one here."

Now of course, I could go on and on with the things that would make you feel happy. However, nothing will make you happy, feel secure, or make you comfortable because you have made it almost impossible to achieve those things. Why? Because you have put so many conditions on what you are trying to attain. You have forgotten that the divine you (the soul), does not need to have anything in life to be happy or feel secure.

The divine you is actually content with what it has chosen to experience in its journey to learn wisdom, good and bad. Therefore, the divine you (or your soul) accepts all things as they are.

You see, the divine you sees the human you as caught up in the drama of, "If I had money or these things of comfort and security, I would be free of wanting things." That is far from the truth!

My dear friends as long as you put conditions on what you want in life, even what you see as your truths about heaven and hell, you will never experience the real truth because you are to locked into what you believe are your truths. By not opening yourself up to who you truly are, your focus on duality, good and evil, will control or rule the way you will find your truths and how you will live your life.

So, I ask you again! What is your truth? Does your truth rest upon what your rational mind perceives in what is right and wrong or is it based on something else that is outside of you, like religion?

Has it ever occurred to you how one keeps repeating a bad situation or patterns over and over? You see, the rational mind cannot single out these types of repeated patterns that one makes because the rational mind only understands them to be beneficial, and that something good will eventually come out of them.

By looking at the rational mind and your physical name as who you are, you will experience life as if you are on a merry-go-round. Yes, you will keep on repeating things over and over because the rational mind is stuck in an energy belief where your reality is built only on your physical name, your genealogy, and what is good and bad, right and wrong, as well as judging what would make you happy and safe.

It takes awareness to make a change because awareness is when you make the choice to get off the merry-go-round of duality, and go outside of the realm of just being a human name that believes in a God that created you and gives you a miracle if you are good.

Most of us have been searching for truth and yet, most of the world population has not found it. Why? Because we don't know enough to get off the merry-go-round of duality living! All that the rational mind knows is that the horses on the merry-go-round go up and down because that is the reality of it. The rational mind can only understand things in a dualistic and judgmental viewpoint where the divine mind sees no judgment, no single philosophy, no religion, and no single truth, only the expansion of truth.

My dear friends, if you are looking for only one truth, then you would have to go back to the first creation where the "I AM" is the "Is-ness" and the true essence of who you truly are. Truth is like a tree where you, as all humans, take for granted what you see with your eyes is only the tree coming out from the ground, and what you don't see are the roots that nourishes the tree.

It is the same with the rational mind and how it complies with the things that are not real and yet, everything seems real. For instance: The out-breath that you take seems very real and yet, it is not real. Just like the truth about good and evil that we all seem to hang onto as being real is not as it seems. Because what we perceive as being real is in truth not our full story.

It has been the rational mind that has been the focal point here and it has drawn our attention for many, many lifetimes as having the ability to create the reality that we perceive would make us happy. Thus forgetting what is on our list of wants doesn't necessarily make the soul happy.

The rational mind and the human ego do a lot of planning on what it wants to experience. The rational mind sets up objectives to target success by looking at each day as something that is owed to you, and therefore should happen. Then when it doesn't happen the way you envisioned it, you get stressed out and angry at yourself and others wondering what went wrong.

That is when the rational mind kicks in and tells you that you are only human thus setting up the need for God, the government, family, or your religion to help bail you out, or give you what you believe is owed to you.

Yes, many of you pray and pray, and you pray even more, until you get disappointed with God, your government, your family, and your religious leaders. Once you realize that there is no single solitary God that is going to answer your prayers by you winning a lottery, or that government, family, friends, and your religion are only looking to control you by giving you things. That is when you can begin to focus on your own choices, and at the same time, take full responsibility for those choices.

My dear friends, it takes making the choice to take full responsibility for your choices that gets you off the merry-go-round. Once you realize that you are more than what you see in the mirror, for you are a Christ also, the potentials that you possess deep within become the pathway to a new expanded consciousness that can lead you to a wealth of wisdom and understanding, thus health and abundance.

This means you don't have to follow or listen to other people, not even to your own family. After all, you have the wisdom of a God!

The time has come to open your eyes, ears, and heart, and make a simple choice that can take you on a new road of discovery. This is a road where you can create for yourself a new energy of expansion that comes directly from you, the "I AM," and not from mass consciousness or from some false God, thus opening up a whole new world for you to see.

You have been programmed for many lifetimes because of the idea of power and control and now, it is time to make a conscious choice to bring in your own "I AM Gnost-Christ" consciousness. I know that making a conscious choice can be very challenging to you because of history and programming. However, it can be done just by doing a very simple step. Learn to take deep conscious breaths through the nose and then let it out through the mouth.

Learn to feel the in-breath of your consciousness calling forth your gnost-Christ consciousness and your spirit to participate in this lifetime. You see, when you learn to take deep in-breaths on a conscious level, you do acknowledge, at the inner levels, that you are the creator and the one that is choosing life and what you desire to experience. Learn to do this for at least fifteen to thirty minutes a day and you will see your life and your reality change.

At first you will begin to open up to your human senses and what they have been telling you to follow, to believe, and what to act on. Then, as you continue your deep breathing, over time, you will begin to move past your human senses and begin to feel your divine senses. Like your intuition, gnost, awareness, imagination, and knowingness. That is when you will begin to sense a better understanding of things around you and why certain things happen a certain way.

You actually begin to observe all the things that are going on in your life, not from a judgmental or rational mind point of view, but from a whole new expanded consciousness. You actually become conscious of what you have been creating for yourself. When you learn to make a conscious choice from your deep breathing it begins to change your life in a very sweeping way.

By making choices from a divine level, leaving out judgment and logic, you are telling yourself that you are not made of energy. You are spirit first and foremost who has a consciousness that can dictate to energy, and to your rational mind to serve you, the creator. Energy, and the rational mind, by its very nature, will serve you if you choose it from a conscious knowing that you are the creator. The Lord of Lords over all that you created.

This is where miracles come from. Even if you are not aware that you are the creator, energy will still serve you, because this energy is under the command of the creator, you. When you are not choosing from a conscious level as a creator or you feel that you are not the creator of your reality, energy will still come in to support that belief too.

My dear friends, if you feel that you are a victim of destiny, energy will come in and support that belief too. In fact, energy has been doing that ever since you left your divine state (the first creation) a long time ago. However, when you make a conscious choice from a knowing that you are a Christ also, equal to and not less than, you are going to attract a new energy of expansion into your life to support your new belief system.

So, learn to take deep in-breaths and out-breathes every day. The in-breath is the creator you at work while the out-breath is you again manifesting your creations on a conscious level. Of course, the important thing here is to make the choice, take deep in-breaths, and then let everything go without trying to help it along using your mental state. Trust yourself as a creator otherwise you don't believe you are the true creator.

Do your deep breathing and conscious choosing, and then go about your normal activities. Don't allow your rational mind to come in and tell you how to go about achieving your choices (goals). You will feel what to do intuitively, you will meet the right people at the right time, and when it is time to start working with your choices you will not be confused with what to do next.

When you make the choice for a better life, abundance, or better health, then you must learn to release it. Don't keep on focusing on it or try to bring in attachments to it! Just release it, do your deep breathing, and watch the flow of energy work. Learn to be aware of how energy comes in to serve you, how it feels, and most of all, don't get discouraged if it isn't happening fast enough for you.

Remember, you are learning to create from a divine level. When the divine level clears up some of the old stuff, that is when you will begin to see a whole new you as well as a new reality. Something else to remember here, make choices for yourself and not for someone else, not even for family members. Everyone is their own creator, and you must understand that, or you are going to struggle in bringing in your new reality.

For instance: This is a big one! When you pray for world peace or for some loved one to be healed of their illnesses, your spirit gets very confused over the prayer because there are many people that do not want peace or their illnesses healed. They are choosing these things from their soul level to serve them. This is why there are many prayers not answered. It is all due to praying for someone that is not choosing, from a subconsciousness level, what you are praying for them to experience.

Have compassion for what they are choosing to experience, and leave the rest up to them. You are your own creator and your own manifester. Learn to trust the process! Also, learn to trust the ups and downs you are experiencing in your life today because they are the results of the choices you made in the past. And sometimes, it takes time to uncreate what you created.

Now, in closing of this chapter, I want to leave you with this. The concept of lying is really about not choosing from a conscious knowing that you are a divine being, and that you are not the creator of your world. When you are not choosing from a divine level, you are in-effect choosing to follow other people and their ideas of who you are and who God is.

The lack of choosing on a divine level creates a deeper cause for you to go even deeper into more lies about who you are, why you are here on earth, and it emphasizes how lost you are because of the way you look at how it takes other people to fulfill you. So, take your deep breaths, trust yourself, acquire your own fulfillment, and discover that part of yourself that solves problems beyond the capabilities of the rational mind.

Chapter 16

Misunderstanding Lucifer's (Satan) Role

My fellow searchers, we cannot leave out Lucifer in this unfolding of soul memories because the time has come to take a good look at him and what he stands for. Many of us associate Lucifer with many different names, such as Satan, the Devil, the Beast, the Anti-Christ, the Serpent in the Bible, as well as with many other names. Lucifer is also a name that generally refers to the Hebrew name "Sheol," meaning hell or the devil, after he was cast out of heaven for breaking God's rules.

Now, I know this chapter may fire up some feelings because of what you have been taught about Lucifer. However, it needs to be addressed in order to help you understand who you are in the scheme of things – for you cannot make a shift from old dualistic energy to new expansional energy unless you know who Lucifer is. Therefore, I ask you to be patient with me in what I am about to say about Lucifer and the role that he has with us.

In fact, as you read this chapter, I ask you to feel into the energy of what is being expressed here. For example: When you say the names Lucifer, the Devil, or Satan, either to yourself or speaking the name out loud, what do you feel? Does it make you feel like a fallen angel or does the name(s) just frighten you? After all, the name itself is tied to many evil acts and effects that you see and experience everyday of your live.

According to most Christians just the name Lucifer itself can stir up a lot of underlying emotions. What if I said that the name "Lucifer" appears only one time in the King James Version of the Bible? It is found in the book of Isaiah 14:12. *"How art thou fallen from heaven, O Lucifer, son of the morning? How art thou cut down to the ground, which didst weaken the nations?"*

In the "New American Bible," written and published by the U.S. Conference of Catholic Bishops, Washington, DC, dated November 11, 2002, the verse reads differently. It reads: *"How have you fallen from the heavens, O morning star, son of the dawn! How are you cut down to the ground, you who mowed down the nations?"* As you can see, the name *Lucifer* was completely left out and the words "son of dawn" was added.

So, why did the Catholic version of the text leave out the name *Lucifer* altogether and add the words *"son of dawn?"* Why is it that most Christian Bibles mention Lucifer's name only once? The reasons are interesting!

You see, the name Lucifer is seen by scholars as being a spiritual ruler, like Jesus, that appeared in heaven before he was thrown out of heaven by God for disobedience. Also, the name Lucifer has a meaning that most Christian denominations don't like because the name itself carries a meaning of "the bearer of light," or "the bringer of light," or the "Day Star," as well as having a meaning, "Of the Light." It all sounds Christ like, doesn't it?

The name Lucifer was originally a Latin word, a word that came to man in the early fifth century. In 2 Peter 1:19 - 21, the Latin word Lucifer is used to refer to the "Morning Star," and with having no relationship to the Devil. It was only in post "New Testament" times that the Latin word Lucifer was used as the Hebrew name "Sheol," the Devil, in religious writings, especially when referring to Lucifer prior to his fall from Heaven.

In 2 Peter 1:19: *"Moreover, we possess the prophetic message that is altogether reliable. You will do well to be attentive to it, as to a lamp shining in a dark place, until "day dawns" and the "morning star" rises in your heart."* Now, who do you believe Peter was addressing here? Who is the "morning star" that rises in the hearts of man? The answer is Lucifer – for the name Lucifer is representative of your own Lucifer consciousness.

You see, the *"lamp shining in the dark place"* is not about Lucifer it is about your own hidden wisdom – for the *"day dawns"* means, for you, the human personality-aspect that is walking upon the earth at this very moment, to understand the wisdom that you possess is beginning to break through to your human conscious level. My dear friends, the angel that is helping you bring in this wisdom of light is in fact, Lucifer.

Now, don't blow me off just yet! You have come too far to be afraid of what I have to say about Lucifer. You see, Lucifer is actually an aspect of "Archangel Luceffa." Does this revelation surprise you?

Look, who is "Archangel Luceffa anyway?" Well! First of all, we all know that Luceffa was given the name Lucifer, Satan, Devil, and Shaitan to the Muslims, once he was thrown out of heaven by God. However, what we have never been taught about Luceffa is that he plays a big role in our awakening to the Christ within us.

Nevertheless, because of the misinterpretation and misunderstanding of the name Luceffa, we, as humans, have become trapped into believing that there is an evil spirit unto himself maneuvering and manipulating our soul and our consciousness in an effort to steal our soul by making us out to be fallen angels. Well, in the truest sense of the name Luceffa, and how we humans interpret the name. The truth of it, "Archangel Luceffa" is one of the 144,000 angelic families that belong to the Oder of the Arc. This angelic family's name is the "Order of Luceffa."

"Archangel Luceffa" is an archetypical angel whose name was later changed to Lucifer for no apparent reason, and then later became known as the Devil or Satan. My dear friends, it is "Archangel Luceffa" (Lucifer) that is the "bearer of light," the "son of the morning," and the "Day Star," and not Jesus – for Jesus is the angel that helps us humans work with our own Christ consciousness once the "bearer of light" (Lucifer) awakens us to it.

Yes, my dear friends, Luceffa and Jesus have been working together for our benefit since the beginning of us coming to earth. You see, Lucifer has no mission or assignment to steal our soul or pour down upon us any evil misgivings. He is there to help us, on a physical and mental level, to become aware of our own demons, which is why there is no devil, Satan, or evil spirit to be afraid of just like there is no God outside of us to be afraid of – for these two characters are much a myth as Adam and Eve.

You see, "Archangel Luceffa" (Lucifer) was entrusted and appointed by the Order of the Arc to shift our energy of positive and negative, and our misunderstanding of its nature, back to its "original form of balance." Hence forth, because of the choices we created while living in an energy of two, a new understanding of positive and negative emerges from the ashes of our evil doings and with it, comes our "original form of oneness and balance" as a self-ruling "I AM" sovereign being.

In order for Archangel Luceffa to accomplish his task he had to have you, and mankind in general, believe and feel that he took a plunge (fall) in consciousness to a "consciousness of deceit and perception," and he did by him taking on the role of playing opposite sides to any given subject, like good versus bad for example. Thus, this action caused you, as in mankind, to feel that you too have fallen in consciousness.

Luceffa became branded as the angel of death and the creator of evil and yet, Luceffa (Lucifer) is neither, for he is an angel of light that helps you eventually bring in your wisdom of light. Look, Jesus, and the family of Sananda, couldn't do it all by themselves or himself. Jesus needed Archangel Luceffa to help him.

You see, since the Christ consciousness (synonymous for Jesus) was forgotten by all of us souled beings because of our fall in consciousness to a consciousness of two, duality. Archangel Luceffa (known as Lucifer) became the "bearer of light" (lamp) and the "morning star" for all of us until the Christ within us, again represented by Jesus, was re-awakened or remembered (resurrected) once again.

Once we, as souled beings, became confused about who we were we fell into physicality to learn who we were, and as a human, we soon became lost in a consciousness of ignorance (darkness) and duality that we literally took on as our reality. Therefore, we needed help to remember who we truly are, and Archangel Luceffa (Lucifer) was the angel who took on the role of being the bringer of light (wisdom), as we went about playing with the forces of positive and negative (good and evil).

As we know now, through time, the forces of opposites became the manner in which we used to bring in the wisdom (light) of our choices and the lack of our understanding of who we are. Once we, as divine beings, took the plunge (fall), the name Lucifer then became synonymous with us, as souls, in expressing our rebellious and unruly nature (disobedient) that eventually became part of a consciousness of judgment and physicality.

Thus, the name Lucifer was changed to the name of Satan, the Devil, Sheol, the "Anti-Christ," the "Beast," the "Serpent" in the Garden, Shaitan, as well as "the King of Babylon," just to mention a few – for he was described as an enemy of God, the Lord of evil, and the tempter for all of mankind. However, it was mankind that became the tempter, because of what we chose as duality (the tree of knowledge of good and bad), and it was that duality that became the enemy of our own Christ Consciousness (symbolized by Jesus and God) and not Arc Angel Luceffa.

Luceffa, like Jesus, became the escape goat for all of mans twisted beliefs and ideas of good and bad – for we, as man, refused to take full responsibility for our actions, and we still do today. When we, as souled beings, first moved from out of our divine essence (first creation) and into our mental state (second creation), we chose not to take responsibility for our actions and our choices, thus creating a force of accountability or what is called today as cause and effect, sowing and reaping in the Bible.

Now, contrast to who Luceffa (Lucifer) is and who Jesus is, it would be appropriate to bring in the "Apostles' Creed" because it is one of the oldest creeds of Christianity, dating way back to the middle of the second century with its roots extending all the way back to the biblical traditions of the Gospels. The creed was able to stay intact even though some phrases were added to reinforce clarity as late as the fourth century.

However, there has been some confusion surrounding the phrase, "He descended into hell." The reason for the confusion is because some churches believe this confirms an early belief that Jesus preached to the dead during his crucifixion and resurrection (1 Peter 3:19, 4:6). Also, we have many churches that object to the phrase "holy catholic church" because it means "inclusive."

Using the web version of Wikipedia Encyclopedia to answer some of your questions about the Apostles' Creed, sometimes titled, symbol of the Apostles, and how it became widely used by a number of Christian sects for religious worshipping and instructions for baptismal purposes, it is one of the best ways to explain the contrast between Luceffa and Jesus.

The Apostles' Creed is evident by religious worshipping Churches of Western tradition, including the Latin Rite of the Catholic Church, Lutheranism, Anglicanism, and Western Orthodoxy. It is also used by Presbyterians, Methodists, and the Congregationalists. The "Apostles' Creed" was based on Christian theological understanding of the Canonical gospels (meaning, conforming to general principles), the letters of the New Testament, and to a lesser extent the Old Testament.

Because of its early origin, it does not address some of the academic study of Jesus Christ defined in the later profession of faith and other Christian Creeds. It thus says nothing explicit about the divinity of either Jesus or of the Holy Spirit. This made it acceptable to many followers of the ancient Greek Christian theologian Arius, who argued that Jesus was the highest created being, but was not divine, and Unitarians (meaning, one who believes in one god but who is not a Christian).

However, it does not address the many other theological questions that did become objects of dispute centuries later. Under the inspiration of the Holy Spirit after Pentecost, the name of the Creed may have come from the fifth century tradition that each of the Twelve Apostles dictated as a governing rule to make decisions or how people should behave.

The Apostles Creed is traditionally divided into twelve articles, which are as follows:

1. I believe in God, the Father Almighty, Creator of heaven and earth,
2. And in Jesus Christ, his only begotten Son, our Lord,
3. Who was conceived by the Holy Spirit, born of the Virgin Mary,
4. Suffered under Pontius Pilate was crucified, dead and buried; He descended into hell.
5. The third day he rose again from the dead;

6. He ascended into heaven, and sits at the right hand of God, the Father Almighty.

7. From there he shall come to judge the quick and the dead.

8. I believe in the Holy Spirit,

9. I believe in the holy catholic church, the communion of saints,

10. The forgiveness of sins,

11. The resurrection of the body,

12. And the life everlasting. Amen

Now, after reading the "Apostles' Creed" one would come to the conclusion that there are big differences between Jesus and Lucifer? However, my "I AM Soul" self, interestingly says, there are no differences – for they are identical in every respect. Let me explain!

You see, before we, as souled beings, took the plunge (fall) from our divine oneness of consciousness, we were all a Christ too (as Jesus is representative of that) that sat at the right hand of the "Spirit of One," which is the "Mother-Spirit of oneself and the Father-Almighty," meaning our connection to universal divine mind. Thus, we, as souled beings, became the "begotten son," for we, as in all souled beings, are the Lord "who was conceived by the Holy Spirit," known as the Spirit of One. It is just that we have forgotten.

"Born of the virgin Mary" is synonymous for our own spirit. However, Mother-Mary also symbolizes the "Spirit of One" (Goddess) in action. What was the action taken? It was the "Spirit of One" giving birth to all of us as souled beings, and not as human beings. Thus, this birth is our awakening to our own spirit in giving us the divine authority (power) to act as part of the Godhead, which is why it was we, all souled beings, and not some lonely white male Hebrew God who lives in the sky, that created the "heavens and the earth." The "Heavens" represents multi-dimensional realms and "Earth" represents our physical realm of duality and form.

Since "Virgin Mary" is synonymous of being the Spirit of One, and also representing the feminine-masculine energy within all of us, then our make-up is of spirit consciousness first (the feminine-Goddess), and that we, as souled beings, used unadulterated energy and our connection to universal mind (God), and gave birth to a son. The "son" was the birth of our outer deceptive and rational mental mind, the masculine, and together, they constitute our "total consciousness" (the Goddess-God that we are).

From that point, both sides of you, which is your spirit and universal divine mind, synonymous for you being a Goddess and a God too (Mary and God), then gave birth to a ego consciousness of a mental nature that ended up giving birth to a lower human consciousness, also known as your Lucifer consciousness, to express the concept of "who are you?"

Mary, according to some religions, was an unmarried virgin at the time she conceived Jesus. The Bible states that Mary was seeded by God and not from physical man. This correlates with Genesis 2:23. *"For out of 'her man' this one has been taken."* However, there is a deeper meaning to this than just the literal writings.

From out of the "Father Almighty," which is synonymous for your own Spirit (Mary) and that of Universal Mind (Father-God), together with the use of unadulterated energy, you conceived an idea that produced a Son, symbolized by the birth of Jesus, a likeness of you, and that likeness was a mental version of you that took on a masculine look that felt real to you and yet, was not real.

I am not saying that Jesus was not real. It is just that the masculine and the mental part of him, and you, are not real, because all that is real is his, and your own spirit consciousness, the feminine. This in effect introduced you, as it did all souled beings, to an outer reasoning and perceptive mind (Adam principle) that became part of a dualistic energy force, positive and negative, that became your avenue to play out opposites, as in one lifetime playing a male and maybe the next lifetime playing a female.

The reason Jesus took on the appearance of a male in the physical sense, as well as depicting himself as the Son of Man and God, was to convey to you, all humans, that you are indeed the creator of your human consciousness so as to learn "who you truly are" by playing the opposite of your divine nature.

Jesus, the Christ, after the "resurrection of his physical body," is symbolic of you resurrecting (ascending) your own human personality consciousness of a disobedient nature (Lucifer) to your divine "I AMness" once you have experienced many different lifetime stories playing the opposite role of your true essence. Thus you, in the human flesh, and as being the son of man, becomes the Lord of Lords (the Son of God) to your many personality-aspects (lifetimes and non-lifetimes).

When your spirit (symbolized by Mary), together with universal divine mind (symbolized by God), split (gave birth) the feminine-masculine within you into a dualistic consciousness, your "consciousness of one" became part of an outer masculine consciousness and an inner feminine subconsciousness level. It was from the outer consciousness level that gave you the feeling of being separated from your inner subconscious level and yet, they are still as one.

The feeling of being separated from your higher subconsciousness level was the only way you, as a Christ also, could move outside of your "I AM Essence" and move into the "abyss of nothingness" for the purpose of experiencing the unknown principle of duality at the time. Thus, this created the avenue for Archangel Luceffa (Lucifer) to come in and bring to you the wisdom behind your choices as you journeyed through many storied lifetimes playing with the forces of opposites (sowing and reaping).

This, in the end, gave you, all souled beings, the route in finding your light (the Christ within) once again. By "Virgin Mary" giving life to a son she is illustrating to you how you, as a human, became part of a outer illusionary masculine aspect of yourself that carries a mind of rationality that perceives itself to be the master and the experiencer for your total being. While your "I AM Christ" essence, the higher you, learns the wisdom of those experiences through the rebellious nature of your human ego personality by playing with the forces of positive and negative, or duality, which is symbolized by Lucifer.

Also, since Jesus, from the standpoint of the Bible, represents the sonship, then the Christ aspect of Jesus and the Holy Spirit, which is your spirit, represents the Christ aspect within you giving life to your choices. Thus, my fellow souled beings, you have never sinned. How can you be divine and sin? It cannot be done unless you take on the belief that you have sinned. Otherwise, there is no such thing as sin.

This is why you, as all humans, can forgive your own sins, because you, realistically and truthfully, are the son that can forgive sins in God's stay, for you are God (the Father-Almighty) and the Christ (Mother). What you are misunderstanding is that Jesus' human aspect on earth as the "son of man" is synonymous for your outer illusionary positive-masculine side of you playing on earth as being the decision maker and the authority for the Mother-Father Goddess-God.

Note: This is why religions interpret the Bible as giving man authority over woman, but in reality there is no such authority. Every person is equal in God's eyes because every person, man and woman, IS God and more!

"Virgin Mary" also confirms that your "I AM Essence" is of a universal divine energy (virgin) that consists of a feminine female quality that is of consciousness and spirit only. The reason Mary conceived Jesus without the help of a physical man is because physical form was conceived (imagined) by the results of your "descended consciousness nature," and not from your "I AM Essence."

It was your outer illusionary positive-masculine aspect (the Adam principle) that gave life to an aspect of yourself called "the descended one," nickname for "Lucifer," the devil, or what is known as your own Lucifer consciousness. It was your outer illusionary version of you, or the mirror image of you (the son principle), that mimicked your spirit and used pure universal energy in manifesting a consciousness of defiance that led to rational thought patterns that became very rebellious in nature (beastly), all because of you wanting to avoid responsibility for your choices and creations.

Of course, what really happened was that this disobedient nature part of you had you feeling separated from the Christ part of you, which is why your outer illusionary consciousness (human you) is now part of an ego personality-aspect that partakes in the physical world of duality, which is illustrated by Adam and Eve not taking responsibility for eating the apple.

Now, it is Archangel Luceffa's task (Lucifer), to reunite you with your demon aspects that you continually refuse to acknowledge as your creations. This is the answer to the mystery of why Mary conceived Jesus without the help of man because physicality was derived from your lower disobedient nature.

It was you, and all souled beings together, that used this pure universal divine energy in creating a solid form (physical body) to play with the perception of duality being real. With the help Archangel Luceffa, also known as your own Lucifer consciousness, you eventually become closer to your "I AM Christ" self with every lifetime. Thus, you, the son, finally "resurrects the body" to an "everlasting body" that holds all of your fears, secrets, treasures, and your inheritance to the throne, which is your, I AM Sovereignty.

So, rather than trying to disown your dark side, embrace it because that is where your divinity (wisdom) resides!

Now, let us look at line 4 of the Apostles' Creed to show you further evidence of there being no difference between Jesus and Lucifer as far as these two angels bringing in your wisdom and sovereignty. The expression of "suffered under Pontius Pilate," is actually about your free will. Why, because Pilate was the Roman governor of Judea in the time of Jesus' teachings and crucifixion.

The name "Pilate" has a metaphysical meaning of being "rulership of the physical plane." In other words, your "free will" in action, for your "free will" is the ruling principle in your physical life, and is what questions the "I AM Christ" principles within you. "*Art thou the King of the Jews*" (John 18:33)?

You see, your human "free will" has no concept of the issues at hand in which you experience in the physical with your inner higher "divine will," and therefore it believes that it is the ruler of the whole you. When your "free will" is challenged it gets jealous of any attempt to override" or seize its power. But when it is assured that the kingdom of heaven (the higher "divine will," representative of Jesus, the Christ) is not of this world, then your "free will" (Pilate) finds no fault.

Of course, there is an age old question concerning the responsibility for the death of Jesus. We have seen it with Hitler, and many others, who blamed the Jews for executing Jesus. However, many have said that there are a number of different people and groups to blame.

For example: We can blame the Religious Rulers of Jesus' time. After all, the religious rulers of the time deserve their share of the blame as much as Pilate. They hated Jesus without any just cause. Their hatred for him caused them to arrest Jesus, find false witnesses, and then condemn him as guilty. They also brought false charges against him in front of Pilate.

Look at Luke 23: 1-2, "*Then the whole assembly of them arose and brought him before Pilate. They brought charges against him, saying, "We found this man misleading our people; he opposes the payment of taxes to Caesar and maintains that he is the Messiah, a king."*

As you can see, blame can be placed upon the religious leaders of Jesus' time as well as Pilate. However, the blame has to be ultimately placed on the entire human race because it was mans ignorance, and not mans sins, that Jesus went to his death on Calvary's cross that day. So, all of us are responsible for Jesus' death. Why? It represented the death of our own Christ consciousness.

The Jews represent two different aspects of the human mind. The outer masculine reasoning side of you, which is the illusionary side of you that is considered as positive and the makeup of form (physical aspect). While the other side of you is the inner feminine soul side that represents the makeup of unity, which is taken as negative. In the mind's feminine soul aspect side, the negative, it is about bringing unity to you because of your beliefs and choices. While in its outer illusionary masculine aspect side of you, it is about diversity or playing opposite.

Because of this belief, we find in ourselves our religious convictions often stand in the way of accepting Christ as our divine state. Instead we, as humans, fixate our dogmatic traditions and beliefs about God and Satan, which is the belief in duality, and follow them as the rule of law rather than seeking to unite ourselves to our own Christ consciousness, which is nothing but us working from out of our "I AM Essence."

Man lives by his harden thoughts when it comes to worshiping outside of himself. The reasons! The Jews were always the hardest to reach with new ideas about Christ. Since Jesus, the Christ, represents man's "divine state," then man is very much set in his dogmatic views when it comes to Christ and the Devil being outside of him and not within him or part of him. Therefore, we all "crucify" ourselves everyday by not seeing ourselves as a Christ also.

This means, if you live life believing only in the rational mind, in your free will, and in your physical body as being real, then you are virtually "dead" because you have buried your Christ identity and your "divine will" deep within your soul consciousness. All because of your "fall into hell," this is nothing more than you descending into human form here on earth.

You see, you don't have to die in order to go to hell any more than you have to die to go to heaven. Both are states of mind and conditions, which you, as a human, experience as a direct outworking of your thoughts, dogmatic beliefs, expressions, and acts. If your mental course of action is not in balance with the truth of you being a Christ too, then the result of pain, distress, torment, and sorrow becomes your outcome, or your hell.

According to the masters, the idea of Satan or a Devil comes from the old Hebrew word meaning "adversary," the *you* who goes against the Christ within yourself, and then accuses the devil (your outer human consciousness), and his army of bad angels (your other human aspects from past lifetimes), for your misery and discomfort. You blame them by not acknowledging them as your creations.

In other words, it was not Jesus that died for your sins! Jesus died on the cross to bring enlightenment to you about your own divinity and how you are responsible for your world and your hell, and not some character called Lucifer or Satan. In its truest reality, there is no such person other than Luceffa, the Arc Angel.

It is you and I, and all of mankind, that dies everyday for our sins all because of our harden beliefs about Christ being someone who is outside of us and a Devil that influences us in making bad decisions. For, we are in denial by not taking responsibility for our choices. You see, death is always the result of the failure to recognize our own spirit (soul) as the source of creation and the wisdom we possess. When we fall short in this respect, we become the crucified Christ, hidden (buried) in a physical form of ignorance (darkness) and a place of torment (hell).

Thus, Archangel Luceffa (Lucifer) is the angel to bring you back around to the Christ within yourself by having you journey through time and space in a physical body playing with the forces of positive and negative in working out the karma (sin) you chose to experience.

Once you journey through many lifetimes in a 3-D consciousness (spirit, rational mind, and body), which is signified by the "third day," you too "rise for a second time from your sleep (dead) state" and move into your Christ state where your consciousness of disobedience (Lucifer) finally ascends to a higher state of mind (heaven) that ends up leading the 'human you' in integrating the wholeness of "all that you are" (all of your demons) back into the oneness of your consciousness once again.

However, this time around, you have the wisdom of your journey at hand to guide you in becoming a self-governing Christ in your own right.

Now, the "right hand" that is mentioned in the Apostles Creed has the metaphysical meaning of you, including your human form, being the co-creator in what has been created since the beginning of your awareness in the first creation – for nothing is left out. You are a divine being that possesses a portion of the Spirit of One, and because of it, you have taken up the crown (co-creator) as being a God in action, thus equal too and not less than. Therefore, the mystery of who you are, who is God, and who Satan is, as well as the meaning of the "right hand of God" have been resolved.

You see, Christ is your first principle, the "I AM" within your own consciousness, and Archangel Luceffa signifies your consciousness in darkness as well as representing you in human form. You, all humans, became the "Babylonian King of the Earth" that is mentioned in the book of Revelation. Thus, the energy of a single solitary Lucifer, like Jesus, does not exist in the way you believe they exist.

Satan and Jesus just represent aspects of you choosing to buy into a belief system where good and evil are viewed as real, which in fact, they are not. Therefore, it is you from the human level that "comes to judge the quick and the dead." The "quick and the dead" are nothing more than your lack of understanding, the ignorance of who you truly are, and your hasty thoughtless dualistic belief systems at work.

"The belief in the Holy Spirit," the "holy catholic church," and the "communion of saints" are nothing more than your own "Spirit" is in a pure consciousness state, and it uses dualistic energy (positive and negative) to serve the real Christ, you. Therefore, the "holy Catholic Church" is nothing more than a group of religious scholars setting up all Catholics to be exclusive and the selective group that Jesus decrees as the right church, which of course is not true.

The reference to the "holy catholic church" is in fact propaganda - for it demonstrates how man and his physical body is the real "church" here, which houses the living Christ and not some building or some religious sect. Of course, the "communion of saints" is not about religious saints or angels of righteousness. They are about your own personality-aspects of many that your soul used to fulfill your need to become a sovereign "I AM" self-ruling Christ in your own right.

"The forgiveness of sins," the "resurrection of the physical body" (or you coming into a new lifetime), and "life everlasting" is about you coming out of your sleep state and into a "knowing" that you are a Christ also. You are the Holy Spirit, you are the church, and you need to trust and forgive yourself – for you have indeed never sinned. You only have been playing with pure energy in order to experience and understand life. Life, where in the end, you become a sovereign "I AM" self-ruling Christ in your own right.

Instead of us taking full responsibility for our creations, we have been avoiding responsibility by convincing ourselves that Satan and his army of bad angels are always around us, pushing us to do his bidding. We can see this by religion teaching us that we will always have sinful tendencies because of our human nature.

However, if we can accept that there is no such being as Lucifer, Satan, or God, other than it representing ourselves, then it surely reflects on those demons (personality-aspects as well as group belief systems) around us that are pushing our buttons to do the things we fear the most.

Look, many of you believe that God gives us all the good things in life, and along comes the Devil and his army of demons to take it all away. My fellow searcher, even the Bible clearly teaches that God is the source of all power and yet, religion teaches that God does not sin.

If God is the source of all power then don't you think he would be responsible for both the good and the bad things in your life? Of course he would, which is why God, Jesus, and Lucifer are one and the same – for they represent the higher and the lower you, or the total you working to become a sovereign divine being in your own right.

In Isaiah 45:5-7, *"I am the Lord and there is no other, there is no God besides me. It is I who arm you, though you know me not, so that toward the rising and the setting of the sun men may know that there is none besides me. I am the Lord, there is no other; I form the light, and create the darkness, I make well-being and create woe; I, the Lord, do all these things."*

If God does all these things, then who do you think is creating your light and darkness? It is you! This is why when your wows or trials come your way, you should accept them as your creations, for they have come from you, the real God, and not blame your wows on some Devil or his army.

Look at Job 1:21, *"The Lord gave, and the Lord has taken away; blessed be the name of the Lord."* Understand that everything comes from you, the creator of everything you experience. It is your spirit that gives life to your creations, all creations, and not some demon or Devil outside of you. It is also you that can take it all away, even your cancer, your hardships, and many other trails.

My fellow searcher, you can pray and pray to a God outside of you to take your hurt away. However, if he doesn't, you can be assured that the hurt you are feeling is actually coming from you in order for you to see the wisdom (light) behind what you believe and choose to create. All that you have experienced, good and bad, since you left the first creation has been created by the "victim" and the victimizer," *you* – for you are both.

The demons are yours and yours only! It is just that you rather deny your demons and place blame on a fallen angel and his army of thugs that really don't exist. The moment you declare your experiences are coming from other people, the Devil, and his army of demons, the more alive the demons within you will take control of your life. The more your demons control you, the more attention you will give them, thereby placing all of your God power in the hands of other people as well as with your demon aspects.

Take note: There is no great evil spirit trying to steal your soul. There are no demonic groups that are trying to control you spiritually, financially, or emotionally. There are no banking groups or persons that are trying to take away your house, your furniture, your car, or your boat. There is no one responsible because you lack abundance, or you don't have a good relationship, or why you have a disease. There is no one trying to make you look bad in front of your boss or steal your job. There is not even anyone trying to ridicule or laugh at you.

My fellow searchers, all of these demons are yours. It is you that is the creator of everything that you feel and experience. Remember, you are, and always have been a Christ, and you have the authority of your spirit behind you. However, you gave away that authority because of your demons and your belief in a God that is not real.

You have placed yourself in a belief system that there is one God, one nation, one church, one race, and one gender that is above another. Because of this type of judgment, these demons have become the major weapons for stealing the authority and sovereignty of your soul.

Therefore, the limitations that you are experiencing today are caused by one of two beliefs that you hold as your truths: that the rational mind is the reliable source of your power, intelligence, and that it creates the authenticity of your reality. Or, that you have no authority in your life because you have given it all to someone or something outside of you, be it God, the Devil, religion, the government, family, or to your beliefs.

My dear friends, when will you wake up from your sleep and see that God does not ask anyone to fight, force, or kill another person over belief systems? When will you understand that God doesn't care if your religion is Christian, Islam, Hindu, Buddhist, Judaism, Atheist, or that you worship at all? The idea of fearing God and the Devil in itself has never come from God. It has come from mankind because you are the creator of your demons.

It is you, and all humans alike, who promote a type of understanding of God and the Devil that brings in war, hate, pride, lust for power, envy, greed, laziness, and the disregard for others. Christians talk about Judas betraying Jesus, not realizing the Judas' aspect within you represents the underhandedness of performing trivial or repetitive actions against your own "I AM Christ" self.

Remember, Judas carried the money bag (energy) for Jesus and the disciples. This signifies that your material desires and concerns are a legitimate faculty of the rational mind and how you understand your beliefs of good and bad. However, Judas' act of betrayal signifies how you, all humans, overstep the divine law and how you become your own betrayer and destroyer. You hang yourself all the time without even realizing you are doing it.

The only focus that the Judas consciousness displays is what is intellectually suitable and our search of physical means. This is because of the betrayal by our own rational mind presenting intellectual reasoning as being truth. Jesus knew (through this part of his mind) that he would be betrayed and yet, he made no effort to prevent the act of Judas. This is because of our own intellect or thought out (reasoned) beliefs about God and Satan will end up betraying us and yet, it is unwise to wholly destroy the intellect within ourselves before its time.

In other words, at its foundation, the belief in God and Satan is good for us. It serves its purpose until we awaken to the real truth. By religions and governments upholding a God of good and a Devil of evil, it guarantees them that we will not dare to question our beliefs or theirs until we are ready to face our own demons. This way religions of the world will maintain control of our energy, our free will, and our creations and reality until we humans finally accept that we are a God also, thus equal to him.

Of course, if you dare to move beyond this hypnotic state, then you are mocked by those who are a slave to the system, to their intellect, to their intelligence, and to their idea of what God wants for you. The big belief in Satan guarantees those in power in keeping you from trusting yourself from knowing your own Christ essence. It is this belief that keeps you separate from knowing that you have the power of Christ in your hand – for, my friends, your mind that sits at the right hand of God.

This belief in a Satan personality outside of you carries a great deal of doubt, fear, and death because the rational mind cannot understand the grandness that you are. The rational mind keeps you in a place of wondering what is right and wrong, who to blame for what you are experiencing, and what you don't have in life.

Of course, no one can take your soul for eternity. Oh, they can hold your soul in a belief system for a period of time but they cannot keep your soul for eternity. Eventually, you are going to awaken from your sleep state because the "order of Luceffa" (Lucifer) will see to it that you journey through many lifetimes working with the energy of opposites (good and bad) in order to see and work out your demons.

Once Lucifer, and group consciousness, helps you, as a human, to understand and acknowledge that your demons belong to you and that there is no outside influence that has control over you, that is when you will awaken to your own wisdom (light) and to the Christ you are. Therefore, there are no demons, Satan, or an army of devils that are going to consume you other than you doing it to yourself.

My dear friends before you can walk into new expansional energy (New Earth), you first must acknowledge who you truly are. You are a Christ that took on the role of being a demon a long time ago to learn wisdom. However, that role was all illusionary because the Christ portion of you could not sin. So, it took you, the creator, to create many lifetime stories where you took on many personality-aspects that dealt with opposites. Now, you are driven by the stories and lifetimes you have created because you believe them to be your reality and who you are.

These storied lifetimes became your demons, and now it is time to let them go. The energy of Lucifer is ready to shine your light of wisdom at the doorway of your human consciousness. Everything that you have been running from, hiding from, and fearing is nothing more than the energy of Luceffa helping you to awaken your Christ self from its deep sleep that it has been in for a long time in waiting for your human self to recognize it.

So, my dear friends, there you have it! There are many roads that lead to your "I AM God" self, as Archangel Luceffa and Jesus are just a couple of them. Yes, I know that some of you may be scratching your head right now just to see if you should even consider in what I described about "Lucifer" and how he took on the same role as Christ but in a different way. Of course, the reason why you might be scratching your head is due to the fact that you, as a human, are more than likely stuck with tradition.

You can say, because of religion, man loves the idea of a Devil. It actually gives him the avenue for not taking responsibility for his suffering. You know the routine! I guess it is better to complain and bitch about what we are experiencing or not getting in life than it is just to create what we want in life in the first place.

In 2 Peter 1:20-21, *"Know this first of all, that there is no prophecy of scripture that is a matter of personal interpretation, for no prophecy ever came through human will; but rather human beings moved by the holy Spirit spoke under the influence of God."*

You see, this verse even says that there is no Devil, Satan, Beast, Anti-Christ, or even this evil person of Lucifer that became Satan, at least as depicted by religion and how they use the name to control their followers.

The *"no prophecy ever coming through human will"* is nothing more than *you* cannot know God (the Christ that you are) through the will of the human mind because the "will of man" is tied directly to the belief that positive (God) and negative (Lucifer) are two different forces, thus two different entities, that battle each other for control.

The true God, and the identity of Lucifer, can only be understood and interpreted by you moving beyond the human rational mind and the belief that God is only good and the Devil is evil.

In addressing the words of, "*Rather human beings moved by the Holy Spirit spoke under the influence of God,*" means that of "human beings" are persons that have been awakened (moved) to their own divinity and spirit, and therefore recognize that their "Holy Spirit" is the source of their expressions (spoke) in bringing to life what is invisible to being visible. For example: Our soul giving life to our physical body, thus enabling us to experience something visible.

My dear friends, it has been, and still is, about learning "who you truly are" and "who you are not." Thus, "Archangel Luceffa" (Lucifer) made the pledge, as did Gaia and other Archangels, to help you see the wisdom of your choices by causing you to journey through many lifetimes learning about the principle of duality in order for you to see your creations first hand and how it affects you, your energy, and others.

By you journeying through time and space, lifetime after lifetime, the doctrine of good and evil becomes the measuring rod for your choices and your actions, which then determines your course of evolution.

So, who is bringing light (wisdom) to whom again? Is it Lucifer or is it Jesus? How about both? The Christ part of you, the real you, became the holder of what you desired to choose and manifest while the Lucifer part of you introduced you to the forces of opposites, sin, and karma. In other words, the energy of Lucifer helps you move through experiencing many opposites in order for you to experience both sides of the coin. This way, in the end, the energy of Lucifer becomes the "bearer of light (wisdom)."

Here is the kicker! Once the wisdom of your choices is known to you on a physical level, you then place yourself into a new expansional energy that comes from your own "I AM Christ" self, which of course is representative of Jesus, the Son of Man (or your outer deceptive mind becoming one with universal mind), and together they all become one with your divinity.

It is your soul (divinity) that holds your memories and then feeds them back to your deceptive and rational mind in order to make a choice of what story (lifetime) you desire to experience. However, your disobedient consciousness, symbolic of Lucifer, interferes and judges your choices and beliefs for you, which then causes you to take on a strong belief in judgment, a believer in right and wrong, and in karma (sin) to finally correct it. Therefore, until you awaken to this practice, every decision you make on earth is artificial and not genuine or true.

To add more about Jesus incarnating as a male was to remind you that it is the rational mind (son of man) that has the authority to master your choices and actions, and bring the total you into balance. Thus, the truths of God's kingdom and "all that was" and "is" are within you, for no real truth can ever be found outside of you or in any church.

If you take the idea of sin and Satan literally, then you are doomed forever. However, the wisdom of the Book of Genesis and that of the book of Revelation illustrates the real meaning of God, Satan, and who you really are. The wisdom of God and Satan is the belief that your everlasting (holy) spirit is the creator of anything disharmonious or what you call *sin*. As long as you hold that belief, you will "carry the guilt of your sin without end."

My dear friends, because of the perception about how "free will" works, your "I AM Essence" cannot free you from your disobedient nature unless you open up to your own demons (beliefs) and free yourself. You cannot free yourself unless your Lucifer consciousness helps you move past the belief that you are sinner and only a human. It is only *you* that can free *you*, but how can *you* forgive yourself if *you* cannot remember who *you* truly are?

Open your heart and feel your own "I AMness" telling you that you are more than human. Do not allow any religion or persons ever tell you that you are a sinner because you will always act in a way that supports what you believe to be. Why would you want to act like a sinner and continue to ignore who you truly are? You are a God also!

As long as you continue with the lie of there being a God and a Satan outside of you, and that one of them created you, then how can your sins ever be forgiven? Sins are only tied to duality. When you move beyond the belief that you must judge what is good and evil, the rational mind and your defiant nature (the false you and the beast) will open up to a new expansional energy of a divine nature.

This will awaken the Christ within you, elevating your disobedient physical consciousness to where you can embrace, embody, and meet your Christ consciousness in the mist of your ignorance by integrating the deceptive mind (the son of man) with your divine will (the Son of God), thereby becoming a true master in your own right.

Now, I do hope that this chapter has helped you to understand Archangel Luceffa (Lucifer) a bit better, and how he can bring to you a whole new world of wisdom, abundance, joy, health, and the know-how in letting go of your fears. When it comes to you moving into a *knowingness* of you being the God you seek. It is the first step in understanding how energy works and how you can transform the old energy of duality into a New Expansional Consciousness of four. The Bible labels it, the New Earth.

By moving into this *knowingness, wisdom,* and *understanding* about who you truly are brings to you what completes you as a Christ also. You become part of a foundation that sets the example for others, thus a servant to others. A servant that is not in the traditional fashion because of what the Bible declares. But a servant that becomes the standard for others to follow in becoming a sovereign being in their right.

My dear friends, when you come to this knowingness and become a sovereign being in your own right, you actually become part of an unlimited energy source in bringing in to your life what your heart desires to manifest and experience. It is just taking the time to learn who you truly are instead of relying on others to tell you who you are.

In the journey to reunite your disobedient Lucifer nature (physical self) with your divinity (Christ self), you had to move through many physical life experiences playing with opposites in order to make significant progress toward the understanding that you are the real Christ, and that Lucifer is the angel that brings to you this understanding in the end.

The fall of man was symbolic of the loss of your awareness of being a Christ also. That you purposely created this defiant and disobedient Lucifer consciousness where, in the end, you knew that it would bring to you the enlightenment needed for you to come back to your Christ "I AMness" again. There is no God who demands your worship and no Satan or Devil seeking to destroy you. It has been about experiencing the energy of opposites and the karma that comes with it in order to become a wiser and compassionate Christ in your own right.

Therefore, there are no messages here of fear, love or hate, right or wrong. It is simply a message saying that it is okay to let go of your old dogmatic beliefs that you have hung onto for so long. Your physical experiences on earth have been the playground for playing opposites, which has now transformed your Lucifer nature into a much higher and wiser consciousness (the Son of Man in the flesh). It was done through the manifestation of your beliefs into linear time and through the sensation of your emotions, neither of which exists beyond the physical realms.

My dear friends, the only Devil that exists is the one that was created by organized religion and those that want to believe he is a bearer of evil. If you have read my last two books, you would know that there is no person called Lucifer, Satan, or the Devil. These names are an aspect of those humans that choose to buy into this powerful lie in order to avoid taking full responsibility for their creations.

It is time to move past your demon gods and the idea of a Satan and his army living in hell, and move into a new consciousness of expansion, comfort, and health. The name "Lucifer," and the angelic family tied to the name, has the same meaning as the name in Christ because they both mean "Morning Star," the Bringer of Light," and the word Christ is the "Bringer of New Consciousness." Therefore, the man named Jesus and the angel of Lucifer are similar when it comes to helping mankind. It is just that they chose to help in different ways and yet, achieve the same results.

Every lifetime that we have had on earth, our Christ Identity has been part of every one of them. Therefore, our Christ identity can only be reached when we expand our consciousness beyond our mental and physical level. This is why God seems so elusive and mysterious because we try to access God through the rational mind.

Feel your spirit and divine self – for they are there waiting for you to call them into your physical lifetime of today. Realize that you have been hypnotized because your rational mind and physical consciousness has been connected to earth through magnetic and electrical impulses of positive and negative, duality thoughts.

By making the choice and acknowledging that everything has many, many layers, including your consciousness, which also means that you are multi-dimensional, then you are able to see more of what you call your reality. By exploring the multi-layers of yourself, you will see more than just your human self in the mirror. There is also something beyond your human self.

Just remember, other than food, clothing, and shelter, we all forgot about our soul consciousness, the real wisdom, and what we truly desire to achieve. The soul is not interested in our catalog of human "wants" that make us happy. The soul is more interested in the human part of us recognizing that consciousness, spirit, and wisdom together is everything.

From all that you believe that your human self needs to survive and be happy, and see it from the perspective of the soul, you begin to see what is important and what is not.

My fellow searchers, Lucifer's message to you today is not about hate or rebellion. It is about him taking your human identity on the path to meet up with your Christ identity. Yes, the time has come now to open up to your Lucifer consciousness and allow it to open the door to a new consciousness of understanding and wisdom. This consciousness leads to New Energy (New Earth) if you are willing to move past the idea of hell and brimstone – for that is what you have been experiencing ever since your first incarnation on earth.

What you see and feel right now is nothing but your fear of change. However, don't be afraid because everything does not appear as it seems. Feel the energy of Lucifer, or this mischievous spirit, this fallen angel, the bad guy, and the devil. But also remember, it was you that became the mischievous spirit, the fallen angel, the bad guy, and the devil that has played on earth. However, because of your dedication and devotion to your soul, your Lucifer consciousness has become the means and "the bearer or bringer of light" (wisdom) in the end.

My dear friends, Lucifer, like war, is about seeking peace, knowing thy enemy, and understanding one's objective. The belief in Lucifer, like war, is a choice that comes from the lower deceptive mind that belongs to the human race. The belief in Lucifer, like war, is the inability to recognize the divine you or the Christ you. Therefore, peace is not the opposite of war. It is the understanding of what is being played out by you, the creator. The lower you always battles against itself because it is incomplete and inconsistent with itself.

In closing this chapter, I would like to leave you with this thought. You have used the rational mind and your idea of God to concentrate on attaining your wishes of wanting to go to heaven, to be healed of your illness, and to be given the things that would make you happy. You live by the good book, you go to church, you pray for and help others, and what do you get back in return, nothing but stress and unhappiness. My dear friends, it is time to see what is important. Is it your dogmatic beliefs and your ties to your religion or what your soul is all about?

New Energy is here and now, and everything has many layers and dimensions to it, including you. So, begin to open up to some of these layers (personality-aspects of many) of you, and as your many aspects begin to come home to you, begin to observe your soul and feel how those other layers of you want to keep on asking for things to make them happy. As you play with this view, begin to observe how much more you truly are – for you are more than just your human identity playing on earth.

Take time to observe how your human identity is still rebelling and refusing to look past the disobedient human (Lucifer) personality because of the fear in what it might find. My dear friends, if you do take the time to do some deep breathing you will initiate this New Energy of Expansion within, and you will see for yourself how your little human self was trying to maintain its little empire (kingdom).

Chapter 17

How Energy Works

In order to understand how energy works and how it relates to your suffering, you must understand who you are, who God is, who Christ is, who Lucifer is, and that energy, before it is put into manifested form, is in a neutral unbiased state. Meaning, it has no positive or negative pattern or configuration to it until you, the real creator, shape it into something using your belief systems. Thus, if you remain unwavering in what you believe about God, Christ, Lucifer, good and evil, and that you are a sinner, then know that you have just limited yourself from receiving miracles in your life that could lead to health, joy, abundance, and great relationships.

Have you wondered why you experience the things you experience? If so, then the first thing you have to look at is what you believe about yourself, about other people, and about the material world around you. You see if you are looking for a desired outcome in regards to solving any situation in your life, whether it is an illness, a financial situation, or any adversity. Then know it becomes very important to review your belief systems because, after all, they are your truths. It is your truths that create your reality.

If you hate, dislike, judge, or disapprove of any person, or group of persons who do not think or believe like you do, let alone blame a devil that you don't even know, then what you will create for yourself is nothing but the same old experiences over and over. By overlooking this truth, you can end up repeating the same behavior patterns over and over all because of not being aware of who you are and how energy works around you. My dear friends, this is the mystery behind your continued suffering.

You have those that believe within their heart of hearts that they are working for God to help mankind. However, what they are overlooking is that God doesn't need help from anyone that is still playing with the lower vibrational forces of positive and negative as their basic truth. All that God needs is Archangel Luceffa (Lucifer) to mirror their own demons (beliefs) back to them as they journey through cycles of lifetimes playing with the belief in sin, and therefore creating for themselves a destiny of karmic experiences.

So, if you continue to fear Lucifer because of misunderstanding his purpose and what has been taught to you about him by religion and your parents, then the path to understanding how "energy works," and how it can bring miracles into your life, will be lost.

You have always been taught that life and God has a certain path for you to follow, a path that would lead you to hell if you did not learn your lessons. My dear friends, your path is not about "learning lessons." It is about experiencing your choices and accepting them as your creations, and then having the ability to understand the wisdom behind those choices.

If you are unwilling to explore the wholeness of who you truly are, who God is, and who Satan is, then how can you ever understand the mind of God and what lessons he wants you to learn? Look, you cannot ever understand the mind of God and what lessons he wants for you to learn if God, like Satan, has no mind of his own. For God, like Satan, is built on the principle of all souled beings as being one body of consciousness, including the human race.

Therefore, the best thing to do right now is take a deep breath, step back, and understand the perfect order of things, because you are the God that created your own divine plan to be sovereign.

As most people know, mother earth is housing about six billion souls, and what does man do? He worries about the survival of earth because of some global warming, the weather, earthquakes, and if he is going to have enough food and money to survive. If that is not enough, he worries about going to heaven if nothing works out. Man pollutes, abuses, makes war against his neighbor and yet, man cannot see that mother earth is far wiser than he thinks.

Mother earth (Gaia) knows how to take care of herself, for she is a spirit unto herself just like we are a spirit unto ourselves. It is just that we, as humans, see ourselves as a protector of earth and a warrior for God and yet, mother earth and God knows exactly what is needed to keep things balanced.

We, the people of the world, turn to politicians, governments, religion, family, big business, friends, and those in the know, looking for someone, anyone, to show us the way. We are so desperate to find a good leader to save us from ourselves because we are so afraid of what the future holds. However, in our search, what do we get? We get leaders that show their ability to stir up our emotions, give us hope, and inspire us to shift in their direction for our safety.

However, when they get into office to serve, they become part of the system that ends up nowhere. Their words sound believable to us. They speak with conviction and charisma from the podium. They speak on the radio, get on television, and they convince us that one political party is better than another. We even have those that hide behind the cloth telling us how God can fix everything if we would just do as they say and yet, all of them do nothing for us but perpetuate their own interest.

These people are not true leaders. They stick to the "old energy" of playing the game of good versus bad, right versus wrong, rich versus poor, God versus Satan, and one religion versus another, competing over who owns God and what he wants for us and from us.

My fellow searchers, the time has come to wake up from your sleep and see the world around you, for you and the world, have not been owned or controlled by some devil, Satan, or Lucifer. You, and the world, have been owned by all those people that seek power, control, and want to maintain their old ways by keeping you asleep. They tell you that it is the fault of the rich, big business, those of Wall Street, or it is the fault of the Democrats or the Republicans. Best yet! It is the fault of our sins and how we have moved away from God.

If I may, allow me to shed some light on the matter. It is not about Lucifer, God, Democrats, Republicans, or those that are rich, poor, or our religions, or even those that take advantage of the system. It is about us, or oneself, for we are the problem here. We stay very stubborn to our beliefs about self, about our government, and about our religion! However, it is us, as a group consciousness that is also the solution.

You see, when you are not accepting your own demons or taking responsibility for your own creations then what you are doing is leaving it up to some religion, politician, government, some rich person, a family member, or friend, to take care of it for you instead of taking responsibility for your own life. It is not even about a Devil trying to influence you in doing something bad. It is all about *you*, for you are the master leader in what you will experience in life.

Don't you think it is time to stand up to our leaders? Now, I don't mean by waging war against them or throwing rocks at them, or through the windows of businesses. In fact, we don't even have to protest, or show our face on the news, or even disclose our identity. All that we have to do is take several deep breaths, and then let go of the belief that we are a sinner, or that we are somehow Gods helpers in fixing things that we think are wrong. Even the thought that Satan holds some power over us and, that we need a savior in order to survive.

My dear friends, you do not need a savior or anything to survive. You do not even need God or the highest Archangel in the land. All that you need is to learn to look within yourself for the answers. For you are the true "I AM" that will never lead yourself down the road of hopelessness. Those that say that they have the answers are those that love to keep you occupied and focused outside of yourself.

It is time to take these false leaders down off their pedestals for they are of the "old energy" of conflict, fear, and confusion. Let us bring in new leaders. Those that understand that power, sin, God and Satan, are an illusion, leaders that are not looking to expand their pockets and their ego. Also remember, it is not about having to protest or declaring war on them. It is about becoming conscious and aware of what your responsibility is and what it is not. By doing this you will create the true leader within yourself.

When you begin to work as a conscious leader unto yourself, which can be done just by learning to take 15 to 30 minutes a day and breathe deeply, you will then allow energy to flow through you without trying to stop it because of your fixed beliefs, anger, and human wants. Know that the consciousness of God (the Christ within) versus the consciousness of the Devil (the lower you) always works from a spiral and continuous circle or cycles (lifetimes) that draws a force toward you that only sees duality as the basic structure of your beliefs and reality. This is an experience that feels so real, so solid, and that is the beauty of it, for it eventually brings to memory "who you truly are."

Because of our strong belief in a dualistic structure it becomes nearly impossible to bring in our divine essence (will) and put it together with our human essence (will). Why? It is because it will create a conflict within us right away, which is why we can see this being played out by our leaders and the mass. Therefore, our rational mind is the battlefield and we, as a human group, reflect that battle outward with our lies, our self-centered leaders, and the wars we see today.

As you know, this conflict between our divine essence (Christ) of no force and our lower deceptive mind that believes in duality, positive and negative, ultimately affects our physical body and what type of life is in store for us as a group consciousness to experience. The doubts, the fears, the controls, our dark creations, and our lack of understanding about how energy works, right from God to Lucifer, become the cause of our suffering and lack of miracles.

Remember, it is also not about Lucifer. Your rational mind is the ultimate place where hell and Satan exists, and you created it all for you to experience! Also, God and Christ is not about one super individual persona unto himself. God is the Goddess and the Christ within you, which is the make-up for all souled beings. Therefore, how can you understand God's mind if you don't even understand your own mind and how it works with the energy patterns of positive and negative?

Many of you go through each day hoping to find the solutions to your problems. However, you will never find the solutions because God himself cannot give you the answers. Now, why is that? It is because God is not there to give it to you. So, instead you look to science, friends, family, and some leader, religion and government, for the answers.

Look, have you ever heard God talking to you like other people claim God talks to them? I don't think so! To those that claim God speaks to you, telling you what to do, especially for you to use the forces of right and wrong as being the framework in what action for you to take, is actually talking to a false God. Why do I say that? It is because there is no such God that will take sides to any situation. The real God only speaks of things as you being the true "I AM God" and the "Lord of Lords" of your own choices, and the actions you take that follow.

Therefore, in retrospect of you being the real God here. Would you like to know "how everything works," which means you have the power to heal yourself. Actually, you will find it to be quite simple! All that you need to do is transcend your dualistic beliefs and move your consciousness beyond the old limited energy of positive and negative, and then awaken to a new understating about God and Lucifer, and what their relationship is to you. Because it is not what you think.

As a human, we are so used to looking at one layer of energy that holds a force of positive and negative, good and bad, and a God and Satan that are at war with each other over our soul. We have, over many lifetimes, become very comfortable with that belief all because of the way we, as humans, have gotten very comfortable with our belief that positive and negative, good and bad, is all that there is. We fail to see how energy actually works.

You see, we, as humans, have forgotten that we are always in motion, which is probably why most people believe that the world is going to hell. If it is not the world going to hell, then everyone on it is. My dear friends, we and the world are not going to hell. All that is happening is that energy is transforming itself from the old vibrational energy of two and moving into a new expansional energy of four, which means balance and completion for those that are ready to work with it.

This "new expansional energy" is the answer to all of our problems and prayers, as it is made up of:

1. Our Positive Consciousness (outer masculine illusionary self)
2. Our Negative Consciousness (inner feminine soul self)
3. Our Consciousness of no force, as it moves back and forth to light and dark without putting judgment on it; and

4. Our Gnost Consciousness, as it is also known as our Christ or Solution Consciousness. This consciousness heals and brings to us the miracles we seek. Also, keep in mind, our soul self is tied to our Christ Consciousness.

If you don't understand that energy and your core consciousness is of a neutral state, before you add your belief systems to them, and that you are a multi-dimensional being that has many behavior patterns to you because of those beliefs, then your human mind becomes very twisted and distorted when it comes to understanding energy, God, Lucifer, and yourself. Why? It is because you are God, Lucifer, and you use energy to serve you.

Since you are God, Lucifer, and your ego, you are, in truth, still one with your "I AMness." Therefore, because of your strong belief in duality and in sin, and that God and Satan are separate from you, you remain in a conscious focus that transforms the energy that you call in to serve you, as a creator, into nothing but opposing belief patterns for you to experience.

Since you are the multi-dimensional being that you are when you bring in this pure unbiased energy to pattern your creations, then those in power such as religion, government, businesses, family, and friends, lock you into a consciousness that only results in everyone and everything outside of you becoming your master in what you will manifest for your reality. This is what you are asleep too!

What you don't realize is that your human consciousness becomes owned and controlled by everyone around you as if you are a slave to them. These groups and more will keep you locked into repeating your creations over and over, all because of your belief patterns. You will do it by following their "will" and not your soul's "will."

My dear friends, you have chosen from a divine level the potential of learning the truth about life, energy, and who you truly are, and now you are experiencing how you got there. This is why there is no such thing as sin or a God that will associate itself to duality. All that is left now is for you to open up to your multi-dimensional consciousness and the belief patterns that each of them carries, for you are God, Lucifer, and yourself and yet, you are one and all of them.

Here is something that my soul opened up to me in my search for truth that I believe is very important to understand and therefore, I pass it on to you. "Consciousness, in its truest meaning, is a state of being aware of your beliefs and your thoughts" because you, as all humans, are programmed into believing that the rational mind is the "master of thoughts". Thus you are robotically programmed to disregard anything and everything of there being something beyond it.

Therefore, you are going to get stuck in a deceptive mind that only understands God and Satan as being limited only to an energy force of positive and negative, without ever becoming familiar with the real truth that consciousness has the potential to expand way beyond the rational mind and that of duality. The human consciousness, and how it has been programmed, deals with just one aspect of itself, and it tries to relate everything that you are experiencing to it from one dimensional phase, thus leaving out all other aspects of yourself from other lifetimes.

When you relate to whatever is happening in your life only to what you are experiencing in this lifetime, then the only outcome that can occur is getting frustrated to the point that you look for solutions outside of you. This can lead to repeating your creations over and over.

For instance: You are taught to always think positive because the experts say that positive thinking is the most important thing that will have an effect on your life. It will but only to a degree! However, in the end, it will have a negative effect too. Why? It is due to the fact that you cannot hold a positive thought by means of the rational mind continually because positive and negative always comes with judgment, fear, and confusion. Thus, it comes hard to control. Once you think you have control over something then sooner or later the reverse happens.

By not taking into account your many past lifetimes, or multi-dimensional self, your negative thoughts will eventually pop up out of nowhere to push you over into judgment, survival, and fear.

You see, no one can come from the rational mind and only stay with a positive or negative attitude for any length of time because eventually your belief systems of the past, and of your current lifetime, will catch up with you, limiting you only to a consciousness that defines you as who you think or believe you are. Don't forget, you come face to face with your choices and experiences every day, and that is when judgment, survival, and fear tend to come in unexpectedly.

What has been forgotten here is that you are a great ray of light sent forth from the Spirit of One before time began and now, you, as well as all souled beings, are the source that can create or uncreate just by choosing because creativity, and you being God like, is already part of your nature. Therefore, you create, experience, and express your uniqueness in a manner of you being a multi-dimensional being and not as a single personality for this lifetime only.

It has been a difficult journey and a long process to experience all of your various parts and pieces (personality-aspects). However, none of it was a test coming from God or Lucifer. It was about expressing and experiencing, and there is a difference. You see, a test is usually given by someone who knows the answers. Since God and Lucifer have no mind, other than the rational mind that comes from you, then it cannot be a test. It is an experience that you chose to learn, and in the end, the experience not only benefits you in human form but all souled beings as well.

What you have learned in the past, and what you are learning today from your many experiences playing the role of victimizer and victim, has been logged into your soul memory as wisdom and not as sin or as positive and negative. Sin, positive, and negative is an indication that "you do not know who you are."

When you look at the concept of reincarnation and how it has not been accepted because of those that love control and power, then let it be known that you have had many, many lifetimes where you did not understand what it was all about, until now. At first, because of religion, you believed that when you died, you would go to some heaven, hell, or somewhere in between, but instead you found yourself journeying through lifetimes playing out many different roles. You have experienced the dark and the light, and it all felt like you fell from somewhere but you cannot seem to remember.

So, after awhile, you came to believe that your day was laid out for you and now, you believe what the day holds for you is nothing but more suffering. My fellow researchers, the day has more to offer than what you think it holds for you, positive or negative. Why? Because of Archangel Luceffa (Lucifer)! As I mentioned before, Lucifer was never an enemy to you. Lucifer has the understanding that your physical lifetimes are on a pattern of cycles (positive and negative, good and bad), which allows him to jump into those cycles right along with you, helping you evolve those cycled patterns of death (unaware of who one is) to a new cycle that goes way beyond death. It is a cycle where you actually become free of your slave owners.

Ever since you moved away from your divine state (left the first creation), you have been on a cycle that follows an energy pattern of positive versus negative, good versus bad, right versus wrong, God versus Satan. Now, it is time for you to move into a new cycled pattern, a cycled pattern where you completely let go of the old you that is controlled by others and your dogmatic beliefs to a new you that understands who you are and your relationship to Christ, to Lucifer, and how energy works.

This new cycled pattern is about becoming a sovereign "I AM" being in your own right as you become aware that Luceffa (Lucifer) was the Archangel that always placed your demons in the doorway of your own consciousness for you to acknowledge and accept them as your creations. Once you accept your demons as your own creations, and then take responsibility for them, the archetypical energy of Luceffa drops his role because now you have become a Christ in your own right. Once Luceffa (Lucifer) drops this old role, you then begin to recognize him as the "bearer of light (wisdom)" instead of him being an enemy.

My fellow searchers, this is when Lucifer will ask you, "Am I still needed because it does appear like you are ready to become a Christ unto yourself?" So, if you are ready, then it is time for you to draw upon your own wisdom of experiences and change your cycle of death (the belief in good and bad, right and wrong) to a cycle of life, understanding, and wisdom (I AM Sovereign).

If you can draw upon your own light (wisdom), then the Archetypical energy of Luceffa will depart, and as a gift before his departure, he will leave you with the understanding of "how energy works." However, before he moves out of your consciousness altogether, he desires to give you a warning about the "consciousness energy of persuasion." Why? Because the "energy of persuasion" can lead you astray because of your fear to let go of the old energy of positive and negative, and that people are either good or evil.

This is why in Revelation 20:2, "*He seized the dragon, the serpent, and tied him up for a thousand years.*" "He" is about you coming into a knowing that you are the Christ, the "dragon," and the "serpent." You see, the "dragon" is referring to your rational mind where you believe in duality. The "ancient serpent" is your lower human disobedient nature not wanting to recognize the Christ part of you, which is symbolized by Lucifer or the "Devil."

My dear friends, it was you that embraced (seizing) the opportunity to move your consciousness outside of yourself. Then, you adhered (tied) to a rational mind (outer self) and a disobedient nature (serpent) that believed in duality (dragon) as being the real you. However, it took the rational mind and your disobedient nature to create many light and dark personality aspects (lifetimes) of you in order to gain the wisdom necessary to answer the question: "Who am I?"

You see, your Christ-spirit (the I AM within) had to restrict (tie) your rational mind (dragon), your disobedient nature (Satan), and your many light and dark ego personality aspects (lifetimes) of you "for a thousand years" (symbolically speaking) to position you in to taking a journey through three cycles of influences, spirit, mind, and its physical component, the human you.

The number one of the "one thousand years" signifies that you have always been a spirit unto yourself. You just took on a belief system that you were not. The first cycle (circle) was where you played in the divine oneness in the beginning of your awakening in spirit.

The second cycle (circle) is when you moved beyond your divine state (the first circle) and moved into a cycle of having an etheric and physical form that played with duality.

The third cycle (circle) is where you learn to integrate all your parts and pieces of yourself and become a sovereign "I AM God" in your own right. Therefore, the one thousand years is a sacred number and not to be taken literally.

Think about it, spending millions of years on earth playing in many different physical bodies and only having one thousand years of peace. Don't you think you are missing the point here? The number one can also signify that everything influences everything because everything is interconnected. After all, everything is one. The essence of life, the collectiveness of the mass, life in every dimension and every form, the total energy of "all that was," all of these things, including you and me, are part of "all that is today."

Now, even though every soul participated in the creation of everything visible and invisible, not every soul has experienced the earth's physical realm. There are many, many souls from the 144,000 different souled groups waiting to see how we volunteers do, waiting for us to show them the way. Believe it or not, we humans on earth are the bravest of all the angels because we all agreed to forget who we are in the quest to bring wisdom and compassion to "all that is" now.

This is why you are a unique and valuable angel, no matter what you think you have done or what station you feel you hold in life. Of course, included in the third zero is about you coming into a new expansional energy (new world) and an awakening while still in the flesh because the first and second cycles are now no longer part of your life, for you have integrated them.

Why? Because now you know who you are? This is what comes after you have journeyed through the first and second cycles (circles), gaining incredible wisdom from your experiences and learning responsibility and compassion. At this point, you move beyond the forces of duality, finally remembering your true identity as a Christ also.

After completing the first two cycles (circles) in not knowing who you are, and with the stuck energy of duality as your companion, symbolized by the one thousand years of being tied up, you enter the third zero and become a complete and sovereign "I AM Christ" in your own right. Now you can create your own universes, dimensions, and realities without experiencing duality. In other words, create your own world according to who you truly are instead of who you think you are.

The rapture in Revelations signifies you coming full circle, which means you can now release all thoughts of destiny and karma (sin) and ascend into a new heaven and a new earth that offers these experiences:

1. Magical energy of healing, abundance, and joy

2. Knowing that you are part of the Christ-Consciousness

3. The balancing of duality, positive and negative, everything is in harmony and unconditional

4. Access to the divine solution-energy of gnost

The journey through the three cycles (three zeros) becomes part of your spirit (Christ self), rational mind (the Anti-Christ), and your disobedient nature (the Beast) and yet, all three levels are as one body of consciousness, for everything you experienced, except for your soul and the wisdom you have learned experiencing them, is an illusion.

My fellow searchers, your soul consciousness is filled with memories of all that you have learned and now, all that is left is for you to tap into your own divine consciousness and reap the wisdom of those experiences. Then you will enter into the third cycle (circle) and become a true "I AM Christ" in your own right just like Jesus (Yeshua) did.

When you awaken to "who you truly are," your outer rational mind (the illusionary you) and your disobedient nature (the serpent) are no longer the controlling factors in your life because now your energy frequency has risen to where you can now work from the wisdom and understanding of your gnost-consciousness. It is from your gnost consciousness that brings in your magic and the miracles you desire to experience.

When said in Revelation 20:3, that Lucifer is "to be released for a short time." It means that, once you move out of duality control (2-D and 3-D energy frequency) and into your new consciousness of awareness of "who you truly are" (4-D and 5-D energy frequency), it will take a little time for you to fully grasp that you no longer need the outer rational mind to control things in your life.

In other words, it may take some time to get used to being free from your 2-D rational mind and 3-D ego personality controlling everything in your life. After all, you have spent perhaps thousands of lifetimes fearfully and emotionally believing that you were part of a dualistic force, a human family, and that your rational mind was indeed the king of intelligence, judgment, and truth.

My dear friends, you know the story of God telling Adam and Eve to avoid the tree with the fruit of knowledge of good and bad, for they would surely die if they ate from it. As you know now, it is evident that this is not a real tree. It is merely your soul telling you that once you shared your "divine will" with your disobedient personality (serpent), you, in fact, did loose (die) your connection to your spirit (God). Thus, you ended up losing your divine will to an illusionary free will that is tied to a deceptive and rational mind, which is again symbolic of the anti-Christ.

If you continue to believe, from an intellectual level, that your name on the birth certificate is all that you are, then you will continue to cut yourself off from the source of life (soul). This will cause you to revolve (cycles of lifetimes) in a mental whirlpool where your dominant beliefs recognizes duality, good and evil, birth and death, as being real.

So, this is why Lucifer gives you this last warning. He is telling you that the only thing real about you is that you are Spirit Consciousness first and foremost, thus everything else is an illusion that was created by you in order to learn the wisdom and understanding of "who you truly are." Once you accept the truth that you are the Christ coming out from behind the clouds of your own ignorance then a new road to the future is created. This road has no struggles, obstacles, or hidden traps. In fact, it isn't even a mystery.

You see, human consciousness is changing. If it wasn't, I would not be able to write this book. Look, human consciousness is at a very delicate phase right now because of the chaos we are feeling around us. This is why we see many out there channeling masters from the angelic realm. Of course, there are many individuals that don't want to hear what they have to say because they are afraid to move forward in their understanding of God and themselves. In other words, they fear God more than the Devil.

However, there are enough humans on Earth who are ready and willing to move beyond their old dogmatic ways of thinking, which is why the masters are coming through to those that are open to them, including the energy of Yeshua (Jesus) and Luceffa.

My fellow searchers, many of you are leaving the confines of your old dualistic structured energy of two to a new expansional energy of four. The Bible calls it, the Old Earth passing away and the New Earth coming in. What Archangel Luceffa is talking about here is that you are feeling this "new energy of expansion" coming in and you may not like it because it feels weird to you. It is because of this weird feeling, the "energy of persuasion" has you feeling that you need to return to the old ways and stay with your old idea of God and Luceffa being enemies.

You know this to be true because you can feel this "energy of persuasion," together with your emotions, pulling at you to throw down this book and return to your old ways of understanding God and the Devil. However, there are some of you that can see this "energy of persuasion" as it comes in through religion, the media, advertising, governments, the internet, your place of work, and even from your family members, as they all work hard to keep you under their control (old beliefs).

This "energy of persuasion" is very strong and all around you, and all that you have to do is stop and feel it. When you do, it feels as if you need to resist, for it has the tendency to draw you in. Of course, the best remedy to overcome this "energy of persuasion" is to allow yourself to feel it.

So, don't run from it. Just understand and know why it is there. Of course, by taking deep breaths every day it will help create safe energy around you. Remember, it is about letting go of your old ways of thinking and then choosing to move beyond this "energy of persuasion" to this "new energy of expansion of four."

Archangel Luceffa, your soul, and the Masters know that you have to let go of so many things right now and it can be painful to you, not only of the physical body, but of the heart because of emotions. Overcoming old belief patterns of good and evil, God and Satan, especially when it comes to family, friends, and religion, it can affect anyone on an emotional level in such a way that you may find yourself compromising what you have just embraced.

You see, if you find yourself compromising with your new awakening to keep peace in the family, then you could find yourself working with the same issues over and over again. Issues pertaining to old belief patterns between you and your family can keep on coming back to you even stronger until you learn that compromising with your new understanding of God is not going to work. Why, because it will prevent you from moving forward into this "new expansional energy of four."

The more you compromise with who you truly are, after being exposed to who you truly are, the more fear you will build up within to where you create an even bigger demon than it was before. You will never understand "how energy works" or how to create miracles in your life if you keep on compromising the point of you being a Christ also, which is why it is important to understand that you are equal to God, Jesus, and all of the Saints, and not that you are an underling to them.

Take the time to allow yourself to feel the essence of your own Christ identity within and follow your own heart. That is where you will come to know how energy can serve you as it will flow easily. This way the forces of positive and negative will have less of a hold on you.

Now that Luceffa (Lucifer) has gotten his warning out to you about the "energy of persuasion," let's move onto understanding "how energy works." However, before we start, you need to understand what it means when you hear our religious leaders say to us that the Bible holds all the secrets of life, including our suffering.

When we get confused about life the first thing we do is look back to our religious studies in hope to find the secret behind our suffering. My dear friends, the Bible holds no secrets! It was written for the times and now, the potential in resolving old issues is here and now. Look, according to my soul, the secret is not in the Bible, the secret is within each and every individual!

For instance: Most of you are familiar with the man Jesus, even though the name Jesus was not his real name. Jesus' real name was Yeshua Ben Joseph. His name was changed by the ruling kings of the world after his departure from earth. However, since everyone knows him as Jesus, I will address him as Jesus in this book to prevent confusion.

Anyhow, Jesus did not come to earth to teach us about God. Jesus came to earth to teach us that we are all Gods and about how energy works. Jesus was not even a religious man as depicted by religious scholars. Jesus was a doctor of energy that learned how to heal the human body by teaching his patients (those that he came in contact with) about how energy worked. His talents and skills were in the framework of manipulating energy for healing purposes.

Jesus traveled to many places, Israel, India, Africa, Egypt, the Middle East, and many other places, to learn about the physical body in order to become a "doctor of energy." Actually, Jesus was before his time when it came to understanding energy and the human body. Also, Jesus was not poor or destitute either as religions describe him, for Jesus had charged for his services.

My fellow searchers, there were many lies put on Jesus because everyone was afraid of him, including the governing rulers and religions of the time. You see, since Jesus had the ability to understand how energy worked and it scared those in power because they were afraid of losing their power, which is why those that were healed, those that knew him, and those that had seen him work with energy perceived him as a God like being.

So, after Jesus' death, these governing rulers felt it better if Jesus looked to be a religious champion sent down from heaven. This way the rulers of the world, and those of the cloth, could maintain their power over the mass by keeping everyone looking at Jesus as a divine being sent down to earth by God. However, what Jesus did over 2000 years ago was not so much about Him healing the body with some type of magic. It was about Jesus explaining to his patients that they had the ability and the potential within themselves to rebalance and rejuvenate their own body, mind, and spirit.

You see, the first thing in understanding energy is that you must recognize that your core essence is of Spirit Consciousness and that you are a divine being first and foremost that holds the authority (power) to create and manifest whatever you please, even the human body. This also means that your core essence is of no form, which also means that you, like Jesus, are not of this world also.

In truth, you don't even have belief systems. Belief systems are what you use to determine what you like to create and manifest. It is that you, as all souled beings, use pure energy and belief systems to experience your creations, and not that you are made of energy. Therefore, since you are not made of energy then the way "energy works" is actually relatively simple! Energy always mimics or copies itself. Let me repeat this! Energy always mimics or copies itself!

You see, since energy is pure and universal then look at it like a river of water flowing freely down in its channel without any obstruction or barriers stopping it from flowing. However, once you, as all humans do, dam up the river with your rational mind of reason and judgment. Then the free flowing waters (pure energy) begin to build up on its river banks causing the river (pure energy) to take on a new shape, like you taking on form for example.

You see, and I reiterate here, in the beginning, the "oneness of Spirit" was "all that was." Some of you called it Home, Heaven, God, the Spirit of One, or just Spirit. Nowadays, you have many names representing this "Oneness." Anyway, no matter how you look at this "oneness," in the beginning, it was the core essence of "all that you are today," including this pure neutralized universal energy of no force that you, and most humans, happens to identify as God.

In that moment of long ago, the core essence of this "Oneness of Spirit" called in this pure energy of neutrality of no force. Once it did, it mimicked itself (copied itself), and then it expanded, and then re-created itself into many aspects of itself. It was an amazing achievement to proficiently re-create itself in its own image so it could see who it was. Therefore, the "Spirit of One" now sees itself as all souled beings. Thus it was you, me, and all of us souls (the children of God) that became conscious in that very moment of long, long ago, as being the Godhead.

Because of that act, you, as all souled beings, are now an "oneness unto yourself," which means each and every souled being (you and I) has a piece or portion of the "Spirit of One" that makes all of us humans a "spirit of one" also. See Luke 17:21: *"For behold, the kingdom of God is within you."* John 10:34-36: *"Jesus answered them, "Is it not written in your law, 'I said, "You are gods".*

Thus, without us, as humans, realizing it, and since we are all a divine being, we too use this pure neutralized universal energy of no force in all of our creations and manifestations. Also, this neutralized energy of no force can never be stolen, or taken away, and we cannot even give it away if we tried. Why, it is because we have, as part of our core essence, the energy of the "Spirit of One" within each of us right now. We may not think so but it is there buried deep within our layered multi-dimensional consciousness (the ego aspects of self).

The explosion that science and religion have told us about creation, and how it was formed, is nothing more than we, as souled beings (gods), playing with this pure universal energy of no force, expanding it, and then producing every potential imaginable for us, as souls, to experience. This was what the "wall of duality," and that of the Atom, was all about, as it pulled all of us souled beings through it as if we had no choice.

Of course, we did choose to move through this "wall of duality" because of the question we asked ourselves, "Who am I?" It is just that we had forgotten that we made the choice.

So, here you are as a direct copy of the "Spirit of One," which again means you are a "spirit of one" unto yourself also that has created a soul identity. You are a divine being unto yourself that ended up creating a Christ like being, and now you have the same authority or power, supremacy, sovereignty, and creatorship ability as the "Spirit of One," and therefore equal to Jesus.

This means you, with the help of all souled beings acting together as one unit (God), manifested all of what you see around you today, including your coherent and rational mind and physical body. If you can understand this from the rational mind level, then you can imagine the miracles that you can bring into your life.

My fellow searchers, you are part of the big "oneness," for the "Spirit of One," who you call God is no longer an "oneness" unto himself but is a "oneness" that has taken up the identity of all souled beings (you, me, and everyone else). Therefore, since you are the "Spirit of One" in disguise, then you too can call in this pure neutralized universal energy of no force and create as many "personality-aspects" of yourself and, at the same time, produce multitudes of potentials, good, bad, and that of a new expanded energy, for you to experience.

In other words, we, all souled beings, take this field of pure universal energy of no force and we re-create it to shape our consciousness of our own "I AMness" to take on any form we wish. Let it be physical or non-physical, male or female, bad or good, and even a form of health or unhealthy. It is all up to each of us. However, and this very important to understand, at its core it still remains pure and neutral, which means you can change, adjust, or replace your physical body, even to the point you can rejuvenate your physical body.

Therefore, the core principle of energy is that it has no force to it, and we, as humans, have to learn to evolve that formed or trapped energy part about us back to its original form of neutrality in order for it to flow freely. By learning to free ourselves from our stuck energy, for illnesses and beliefs of all kinds, are nothing but stuck energy, it then sets up the rejuvenation process in your body to heal itself.

Let me expand on this: Since you, as all souled beings, used this pure universal energy of no force and became a carbon copy (a mirror image) of yourself. You then created every possible situation imaginable of an opposing nature that could ever happen, like be a male or female. You also created a potential where you could create out of thin air "new energy" that expands beyond the customary dualistic energy of positive and negative.

Of course, in order to reach this potential, we had to devise a plan to create a structured physical body and universe, including earth, that would become our encoded path (DNA) and predictable choices of experiences in order for us to evolve back to our original oneness of no force once again. As a result, this allows us to move into this "new expansional energy of four."

In other words, the "law of destiny" and "Archangel Luceffa" (sowing and reaping, cause and effect, what goes around comes around) became the vehicle for all of us to evolve back to our own "spirit of one" that holds all the wisdom of our choices and experiences. Thus, eventually bringing us back to a thought pattern that carries no force to it. Not even positive and negative.

You see, from these billions and billions of potentials that we all created together a long time ago, the greatest and grandest potentials we, as souls, chose to express and bring into our life to experience first was "belief systems," and with the creation of it, came the belief in duality. Through belief systems we found that we could structure our creations in a manner where they feel very real to us. So real that we could lose ourselves in our own creations, which we did.

Therefore, it is your dogmatic belief systems that are preventing you from rejuvenating your physical body because you are not accepting "who you truly are" and "how energy works." You see, once you understand "who you truly are," and that you have the oneness of your own divine essence, you would actually see and understand that you did expand your consciousness to the point where you re-created yourself into something you were not.

The human body that you find yourself in is not the real you. The real you has been layered and layered with many images (copies) of yourself because of belief systems, which is why you suffer in life. Now, because of energy having to come back to its original form of pureness and oneness again, you journey through many lifetimes peeling away those copies (personality-aspects) of yourself that have become stuck in a belief that you are only human.

Remember, you are a God in your own right, and you have always been looking to explore all possibilities of life, but you also must remember that you have the tendency to use pure energy in such a manner that it becomes stuck within you. Since energy has to evolve and come back to its original form of neutrality, then your spirit, rational mind, and body, have to evolve and come back to their original form of neutrality and oneness as well.

This is why you question yourself in regards to why you experience things over and over, even the whys of having to experience diseases, be financially broke, and many other calamities. You may have even asked yourself the questions: "Why can't I be healed, win a lottery, or just have things go well in my life?" Or, "What is holding everything back from me being happy and healthy?" Of course, when you asked these questions, either to yourself, to someone else, or through prayer, you seem surprised when things don't go well, or if you don't hear what you want to hear.

Look, your physical body, and all that you believe you need in life to survive, is made up of nothing but energy, even though at your core you are not made of energy. It is that you, as a God also, use pure universal energy for your creations, and once you consign a potential and a belief to it, it takes on a force of either being positive or negative. The reason for it taking on a creation of positive or negative! It is due to you having a strong belief in positive and negative that reaches as far back to your beginning stage where you moved your focus outside of your divine state (the first circle).

Since your physical body has the make-up of a dualistic energy force, because of your beliefs, you have the tendency to believe that everything, including God, is in a state of having two parts, one positive (good) and the other negative (bad). Therefore, it is the doctrine of opposing forces where good and evil always determines the course of your thoughts, beliefs, and the actions you place on this pure unbiased energy coming into your consciousness for expression.

So, knowing from a soul level, that energy has to evolve back to its original form of oneness and neutrality we, as souls, chose the path of evolution (soul growth) as the means to move forward in our quest to answer the question, "Who are we?" It was from this question we chose to follow the path of opposites. This way, when our energy got stuck, because of forgetfulness being part of our consciousness, we knew that energy would go back into itself to explore the reason for it being stuck. Hence, this is where our diseases, suffering, and imbalanced cells in the body come from, for it brings to our attention the question, "Why me?"

You see, what is the first thing we do as humans when we develop a deadly disease, have a bad accident, find ourselves broke, lose our home or job? I am sure there are many other things that could happen to get our attention. However, the first thing we all do, other than praying, is reevaluate our life. We all begin to ask the why of it all and what caused it. Well, the answer is quite simple!

Understand that energy, like water, in its beginning stages, has no force to it. Energy always begins in a natural or free flowing state, until you, the true creator, take on a desire to experience something. Once you make the choice to experience something that is when you call in to yourself many, many potentials that exist in a state of neutrality, for they exist outside of your core essence.

You see, they are potentials that can be brought in by *you* to be lived out, which is why your *spirit* is the source of all energy and not the rational mind or the human body. This is very important to understand. It is your spirit that calls in the pure energy needed to experience the things you choose to experience. This also means that your spirit can bring in the energy required to bring you wealth, understanding, and even the energy to rejuvenate your physical body back into balance, thus a healthy state.

The reason why many of you are not healed of your diseases, or that everything stays the same, is that you believe that your soul, spirit, and your core essence are made up of energy, and that you are only human. This is not the case at all! It is that pure energy is brought into your human reality through belief, desire, and passion.

However, once you bring pure energy in, it passes through your rational mind because of it being part of the second creation. Therefore, if you have the tendency to believe in good and evil, or sin, then you contaminate (adulterate) this pure unbiased energy coming into your body in such a way that the energy ultimately becomes stuck, thus creating all kinds of problems.

You see, it is the desire and the passion of your soul to experience as much potentials as possible in a lifetime. It does not matter to your soul what you experience as long as you are choosing something to experience, good, bad, or evil, for it simply doesn't matter. Since it is your soul that calls out for pure energy to experience things then understand that your soul has different beliefs, desires, and passions than your human ego self.

In fact, your soul's beliefs, desires, and passions have nothing to do with your human life because your soul operates on a higher state of consciousness. This is why your soul doesn't understand or care about your human list of wants (prayers) because all that they do is keep your energy stuck. What is relevant to your soul is the experiences you choose, the expressions you put into form, and the wisdom found in the experience of it all. It is about your soul desiring to seek its freedom and sovereignty while your human self is here on earth listening and following those that believe they have all the answers to your problems, including how to save your soul.

This means the connection to your soul's desire of becoming free and sovereign has no connection what-so-ever with your human desire to be healed from poverty, diseases, sadness, or anything else that seems to be wrong with you. Of course, my hope in writing this book is to change that type of thinking.

So, if you look at your human self and how you call in energy to create what you desire to experience, then you can understand how your soul will bring to you that energy in a raw neutral state. Once this raw neutral energy of no force is brought down to the human level, it then aligns itself with your layered beliefs of many lifetimes past, eventually mimicking itself (energy that is) to adapt to its new lifetime beliefs, and with the environment of two parts, positive and negative.

In other words, when pure energy comes into your life it automatically takes on the similar energy patterns that you are already experiencing right now. For instance: If you are experiencing poverty, illness, or some other calamity, like a disease, then this pure energy you bring into your life will automatically take on the same pattern as the old energy, positive and negative, which is why you journey the same road of suffering over and over. Why, because you believe in good and bad, right and wrong, and most of all, sin and a devil that is forever after you.

Maybe now you can see why, we, as humans, repeat our history. We never learn to look within ourselves to find the cause of what we are experiencing. Instead, we look outside of ourselves to government, religion, family, friends, science, and a God outside of ourselves for all the answers, even our cures to our diseases. We just cannot understand and accept that we are the creator of our disease, accidents and our greatness in life. There is no such thing as an accident or someone becoming rich overnight without one creating it for themselves.

So, if you continue to believe that you are not the creator of your own accidents or what you are experiencing today, then this pure energy you bring into your life will always follow the old pattern of duality. This pure energy of neutrality will always mimic what you, the creator, believe to be true for you. Therefore, you will keep on experiencing the same things over and over until you finally learn to let go of the belief that you are only human and alone.

However, if you can move past the idea of being only human and alone, and see yourself equal to God, for you are a Christ too, in every way with no exceptions, then you are ready to change the repetitiveness of the energy coming in, and therefore your experiences.

For instance: Let us take the cells in your body. Your cells are all particles of energy that have been brought in from this field of potentials of pure raw neutral energy and, when you first brought these perfectly healthy cells into your physical body they were free of any disease. But, because of your strong belief in duality, these new cells will mimic the old cells in taking on the same energy pattern. Therefore, if you have a disease, like cancer, then all those new healthy cells will mimic your old cancer cells, thus the energy of cancer becomes the prevailing force in the body, no exception.

You see, once these new healthy cells become part of your physical body, they begin to communicate with the other cells that are already there. If you have diseased cells, then the new energy cells will take on the same pattern as the diseased cells.

Science says that our body changes every seven years. This means that billions and billions of cells in our body have died and new ones have taken their place. However, how is it that our scar or some illness that we have had for years and years still remain? Well! It is because of what I just mentioned above.

You see, every part of you is connected to every other part of you, including all those other "personality-aspects" (lifetimes) of you living in other dimensions. All the parts and pieces of you are communicating to some degree with each other. Oh, you have some parts of you that die off but when they do, they truly don't die. They either integrate with you, the creator, or they move off into some dimension waiting for their turn to integrate. This means that you have all around you many, many potentials, parts and pieces of you that have the ability to rejuvenate energy on your behalf.

In other words, if energy mimics itself, expands, and then re-creates itself, then you, as a human, have the ability to bring in this new energy of neutrality and have it communicate to the old sick cells and rejuvenate themselves to being healthy cells. If you can accept yourself as being a Christ too and that your soul is the prime creator of pure raw energy, and then allow this wisdom to follow through to all parts and pieces of you, this neutralized energy that comes into your physical body will take on the pattern of your new belief. This is what brings healing.

This new belief, without any doubt on your part, followed through with deep breathing, will actually set your life straight and put you on a course that can bring you great abundance and happiness. It is your consciousness that activates energy and energy potentials all the time. If your consciousness is only focused on this very linear and limited physical dimension, then all that you will do is repeat what you are experiencing right now. The choice is yours!

Your rational mind doesn't see the other things that are moving in and out of your reality because your rational scientific mind is not geared to expand beyond what it knows as its truth. When you finally make a choice to open your rational mind, heart, and awareness beyond duality, then things will change. Of course, the first thing to change is how you perceive and judge things.

Hmm! Keep this in mind! You are highly trained already to focus your consciousness on this reality, and therefore it becomes very important for you to move past this type of thinking. You know this to be true because you can feel it in your heart that you have locked up within you a belief that has lived its course. Now, it is time for you to free yourself and move into a higher state of awareness.

It is about making a choice, sitting quietly and taking deep breaths at least 15 to 30 minutes a day, and then allowing the shift from old to new happen within you without putting a force onto it. Once this is done, it allows this "new expansional energy" to make things happen for you, and as you know now, it is different than the old energy of positive and negative.

In the old energy, if you force or perform in a certain way (good or bad, or like visualizing what you desire), you know basically what the reaction will be, thus predicting the outcome. Those in power know that certain things happen in a certain fashion, that it is repeatable and predictable, which is why it is important to them to keep you in fear and focusing outside of yourself to a God that really doesn't exist.

My fellow searchers, I know that this concept about energy has to be worked on because it is something that has to be developed and expanded by you, the real creator. However, this "new energy of expansion" is all around you now, and the only thing left for you to do is learn how to tap into it. The choice has to be yours if you have the desire to let go of the old.

All I can tell you is that you have both the old and the new energy around you in a neutral state, waiting to be activated by you, the real creator. Of course, once you become aware that there are many parts and pieces of you, it becomes much easier to activate the energy you require to help you in life the way you want to experience it.

Chapter 18

Understanding Your Soul

Religions teach that we have a soul but a soul that cannot be understood in a positive or in a pure way because it cannot be seen or witnessed. Religions supports the concept that as long as we are alive here on earth the soul is with us but once the body dies the soul departs, either moving on to heaven, to a place of torment and anguish, or somewhere in-between. For this reason, the soul is seen by mankind in a more negative way more than a positive because of the way we, as humans, have been taught by our religious upbringing.

Religions also declare that the soul is what causes the body to grow and have animation because without the soul the body would deteriorate and die, which is partially true. It is the spirit that injects the life force into the soul that animates the brain-mind and the ego personality (human body) into taking action for the sole purpose of soul growth.

Most adults, because of their religious nurturing, believe evolution has never played a role in shaping mankind. However, according to creationists, those who believe that God created everything also believe mankind was created fully formed with having no previous related life or biology that belonged to other species of the past. For instance: Man evolving from the ape. Religion holds the belief that there are some parts of nature that are too complex and confusing to be explained away by evolution, and therefore must be the handiwork of an intelligent designer.

However, what might be overlooked by religion and creationists is that evolution could be God's tool for soul growth. Many scientists and some of our religious leaders would admit that it is perfectly logical to think that a supreme being would use evolution as a method to create the world for man's soul growth. How else could man get to know who he is, the wisdom he possess, and the choices that he makes?

According to the angelic realm, the earth was formed about 4.5 billion years ago, and that life appeared upon it about 2.5 to 3 billion years ago compared to the belief of the creationists where man first appeared on earth less than a hundred thousand years (100,000) ago. Therefore, who do you believe is right, is it religion, science, or the angelic realm?

From my soul to yours, the Bible should not be taken as factual proof when it comes to the creation of the earth and when man first appeared upon it because of its often contradictory verses. The Bible needs to be read allegorically in relationship to the soul, earth, and all that is upon it, as it gradually evolves. Of course, scientists will not completely rule out the abstract thinking of a supreme creator because it takes science to answer the "how" questions and religion to answer the "why" questions.

My dear friends, why is there an earth, a universe, a galaxy, or even humans anyway? Why is it that most people believe that religion is in a better place to answer this question than science? If any of you have read the Bible, then you would know that religion is about ethics, beliefs, and faith in a white male God while science is all about what is truth and what is not, as both in a way, is all governed by logic and rational thought.

However, even with all the differences between science's thought on evolution and religion's belief on intelligent design, there is one thing that they both overlook. We, as humans, like all other living things, are a product of over four billion years of evolutionary progression. We have been shaped and broken up by the measure of our soul's study of itself, and by the continual interplay among our own biological bodies in different lifetimes.

We, as souled beings, are the unspecified and nameless intelligent designers that have chosen to evolve through the process of evolution, and not that we are a product of a white male God or a product of an Ape. We, as souls, are a product of a series of learning experiences that are designed to repeat itself using the human body as a prototype until it gets to know itself and what its purpose is.

Therefore, religion is correct as far as there being an "intelligent designer" but fails to recognize the "intelligent designer" as being you, me, and all souls alike that are equally acting together as the Godhead in forming a divine plan to know ourselves. However, science is also correct in their theory by saying mankind evolves as a species. Yet, like religion, they too fail to recognize the "intelligent designer" behind the species evolving. Science and religion always looks outside of themselves for the answers.

It is not that mankind evolved from the ape or any animal. It is about your soul learning how to intermix with materialism in order to emphasize the soul's divine sovereignty through the mental nature of the mind that occupies a physical body. To do this, it takes several lifetimes of soul growth, maturity, and experiencing with self and others.

We, as souled beings, have gone through many versions of ourselves in developing our brain-mind, spirit, and physical body. Even to the point where we finally emphasized brains or mind over brawns, which gave us language, creativity, reason, curiosity, and the most complex social system that we can ever imagine, including the illusion of money having power.

For instance: Because of how we developed our mind through time we, as humans, took on the belief that "like attracts like" or "thoughts of good and evil attract thoughts of good and evil," which was delivered to us by our religious leaders. Therefore, we can also say in what we reflect or assign to money then attracts to us what we understand about money. It is the same way with religion! If we assign power to money in the same way we assign power to religion then we are assigning how much power religion has over us. This would be the same for governments, family, family, and businesses.

My dear friends, it is not that money has power or is the root of all evil. It is that we, as humans, give money, through our belief systems, the illusion of it having power just like we give away our own power to religion. Money, like power, changes our thoughts about who we truly are and gives it to those that say we must fear God, which is why most of us don't have money.

When religion teaches us that money is the root of all evil they are actually teaching us to attract to ourselves the fear of not having money. It is not that most of us lack money. It is that we lack the understanding of who the source is. If we look at money and earth as conditional, then how can we look at a God as being unconditional?

When we hold a belief system in a God of unconditional framework then we will constantly battle ourselves from every level of our being, which is why we attract to ourselves conditional experiences that hold back our creativity, even money. We, as humans, have even come as far as locking our reasoned mind into a belief system that battles between who we truly are and the philosophy that physical matter is the only reality there is before we can enter in to any type of heaven where God dwells. It is because of this conflict that we can better understand why religion has held such a grip on us, for the philosophy of heaven must fight to be heard from the ego's perspective.

Because of the soul's path of evolution that it took in the beginning stages of swimming with the dolphins and whales to where we have incarnated from dinosaurs to mammals, and then to primates, has left a deep-rooted mark on our soul. This grip also includes the theory of humans evolving from the ape.

When we take a look at how our physical body is put together today, an intelligent designer becomes ever more indisputable to us. This is why science and religion have a hard time agreeing because they see too many flaws from our past. And yet, both science and religion cannot see the perfection of the physical body and how it serves the soul so well in speeding up the process by which new and different organisms develop as a result of our genetics (heredity).

For instance: As I have evolved to the more modern version of myself, I have acquired with no doubt the ability to express something that can only be treasured intellectually and with enlightenment. In other words, from my intellectual and enlightenment point of view, I could not write this book without the ability to express myself using reason, intuitive feelings, and wisdom, and I could not comprehend what I am writing without these abilities either. To think in this manner is quite unique in itself from when I first came to earth a long time ago.

It is like a pre-adolescent child not having the wisdom and the mind configuration to understand what I am writing here because the mind of the child is far different than the mind of an adult. From my understanding, it takes about twelve years or so for the frontal lobes of the brain to develop fully after puberty. You see, according to science, our frontal lobes are the key to social behavior, abstract thinking, along with planning and solving complex problems. Because of our evolution from the primitive state of mind to where the brain is highly developed today, they both end up competing with each other over their survival.

For example: Let's name your highly developed brain of today the "grown-up you" and name the more habitual and customary you, the "pre-adolescent you." The "grown-up you" knows, because of wisdom (other lifetimes), that over-spending and under-saving is not going to be good for your financial sovereignty in the future and the freedom to stand on your own. However, the "pre-adolescent you" (one lifetime as religion believe) is still primed to spend money on what you want today even if you cannot afford it, for it lacks the wisdom to understand.

Thus, the "pre-adolescent you" simply doesn't understand why the "grown-up you" would deny you a trip to the new car lot to buy that nice looking vehicle you always wanted. Therefore, the "grown-up you" is just not designed (planned ahead) to prevent the "pre-adolescent you" from taking over your thought process, all because of the easiness to open credit in fulfilling your wants.

The point is that there is an instant conflict within yourself between what you know would be beneficial for you and what you feel emotionally in regards to satisfying the ego's self-worth. What happens is that you often fall victim to your "pre-adolescent you," even when you know that you cannot afford it.

When we look at government and how they spend money that they don't have, then we are looking at our own "adolescent self" playing in a culture of blame, spending, and not taking full responsibility for our acts. As we can see, in every corner of the world government and religions spend billions and billions of dollars every year on building a society that must rely on them for our survival.

It's the same way with our financial security, for their goal is to keep us all in as much debt as they can without us missing a payment. This way it becomes very easy for them to control us in order to maintain their hypnotic effect on us, thus their power.

You see, we give up our individuality, sovereignty, and freedom in support of our religious faith and our political doctrines for the benefit and comfort of some superior being (God) that doesn't exist, and that our politicians will come and save us, even to the point that we are willing to give up our sons and daughters to them for the benefit of keeping us dependent on them. Yes, some of us are even willing to kill for them.

It is incredible how we took on a belief long ago about a white male God that created us, and now we cannot get out of this belief because of its strong hold on us. The state of being controlled by the hypnotic effect of governments, religion, big business, family, and friends are so overwhelming and powerful that we easily fall prey to them all because we are not willing to take full responsibility for our own acts (creations).

You see, the reason why governments and religions are so successful in keeping us in a hypnotic state is that they tap into our primitive mind, the "pre-adolescent self", in much the same way they buy our votes with free programs that keep us relying on them, only more so. Both government and religion gain their foothold by taking control over our desire to feel worthy because it is our deep self-worth, the "pre-adolescent self," that seems to give us some purpose in life.

It is religion, government, family, friends, and big business that keep us in fear because they are our monster. Like vampires, needing to feed of us, needing more of our energy (blood) in order for them to perpetuate their own agenda to maintain their power.

My fellow searchers do not discount what I am saying here because your sovereignty and freedom is at stake. Remember, love is multi-dimensional like you are – for in its truest state, love is unconditional and it has always been because true love lets you be who you are and express who you are in any way you want without being looked at as a fool, some nut case, or someone that seems selfish.

You see government and religion are very good in sucking the energy (blood) right out of us, and they do it by explaining our illnesses away by stating they are caused by bacterial diseases and genetic disorders. They explain why we are poor by blaming those that have it all. They even say that the earthquakes, volcanoes, floods, and droughts occur because of God raining down his wrath upon us because of not taking care of earth.

It is through your 'pre-adolescent you' where government and religion easily hijack your freedom to become sovereign and an independent soul. Religion uses terms such as "god the father," and their rituals of worship, and ceremonies, to reinforce their hold on you despite your "grown-up you" being able to recognize the difference between the real soul and the soul that is created by religion.

For instance: The real soul is, in effect, the wisdom of your own "I AM" speaking and expressing through your human consciousness. Look, I am able to write this book, and the material presented in it, because of the wisdom of my soul's passage through many lifetimes and experiences filtering through, from my first to my last, to my human consciousness in this lifetime.

My soul's wisdom is the result of condensing all of my choices and experiences since my awakening in the first creation eons ago, then squeezing out the best of all my lifetimes where my focus was not on drama, heightened emotions, and my negative experiences thus, in the end, my *soul* became my *enlightenment* and my *wisdom*.

In other words, it was I (me) who created my soul, not some God outside of me, for my soul became part of my divine plan to fragment my consciousness into multiple lifetimes to learn about health, wealth, illness, poverty, lack of common sense, death, and many other things including getting totally lost. By my spirit creating my soul it gave me a chance to pretend that I didn't know who I truly was and where I actually came from. Hence, it was my soul that gave me a chance to enter many physical bodies so I can evolve in wisdom and enlightenment.

Once I, my human self, became enlightened to my soul's divine plan. My human consciousness ascended to where my wisdom moved beyond my soul's agenda to create more lifetimes for me to experience being lost and alone. Thus, as a result, I have made the choice not to experience anymore duality and me being lost. I have also made the choice to let go of human drama, for I have learned to integrate all aspects of duality, the light and dark, the masculine and feminine, the good and bad, right and wrong, and most of all, no more judgment.

I have remembered, while in human consciousness, that creation was all based on duality, forgetfulness, and experiencing for the benefit of soul growth and learning "who I truly am." However, in the process, I also learned about the wisdom of those experiences, good and bad, and how to "trust in myself as a living God" because without "trust in myself as a God also, I wouldn't have been able to integrate "all that I am."

Look, the media constantly bombards us with negative material to the point where we eventually become very pessimistic about life, love, and how it treats us. Thus, we begin to blame and fear everyone that thinks differently than those of us that are awakened to the real God.

My dear friends, religion, government, and the media all know that most of us are intellectually lazy and largely uninformed when it comes to God, his love, and the workings of government. Therefore, they use scare tactics and sensationalism because it works well in such an environment. It keeps them rich and powerful, and for us, we remain poor, uninformed of who we truly are, and therefore prone to illnesses and choices that are not really ours.

As you all know, leaving one's faith (traditions) and family that one was born into certainly leads to being shunned by those that hang onto their religious beliefs about God and their family as a life support, if not worse. In Islam, you have seen honor killings and in the Christian culture, it is not uncommon to hear of individuals whose families and friends have turned their backs on them because they have abandoned or renounced their family's religious beliefs.

Religions know that losing family and friends is a powerful tool for keeping everyone under control. It is far easier to ignore even the slightest evidence that we are a God also than to give up the love and friendship of a community of people that share the same common belief or background, especially family members. People fear so much because of what they believe their survival depends solely on being part of a family or church that shares the common belief that they will be saved.

Religion has always offered a ready social network for families to join them in maintaining a kinship that is designed to keep you in a primitive state of mind, even to the point that you are willing to commit a revolting act to protect the faith and the leaders of that faith. Now, because of this kinship to others, your "primitive mind," which has served you so well during your evolution, threatens your very existence.

However, the "grown-up you" has given you some new understanding of God and Christ, it has also given you new technology to understand the universe, the earth, and even your soul. However, the "pre-adolescent you," the primitive mind is stuck in a belief that you must, at all cost, fight to maintain your deep-seated beliefs when it comes to God.

My fellow searchers, most of the world today still believes that God is a solitary supreme being unto himself that must be feared, and those that disagree must be converted at all cost, either through discrediting, or making fun of, or making one look ridiculous, or even experiencing death. Therefore, religion, government, family, friends, big business, and the media need to be taken seriously if you have a great desire to understand the real truth about God, Christ, the Devil, and who you are as a souled being.

Take time and understand their root purpose and how they can seize command of your mind, thus leaving them in control of your soul (wisdom) for a long time. If you do not take the time to acknowledge your own wisdom (soul) and stop this 'pre-adolescent you' from overriding your new understanding of spirit, you are surely destined to repeat what you are experiencing over and over, again and again until you do.

Why? It is because your soul does not want to be controlled by anyone other than its own wisdom, not even your human self. Most everything that is happening to you today in life is all due to the 'pre-adolescent you' refusing to grow up and see the wondrous workings of your own soul (wisdom).

It is you that is the 'intelligent designer,' the boss, and the owner, who is in charge of the essence of God and not some deity or church outside of you. Instead of honoring your religion, and the God it presents, learn to honor yourself. After all, it is *you* that is the divine and the Christ. Don't ever think that God doesn't love you anymore because it is not about God loving you. It is about loving and honoring yourself as God and a Christ also.

In honoring yourself first, keep in mind that your soul doesn't care about what experiences you give yourself, like being financially poor, not having a relationship, your life being in chaos, or what your body is going through. What your soul cares for the most is the experiencing of what you are choosing.

Of course, it doesn't mean that your soul is uncaring or heartless. It is just that your soul loves you so much that it has complete compassion for what you are creating for yourself. So much so, that your soul allows you to go through anything you choose to experience. Your soul is just waiting for the time where you become aware of its wisdom so that you can become a free sovereign God in your own right.

Now that you know how much you are hypnotized and controlled by your own beliefs and those of others, it is time for your soul to come in and give you what you have been seeking for many, many lifetimes. Your soul is ready and anxious to give you the secrets and the circumstances on why you suffer. However, before we start, the first question you should ask yourself is, "What is the soul anyway?" And second, "Why do you call it the soul?"

First, you must understand that your soul is real. The soul is actually your wisdom or you in your divine state. It is actually you in your completeness as a sovereign self-governing Godlike being where your wisdom is right here and now.

Second, it is your wisdom that highlights your human consciousness not to be ruled, enslaved, or controlled by belief systems, government, religion, friends, family, or by anyone else or thing. Understand that the physical body is merely a temporary vessel for your soul, while you, the three-dimensional holographic version of you, journeys through many lifetimes on earth.

The holographic human ego (personality traits) gets its power and the freedom to choose from your soul consciousness because it is connected to all life, your spirit, and your wisdom. Since your spirit is the source of all what you bring to life than your soul knows no end, no death, no sin, and no limits, for your soul, and the wisdom it holds, is an extension of your spirit that is forever eternal and divine.

As said, your soul manages its evolution through a series of creating incarnations. It has the ability to transcend itself a little at a time into material form as you journey through many lifetimes. Your soul looks at physical life as a glorious thing because of what physical life offers your soul. It is your wisdom that is the Christ coming from out behind the wall of ignorance to integrate with the human you. It is the "pre-adolescent you" becoming the "grown-up you."

Of course, even before your soul commits to an incarnation on earth, your soul arranges the criteria that has to be met by you before you are born in the flesh. After all, your soul has a purpose, which is to experience life through your physical hologramic aspect.

What makes a lifetime purposeful is not about what you do in life, or how you strive to gain favor with some God by trying to serve other people before yourself, or even compelled to do, even if it is good or bad. It is about the experience of the act that the soul is interested in, because that is what brings wisdom to your soul and not so much the act itself, no matter if it was good or bad. This is why, when you get to understand how energy works, you can heal your body, mind, and spirit.

Remember, in the beginning stages of your awakening a long time ago, you used the life force (spirit) to create a soul that felt a great urge to move the hologramic version of you outside of the oneness of your consciousness to explore all possibilities of life. The soul, despite being a piece of the divine, was truly limited. Thus, your soul threw itself into a creation, physicality, where it could learn to become unlimited, which is why, in the eyes of your soul, you have never sinned, for that is the wisdom of your soul revealed. This is very important to understand.

For instance: Using the soul in a mathematical formula that represents one hundred percent (100%) as an example for your completeness it allows me to communicate to you on an intellectual level how your soul allocates part of its consciousness, like one to two percent, to incarnate into a hologramic physical body to explore all possibilities of life.

Thus your soul created the environment, a physical body, and a story (lifetime), many of them, to perform the task in exploring those possibilities. To help your soul in performing its task, the soul created the illusion of a force that is made up of opposites so the human you would oppose the true desire of the soul. As you can see, your soul designed it that way so as to evolve in wisdom without you, the human aspect, interfering with it.

By allowing the physical hologramic human you, which houses one to two percent of your soul's total consciousness, to move forward with its outward agenda, it allowed the hologramic human you to forget the other ninety-eight percent of your total consciousness. Because of it, everything the human you experiences is an illusion other than your soul becoming the beneficiary of the wisdom of what you are experiencing.

You see, the human part of you, the one to two percent, feels that it has its own desires that it wants to enjoy, and therefore has no sense or clarity of what your soul had planned for its (your) own evolution. Once you are born in the physical realm, the human part of you, the one to two percent, begins to relate only to the physical world and what is in it. It looks for its pleasures through the mind, food, drink, money, intelligence, music, religious literature, and aiming to gain favor with a God that really doesn't exists by servicing others.

Now, these things are not evil in nature, it is just that the human part of you gets stuck in the hypnosis of pursuing worldly pleasures, and that the idea of servicing others gets you to heaven. However, what you should take pleasure in is not trying to get to heaven by servicing others before yourself but have the human you become awakened to your soul's agenda and the other ninety-eight percent of you.

As said, the earth, as well as all dimensions, was created by all souled beings acting together as the Godhead to resolve the issue with our stuck energy and our belief that we are not a divine being. However, that was only part of it. We all personally came to earth to launch the underlying agenda of our soul so that we could take on a whole new level of understanding life and to answer the question, "Who Am I?"

Now, how did the soul accomplish this? It did it by disguising, or masking, or hiding itself from itself. This was done by allowing us, as souls, to take on a human body, to take on the belief in positive and negative (duality), and to take on the veil of forgetfulness so we could follow through with our soul's secret plan in achieving its underlying agenda to become an "I AM" sovereign being in its own right.

My dear friends are you ready to hear the vibrational wisdom of your soul for the very first time since you leaving your divine state (first creation)? Don't you think it is time to know how to move past this old hypnotic trance that you have been in for a long time? For many lifetimes Lucifer has come in and helped you balance your energies of light and dark. And now, you may be ready (the choice is yours) to move from this linear path of duality living to a multi-dimensional living. It is time for you to move past the illusion of duality, the separation from your soul, and to understand where your demons come from.

So, if you believe that you have to hear words in your head about moving forward in your understanding of spirit, then what you are hearing is *not* coming from your soul. All that you are doing is connecting to the old intellectual system of duality trying to keep you locked in to the hologramic world of illusions, locked into your one to two percent of consciousness. Also, if you believe that you have to hear words coming from God in order for this to be real, then you are being set up to fail.

My dear friends, you will not hear any words. The soul will come in through your heart by way of movement. By allowing yourself to be in the now moment, it gives your soul the chance to convey to your heart that it was your spirit that gave the hologramic human personality the same creator abilities that your soul enjoys. That someday, after all of your many lifetime experiences playing throughout all of the dimensions, including earth, the human you integrates the completeness of your soul's wisdom with the physical you of today.

Thus, the hologramic human you inherits the throne (all wisdom that your soul possesses) because the hologramic human you and your soul's wisdom becomes one and the same, you; thereby leaving behind the hologramic version of you with only the real you left, as a living God. Once this is done then all fear of death and your treasures of material wants disappear from your human consciousness. In its place, you take on an expanded consciousness that brings in the Gnost (Christ) in fulfilling any desire (miracle) you wish to experience, even if it means the desire to heal yourself or become very wealthy, or both.

Your soul knows and understands that you, from the human level, have been dormant for a long time because your soul has allowed the hologramic human you to do as it pleased. Your soul allowed the hologramic human you believe in many things, like a God that created you, that you are a sinner, that you are not worthy of God, and many other things that made you feel incomplete.

It is because of these strong beliefs, you have lost your creativity, for it is your birth right to become the spiritual artists that you are in your own right. You have forgotten that you helped create all the stars, all dimensions, earth, and even the physical body you occupy today.

It is not that you are foolish, unworthy, or unwise, or that your life was predetermined. In fact, you don't even have to fall to your knees in prayer, or give the sign of the cross, or say your prayer beads to prove yourself to God. It is about releasing those old notions, for you are the creator God of every moment of your life. It was you from the soul level that created the pathway that led you to where you are today.

My fellow seekers, if there is one thing that I would love to get through to you it would be this: understand that you (your soul) created the rational mind and your human body to serve you until you was ready to move into your creativity cycle using your wisdom and new expansional energy. You see, this new expansional energy is essentially the human you, without the hologramic you, allowing your soul (wisdom) to join the human you in the physical form in a more complete and profound way than ever before.

It is about the joining where you, in human form, can express the natural flow of your creativity in the now moment without putting a force to it. Instead of trying to figure out how to have a good relationship, how to heal yourself, how to make money, create happiness, or how to serve others to gain favor with God, just allow your soul (wisdom) to come in and help you create these things using new expansional energy.

Remember, you will never figure out God using your rational mind, and you will never be able to heal yourself, be happy, or create the peace within if you continue to use rules and the structure of duality as your means of creativity. If you define God and Christ like you do religion, then you will hold back the natural flow of your soul's wholeness and sovereignty from coming into your life.

Look, it is not about trying to impress some God outside of you or gain favor by what you do for him, because this kind of God cannot help you. It is the wisdom of your soul that will help bring you back to the appropriate place in consciousness where you can change your old story (life) to a new story (life) of creating miracles of peace, love, abundance, health, and joy.

I know that many of you have been going through health issues, job worries, money problems, family problems, worrying about loved ones, and on top of it all, wondering what this world is coming to. Yes, many of you are scared to death about what government is doing. We can get very emotional and mental with all of these things that are going on right now. What a combination this is when our emotions and mental state come together in trying to figure this mess out.

We all pray to the heavens trying to get God to come into our lives to feed us, heal us, and protect us from the bad guys. Well, the truth of it,

God is not coming to help us, which is why there is no right time other then now to call in our own wisdom to help bring in those wonderful potentials that most have not yet experienced. Remember, this God of the Bible is not real.

The energy of every potential created by you, and all souls, still exists in a dormant or neutral state waiting for you to bring them into your human level and experience them, even the healing of your body. Since energy is neutral in its beginning, then energy is nothing until the imagination of the creator (you) triggers it to serve, and then it goes to work to accommodate you.

This means that you have, at this very moment and at your disposal, multiple potentials for abundance, healing, and the heaven on earth you seek waiting to be expressed and brought onto earth by you. By understanding that your spirit is what gives life to your creations, it then becomes very important to understand how energy works.

When you understand that energy at its core does not have a positive or negative charge to it, you then can begin to understand how the material world around you, including your physical body and this God of duality, is nothing but pure illusion. All that there is that surrounds you, is pure neutral energy that has been formed by you, the real creator, and now it seems like you are trapped into something that is not real. Trapped to the point where you fight with your beliefs, with yourself, with others about who is right and wrong, and why Jesus does not come down and save you or give you a miracle.

When you live from the mind of reason, logic, judgment, and that your mind is the master of intelligence, your soul cannot bring forth to you the wisdom that you hold hidden deep within your consciousness. Thus, you become more and more separated from your soul, or the Christ that you are, and the wisdom you possess.

My dear friends, it's not just about the economy and what government can do for you. It is about "awareness," for it is a far greater treasure than what government can do for you, even a greater treasure than all the intelligence and brainpower you could ever learn from books. You can be a very intelligent person because of book study but if you are not "aware" of your soul's wisdom and your divine state, then the working of God, the government, and what you are experiencing does not mean anything.

It is "awareness" and the "understanding of consciousness" that your soul seeks, not intelligence, or your ability to be smarter than someone else, or if government can help you. The real treasure is being aware of your soul, who you truly are, and how the body relates to your soul's wisdom. It's all about being aware of all your creations, from the food you eat, to what you believe in and everything in-between. Being aware of who you truly are is everything, from the awareness of your body, the wisdom you possess, the density of the air you breathe, and the life you chose to live upon the earth.

Being aware is not about how much money you have, how educated you are, what type of car you drive, or how many friends you believe you have, for these things come to you automatically as a result of being conscious and aware of your soul's wisdom.

When you ask yourself who you are, then understand the relationship between your soul's wisdom and your hologramic human you. The human you were created from the love that came from your soul as an expression to walk upon earth. Your soul gave the human you an identity and the freedom to discover what your heart desires. Otherwise, without your soul giving the human you freedom, you would never have the overwhelming wisdom that you posses today. Always remember, wisdom is not tied to your intelligence, only to your soul.

Here is another thing to keep in mind. Before you incarnated into physical form, even though you forgot, you made an agreement with your soul to come and get you if you became lost or have forgotten who you were. Even if you strayed from the path of becoming a sovereign being in your own right, you asked your soul on a subconscious level to come in and help put you back on track.

My dear friends, this explains the mystery behind why you have an accidents, have an illness, have financial problems, along with having many other good or bad things happen to you – for what your soul reflects back to you it has already been chosen from a mental and human level.

Your soul does not interfere with your human identity, the story you chose to play out in this lifetime, and what you choose to create now (good or bad). Everything you choose to do come with it a great love of compassion and honor. The job of your soul is to have your human you understand the beauty of your journey by learning to acknowledge your spiritual lineage where you have had many lifetimes.

Now, the human you, is at the point of bringing together "all that you are," for you are the ascended one that the Book of Revelation is talking about as coming from behind the clouds to save you, for you are a Christ too. Your soul, with the help of Lucifer, has created an opening a long time ago where you allowed your demons to come through, and now you can integrate those demons by choice. When you do, the choice will allow your soul's wisdom to join you in your human form. This way never again will you wonder where your soul is or who you are.

So, I ask you again! Are you ready to allow your soul's wisdom and the Christ within to come in and be part of your life? Your soul doesn't need you to straighten out your act or be perfect first. All your soul wants is to enjoy and feel everything you are feeling and experiencing right now. In fact, the whole routine in allowing your soul to come in is quite simple!

Remember, it is not about resolving your sins because there are no sins to resolve. Your soul's wisdom just wants to come in and be with every breath you take for the rest of your life and more. If you could hear your soul it would say, "Beloved one, what makes a lifetime purposeful is not what you do, or how intelligent you are, or are compelled to do that gives life purpose. It is when you call in your soul's wisdom to engage in that purpose."

It is only here that your soul can unite with your dense physical body and use it to bring your body, mind, spirit, and your wisdom to its ultimate perfection of one. Therefore, the ultimate purpose of physical creation is for the soul to achieve the ultimate union with you while in the flesh. This is the purpose and the secret of the soul.

Chapter 19

How To Create Miracles

Now, if you are ready, I will take you further into this "new energy of expansion" which will aid you in mastering the art of creating miracles for yourself to experience. In fact, let us look at what a miracle is anyway? Some would say that a miracle is an effect manifesting as an act coming from God or an event that appears to be contrary to the laws of nature. It can also mean something that shows the intervention of a power that is not limited by the laws of physical matter, including the mind. A miracle can also mean a power that interrupts the fixed laws of physical nature that are governed by a supernatural power that exceeds all known human power.

All that we know about miracles is that they are wonderful and marvelous happenings that are hard to explain. At least until now! To understand miracles and how they happen, you must understand that miracles don't come from God because the God you know is not real. In actuality, miracles come from you.

It is *you* that create miracles, for *you* are a divine extension of the Spirit of One. It is *you* that has the power and the freedom to become conscious of your choices. However, it is also *you* that have chosen to close yourself off from receiving any miracles all because of your belief systems about a white male Hebrew God that created you, and all that you receive in life.

There are people that suggest that the world around you is controlled by a supernatural being that is beyond your understanding, and you can either go along with them or you can say, "No, I am finished with those people that suggest God is impossible to explain or that he is a mystery." I can also illustrate, which will seem miraculous to those people that will not look beyond their old way of thinking, "that God is nothing more than *you* creating your world of possibilities and probabilities. Thus, it is you that creates your own miracles."

When Jesus walked the earth he showed us his miracles and he was able to perform them because he understood the dynamics of the 3-D world and how everything in life is nothing but potentials (miracles) that become a reality just by making conscious choices. Jesus knew it was his conscious connection to the "Christ I AM" within himself that activated his authority (power) to create miracles, and not his 2-D rational mind, or his outer physical personality, or some supernatural power outside of him.

Jesus had the ability and the knowledge to recognize the physical world as something that deceived the physical senses by everything appearing to be real, when in truth, it is not. As a result Jesus could manipulate the forces of duality, turn it into the new energy of four, and with the help of his divine imagination, he manifested the outcome of his choices, and so can you.

To master the art of miracles you have to change your views about who you think you are, that you are only human, and then change your belief patterns from focusing outside of you to focusing on *you* as being the source of your creations and not some God above you. This is when you will open up to your true spiritual heritage, be crowned as the Christ, and that is when you will begin to perform great miracles, even greater miracles than Jesus'.

Remember Jesus saying that he was not of this world (John 8:12)? Well, neither are you! Besides, even the name Jesus is not his name. Your world, like Jesus, is consciousness, pure spirit (light), and expressing and manifesting your choices for soul growth. When you look at the disciples when they approached Jesus and asked, "*Why do you speak to them in parables*" (Matthew 13:10)? Jesus' reply was:

"*To you it has been granted to know the mysteries (miracles) of the kingdom of heaven, but to them it has not been granted. For whoever has, to him more shall be given, and he will have an abundance; but whoever does not have, even what he has shall be taken away from him. Therefore I speak to them in parables; because while seeing they do not see and while hearing they do not hear, nor do they understand (Matthew 13:11-13).*"

If you take a look at human consciousness in general through the eyes of you being a Christ also, you will understand why it has been very important to evolve gradually into a deeper understanding of "why you are the way you are and why you experience the things you experience, for you are *not* your name nor are you of this world."

Your consciousness is the house of the "I AM." Therefore, it is your soul's consciousness that calls up energy in its pure unadulterated state, and when you place a desire or passion to it, you, without doubt, call in your history of truths (belief systems). This then creates your experiences and your reality the way you understand it. That, my dear friends, in itself is a miracle.

So, if you connect your human consciousness everyday to the beliefs of others and to your own history (lifetimes) of beliefs (lies) about some God who created you, then by natural physics you will create your world and experiences accordingly. Thus *choice* and *free will* are not being expressed and manifested in the manner of "who you truly are," which then prevents you from bringing in life's miracles of health, abundance, and joy because you cannot see, hear, or understand that you are the source for your miracles.

If you cannot understand that most of what you believe today comes from others, such as religion, friends, family, politicians, and from your lifetimes past, then you are lost in a world of perception, susceptibility, and lies that keep you wrapped and locked into a consciousness energy called "emotional control" without you even realizing it. Thus, in an effect, your emotions become the standard (parables) that takes the place of your real choices and the free will to carry them out, for you are blind to them and to the Christ you are.

Most all choices that come from the human level are usually based on emotions because everything about us is based on our connection to family, history, friends, religion and our so called truths, and how we understand them from the rational mind. Therefore, all that we believe about self and others comes from our mental level and from our human consciousness, and *not* from our "I AM Soul Consciousness."

It is by way of our emotions why we feel that we must pray to a God for a miracle instead of just making the conscious choice to bring what we desire into our reality. It is that simple!

So, my fellow searchers, if you are ready to listen to your soul instead of your emotions, then your soul will make it clear to you how to master the art of creating miracles for you to experience, even the miracle of healing your illness, your financial problems, or whatever you feel needs changing in your life. Of course, the first thing you need to do to bring in these miracles, which is very important to understand, is to commit and trust, without doubt, in yourself as a Christ too, thus equal to God.

It is about honoring and becoming aware of your emotions and the many lifetimes of your past, whether they were good or bad makes no difference. It is about the contributions you made while living in the flesh and not seeing yourself as a sinner or that you are unworthy of God's love. It is also about accepting full responsibility for what you are experiencing today. No one has placed upon you what you are experiencing right now but *you*. Let it be suffering or happiness. For all calamities in life that you have experienced, or are experiencing now, did come from you, no exceptions!

For instance: When I first began communicating with the angelic realm in 1975, more-so in 2004, I wanted to fall to my knees in worship all because of my religious upbringing in understanding God, Jesus, and the Masters as being above me. I remember having thoughts of something akin to intimidation when these angelic beings began presenting themselves to me! Yet, when I communicated with them, they always assured me that they are no better, or saintlier, or higher than I am, for we are all Masters and Gods in disguise.

In fact, I remember them saying to me, and I write it here for you, word for word, *"That it is us humans who are at the top of the angelic realm because of the work we are doing."* My dear friends, this means you are higher in wisdom than those angels that have never experienced earth or even those extraterrestrial beings that you seem to think of as having higher intelligence than you.

These angelic beings see us humans as perfect already and without sin. For we are beings of light and the only thing that is real because everything else about us is being projected out of our consciousness as if our consciousness is a projector that is producing a three-dimensional image. Like a hologram of something that feels real to us and yet, it is not.

You see, since energy is pure and neutral and ready to serve us according to where we are directing our consciousness (projector), then we get to choose what hologramic three-dimensional story to create outside of us to manifest and experience. However, because we are asleep as to who we truly are and how we perceive our belief systems as to who we think we are, then everything outside of us, appear incomplete, problematic, and separated.

Therefore, to help you understand miracles and how you are responsible for them. I would like to mention something that was given to me by Jesus (Yeshua) himself back in 2004. Now, before I give you the crux of the communications that I had with Jesus, please remember that Jesus does not want to be worshiped as a God because you are a God as much as he is, and even more. But that is another story.

Jesus wants us to understand that the idea of him coming to save humanity is false because every one of us is a Christ also, and therefore we, each one of us, hold the power of the Spirit of One within us to save ourselves. All that is needed is for us, as humans, to awaken to this truth.

My dear friends, you are a God also, and therefore your own rescuer. Like Jesus, your name too has been changed to a conditional name that holds the belief that you are only human. Like Jesus, his name was also changed to accommodate the Kings of the world, for Jesus' real name was Yeshua Ben Joseph. Why would Joseph and Mary, born as a Hebrew, give Jesus a Greek name?

If you look in the Bible on the subject of names you will find names like Elijah, Isaiah, Zechariah, and Ezekiel, and many more that carry the Hebrew name. We all know Jesus was a Hebrew, so why would Joseph and Mary give their son a Latin name from the Greek God Zeus.

When you refer to Acts 26: 13-15 as the Apostle Paul is speaking to King Agrippa. *"At midday, along the way, O king, I saw a light from the sky, brighter than the sun, shining around me and my traveling companions.*

We all fell to the ground and I heard a voice saying to me in Hebrew, 'Saul, Saul, why are you persecuting me? It is hard for you to kick against the goad.' And I said, 'Who are you, sir?' And the Lord replied, 'I am Jesus whom you are persecuting.

May be some of you have noticed that Saul said the Lord spoke to him in the Hebrew tongue. If this is true, then the Lord could not have said his name was Jesus, because Jesus is not a Hebrew name. During that time, the Apostle Paul wouldn't even know or recognize the name Jesus. Therefore, Jesus' name was changed.

Now that I got that out of the way, here is the conversation I had with Jesus, or should I say Yeshua Ben Joseph. By the way, I have also written this message in my first book, "Genesis: Your Journey Home, 2nd Edition, Chapter 10. Now, I give this message to you like Jesus gave it to me at the time, word for word:

"You have the authority of the Father to create greater miracles than even I did because you are a Creator God. You are whole; you are a divine Souled Being. I, Yeshua (Jesus) was the example of your living Christhood for it was you "who gave life to me."

"My energy and my life are born of yours, because you are God. It was your choice to manifest the Christ Principle within me, here on earth, in order to introduce the Christ Consciousness to humanity. Therefore, indeed I am the true Son of God because all of you, together as one, are the God who gave me life. I say unto you, it is time for you to feel your wholeness of Spirit, trust it, and let me go."

"The Bible was written a long time ago to help you with your education and evolution in becoming a fully evolved God. The harvest not only means ascension to higher understanding; it also means you are now complete, for you are ready to move into a new cycle of creation and become a full creator God in your own right. You have come full circle and you are now complete, if you so choose, for the fullness of time have come. The second circle of creation has been your field of learning in becoming a true Creator God.

"The harvest is for those who are ready to move into the third circle of creation where you are absolutely limitless and without restriction. I know that religious groups and even your own family would say that you are listening to the devil. But, I say to you to trust your own heart. Listen to the voice of your own Spirit telling you it is time to harvest the seed of the Christ consciousness that I planted so long ago."

> "When I walked the earth I planted the Christ seed, but most of it fell on dry ground for man was not ready to accept my message. Dear ones, you do not need to be saved for you already are. You need only to find yourself and remember who you are, for you have never been lost to the Father. Search your heart, be still and know that you are God."

As you can see, Jesus is saying that *you*, and all humans, are the Godhead for the Christ consciousness. He is also telling you that it is time to feel your own wholeness of Spirit, trust it, let him go, and allow yourself to enter into a new cycle, a new expanded energy. It's a cycle where you, by becoming aware of who you truly are and what you are choosing, can become completely unlimited without having any conditions to your creations.

Thus, you can create all the miracles you desire to experience. All that it takes is for you to let go of your current reality base belief systems of opposites and your emotional ties to them. By having the belief that you need a savior keeps your attention on what you don't want, which is some type of salvation rather than what you really desire.

You are nothing but light (spirit), consciousness, and you are a divine being that possess the secret code of understanding unconditional love as the framework of your total being. Thus, everything else is an illusion, including what you see with your eyes and hear with your ears, which is nothing but a 3-deminsional image of something that feels real and yet, it is not. When you become clear about who you are, which is, love already, you are then free to create anything you desire.

By having the courage to explore things that go beyond the old fears and limitations of religion and their ideology of good and evil, it takes you to move from your mental consciousness (analyzation, control, emotions, perception, power) to your divine consciousness (awareness, focus, compassion, imagination, and expression, unconditionally). Why? It is because the challenges that you face every day in life is about drama, worry, fear, uncertainty, and emotions that produce the perception that you need someone to love you or save you.

If you do nothing but process your beliefs through the ideology of good and evil, then all that you are going to do is create more drama, more worry, more fear, and more uncertainty. Why? Well, it starts with your consciousness, which is in essence your awareness. Again, your consciousness has no form to it and your spirit is not made of energy.

You are a spiritual being of light that loves to express, create, and expand beyond your accumulative wisdom of understanding. Since consciousness is all who you are, then you attract energy from what the Tobias called the field.

The field is a reservoir of pure neutral energy that exists all around you no matter where you are in your evolution, even in hell. Since your consciousness is connected to everything, including your many other "personality-aspects" (lifetimes) of the past, to your human-aspect of today, to all humans, to angelic beings, to your angelic family, and to "all that is and all that was," meaning just about everything, then what do you think is going to come into your life if you are stuck in a belief system of everything having a framework of duality? You are going to suffer!

My dear friends, there is only one way to move past the framework of positive and negative, and that is by learning to become unconditional with your beliefs. The more you unlock your soul consciousness and its wisdom. You truly become an ascended master in your own right. To the point where you can disconnect yourself from the field of the mass consciousness and its adulteration of this pure energy, and create for yourself a whole new reality that comes directly from you.

Consciousness is always looking to discover itself by means of using energy, and if you are stuck in a belief system for too long, then your soul calls in the energy required to help you become unstuck, to get you moving again. This is where your Lucifer consciousness (figuratively speaking) comes into your life and draws in the energy needed to make a connection to multiple illnesses, drama, poverty, bad relationships, sadness, accidents, or whatever it takes to get you out of your basic belief in duality. This sometimes can take many lifetimes.

Because your soul is always looking to expand in consciousness, it takes your Lucifer consciousness to jump kick your human personality into taking action. For instance: the human ego believes that you are *not* worthy of God and that you are foolish to believe that you are equal to him. So, your Lucifer consciousness calls out to your soul the energy of opposites to get you to look at your layered belief systems to see what it will take to move you beyond them.

This means the energy that you are using right now for your physical body, and the reality that you are playing in, is coming from contaminated energy (figuratively speaking) that was once pure and unadulterated.

For instance: Every one of us carries all the diseases known to man within the body, including cancer, all because of the belief in opposites. Of course, most of us keep our body in balance by evolving and letting go of old belief systems that don't serve us anymore. However, there are many of us that will not let go of our dogmatic beliefs about a God that is separate from us, and that we are flawed at birth because of our strong belief in sin.

Therefore, we contract many lifetimes having many types of diseases as well as accidents to help us change our way of thinking and believing. When our soul calls out to this neutral energy to serve us, and because of our strong belief in opposites, we send the signal to our good cells in the body to move and shift this pure neutral energy coming in to our consciousness to be processed according to our conditional and limited beliefs about God and what He wants for us.

Since energy will mimic itself right down to the subatomic level, this means everything about you, your history of lifetimes, your conditional beliefs, past and present, and your fears, past and present, are contained within each new cell that comes into your body.

For Instance: I mentioned in the last chapter that we have billions and billions of cells in our body and some are being birthed while others are dying. Some cells are diseased while others may be imbalanced, and they can linger in sickness for a long time. These diseased or imbalanced cells won't leave because the flow of energy coming into them is not right, so they stay in our body.

Now, at each cell's core they contain all the essence of you being the creator that has the divine understanding of you being unconditional. However, in their reality as a cell, some of them are diseased because of the way you look at duality as the basic structure of your reality.

Nevertheless, you can heal your body of any disease, including cancer, aids, multiple sclerosis, and more, just by remembering and trusting who you truly are and who you are not. By recognizing yourself as "spirit and consciousness first and foremost" that has a rational mind and ego as a way to reassure yourself that you would have no recollection as to who you truly are, you then can expand your consciousness enough to realize that you are the creator of your world, thus the creator of your miracles.

In other words, you, and not some God above or outside of you, are the master manipulator of energy. If you do not truly believe this then what you create for your miracles become conditional and limited only to good and bad. You take on the belief of God having conditions and rules to follow because that is how you look at yourself. If you look at a God that is conditional then the God you believe in holds your creativity and your miracles, and not you as a God.

Again, energy is always neutral and unconditional, having no agenda, and when you call it in, it's there to serve you the way you choose it to serve you. If you are not aware or awakened to how energy works, then what is going to happen is that energy will serve you according to your layered belief systems and not what you desire for an outcome.

The cells in your body have a communication system within each of them, and if you, the source for your miracles, send out signals that are misinterpreted because of your strong belief in opposites, then the whole process of every cell becoming balanced will be lost.

For instance: When you pray or ask God for healing, for yourself or for someone else, all that you are doing is working from an emotional and conditional consciousness that is pleading with someone to do it for you.

You are the real creator here, and you have the authority as a living divine being to call into your body those cells that are filled with a life force that comes from the real creator, *you*. When these healthy cells come into your body, they are completely balanced physically and energetically, and without conditions put on them, and all that you have to do is understand that they are perfect just like you are perfect already.

Thus, these cells can create the perfect setting where your physical body can return to a condition of nothing but health. All that it comes down to, and I am sure that you must have heard this saying before, "is recognizing yourself as a divine being having a human experience." It is up to you to make a conscious choice where every single cell in your body communicates with each other to restore your body back to health, and the best way to do this is through deep breathing and learning to look at life and yourself as being unconditional.

You see, and this comes hard for everyone to understand. Your spirit and soul (wisdom) do not really exist within anything that is of duality or comes with a set of rules to follow. All of what duality and conditional beliefs brings in is just a three-dimensional image of you that seems real but it is not. The only thing real is your spirit and the wisdom of your soul's consciousness, which makes you a grand being that is cloaked in a human body.

What is forgotten here is that your natural state of being, believe it or not, is actually joy, health, unconditional, and having abundance already just because of you being a divine being. However, because of your many layered belief systems, you have chosen conditional beliefs that bring nothing but pain and suffering as the means to feel alive.

This means you live in the past more so than the present. Because of you not being aware of your divine state, you choose to find your solutions to your suffering through the rational mind and from an outside God that has placed conditions on you to follow.

Since you have given your rational mind and this God of conditional beliefs complete control over your creations, the rational mind can then manufacture your emotions in such a way to help save you by looking for others to cure you. However, the opposite happens, for others cannot save or cure you, only you can save and cure yourself.

Also, the biggest emotion we, as humans, have created is drama. Drama gives us a sense of purpose because it provides a belief that something needs fixing or solving. We have given up our divine identity (will) to the rational mind so that we can feel our emotional creations on a level that represents two ends of a scale that consists of positive and negative.

If you actually believe or think that by staying positive about your situations, be it a disease or something else, you are actually doing nothing for yourself but giving away your power to create a miracle. You give it away by having no awareness of your soul's role in creating personality-aspects (lifetimes) to serve you. When these aspects show up energetically in the form of emotions, you automatically connect with them. Thus, you cannot heal your body, have joy, or have abundance in your life if you get lost in your emotions.

Look, while you have been evolving through time and space, lifetime after lifetime, experiencing the forces of opposites, you have been attaching yourself to vast amounts of emotional viewpoints, and with many aspects of you that now identify you as who you are, only human.

You, without realizing it, have become cut off from any awareness of who you truly are. So much so that everything about you on an emotional scale becomes very complex.

This is why many people can get very distressed with life and find themselves going to professionals for help. However, how can these professionals help you if they themselves don't know who they are? So, instead they give you medicine to calm you down.

My dear friends, the solution is not about medicine! It is about knowing who you truly are and your connection to your own soul. By slowly integrating all of your emotional aspects, including your misunderstood "free will," you begin to remember who you truly are, thus reclaiming control over your life, your rational mind, and over the flow of energy.

For instance: To become a sovereign "I AM" being in your own right requires going beyond your rational mind and your idea of what free will means so that your divine will of unconditional love can take over the controls of your life. However, your rational mind has played the role of protecting you for so long that it has become quite comfortable doing it. Therefore, the rational mind, and your idea of free will, is not capable of just standing aside while you play a new game that may or may not be true according to your dogmatic beliefs.

So, to the rational mind, enlightenment is a frightening thing because how does the mind explain enlightenment? All that the mind will do is give you the feeling that the rational mind, and your idea of free will, is going to die, or that you are going to lose your individuality. Therefore, the rational mind, along with your free will, says, "Not so fast here, you are not going to get rid of me just like that. Therefore, I need more enlightenment."

Remember, the rational mind has been taught well by our religious leaders to turnover our free will to a conditional God that sets rules for us to follow. If we see God as a being unto himself who is outside of us, then the rational mind kicks in and says, "I cannot do that because I will lose my individuality and my place in heaven when I die." This of course creates an emotional battle deep within you between your rational mind, free will, and your idea of spiritual enlightenment.

Instead of listening to your rational mind, and how it needs to win to survive, see the rational mind as an incredible creation that you gave yourself to serve you in your development toward sovereignty. The rational mind just worries that if you let it go, something bad is going to happen. So, it becomes afraid of what you are thinking to change. Whether it is about a job, your position in life, your idea of religion, your physical survival, or that you are not smart enough to do the one thing that you always wanted to do. It just comes down to all of it, no matter what that is, is just fear and misunderstanding.

So, how you perceive life, and what you think it should be, constitutes the type of choice you will make even though it is not a reflection of who you truly are. It is a reflection of the viewpoint of what you have chosen to act on as being real. To understand what is real and what is not is to feel the difference between what the rational mind is doing right now and what is coming from the heart of your full self. If thoughts come into your head as conditional thoughts then you are stuck.

Because we identified so strongly with whatever thoughts and emotions our rational mind considered truth, we have become caught up into believing that we are the character that we are playing rather than seeing the true actor that each of us are.

We have played many roles (lifetimes) and many scripts (stories) in the past, and we have played them out as if we truly believed that was who we were. And now, there is an opportunity for a new story (lifetime), a new life, a new family, a new place, and what we do is hang on to the old stories even though they don't serve us anymore. This causes us to layer our beliefs so much so that we have no idea who we are.

By understanding that you are *not* your rational mind or human personality, then you can make that huge leap beyond what you fear the most. Since the rational mind is where you play your games of make-believe that results in becoming emotionally tied to your past, you create drama so the rational mind can provide you with a sense of problems to solve. This then creates a challenge to the rational mind to find a solution, thus the deceptive mind (Anti-Christ) maintains its control over you.

The rational mind was designed by *you*, the creator, to provide protection from what could be considered as truth, falseness, good and bad. In other words, you created the rational mind to judge, and therefore you created a God that comes with conditions from the perspective of duality and not from the heart where your soul is. Therefore, since you created the rational mind, then you are responsible for all of your games that you have played out, including the one you are in now.

The physical body that you find yourself in today is nothing really other than you playing out a story. It will be gone someday just like the story of you living in a certain place, having a certain skill, the family name you are tied to, all will be gone. What will be left then is the *real* you and the application of the experience that you had. The character that you have created and the illusion of it will be gone. It will be nothing more than an experience that is now part of your soul memories, part of the wholeness of who you are, and part of your I AMness.

Is this hard to understand that the part that was you in this lifetime is not you anymore once you die? You only pretended that it was you that was married, had cancer, needed healing, had kids, that you needed a job, a house, a car, or that you needed salvation. You even pretended that you needed to have your prayers answered about you going to heaven.

Most of us pray for truth. Some pray for answers, and some say show me the way. What do we do? We continue to ignore the truth even though we can feel the real truth within our heart, that we are a divine being having a human experience. We hesitate to listen to our soul, or to our divine self, because of our family beliefs, our religion, and the fear of some God getting upset with us if we stopped believing in him.

The best thing for us to do is listen to our heart and then talk to our rational mind. Now, I don't mean argue with it or boss it around, or even try to control it. Just talk to it! Anytime you try to control, use logic, or reason with the rational mind, you are not going to get anywhere other than repeat your experiences over and over.

Allow the rational mind to think its thoughts of worry, its unworthiness, or that it is not good enough in measuring up to others. Just sit back, take deep breaths, and observe when the rational mind goes overboard with its thoughts of judgments, its fear of God, and its conditional ways.

Instead of trying to control the rational mind and your emotional thoughts, just tell the rational mind that you understand it in a deeper way than what it is judging itself on. Tell your rational mind that it is safe, that you value its service, and that it is not going to die, or be lost in some place of nothingness. Be strong but loving and direct, and then tell your rational mind that you are in charge and now it can rest.

Also, do not allow yourself to reason with the rational mind or talk it out of its fears; just understand that the rational mind was designed to protect you. But that doesn't mean you don't have to take these fears on just because the rational mind has doubt. Just remember, what is yours to experience is what you choose, and not that someone is placing it on you.

It is the rational mind that creates the belief system first and then it questions itself later, which then causes you to have emotional struggles that lead to finger pointing, like putting the blame on someone else or on something if things go wrong. It is the deceptive and rational mind that tricks you into thinking that someone is responsible for your acts, thereby allowing you to take the position that it is not your fault.

The rational mind is very persuasive because it will trick you into drama and that judgment is good if God is on your side. That is the mind's way of guaranteeing its continual existence and its control over you.

In order to shift your perception of truth, the divine part of you has recorded into your soul memories all that you have done and believed in from the time you left the first creation up until your now moment. In this way, the Christ you and your Lucifer consciousness are constantly at work causing your outer world to reflect back to you just who you have become. This is why you meet people and situations in your life, even family members, that causes you pain and suffering as well as joy and abundance.

What you are experiencing today is nothing more than your emotional personality-aspects (lifetimes) of your past that you have pushed away and ignored because of you not believing in reincarnation. This causes you to experience more and more shattered and violent circular (over and over) lifetimes of nothing but turmoil and instability until you finally have had enough where you begin to acknowledge, embrace, and honor your lifetimes past as something that was scripted by your soul.

When you begin to remember that you are the creator soul, you also get to remember that you are not those past emotional-aspects either. You are the parent that created them as your children to bring to you wisdom and understanding. Now, some of these emotional-aspects (lifetimes) of the past are knocking at your consciousness, wanting you to accept them as your creations. However, because of your strong belief in duality, and that there is only one lifetime, there is that chance of a missed opportunity to excel as an unconditional loving parent to welcome home those emotional aspects of yourself from past lifetimes.

It has been your lack of awareness, understanding, and your religious dogmatic views about good and evil, God and Satan that has caused you to play out your mind games for so many lifetimes. You, without realizing it, have believed everything the rational mind has told you about who you are and what to believe. Your focus has been completely about the rational mind and how it gets caught up into all kinds of drama, disasters, and situations where you must choose between what is right and wrong. Instead of you choosing who you truly are.

For me, like you, I have played this game of duality (this rollercoaster ride) for a long time and I have examined it for many lifetimes and now, in this lifetime, I understand the nature of the game, and that it is just that, a game. Of course, I have the opportunity to continue the game of duality using my emotions, and that of drama, or choose to be aware of the game that I am playing.

By accepting "all aspects of myself" and "all that I am today," as well as "all that I have created" along the way, then it becomes the first step in allowing my divinity (Christ self) to meld with the human me, which is the greatest achievement that I can ever make in this lifetime. Of all the successes I have had with my business, my writings, and the healing of my body, nothing can compare to me identifying myself as the Christ that I AM.

I have been an actor on the earth stage and my rational mind has been playing many different roles that see everything it has experienced as being real. Now, by accepting my soul's role in all that I have created, good and bad, I bring to myself tremendous clarity and knowing that I am the real creator of my world. This clarity and knowing brings to me the remembrance of my natural state of being, which is nothing but joy, healing, and abundance. No one has to convince or persuade me about my divinity. I know without a doubt that I AM the "prodigal son returning home" to my higher soul-self.

So, you can say that my consciousness, because of my desire to expand beyond the old dogmatic views to explore my rational mind and how it kept me limited for so long, has affected the way I receive energy today. Yes indeed, energy is changing for me through the circuitry components of my being, the plug-ins of my emotional personality-aspects of my past, the connection points that link me to my "I AM" soul or Christ self, and the points of separation that have kept me from my divinity.

My dear friends, this simply means when my energy changed from its vibratory nature of duality and conditional means, everything changed for me. All I can say is that it is a wonderful and beautiful thing if you understand what is going on around you. My human understanding of God, Satan, and my religious views have changed, and with me having no emotional ties to them, for they drew in vibrational energy of judgment, good and evil, and the thought of right and wrong being real. That itself created a belief system that created my reality as if I was only human and alone.

But because of my consciousness has expanded beyond organized religion and how I understand God and Satan on an emotional level. I am now reconnected to my soul (Christ self) and to all the personality-aspects (physical and non-physical) that my soul projected out on earth to be played out. Now, I cannot be swayed by my rational mind or other people that say I must always choose Jesus as my savior, or that I must attend church, or that I must help others before helping myself if I want to receive my rewards in heaven.

I know without any doubt that if I want to see heaven or experience any healing, then all that I have to do is choose it, take deep breaths, and create the miracle of my choosing. It was my soul (wisdom), and not my human self, that created my body and my temporary identity. My dear friends, it is not what I learned about God, my intelligence, or if I was educated in this lifetime. It is about the wisdom that I extracted from my many lifetime experiences that I had along the way and with all those that I came in contact with.

It is about understanding the soul and how I separated myself from the loveliness of my own wisdom. Because I was so much in my rational mind, so bent on living in duality of conditional rules, or that my rational mind knew all the answers, my soul could not bring forth the wisdom of my total consciousness or self.

My fellow searchers, what my soul seeked was experiences and now, my soul is inviting the human part of me to become *aware* of who I truly am. My soul didn't care about my intelligence, my business, or my ability to analyze or solve problems. All that my soul cared about in this lifetime was for me to become aware of who I truly am.

My soul has looked for me, the human aspect, in this lifetime to connect my rational mind, my physical body, my spirit, and my Christ (Gnost) consciousness to become one consciousness unto myself that no longer needs the old vibrational energy of two as my basic structure of reality. As a result, no longer will there be a veil over my future, a veil to prevent me to contact my higher "I AM" soul self, and most of all, no more limits to what I can experience or accomplish, for I am a true master that is equal to God and not less than.

Chapter 20

The Importance Of Deep Breathing

Because we live in a society that is very over sensitive in reacting to remedial solutions, it becomes necessary for me to make this disclaimer. "This book, and the chapters herein, is not intended as a substitute for medical advice. The reader should consult a physician in matters relating to his/her own health, and particularly with respect to any symptoms that may require diagnosis or medical attention.

Therefore, I, the author, or my publisher, do not dispense medical advice nor prescribe the use of any technique as a form of treatment for physical or medical treatment without the advice of a physician, either directly or indirectly. I am only offering information of a special nature to help those in their quest for understanding "who they truly are," and how deep breathing can carry a high potential in affecting their health, abundance, and joy."

That said I now will move on to the subject matter of deep breathing and how it can affect your quality of life.

What is the importance of deep breathing anyway? John 1:1, *"In the beginning was the word, and the word was with God, and the word was God."* When looking behind the *word* of spirit you will find an even greater power than the *word*, it is the *breath*.

My dear friends, it takes the *breath* to reveal your manifestations. Even in most religious writings, old and new, the use of the words air, wind, and breath, and how they are used in the same manner as for life, energy, and spirit is revealed as the principle in creating life. This means the principle of your spirit's divine presence is used to call in the "breath of life" in whatever you, the creator, choose to create.

The breath that we take from the time we are born until the day we die is very much overlooked, misunderstood, and underestimated when it comes to searching for the source of life, our spirit's existence, and the meaning of life – even though Genesis 2:7 tells us that, *"The Lord God formed man of dust from the ground, and breathed into his nostrils the breath of life, and man became a living soul."*

My dear co-creators, it was not a white male Hebrew God that formed your body from the dust of the ground. It was your own spirit, which is why, by that same breath, *you* can find your way back home to your own "I AM God" identity. How is this possible? It is possible because your spirit's presence is within each breath you take. If your spirit was not in each breath then the physical body would die.

You see, the movement of your spirit in the physical body is reflected in the art of how you actually breathe. If you breathe with a shallow breath then the space between the top and bottom of your breath can confine and suppress your spirit in giving life to your creations such as, causing the cells in your physical body to suffocate, thus creating for yourself many physical problems.

By taking shallow breaths you partially fill the lungs without realizing that shallow breathing can cause headaches, dizziness, high blood pressure, feeling fatigue, memory difficulties, numbness, irritability, chest or heart pressures, and many other irregularities. Then to top it off, to correct or control your health problems you take pharmaceutical drugs that translates to even more physical problems.

The power of breath is the answer to your health problems than taking all kinds of medicines that do nothing but harm the body. What if I said that you can miraculously heal your health problems, including memory loss, just by spending at least fifteen to thirty minutes a day for a few months doing deep breathing? Now, on the other hand, you can always choose to take the remedially drugs and let someone else control your life and your health.

Look, deep breathing is not just about the Bible. It is also a science that is long established in promoting health and longevity. Deep breathing has been part of the Bible since its inception. Even the prophets who wrote it referenced the art of deep breathing for a reason.

When you take deep breaths and then let everything go, including all your emotional attachments, and then invite in your soul-spirit back into your human life that is when healing and rejuvenation can begin to take place. By letting everything go on an emotional level, and then add deep breathing as a life line, that is when you bring in no fear, no stress, and no judgment. Even the healing power of Christ mentioned in the Bible was attained through the art of deep breathing.

If you choose to do deep breathing, then be aware of your worries and concerns without judgment and then allow yourself to meet your identical twin by looking at your human self and your soul self eye to eye, heart to heart, and soul to human. That is when you will see that it has been a long time since you have felt your spirit, your soul, your divinity, and that you allowed it to be fully present in your rational mind and body. Which is why, at first, it takes awhile to fully feel their presence.

In the Book of Secrets, Osho Rajneesh writes: "If you can do something with breath, you will attain the source of life, you can transcend time and space, you will be in the world, and also beyond it." He also wrote, "There are certain points in the breathing which you have never observed, and those points are the doors, the nearest doors to you, from where you can enter into a different world, into a different being, a different consciousness."

From my research, deep breathing is the quickest and easiest way to clear your rational mind, calm your emotions, and open your heart to a new understanding of who you truly are, for you are Christ in manifestation. Deep breathing uplifts you, balances you, and then grounds you to the effect that you can open yourself up to receiving your Christ self because it has been absent from your human self for a long time.

It is through deep breathing where you will find your true connection with the God that you are coming through to your human level. When you allow yourself time for deep in-breaths then the out-breaths will reconnect you to your soul, and to the awareness of you being a Christ also. Thus, the reconnection of your soul is the "human you" becoming aware of your journey through time and space finding its way back home to your "Christ I AMness."

Your soul is a divine Christ like being that created many false you's, good and bad, in order to explore the question, "Who Am I"? Maybe that is where the word "rebirth or rebirthing" came from in the Bible. It offers a conscious awakening to your many former lifetimes and then finally to a physical lifetime where you encounter your own Christ essence by way of your soul coming into your human body in this lifetime.

You can find in the Bible the basic doctrine that brings out the variations between you and the "whys" in which you experience different things, good and bad. This is why you are born in many diverse physical bodies to learn the lessons related to those "whys" in which you experience. This then eventually leads to you opening up to your own divine essence, the grander you.

It is quite evident that the Bible speaks of rebirth. For instance: the Jewish priest asked John the Baptist, *"Art thou Elijah"?* (John 1:21). In Matthew 11:14, you have the words of Jesus relating to John the Baptist as Elijah, which is explicit and clear – for Jesus said, *"this is Elijah."*

Then later in Matthew 17:1-13, at the time when Jesus took Peter, James, and John his brother upon the mount of transfiguration. Jesus said, *"Elijah has come already, and they knew him not, but done unto him whatsoever." "Then the disciples understood that Jesus spoke unto them of John the Baptist."*

In Matthew 16:13-17, Jesus asking his disciples, *"Who do people say that the Son of Man is?"* The disciples replied, *"Some say John the Baptist, others Elijah, still others Jeremiah or one of the prophets."* Then Jesus said to them, *"But who do you say that I am?"* Then Peter replied, *"You are the Messiah, the Son of the living God."* Jesus' reply to Peter was, *"Blessed are you, Simon son of Jonah. For flesh and blood has not revealed this to you, but my heavenly Father."*

Have you noticed from these verses from the Bible that Jesus did not disagree with his disciples when they talked about rebirth, which is very noteworthy here? After all, according to the Bible, Jesus was a teacher, and he was celebrated as being the Christ. Therefore, if his disciples had entertained a wrong view concerning the idea of rebirth, then it would have been Jesus' duty to have corrected them.

However, Jesus did not indicate that there was any need to correct them. Also, Simon Peter's reply to Jesus does convey an understanding of a deeper truth when it comes to the mission of Jesus, the Christ.

We can even go further into the biblical support for the doctrine of rebirth. We can find cases mentioned where an individual was chosen for a certain undertaking before their birth. Look at Samson and his undertaking, as an angel foretold his coming and his mission to slay the Philistines (Judges 13:1-25). In verse two and three it reads:

"There was a certain man in Zorah, of the family of Danites, whose name was Manoah, and his wife was barren." "And the angel of the Lord appeared unto the woman, and said unto her, Behold now, thou art barren, and barest not; but thou shalt conceive, and bear a son…and he shall begin to deliver Israel out of the hand of the Philistines." "And the woman bared a son, and called his name Samson."

You can find in Jeremiah 1:5, *"Before I formed you in the womb I knew you, before you were born I dedicated you, a prophet to the nations I appointed you."* As you can see, most of us are familiar with some of the Bible stories telling us of the coming of Jesus, John, Samson, and many others to perform special missions for mankind.

An individual is chosen for a special mission because of one fitting the purpose for a particular kind of work to be done in order to advance mankind in consciousness. As you can also see, the ability, skills, and the capacity to fulfill their missions were not handed out by God on a silver platter. They all had to work hard with other lifetimes prior to their rebirth in those lifetimes in order for them to accomplish their missions.

You can find in the Bible many places of the doctrine of rebirth and how it was taught in the events that were mentioned. Just look in the first Psalm, for instance, which can be wisely interpreted only by using a belief in rebirth as a basis.

Look at the "law of cause and effect" or what the Bible calls "sowing and reaping." When you work with the law of rebirth to bring about perfect justice and fairness, or the law of consequences, then you can see the law works perfectly on all levels including the earthly realm.

Look in Galatians 6:7-9 where you are told not to be deceived – *"for God is not mocked because whatsoever a man soweth that shall he also reap."* This includes whatever one soweth in the flesh shall of the flesh reap as well as in spirit. The chapter also talks about not being weary in what you do – *"for in due season we shall reap."* Due season is not spring, summer, fall, or winter or later in life. It is all about other lifetimes paying the price for what you did.

Look in John Chapter Nine in its entirety – for we will find the story of the blind man from birth and Jesus' disciples asking him who sinned, the man or the blind man's parents. As Jesus' reply was, *"Neither, but that the works of God should be made manifest in him."* From these passages Jesus is making a great effort to make it clear that the law of sowing and reaping behind our physical limitations is not about sin and punishment, but about experiencing, clarification, and enlightenment.

Here we can find the perfect justice of the law of cause and effect at its best, which of course brings about all calamities, accidents, disease, and wrongdoings. When we, as souled beings, separated ourselves from our own oneness a long time ago as a massive group consciousness, we created the law of cause and effect in order for us to return in another lifetime with all of our limitations to face head on that were the results of us violating the law of consequences.

It was, and still is today, the transgression of divine laws that lead us, as humans, through many sorrows and sufferings that accompany our limitations as a human. Of course, in doing so, we learn our lessons, and then the character flaws within our human personality are then removed. Thus, the freedom of our soul is a condition that begins within us.

It takes the breath to explore the mystery of rebirth, that of consciousness, and the mystery between the first in-breath and the last out-breath that we experience as a three-dimensional being. It is the breath that brings in our spirit and our soul into biology.

Let's look at the element of air, which is also known as breath, and is the most mysterious element on earth. Why? It is because, like spirit, air cannot be seen. However, we can experience both and see the effects of them. You see, it took the first in-breath to set up the substance of matter or the biological body in which part of our soul became enclosed, and with all of spirit's ability to animate (bring to life) the body in doing things.

Thus, the in-breath of your spirit set up a powerful impact within the physical body that strongly affected your nervous system where each successive in-breath had repeated itself and then reflected back to you what you have chosen to act on, good or bad. Therefore, the energy of positive and negative, whichever was used to produce or manifest the choice, remains until you finally clear all circumstances that allowed the origin and growth of the interconnecting energies that manifested the choice. This is why the Bible states that "thoughts are things."

For instance: Let's say that your first in-breath, once you came into a physical body long ago, was based on fear, and this fear empowered you to force things into your life because of feeling so much anxiety in not knowing what is going to happen. Well! The first imprint, first pattern, and the first lasting effect into your nervous system is all about fear, and now this fear is stamped (sealed) into the memory cells, the organs, and the tissues of the physical body.

Thus, you have become unconscious of the mix of things that you have created, positive and negative, good and bad, since the time you left your divine state (the first creation). Because of the impact of the first in-breath being about fear and how you, from a mental state, acted toward pure neutral energy, you have placed a number of recurring mixed thought actions that have formed a number of dissimilar personality-aspects (lifetimes) that differ in many respects.

Now, these differing personality-aspects of cruel, immoral, depraved, merciless, liars, as well as with your aspects of good, decent, moral, upright, worthy, pleasant, and skillful ones are still part of you. Of course, let's not forgot your many religious aspects from many different religions. They too are all part of your lifetime of today.

All of your human personality-aspects of the past are still with you by means of the cells, the organs, the tissues of the body, the nervous system, and even the blood that flows through you. It is just that you have forgotten them. Now, the out-breath you take each time you breathe-in this lifetime in a way is preparing you for your final out-breath.

Now, this final out-breath is not about your death here in this lifetime. What I am referring to here is you, as all humans, need to integrate all those human aspects (lifetimes) of yourself with your human self of today, which in turn is followed by your freedom to create all the miracles you desire.

So, looking at fear and what you have attached yourself to in bringing about your fears is a good place to begin if you are ready to meld back into your spirit "all that you are." In other words, are you ready to make the choice that will benefit the wholeness of you and not just the human you of today? If you are, then first, never play down the story told by your rational mind, and that of others, that you only live one lifetime.

Instead, allow yourself to feel your human ego personality-aspects of the past desiring to come home to their creator, *you*. Feel what brings you joy, unconditional love, forgiveness, and compassion, for that is the divine you that is reaching out to all your other human personality-aspects to come home to you.

Secondly, take deep in-breaths and out-breaths several times and then feel your heart telling you that it knows the divine you. When you do take the in-breath and out-breath, don't concern yourself if you feel the two polarities pulling at your rational mind trying to stop what you are doing and stick with what you have been taught.

However, when you do take your in-breath and out-breath watch, at the top of your inhale and at the bottom of your exhale, how it pauses for a minuscule of a second where there is no breath happening at all. I mentioned this because you can feel at the top of your inhale, and just before your exhale, and vice-versa, you are actually going in and out of your truths. If you will allow, you will come back into a new truth at a different place in consciousness every time.

Why is this? Well, from what I have found on a personal note is that the in-breath, along with the short pause at the top, followed with the out-breath and its pause, becomes my entry way into my total consciousness, my wholeness, including my memories of the past, present, and future. It is through my in-breath and out-breath where I find timelessness, memory recovery, my emotions that I have not yet let go, and the influences of my past lifetimes.

Through deep breathing I have been learning how to feel those lost deep emotions because all of them are connected to some past lifetime where I have played them out as a story and as my truth. By becoming aware of all parts and pieces of me, I began the process of redesigning myself by accepting them as my creations. Once I did, more light moved into my body cells in redesigning the energy coming into them. Thus healing and memory began!

However, before this can happen for you, the basic interconnecting patterns that are of your emotional and intellectual beliefs (truths) must be let go before you can move into any type of healing and memory gain. Another thing! Allow yourself a period to do your breathing that is not based on a time limit before you are healed. Sometimes it can take weeks, months, and even years before you finally make the connection to your soul.

Often when you begin your focus on breathing, the old energies that have been held in the body for a long time will be the first to release. This is when you will have all kinds of feelings. A whole range of them coming out, like sadness, not being worthy, hate, resentment, anger, jealousy, and a whole lot more before you begin your healing.

This is when you need to take note here because when those things begin to release from your consciousness that is when you are very highly susceptible to getting stuck with them all over again. Just keep on taking deep breaths in and out, and allow yourself to understand that you have been playing with many human lifetimes for a long time and it can be difficult releasing those old beliefs (truths) about yourself let alone this idol of a white male Hebrew God that created you.

As you can witness for yourself! It is easy to control people by using emotions as the trigger, because this is how governments, religions, family, friends, and the media control the masses. They feed us with beliefs that tell us not to feel our feelings or go within because it is through our feelings and going within where we find the real truth that the rational and deceptive mind are the driving force that determines our lifetime and how we are going to live it.

Just remember, there is no outside force like a God, the government, job, church, or money that is the source for your miracles. Rather, you are the source for your miracles because it begins within you and your ability to change your inner world first, not your outer world.

For Instance: Allow me to tell you a story that I once read somewhere in my discovery of spirit. However, my version of what I got out of the story is a bit different than the one I read.

There was this person who wanted to learn the process of breathing. During his first encounter of deep breathing, he had many deep feelings of anger and resentment moving through him. So, he went to his teacher for advice. All that his teacher said to him was to just keep breathing and observe his emotions and feelings. Hence, when he got through that he also managed to get through the stage where he was starting to burn up a lot of karma. You could say that his whole body was being consumed by the flames of preprogrammed consequences.

When this person was having internal visions being consumed by what seemed like fire and brimstone, he became very distressed. So, he again went to his teacher to ask what was happening to him. All that the teacher said to him was to keep on breathing and observing. When he finally managed to get through that, his own divinity (his Christ self) came to visit him and asked if he was now ready to dance with his soul as one.

Now, when this person accepted the dance with his divinity that is when his "I AM" entered his physical consciousness, along with his other human personality-aspects of the past, filling him with glorious wisdom, memory, and understanding. Even then, his teacher came along and said for him to keep on breathing and observing.

The meaning of the message: When you learn to breathe from the standpoint of observing and being aware of yourself as a conscious creator. You will learn the "whys" of creating many human personality-aspects of yourself; the "whys" of you choosing different lifetimes where you played with the energy of good and bad; and the "whys" of you experiencing the suffering of those so called accidents or bad things that came into your life unexpectedly. Thus, the bringing in the "understanding" of miracles! The conjecture of the word "miracles" is nothing more than you not knowing "who you truly are" from the standpoint of awareness.

It is "awareness" that makes itself known to you as wisdom and, if you are *not* aware of who you truly are then you are hidden from your wisdom. When you finally accept responsibility for yourself and allow others to do the same. Then trust yourself as a creator and let go of all your fears, and that will be the time when true healing will come to you.

Healing comes when you no longer have the need to tell your story about what made you suffer in the first place. So, if you feel alone and depressed right now about puzzling events in your life or that you are looking for understanding in what is happening to you, then I would consider the importance of deep breathing.

Through deep breathing you will see, hear, and feel things that you have never experienced before. Like for example: No religion, no God or Satan pulling at you, and no sinning, just forward movement in understanding your creations. Deep breathing is powerful, intense, very confronting, fun, and it is the magic that brings in healing, abundance, joy, and the secrets of your soul. Therefore, never underestimate the power of breath.

Just by working with breath alone you can do amazing things. If you focus on deep breathing and the letting go of your fears, it is possible to do even greater things, for greater secrets and wisdom are revealed. It is not God, religion, science, governments, or your guru, not even those that have money. It is you that contain the wisdom of who you think you are and no one else. If you believe that you are limited and need saving then so be it.

My healing came from freeing myself from the belief in sin, the belief that some white male Hebrew God created me and gives me things, taking full responsibility for my life, and becoming aware of my soul, which then led me to my wisdom. It was from my soul introducing me to my past lifetime aspects that released me from my karmic conditions of the past and present, which then led me to my true essence and to my wisdom.

By me letting go of the idea of sin, the worry of failure, and the feeling of being unworthy to some single white male God released me from my deep hidden secrets that I didn't even know that they were there. This new awareness launched me into a new energy that set the stage for the rejuvenation of my cells in my body, in my mind, and in my human personality of a 5-D consciousness.

When you are aware of being a Christ in your own right, you expand your 3-D consciousness much faster and much easier to the 5-D consciousness. Breathing is the purification and the awakening of the human you where you automatically ascend and develop the skill to walk your own path as a sovereign being and a genuine Master in your own right. That is the empowering aspect of deep breathing, for no one can do it for you but you.

It is through deep breathing where you will awaken to the highest of realities of life, wisdom, and of a 5-D consciousness, thus coming to know all the deep secrets of your soul, thus answering your own questions. Deep breathing is the pathway to your divine essence, your soul, your spirit, your Gnost, and your Christ identity – for they are all the same, *you*.

I kid you not! Deep in-breaths and out-breaths lead to the healing of stress, emotional problems, substance abuse, and to the healing of all fears and anxieties. Through the angel of Luceffa, breath has been the technique for a long time that brings to you the fire of karma and the awareness by evolutionary agreements in the form of natural disasters, social upheavals, and wars. These things are doing the work of pushing you out of your comfort zone and into a spiritual awakening, purification, and rebirth.

Deep breathing can move you through the eye of any storm in your life with great ease and comfort because it will bring to you peace, balance, and power. All that it takes is trust. Trust in yourself as being the creator of your world. Understand that your human existence on earth right now is actually less than two percent of all that you are. This means the grandest of you is not with you one hundred percent of the time because you refuse to let it in.

The reality of pain, disappointment, and self-doubt is always present at the doorway of your rational consciousness, filling you with distractions, excuses, complaints, and impatience. It is your fear of life that constricts the natural flow of your energy, which means you move even further into restriction, and that of a 3-D consciousness. In order to understand what is happening right now is that you need to think outside of the box and to think outside of your current way of doing things.

Don't get caught up with mental analysis of trying to figure out God or Satan, and why things are happening to you. Stop all of this running around trying to figure out what to do, and understand that it is all a natural process in order for you to move forward in consciousness. Oh! You may argue with me on this point. However, evolution of your soul is natural. Your life, health, body, joy, and your abundance will all take care of itself if you would just let it. Nothing new can come in to your life if you keep on forcing things in your life.

Understand that you are already connected to every piece of wisdom, abundance, and all that you are, and all that you have to do is make the conscious choice and allow it in. If you keep up your deep breathing and follow your heart instead of worrying all the time, you will eventually open up to a whole new 5-D world of wisdom and experiences.

So, stop your complaining and make the conscious choice to become a sovereign and free being that needs nothing to make you happy. Everything you need to make you happy is there already waiting for you to bring it into your life. Remember, deep breathing, like intuition, is something that is very difficult to define because you want to use words of a mental and rational nature to define it. Deep breathing, and its effects on you, cannot be reasoned with about why it works. You just know that it does.

My fellow searchers, your divinity is very much a part of you but you have separated yourself from it because you were sold a bill of goods that Christ is only of one man. Therefore, your divinity and soul have been very much ignored for a long time, which is why you don't trust yourself in bringing in your creations of health, joy, and abundance. Instead you choose to follow your rational mind, the professionals out there, and your family as if they know what is best for you. How do they know what is best for you if they don't know what is best for themselves?

As you can see, breathing is a good friend of your spirit because they work well together. Your spirit is the identity of your soul, for the two have always worked together because your soul is the voice, intuition, and the wisdom of your spirit. It takes deep breathing to trigger your soul, spirit, and intuition in order for them to become a permanent residence with your human consciousness. Once they become a permanent residence with your human personality, you ascend to a whole new 5-deminsional world of joy, abundance, and health.

You don't have to prepare your body and rational mind, or do a lot of processing, thinking, or philosophizing. All that you have to do is invite your spirit and soul into your life. It is when you are not aware of your divinity in your present reality that allows the diseases, your suffering, and your fears to take over, all because of your dogmatic beliefs.

Remember, the 2-D rational mind will always try to run everything in your life because the 2-D rational mind does not understand the ways of your spirit and soul and how they work as one unit. By observing your deep breathing, pay attention to what is happening within you and around you in each moment. Breathe with awareness and do it with self-assurance that you are a living Christ in the flesh.

Feel the expansion of your wisdom, and at the same time, feel the narrowing of your problems. Breath in your I AMness and watch the world around you change forever. So, invite your divine essence in and you will be amazed about how much you can do as a true creator. As you breathe deeply for those fifteen to thirty minutes a day, feel the essence of your spirit-soul come in. Then keep breathing and know that you have been away for a long time.

All I can add now is that it does go beyond words. It is an experience that turns into a knowing that you are no longer operating within just a small portion of your total consciousness. It is about opening the door of your 2-D consciousness widely and you moving into a new doorway that consists of no duality. To get to this 4-D and 5-D doorway of non-duality, you must understand that your divinity has never judged you, and it never will because your divinity understands that you have been operating with a limited 2-D mind that only knows itself as being the bread winner.

Only an invitation from the human you can bring in your divinity. No church, religion, or any Christ like being outside of you can bring your divinity in, only you. So, take several deeps breaths every day for at least fifteen to thirty minutes. If you have the courage to let go of your fear of God, Satan, and your anxieties about life, then take the next step and invite your spirit-soul in, and then watch what happens.

With allowing your spirit-soul (divinity) and the wholeness of your being back into your human self in this lifetime, you are going to find yourself moving beyond the 2-D rational mind, your fears, and most importantly, your 3-D philosophy of God and his mystery of distractions.

My dear friends, the mystery of God no longer needs to remain a mystery because the divineness within you no longer needs to be hidden. Your spirit-soul wants to share your life with you because it is your real essence, and it has been part of you for a long time but your human self has been keeping it away because of your belief that some white male God created you.

It took the spirit of life, the Christ part of you, to breathe in your human consciousness, and now your human consciousness has come to a point where it can invite your spirit in through that same breath.

Chapter 21

Learn To Be A Conscious Creator

How do you become a "conscious creator"? It is by accepting the fact that you are responsible for everything that comes into your life. Nothing is left out, not even the excuses of being born poor, rich, sexually abused, being a raped victim, or any other misfortune that you have experienced, not even cancer. You cannot be a "conscious creator" and a "true master" if you are still blaming yourself, other people, and circumstances for what happened to you long ago or is happening to you now, even if you truly believe it is not your fault.

Understand that in some unspecified life or distinctive manifestation in your journey of life, you have made the choice to experience what you are experiencing today even though you cannot remember the choice. By accepting this truth it becomes the first step toward your healing. Can you imagine at a deep level knowing something that feels so profoundly true about yourself but not accepting it because of fear? So, what do we do instead? We learn to blame others for our misfortunes in life. My dear friends this is living in hell at its best.

For instance: You have the poor blaming the rich, others blaming their parents, or where they grew up, or that it was just the cards that they were dealt. You have those that were sexually abused blaming their parents, relatives, or their parents' friends, not realizing that sex abuse is a virus of the mind that is carried forward from another lifetime, thus not a wrongful or right action. It cannot be wrong or right if it is looked at as an experience that was chosen from a deeper level in order to understand oneself.

You also have those that identify themselves as middleclass blaming their misfortunes on their education, spouse, siblings, bad relationships, their job, the government, an illness, and even karma. You have the rich saying it is the fault of society, a competitor, government, employees, the stock market, as well as many other things.

You have those that say they had no choice about what family they were born into, and therefore had no choice in the matter about their family being abusive, cold, and uncaring. When they see families that appear kind, loving, warm, and supportive toward each other, they either feel sorry for themselves or they are angry and jealous at them because of their lives seeming so effortless.

Some people are born into a family that prepares them for the future while others are born into a family of alcoholics or dope-attic parents, and the ignorance that surround them thus giving them the impression that there is no chance at life anyway. All of this becomes very taxing to them because of carry within them the mental problems into adulthood trying to overcome them.

My dear friends, it is not about losing the lottery, or where one is born, or what journey one undertakes to make them stronger. Life is not about God's lessons. It is about becoming aware of your soul's journey in answering the call to come to earth to answer the question, "Who Am I?"

You can find everywhere souls that went through some very dark times feeling alone and betrayed by those that were closest to them and yet, it was all part of everyone's plan to become a "conscious creator." Earth is the playground to learn how to be a true creator in your own right.

We all have been in creatorship training and we have been doing it in various ways using multi-dimensional realms and creating many human personality aspects of ourselves because earth and duality has become a dimension where we could experience very harsh realities. However, the time has come for us to forgive ourselves, to forgive others, and learn to trust and love ourselves. Earth and duality is the last step before going on into the third circle of no-suffering and yet, to get to this no-suffering, we must learn to let go of our story and what we believed happened to us as not being our fault.

It is not about your fault! It is about "choosing" because of the desire to know "who you are," and therefore it is about taking full responsibility for your choices and your creations. You see, the third circle is a place for full creators without having limitations put on them because of the mind-set of victimhood and their highlighted emotions due to duality thinking.

It is not about victimhood. It is all about your experiences that you took from every different direction in order to understand how energy and power works, and in the end, learn who you truly are.

So yes, it is about letting go of our story and our dogmatic belief, for that is the part of us that played with the forces of opposites. Know that we truly embodied our creations of duality and the power that came with it. We brought them to life, manifested them, and had it feel so real that we got lost. Now, we carry the wisdom of those dualistic experiences and the meaning of power within us, and into this third circle as a sovereign conscious creator in our own right.

My dear friends, the time has come for you to look at who you truly are and accept full responsibility as a creator. When you do, you are going to find your soul knocking at the door of your Christ consciousness to unify all parts and pieces of you that are confused, angry, and frustrated because they have felt left out when it comes to you loving them. Understand, before they can accept you as their creator, you have to accept the "I AMness" of you being a Christ also that created them.

It is not about your excuses or the words you come up with anymore to justify what you are experiencing or feeling emotionally. It is about accepting no more "what if's," or "but I was" excuses, or "being unworthy" of having a high meaningful life. Every part of you wants to come back home to the real you, the true executive administrator of your life. If you are not clear about who you are, because of your emotions and dogmatic beliefs, then it will be difficult to move to the next level.

All of your human personality aspects (lifetimes past) are looking for a good leader. A leader that will not demean them and the present you because of karma, your parents, your education, your lack of money, you feeling unworthy of having a relationship, or even you pretending that you don't know the answers to your problems. You do know the answers because you can feel them! It is about you moving past the empty pointless comments of not being good enough because of "who you think you are" versus knowing "who you truly are" in the greater scheme of things.

If you haven't totally accepted the "I AMness" of your soul, where you know that you are a Christ also, then all I can say is to expect your accidents, ups and downs, dramas, and your crisis in life to continue. Don't expect your cross on the wall or around your neck to save you, or wait for God to tell you he loves you because you will wait a long time.

Just admit that you are loved dearly by your own soul (Christ self) even if you don't go to church, help your neighbor, or love some pretense of a God outside of you. Step out of your hopelessness state of mind, take responsibility for yourself, and become the owner of your creations, good, bad, past, and present. Once this is done, then all human aspects of you (other lifetimes) will feel your love for them. Thus creating an avenue for them to come home to their creator, *you*.

Remember, a true creator only takes responsibility for oneself and not for anyone else's life, such as a father, a mother, a son, a daughter, a brother, a sister, a spouse, a friend, or even a foe because of feeling obligated or feeling guilty because of one's faith, duty, or honor. It is not about your faith, duty, honor, or praying to God for them, or trying to heal them because you love them. It is that you cannot be their co-creator because you "know not what they have chosen" from the soul level to find their own balance.

If the co-creations are only based on prayer for one to heal because of missing them or losing a great friend or relationship, then all that is going to happen is that your life and energy, not theirs, will disintegrate and fragment even more because of trying to interfere with their choices. Of course, not praying for them does not mean that you do not love them. Praying for them only shows that you do not trust their own soul in what it is doing.

Try to understand the bigger picture here as to what is going on in their lives. Yes, it is okay to show your love for them but do it because you choose to not because of feeling obligated. However, let me warn you. Your soul knows if it is unconditional love or obligation. So, have compassion for them and let go of trying to run their lives and choices – for they are a creator Christ unto themselves.

I know that we can feel hurt and upset when things don't go right in our lives including what happens to our loved ones in getting sick to the point that it seems like God has forsaken them. God has not forsaken them, you, or anyone! Have compassion, for their own soul is bringing in the carefully worked-out formula to end their causes of mental and physical torment that they put on themselves in order for them to evolve into a sovereign being. Where they know they are a divine being also.

Look, I know that it can come hard for us to let go because of our emotional ties to them. However, we must learn to let them go because it is not up to us, or anyone for that matter, to understand their soul in how it will carry out their divine plan that will eventually give them freedom. The worst thing we can do is pray for them and place our will onto them because what will happen is that we will end up with a need to blame someone or something if they are not healed or helped, even God or the Devil if it makes sense to us.

You see, when it comes to prayers not being fulfilled fast enough, and if things don't go the way you have planned it in your head, the rational mind will automatically look around for someone or something to blame. Of course, it is those that you love the most and are closest to you who are the easiest targets, especially God and your spouse.

So, what happens when you have been seduced into the trap of playing the blame game? Of course, you become a victim unto yourself, a victim of your own making where you bring to yourself nothing but more and more ups and downs in your life. So much so, that it can cause you financial hardships, bad relationships, poor health, so called accidents, and many other unhappy events.

Look, a few years ago I lost my sister-in-law to cancer. Despite my sister-in-law's surgery and treatments, the cancer spread throughout her body. After accepting hospice for a bit, she finally died at home with her family at her side. She was fifty-seven years old, and by all accounts, my sister-in-law was very active when it came to learning about herself and to her relationship to her soul. She lived quietly with meaning and purpose, and her death is a prime example of how short life can be.

I mention this to help you think about what you would feel in relation to how you have lived your own life when your time comes. Will you take ownership of every comment that you have made about someone? How about the deals you have made in life? Will you take ownership of your achievements as well as all of your screw-ups? Will you feel like you have lived life on your own terms or will you blame others and circumstances for what has happened in your life?

We all know people who have consigned themselves to living half-healthy lives, emotionally and physically, by continually choosing to blame other people for their health, their position in life, their financial situations, why they lost their jobs, their homes, their cars, their spouses, sons, daughters, and many, many other things.

For instance: Look how we blame companies of food products for our obesity instead of taking full responsibility for the food we eat. To me, it is unconscious living and all that we are doing is passing the blame onto someone else instead of owning our own lives, health, and a chance to be happy and free of worry.

Yes, we can blame the stock market, our financial situation, our boyfriend, girlfriend, spouse, kids, our work schedule, our job, our boss, the activists, the terrorists, and even the demands that are put on us every day. And all that it does, we suffer even more because it puts us in an unimaginative and uninspired state of mind.

By blaming other people for our pain and suffering just keeps us from becoming a true "conscious creator" that can bring into our lives nothing but miracles to experience. Remember, greed works both ways! Greed is not just about the rich. Greed is also the poor living of the government and its people because of not willing to take full responsibility for their choices to live that way.

In other words, a lot of us just can't find our way out of the box that we put ourselves into because we refuse to imagine anything else but what we are experiencing. Yes, we can always find situations to slow us down because of money, a death in the family, or some illness, or maybe an injury that inflicts extensive exhausting treatments, or not finding our soul mate. Of course, these events can leave us emotionally confused, for it is natural.

However, when we allow ourselves some time and space to get our act together, we can recreate a whole new version of ourselves that can finally release the blame game. No one has to live life with complexity, difficulty, feeling sorry for oneself or even the role of trying to be a martyr for some cause. It is about *awareness* and *knowing* who you truly are that brings you grace.

You see, most everyone works with sin and karma on a daily basis with confusion, aggravation, and with feelings of unworthiness. Everyone, at some time or another, has faced desperation, depression, lack of funds, grief, and loneliness of some sort in their lives, and then turned around and said life isn't fair because we don't get to choose our circumstances, our surroundings, or get to control the people around us.

My fellow searchers, life is fair! The reason we don't see it as fair is because we see life as not being perfect. Life is perfect! Because we are perfect! It is perfect because we are the ones choosing what experiences we want to experience. There will always be obstacles, annoyances, and limitations to challenge us on an emotional scale. However, it is how we accept these challenges that separate us from receiving a high meaningful life of clarity and simplicity or receiving life as desperate and discouraging.

The miracle of a high meaningful life requires commitment from the heart that you are the creator of your life and the world you live in today. If not, you will receive a low meaningful life of despair and anxiety because of those challenges. Just because things don't work out the way you think it should in your life is no excuse to get emotionally frustrated because of having certain expectations about someone owing you something, even government and its people. Does it come hard for you to understand that government gets its money (energy) from the people?

Look at it this way! No one owes you anything, not even a living. Where do you get that the people of a government owe you a living? Do you belief it comes from the Bible or is it just morally and ethically right to give to others that can't help themselves? Everyone, rich, poor, sick or healthy, are all equal in God's eye, and are therefore connected to the same potentials and opportunities just by being divine in nature.

Looking at oneself as uneducated, unworthy, and being born poor is no justification to belief someone owes you something. Oh, one can hope to get out of poverty. However, hope itself is nothing but mental images of limitations, fear, and wishful thinking. Not that hope is a negative thing but it can be, for hope can keep you working in a cycle of its own. It is about taking full responsibility for you and becoming stronger because of it. By doing this, you will find the magic within you that creates exactly what you desire. (Let it be health, money, moving out of poverty, a new car, home, or whatever).

When you sign (figuratively speaking) your own proclamation that you will take full responsibility for yourself, and that you are the creator of your world, watch what happens. You will automatically understand that you are not a victim but are a true creator in your own right. If you acknowledge your divine creatorship authority, you will bring into your life completion. Consider Jesus, he did not blame anyone for his crucifixion.

This completion means you love and trust yourself as a true Christ in your own right because you will never have to fix anything again. Why? Because you will have the understanding that you don't need anything, not even those extra materialistic goods to keep you alive and happy.

When you realize that you have nothing to fix because of sin, karma, or guilt that is when you will begin to create the miracles of abundance, health, joy, and a knowing that you no longer have to fear God or control your life. God is not the God you think, God is about you learning to be a sovereign Christ in human form instead of trying to preserve your human identity as who think you are. It is about operating in the moment of pure trust in being a Christ unto yourself.

Let's look at money for instance: You control your money as if it hurts when you buy something for yourself or for someone else. You act as if money is the only thing that is going to make you happy just because it brings comfort and security. Well, it's not! We try to control money because we are so afraid that we will not make enough to support who we are.

Some of us are always looking for ways to impress someone because that is the ego's way of telling someone that we are someone to be reckoned with. My dear friend's money is nothing but potential and energy waiting to come in and serve us, the true creators.

Remember, money, like energy, does not have a vibrational imprint on it until your consciousness brings it into reality. Therefore, the more you control money, what you eat, what you think, ways to impress, what you do to control others, even the controls that say you are getting older, and especially the controlling of your body because you don't like what it looks like, the more your life will become confused, complicated, and harder to understand.

When you learn to let go of all these controls, especially the control of right and wrong and that you need money to feel safe, then the more your divine inner knowingness can become synchronistic with your outer human identity. My dear friends, this means your life becomes more in line with you inner soul self. Thus life, money, health, relationships, and many other things come to you as if they simply appear out of the blue.

You see, all that these controls do is reflect back to you what you are embracing in life. The more you try to control things in life, the more restrictive and limiting you become! It is as simple as that! There are many changes going on around you right now, not just with the world but with your soul. The last one to know this is your human ego with all of its emotions and needless claims that someone somehow owes you a living or an apology. No one owes you anything, not your father, mother, spouse, family, friends, your boss, government, or your church.

Look, when you look at yourself in the mirror what do you see? Do you see a physical body that has a spirit, mind, and soul or do you just see the human part of you and the story you are living out right now? This is a very important question to understand, and for you to answer.

Most of us fail to understand or even acknowledge our own evolving energy network of inter-connecting lifetimes and the stories that we have played out, let alone what we are playing out now in our present lifetime. This active energy network of joined lifetimes (other human personality aspects) allows us to speak to all parts and pieces of ourselves - to every organ, molecule, and atom in our body including our DNA, and to every dimensional corridor that our human personality-aspects dwell.

It is through your DNA, as it expands and grows because of your many lifetimes that help you take the first step in bringing in your divine soul to communicate with your human self in understanding your own "spirit of one." The more you persist in keeping all parts and pieces of yourself separate, including seeing your spirit, rational mind, and body as different parts, the more challenges that you will have in life.

Why? It is because you have forgotten that your many different human lifetimes (stories) of the past are still part of you in your now present lifetime. These parts and pieces of you had their purpose in each of those lifetimes, and all of them performed wonderfully no matter what they (you) did. Now, they are seeking to come home to their creator, *you*. The time has come in your present lifetime to bring all of these lifetimes (parts and pieces of self) back into your wholeness.

Take a deep breath right now and feel every part and piece that is part of your present lifetime including your physical body. Feel all the organs and how they function. Feel the rational mind and how it loves to control your human focus on things like responsibility, emotions, your beliefs, state of affairs, and how it protects you. Once this is done, take another deep breath and feel your divine intelligence, your soul, other personality aspects of you, and then your "I AM Christ" consciousness.

These are the things that you have been overlooking because of your focus on the mental and physical aspect of you in the present. You, or your rational mind, have been hypnotized to separate your human ego from your complete self including your soul. It continues today through religious doctrine, the media, family, friends, and the government.

Religion hypnotizes us by having us search for God as a persona unto himself. The media and the government use fear to keep us in line with their ideology, and family and friends try to keep us in line with traditions. This way when we stray too far from the fold that they uphold and defend to stay in power, they reel us back in by declaring someone or something as being an enemy.

Look, most of us are blind when it comes to ancestral (family) karma just because of feeling obligated to them, which is why we feel responsible for them. After all, we have been traveling with them now for many lifetimes. So, because of this deep connection with them, we say that we love them and therefore we will do our best to help them until they are healed, or enlightened, or until they are happy.

My dear friends, in reality, they are not even family. They are angelic beings like you working out what their soul wants for them. So, why do you interfere with their soul growth? It is because you, down deep, feel that you have a loyalty to them. You owe your family nothing but a thank you, and all that they owe you is a thank you. All that we are doing together is working out our own belief systems in trying to find out who we are. It's up to you what you want to choose, fulfillment and completion, or being lost in a world of make-believe.

However, because of the rise in consciousness that Jesus (Yeshua) initiated over 2000 years ago, the connection to earth, our physical being, our higher soul self, and all parts and pieces of us, including our ancestral ties, are now becoming aware of the truth that we are a divine being that is simply playing out a story right now. Through many lifetimes, we have been experiencing and expanding toward the divine melding with our human ego, and now, for millions of us, there is no turning back.

Therefore, the best choice you can ever make is to just accept it and allow yourself to feel your many human aspects while choosing to be a "conscious creator" in your own right. This will allow you to meld fully with your soul, the divine you. In the end, you become the master and the Christ-messiah of your life, to your many aspects of the past, and to the world around you.

You can say that the energy of duality was allowed because your connection to it was on purpose. It was the soul's plan to limit you, and then you to become a sovereign "I AM" being unto yourself. No matter what you believe right now, you are changing because the DNA in your physical body is beginning to rewire itself so that you can make your connection to all parts and pieces of you, including the connection to your soul self.

Once you make the connection to all parts and pieces of you, then it becomes a choice to integrate "all that you are" into "one body of consciousness," which is your Christ consciousness." Thus you are no longer pulling in the dualistic energy of opposites that keep you suffering, and instead, you gravitate toward expanding your rational mind and consciousness beyond the polarity pull of having distinct aspects that keep you separated from your own "I AM Soul" self.

Once you become "one body of consciousness," your "I AMness, the Christ that you are," changes the way you are connected to the energy of opposites (duality), to the mass consciousness, and to your ancestral family. As you learn to develop your "oneness of consciousness" in physical form, you will find it getting easier and easier to release yourself from the belief of duality, human judgment, family, friends, and human traditionalism as far as blame and religion go.

Once you begin to take full responsibility for yourself, and not pass it on to someone else or some God or Devil outside of you, you will start to discover a new freedom that can be very overwhelming. A freedom where you can expand your consciousness into other dimensions where you can bring back with you all the riches, health, and joy you can stand.

But keep in mind, this freedom does not come in through force. It comes in through the breath. By being aware of who you truly are, and by allowing yourself to feel the "wholeness of your I AMness," you will literally free yourself from trying to control everything. When you understand this, you become aware that you are not your rational mind but a souled being that allowed yourself to open your heart to your soul.

By opening up to your soul in complete trust it will help the rational mind see mass consciousness and your wants as a way of validating its reality. Your rational mind will understand that due to expansional energy and your wholeness of consciousness becoming one again, you will not need to worry anymore about money, health, joy, or any other material thing, not even life, because the rational mind will be literally re-programmed to work with your soul in a matter of balance and oneness.

Your rational mind will begin to understand that everything you need in life can be found within yourself, and therefore you have no need to blame yourself or others for your lack of anything. And that my fellow searchers, is when you will not have to force yourself to trust yourself because "trust in yourself" will come natural.

Therefore, search no more for God or Christ, for you are God and the Christ that you have been waiting for. You are the magic that can bring to you a life of freedom, abundance, joy, and health. So, awaken to the Christ (soul) that is you and create the miracles you seek. Remember, to bring in this New Energy (New Earth) and the miracles that the Bible mentions is about opening yourself up to trusting and loving yourself unconditionally without ever thinking that you were or are a sinner.

If you don't have trust, love, and have compassion for yourself first, then everything else you do for others become meaningless. When you truly trust and love yourself first, and accept everything about you, including being a Christ also, thus equal too, it all comes to you. The healing of your spirit, rational mind, and body, and everything you need in life to survive, including the answers you seek, will happen.

Also remember, it is because of habit, we continue with our positive sayings and our prayers every day, which means, along with this belief in positive comes the negative. Even with hope comes despair. So, you see, if we continue on the path of playing the game of positive and negative, right and wrong, good and bad, then no matter what we do, we will trigger all of the memories tied to the system of duality to serve us.

When you let go of this false optimism along with your false pessimism, and allow everything to come into your life without forcing or denying it, you are going to discover miracles. So, stop building your foundation with a God that only understands duality as something that is good and evil, positive and negative.

Also, stop building your miracles on Jesus as the only Christ that can grant you those miracles. Instead, build your foundation on understanding that God and Christ is *you* in the present, the one that can truly save you, give you freedom, and create all the miracles you want.

Remember, the rational mind, through default, became God, and because of our religious training, Jesus became our way of miracles, which is why we will never understand God, Jesus, good and bad, or miracles using the rational mind. We wonder why we don't experience enlightenment, or have an experience with a master, or an experience with the angelic realm, or even have an experience with our higher self. We are so stuck in the false mind fighting for a God that is so mental and tied to positive and negative that we overlook how much we are battling our own spirit.

I know that most of us are afraid of moving past this God of the Bible and how Christ is depicted because of somehow losing our place in heaven after all these years giving him our love and worship. I also know that there are lots of people that believe there is nothing beyond this life. There are those that even believe that there is no God and no Christ, just nothing but darkness and non-existence, while others believe there is a God, a Christ, and some type of heaven and hell.

My fellow searchers, going beyond the rational mind and this God of the Bible takes real courage if you are looking for grand experiences, having overwhelming potentials to choose from, and you living without limitations. You see, it is not about giving up God, Christ, or you finding your place in heaven, because how can you give them up if you are already God, Christ, and in heaven?

Moving past the rational mind and this false image of God, heaven, and how Christ assists you in your hour of need is not about Jesus but is about bringing in your own divinity to earth in this now moment to work with you. However, it becomes a great challenge for you because the rational mind is programmed for control, judgment, and duality.

For instance: The rational mind loves to control the philosophy of God, the philosophy of money, of health, and life in general by placing these things as something right or wrong, good or bad. Therefore, you set yourself up for failure because you are always looking for the next thing to do under the guidance of a God and a Christ that is totally mental, dualistic, and outside of you.

The rational mind has a hard time to understand the wholeness of your "I AM Consciousness." Why? It is because the rational mind feels it will lose control and go out of existence, either by a God sending it to hell forever and ever or by losing its awareness of being. So, how do you get beyond your rational mind and those emotional feelings? Well, the first thing is that you cannot use the rational mind to figure this out. Second, having the rational mind trying to figure out how to get out of itself is actually setting you up to never getting beyond the rational mind.

Look, the rational mind will always stay within itself because of being to busy with everything that brings in doubt, control, and mistrust. Your rational mind will argue with you constantly, telling you what you have been taught by religion, your forefathers, and by society in pointing out that you have been on the right path, especially when it comes to God and his miracles.

So, how can you escape the rational mind's grip on you? Especially, when you have family and close friends that will mock you just because of what you say about an incomplete God that is purely based on the principles of duality, religious training, and intellectual thinking. What can you do to escape this propaganda machine? You take deep breaths (several of them) and call in your own Christ-Spirit (soul) to be present in your life.

Now, since the rational mind cannot see your soul, don't worry about the method in which you to take these deep breaths. Just breathe! Breathe in through the nose and exhale from the mouth or breathe in through the mouth and exhale from the mouth, it all doesn't matter. Just allow yourself at least fifteen to thirty minutes a day to take deep breaths. That is the way your soul identity will come into your heart to serve you, the real creator.

You will know that it's working by everything in your life beginning to shake-up around you. It's a shake-up that will bring in major changes to your life. The first change you will experience is about taking a quantum leap in consciousness that brings to memory your ability to take full responsibility for your life and what you are experiencing right now.

The second change you will experience is a call to mind asking you if you are ready and bold enough to let yourself be the creator. The third change you will experience is a call to mind to accept the plain truth that you are a divine being, that you are equal to God, and that *you* are the *Christ*, and not that you are just a human seeking out Jesus, the Christ.

In fact, there will be changes going on in your life every day as long as you continue to take deep breaths and allow your soul to come into your physical life and become the owner of everything in your life. Of course, the most important thing to remember is that doubt can always creep in at anytime telling your rational mind that "you cannot do it" because you are no Christ, for Jesus holds that title. There you go, back to the old programming where you will always look for something to be wrong.

Once this occurs, the old dogmatic recorded memory tapes comes out searching the rational mind to play the game of "what if" all over again. Now, don't fret over it because it's natural anyway. Just calm yourself down and begin to take several deep breaths again and again. Before you know it, your soul is right there at the doorway of your consciousness ready and willing again to come into your life to help you become that "conscious creator." All that it requires is your stillness, wiliness, and the ability to receive (through breath) your soul without saying anything.

Just allow your consciousness to respond to your soul directly without any interference coming from your rational mind because your soul will come in through the in-breath. Now, to keep you in the heart center, where your soul comes in to engage you, I do want to remind you that it takes a belief in something that causes something to manifest.

For example: We, as humans, have collectively agreed to believe that everything we see around us is real and true. Even though the greater truth is that it's all just neutral energy that has been changed to a mental base, and then to a solid base. This means everything we see around us is an illusion. Remember, we, as divine beings, created it all in order to have incredible experiences that will one day help us remember who we are while under the illusion of being separate from our own divine self.

It was from this illusion of separateness that produced a force of opposites that caused us to look outside of ourselves for meaning, purpose, and the acceptance of being a creator. Therefore, because of our strong belief in separation, our physical world became our reflection in whatever we chose to do, which is how we now define ourselves instead of looking within to find our inner importance.

My fellow searchers, how can we bring into harmony "all that we are" if we keep on rejecting who we are? We will never find balance in our life or in ourselves by pushing away what we believe to be bad, negative, or evil, or that we are unworthy of being a Christ also. The reason why? When your focus is sole on these things of bad, evil, and negative, as well as good, pleasant, and positive, and that you are not a divine being, all that you are going to do is add more energy to them and none for the real you.

Balance in life can only come by way of integrating "all that you are," allowing everything that comes into your life as an experience and not that it is right or wrong, good or bad, or that you are just human. Allow your emotions, your frustrations, and every thought of good and evil be felt, and then let them pass through you without shaping them as something is wrong with you. This will begin the balance you are looking for without distorting who you really are.

So, don't despair! Learn to take deep breaths every day, and then say thank you to yourself, to your soul, and to all the parts and pieces of you including those that you meet in life, and not to some God that is outside of you. Remember, no matter who you meet in life, they are just players that you allowed to bring into your life as a reflection to lead you back to yourself.

For Instance: As you can see, the world and our country are changing fast. There is much that we have felt from vibrational changes and yet, without realizing it, the news media brings into our consciousness many suggestions that reflect our duality and our own lack of leadership. We are seeing within our political parties a great clarity of how we, as a group consciousness that lives in the United States, even thought we humans are all divine in nature, reflect our beliefs in an outward doctrine of opposing principles and how we all lack direction.

How many times have we asked ourselves and others, "Why is the country so divided?" Why is it that we fault this one, or that one, or this cause, or that cause? But truly, what is really happening to us is that our soul is just reflecting back to us our ignorance in great clarity in what we call our politics, in the choices that they make, and in the voices that they sound out. It is showing us all unquestionably, as a group, the long-held belief in duality, and that we are only humans that need direction and supervision.

So again, take deep breaths and say thank-you to your soul, to your former partners (relationships), and to your country for the experiences because it helps you connect to your divinity and your soul.

Now, to sum up this chapter, allow your emotions and experiences of pain be felt without blaming yourself and others, for it must be real. It is not that you can just say, "Okay, I will say yes, that I am a divine being and that everything you are experiencing will go away." My dear friends, it has to be a genuine *yes* in accepting who you truly are. A genuine *yes* to accepting full responsibility for yourself, a genuine *yes* to everything that is happening in your life, and a genuine *yes* to releasing old dogmatic beliefs about a white male God that is separate from you. This allows the energy around you to become balanced.

Because of how dualistic vibrational energy works as an opposing energy in a 2-D and 3-D world, if you try to push it away because you believe that you are not the creator, and therefore not responsible. It will work against you and grow even more. This is why people that have fear-provoking diseases, that have no money, no job, no relationships, and so forth, the energy of positive and negative grows even stronger within and around them because they are adding more opposing energy to their situation.

In other words, you don't have to fear saying *yes* or *no* to something if you don't like it. That is not how dualistic vibrational energy works. It is when you say with genuineness and trust, yes to accepting full responsibility for what is happening in your life no matter what that is. It releases your attention and your ties to that something, which then allows your divinity (soul) to come in, raising your vibrational frequency, and then joining your human ego in a new expansional energy of a 4-D and 5-D world. This then sets in motion everything in your life to find its balance, which can include healing, abundance, great relationships, and overwhelming potentials to create.

This is true even when you say yes to your rational mind for judging others and yourself because your rational mind will race around as if its tail has been cut-off. Just know that you are the "I AM of your soul" and the creator of your world. Just know that the rational mind will eventually calm down once it gets to understand that it is futile to continue with judging itself and others. It did for me and it will for you too.

Make the "conscious choice" in taking deep breaths until it becomes habit forming to choose unconditional love without judgment or concern about what you think you did in life. Keep focused and choose to return to you as a Christ and not one looking for Christ. Do not get into second guessing or judging yourself about why you made a certain choice. Just remember that your soul will only bring to you whatever you are ready to handle because you are on the path of integration and awakening.

Chapter 22

Moving Beyond Perception And Lies

Perception is a great word to describe the process about how we, as humans, use our rational mind and our five physical senses to acquire information about how everything works including the planet, the physical body, how we live, form our truths and opinions, make decisions, how we understand God, and how we connect to our belief systems. Perception by and large is understood on what is observed by the rational mind as being traditional and long established, therefore looked at as reliable, logical, and as truth because of how the rational mind encodes it that way.

For Instance: When we see someone that we did not see for a long time, or smell our favorite food, or hear the voice of a close friend, recognition is almost immediate. It is within a fraction of a second after the eyes, nose, ears, tongue, or touch, we know the entity (or an object) that is familiar, and whether it is pleasing or dangerous.

How does such recognition happen so accurately and quickly, even if the cause of physical response is complex and the context in which they arise varies? It is because of the way in which the rational mind takes it in as being valid and believable, therefore "all that there is."

Perception is what we, as souled beings, use to develop our awareness, to attain understanding of the environment around us, and to come face to face with our dogmatic beliefs. We do it by organizing and interpreting what we are seeing and experiencing using our five physical senses. For perception involves signals in the nervous system that result from physical stimulation of the five senses.

For example: Sight involves light striking the retinas of the eyes, smell is mediated by odor molecules and hearing involves pressure waves. All and all, perception is not so much influenced or shaped by the receiving of these signals but can be shaped by learning, memory and expectation. This is why we, as humans, can trap ourselves into a belief system so strong that it takes an accident of some kind to get us out.

This is also why we have our illnesses, misfortunes, and many other so called bad things that happen to us in life. It happens so we can get out of the perception of what we are seeing, tasting, touching, hearing, and smelling as being "all that there is," and then interpret it as our truths, for that is not "all that there is." There is more to life and what we are experiencing with our five physical senses then we think. It is just that most of us are not aware of it yet.

For instance: How many times have you asked God in prayer saying, "Enough of this suffering, chaos, turmoil, punishment and judgment? Is it not time for me to respect, love, honor, and understand others, to live in peace and in harmony?" However, the answer you get does not really come from God. It comes from your religious leaders saying that it comes from God and yet, it is just how the rational mind encodes it that way. You have been told for centuries to be unwavering about your truths because Jesus or someone of holiness will deliver you from evil.

We hear it all the time by those that say they are in the know, that the world is falling apart, that humanity has reached a point where God has had enough of sinning. Our religious leaders are comparing from events that have already happened and from what they have interpreted from the Bible, and now they forecast what God is going to do to us, to the world, and how he is going to make it happen if we do not repent. All of this brings great fear into our heart and we don't know what to do about it.

My fellow searchers don't fear! What is really happening is that things are not falling apart. Religion, and their leaders, does not know what they are talking about. It is that we humans and mother earth are just going through an incredible change, an "awareness change," where we, as a human group, are beginning to open up to the idea that something that appears beyond our reach may not be after all.

Most of the world today perceives and understands that nothing exists beyond what they have always thought of as positive and negative, God and Satan, sin and suffering. As you can attest to your own personal experiences, many of you are having a difficult time handling this continued vibrational energy of duality. It just seems to bring to you nothing but fear, suffering, and confusion.

There are many of us today that are becoming *aware* that this strong energy of opposites is certainly affecting the rational mind and how it has been very challenging to our truths. Because of this, we are now feeling some doubt about what we, or at least for most of us, have been taught by our religious leaders, our educational system, our parents, our government, and even our science.

Yes indeed, we are living in changing times alright, and we have to admit that we are having a difficult time in dealing with it. The trend of drama, anxiety, panic, fear, concern, and doubt, all of these emotions are now coming to the forefront of our mind, challenging us to look at them.

When we look at the rational mind of a believer and how they judge, let's say, extreme weather, record highs, lows, droughts, earthquakes, floods, chaos, global heating and cooling, and many other unpleasant activities around the world, the rational mind believer will automatically place the event on the end times or that man has gone crazy instead of looking at himself as the creator of it all.

Why is that? It is because of how the rational mind loves to wrap itself around what it doesn't understand about its environment, what is happening to it, and about how God and man really deals with issues. Because of our physical senses, we wrap ourselves around our emotional and mental consciousness in such a way so as to make sense out of chaos and to why we suffer and yet, it is not about those things at all.

It is about human consciousness finally changing from the old way of thinking to a whole new way of thinking and, what it's causing is immense confusion, doubt, and fear. Of course, this confusion, doubt, and fear are actually leading to a clearing out of things that no longer are appropriate for us to believe anymore.

Yes, we have seen in the past few years the intensity of how everything on earth, including the questioning of Jesus' arrival, seems to be getting more chaotic and disorganized. Just look at the financial system, the politicians, not just in the United States, but throughout the world. We even have some religious leaders trying to predict the time and day for the coming of Jesus. And now, it seems that everybody is ripe for following some leader that will do nothing more than lead us to more lies, pain, and suffering.

From my understanding of what is coming from the angelic realm and from my own soul, the year 2012, and going into 2013, may even be worse than the previous years from all aspects. However, because of these things happening around the world, it is going to bring to us an outburst of some kind that will open us up to a "new awareness," an awareness that will unlock the consciousness of our own soul.

Now, this outburst has nothing to do with bombs or catastrophic happenings around the world, it has to do with those of us that are suddenly beginning to feel our dramas, anxieties, losing control, our fears, and our doubts on a whole new level, a level that will bring us face to face with our core beliefs. Beliefs that have held us stuck in the vibrational energy of duality (opposite) for so long that we have come to believe that this energy of positive and negative is "all that there is" and yet, it is just how the rational mind perceives it that way.

There are many of you that are now searching your heart and are asking if you have been honorable and worthy enough to make it to heaven if something bad happens. The chaos and confusion that you are seeing and feeling around you has you feeling vulnerable and helpless, for you are now questioning your heart saying, "I wished I had treated my parents better." "I wish I had treated my wife better." I wished I would have been a better parent to my children." I wished I would have prayed to God and gone to church more." You could go on and on with this "I wished syndrome that you could have done better."

Yes indeed, what we, as humans, fear the most is "judgment day" that has been ingrained within us by our religious leaders for centuries. Now, we are afraid to die because we are afraid of what God will do to us. All because of this belief in opposites, sin, and retribution that has been brought forth by our religious books. My friends, it's all lies!

Now, why then are we so afraid to come face to face with our maker? It is because of how we perceive and identify the forces of positive and negative as being good and bad, and because of what we believe about sin and our truths. Because of this fear in meeting our maker and how we perceive the vibrational energy of duality, sin, and our truths, we feel that we must go into punishment while we are in human form so that when we do meet our maker he will be kinder and easier on us.

In fact, we put ourselves in a dark place in our consciousness where we surround ourselves with nothing but drama, fear, doubt, and self-inflicted punishment for all the things we *think* we did wrong. My dear friends, it is not about right and wrong, or good and bad, or what we think we did in life, or even about facing God. It is about us becoming *aware* of who we truly are, and then having the courage to face ourselves. There is an expanded truth that goes far beyond the forces of positive and negative, beyond God and Satan, and beyond religion.

Yes we, the people of the world, have been lied to for a long time and now our belief systems, and how we perceive things in our life, keep us trapped into a principle belief that the forces of positive and negative (God and Satan) is "all that there is." Yes, we have been for many lifetimes following a core belief that our physical reality, and how we understand God (atheist or believer), is all that there is. It is not "all that there is!"

If by some strange reason, we believe that there is an afterlife, then this afterlife comes with a "day of judgment" where we, go to heaven, hell, or somewhere in-between. We, as mankind, have always failed to go beyond our rational mind and our ability to discern duality when it comes to the forces of positive and negative, God and Satan. We, as humans, fail to see that Adam and Eve and the biting of the apple was nothing but a metaphor telling us that we took on the belief in duality in order for our spirit (the I AM) to learn and know all things.

This belief has led you through many lifetimes being part of something that is actually not real. If everything is just a perception and an illusion, including what you see as positive and negative, and what you understand as sin. Then it is just a way for the rational mind to process what you have created as an individual and as group consciousness. As long as you buy into this belief in sin and duality, there will always be a plus and a minus, a right and a wrong, a good and a bad, suffering and non-suffering, and it will always be this way until you move past this old way of thinking.

Ever since we were in our spirit's youth back in our divine state (first creation), the only thing that our spirit wanted to do was to experience itself through its son, which is nothing more than a metaphor for the rational mind and your human personality. Therefore, we became nothing more than our desire to experience no matter what we experienced, good or bad.

In fact, your young spirit had no agenda at the time. All it wanted to do is discover itself by creating an aspect of itself, which is the human you. Now, that you have had many lifetimes playing on earth, you have been told that you are damned to hell by some God because of your sins. This belief in sin, and in karma, and the perception of them, because of memory, has been part of your consciousness ever since.

When Jesus came to earth over two thousand years ago he planted a new seed (belief) within our memory hoping that one day it will take root. Well this seed has stayed under the surface of our consciousness for a long time and now, there is a more fertile environment where we, as humans, are free to choose to let go of our dogmatic beliefs, and therefore our suffering, which then changes our reality.

Many of you have been crying out to God for many lifetimes asking what is real, what is truth, and why do you have the reality you have, such as being poor, having an accident, an illness, and many other things that confuse you. Oh, you have tried to shape and define your reality from what you knew of the forces of positive and negative, God and Satan, and that of religion. As you can see, it doesn't work anymore. You even tried to do it on a mental level and that did not work either.

So, what can you do to overcome this suffering and playing in duality? There is only one thing you can do and that is, go within and blow up all that you took on for belief systems including your religious ones. Learn to empty your glass and let everything go.

To understand everything that is of duality, all that you have created and learned, including us souled beings leaving our divine state and how it is all interconnected, we need to understand that we all moved from a oneness consciousness to a 2-D and 3-D consciousness that holds a belief that duality is in everything, such as air, the trees, water, animals, fellow humans, ourselves, our bodies, our mind and yes, we even can find it in all of our other human personality-aspects (lifetimes).

Everything of a 2-D and 3-D world, for nothing is left out, was created on the basis of the influences of positive and negative, duality. In fact, we were told a long time ago that if we could not see, touch, smell, taste, or hear it, then it is not real, and we believed it. This is very important for us to understand if we want to move forward in our understanding of God.

I understand that some of you are afraid to look at your dogmatic beliefs because of how you were brought-up, how you were taught by your religious leaders, society, and how it is wrong to go against them or God. However, I ask you to take a moment and feel into your beliefs, feel into your fear of God, and feel into what you perceive as sin. And when you do, you are going to find that ninety-nine percent of your fears come from the rational mind and how it has been trained that way for millions of years.

This means that ninety-nine percent of your choices in life come from the rational mind and its emotional footprint of lifetimes pasts, and not from the "I AM" part of you or from your now moment. For you have expressed all that you have done outwardly from a mental and emotional level that has come from other lifetime experiences. This is why you have never sinned. It is and has been your agreements, beliefs, your human aspects of the past, your perception of God, and that of mass consciousness, that reinforces the vibrational energy of duality as being "all that there is."

Because of this hypnotic layering and layering that has been going on in your consciousness, lifetime after lifetime, you maintain your belief that nothing exists beyond duality, or God or Satan. To you, it has to be either good or bad, right or wrong, up or down, heaven or hell, because you see it, as there is nothing in-between or beyond.

It suggests that every thought pattern that we have is likely to take on an emotional response pattern that places us in a dualistic reality that takes on the form of suffering. So, because of this, we fear what goes on around us, and what we do not understand is our consciousness is expanding and changing. However, we are beginning to become aware of who we truly are. We have been overlooking our consciousness and how it has been evolving and expanding slowly ever since we asked ourselves, "Who am I?"

You see, when our consciousness evolves, and since everything is connected to everything, then everything has to change around us as well. That my angelic friends are why the things we see and are experiencing is happening right now. Everything around us and within us are spiraling upward in a circular motion, and therefore what is left behind, either outward or inward, has to explode or collapse, and this includes our old dogmatic belief systems. Even if we do not accept this truth, we will journey through many more lifetimes until we do.

So, the best way for me to describe what is happening to you, and to the world, is that you and the world are not falling apart. You and the world are simply changing the way you connect to your consciousness. It may seem like its dooms day time here on earth, but be assured, the only thing that is happening is that all energies and personality-aspects of you, like for the world, are reconnecting. Once you reconnect, you will be able to look far beyond the old energy of duality as being "all that there is," for the old world is making a transition to a new world.

Better said, the "old vibrational energy of duality" is now in the process of making a transitioning to a "new expansional energy" that far exceeds the vibrational energy of duality.

For example: Here is how perception works: All of us have made life contracts with our spirit a long time ago, before coming into the flesh, and these contracts, other than looking for the answer to who am I, was about learning how vibrational energy works and how it affects us on a soul level. And yes, many of us have had many lifetimes playing out both sides of the coin and yet, we do come to a point in playing with energy where we choose a lifetime where we desire to learn the *real* truth about "who we truly are."

Life contracts can be relatively easy to spot or understand as long as you don't get too mental about them. If you stay within your heart and take a look at some of the most memorable events that have happened to you from birth through the present now, you may be able to unmask your life contract.

For example: I will use my life contract as a platform to help you raise your awareness to help put your own life contract together. From my birth to now, I will give you my memorable events that have taken place in my life to where I know now what my life contract is, and what I did about it once I learned of it:

- First, I chose to incarnate at a time of great transformation that was taking place on earth. Therefore, I was born in 1948, just a few years after the Second World War.

It was a time when humanity was going through a lot of old energies of light and dark, and it was a perfect time for many souls to come back to earth for an incarnation. It was during this era that many souls knew the time of the millennium in 2000, prophesied by Jesus, would bring in incredible times for Earth, to either go through great catastrophic events or move into New Energy.

- Second, I chose to come back to earth as a son of a Maine Catholic family, somewhat conventional in terms of traditions, and what better way to come into this world as being penniless, having no means for a higher education, and having siblings that are traditionalist as far as their core beliefs. My father was a steamfitter that worked on Loring AFB and my mother was a stay at home mom.

When I reached the age of knowing that my desire was to become a business owner, seeking financial independence, I observed that I was the only one in the family that thought that way. I also found, at a very young age, that I was the only one in the family that could feel and see spirits around me, even though my mother seemed to display some psychic abilities, she never did develop them.

- Third, in 1971, twenty-three years old, married and with children, I found the financial support, even though it seemed impossible at the time, to enter the business world. However, because of very trying circumstances, I personally, along with the company, went bankrupt three and a half years later. The ordeal was devastating because I felt I lacked the intelligence and the education (high school level) to operate a business.

It was very challenging times because of how I looked at my religious training, where I was born, and how I had seen myself. I felt, on a subconscious level, that I was not worthy or intellectual enough to succeed in business.

- Fourth, something happened that changed my thinking, or I thought it did. It was in early 1975, while lying in bed, looking up at the ceiling, trying to go to sleep, I unexpectedly saw three Franciscan Monks (like an apparition) dressed in their traditional attire emerging from the darkness of my bedroom.

Then, as they all walked toward me, one of the monks moved closer to me and said that, "I was with them in another lifetime and now, in this lifetime, it is time for me to know the truth." However, it took me about thirty years before that truth came to me.

- Fifth, a few months later (late 1975), and after seeing the monks, I again found the means to go back into business for the second time. However, this time around with only one partner, as with my first business undertaking I had three partners. This partnership lasted eighteen years before my world once again come tumbling down – for I was kicked out of my own company by the person that I thought I could trust the most because he showed, on the outside, that he was a highly spiritual person.
- Sixth, even though I prayed and prayed for help, I found that this time around there were no monks and no spiritual vision to help me get through the ordeal. It was as if I was alone this time. In fact, I visited many psychics within a short period of time hoping that they could direct me through this mess that I found myself in. I was hoping that they (spirits from the other side) could tell me what to do.

Now, I do not discredit any psychic or clairvoyant person in their ability to channel those from the other side of the veil because they are a lot of goods one out there that do great work. In fact, the psychics I worked with are decent and wonderful people. They all worked hard to help me as best they could and in the end, they brought me hope and optimism. It was from this hope that gave me the courage to file a law suit against my former partner for my half of the company.

- Seventh, after a few months of deep breathing, fighting with myself, and with my former partner, I again was finding myself wanting to go back into business for the third time. Even though I had no money to speak of, a family of six to care for, feeling a lot of emotional pain and stress, and the thought of finding someone once again to help me financially, I pressed forward the best I could.

- Eighth, in spite of what I was feeling and going through with the lawsuit with my former partner I found a corporation that decided to help me financially to get back into business by me offering them twenty-five percent ownership in the company. This then enabled me to open the doors of my company for the third time in April 1994.
- Ninth, because of my court battles with my former partner I was utterly unaware that I was neglecting my new formed company. Actually, to the point that I thought I was going to lose it. Because of my former partner's actions, I chose to battle back, and in doing so, I brought out some of my past human personality-aspects where I expressed very aggressive tendencies, all due to not wanting to be seen as a victim.

However, in the end, and after eight years of court battles, it cost my former partner more money than what he would have given me for my half of the company, and that he eventually lost the company due to bankruptcy.

- Tenth, after seven years running my newly formed company, I made enough money to buy out my twenty-five percent partner. This allowed me to sell my company and leave western Pennsylvania and move to northeastern Tennessee in September 2000, the year of the millennium. I then reopened a new business in Tennessee as a ninety-percent owner, giving up ten percent ownership due to needing help in securing my future in a new city and a new state.
- Eleventh, from this new location in northeast Tennessee, my company developed an electronic web base procurement system that became very popular with the U.S. Military. So popular, the company's annual sales moved past the three million dollar mark within two years of my opening in 2000.
- Twelfth, because of my new company performing well, I found myself joining up with a highly educated and intellectual person that was very well versed in traveling around the world helping large companies market their products, and therefore thought that this person could do the same for me.

- Thirteenth, because of his expertise in marketing and his academic and intellectual understanding of the business world, I decided to launch a LLC Company (Limited Liability Company), financed by my ninety-percent ownership, thus giving this highly educated person, and to those that worked with him, forty-nine percent ownership of this newly LLC Company, leaving me with fifty-one percent ownership. The purpose was to join together and see if this man could sell my e-procurement system to state and city governments across the nation.
- Fourteenth, the best quality I had seen in this man, other than his intellect and higher education, was that he had a very persuasive personality. So persuasive, I found out to late that he actually drew me into his web of trumped-up stories thus persuading me to give him thousands of dollars to investigate the feasibility of my company's e-procurement system being used by state and local governments.
- Fifteenth, because of this man's persuasive personality, I actually came very close to losing my company of ninety-percent ownership, as everything that I made in profits from it was given to this man to be used to build up this new LLC Company.
- Sixteenth, by year's end 2004, I found myself and my company of ninety-percent in the red for the very first time since I opened the doors in 1994. I was nearly broke and just hanging onto my company with a very thin thread. I really didn't know what to do.

So, again my thoughts went to religious training, where I was born, my educational level, and I felt like I was not intellectual enough or worthy enough for success. After all, this would have meant that I have failed for the third time.

- Seventeenth, because of my naiveness in trusting people and my unconscious belief in predestine, because of where I was born and what I was taught about God, I began to pray again. However, this time around I found myself not praying to some white male God in heaven. I prayed, or I appealed to the three monks that I had seen back in 1975 to hear me out.
- Eighteenth, out of the blue, year 2004, about seven o'clock in the morning, and just before getting up out of bed, I was overwhelmed

when Jesus (Yeshua) himself appeared before me, revealing himself to me in material form, telling me that everything will be fine.

Once Jesus gave me the message he then transformed back into nonphysical form. Also, to my surprise, he stayed around and talked with me for a couple more minutes before he finally left.

Now, I mentioned this not out of thinking that I am special or better than anyone else. I mention this to illustrate how we are all special and that we all can experience Jesus. In fact, Jesus is available to anyone that seeks their own "I AM" sovereignty. Remember, we are all divine.

- Nineteenth, after the visit from Jesus, I closed down the LLC Company since I was fifty-one percent owner, and then fired this highly educated intellectual and persuasive person, took the loss, and began to focus my attention on the things that were important to me and my ninety-percent ownership of the company that I opened up in 1993.

It was the very first time in my life, after thirty-three years of struggling with business, where I felt extremely liberated, where I believed in myself, and where I trusted in myself to be the perfect person to plan and make decisions for myself and my company.

- Twentieth, it was a time when I finally let go of all my fears of God, the Devil, sin, and that I was doing something wrong because of never attending church. I even let go of the idea that I was not intellectual or educated enough to run a business because of where I was born.

Now, ever since I let everything go, including the belief of being unworthy of success and the fear of not being educated enough to manage a business, my company's annual sales today are in the millions, and to top it off, this is my third book that I have written.

So, as you can see, my contract for this lifetime was to learn the real truth about "who I am" and "who I am not," for my soul's greatest secret is that I am a Christ in my own right. What better way for me to learn this lesson then for me to be born into a Catholic family that was penniless, me being so different from my family in all aspects of life, and then meeting and working with people that had a personality nature about them that ended up challenging me to my very core.

From the family that I was born into, to the individuals I met and worked with in this lifetime, including the visitations from the monks, to seeing Jesus, I had to experience the untruths, the deceptions, the lies and cover-ups, and all that was hidden within my soul memories from my past lifetimes before I could come into the discovery of the real truth in this lifetime that the Monks talked about over thirty years earlier.

By going into business three times and experiencing firsthand the manipulation of truth, I found myself, at many levels of my consciousness, being challenged with it. It was from this contract in this lifetime that eventually led me into the study of Biblical scriptures. Thus discovering how religion, government, businesses, the media, family, and friends, consciously and unconsciously, present themselves in an unenlightened way, for the real truth can only come from within oneself.

My dear friends, this is why we contract illnesses, have accidents, and meet those in life that will challenge us to our very core, for all of it brings to us an awakening. It was this contract, and coming into the direct opposite of truth for my first half of life that eventually helped me to uncover the real truth, and become aware of the greatest secret ever devised by my own soul. It was my soul that planned the whole event out for my human self to discover.

It was through family, religion, the place and the conditions of my birth, the struggle of becoming financial independent, and the business people that I met along the way that became my ticket for learning the real truth and my freedom in this lifetime, which is why I thank them, and not judge them or rebuke them. It was from the constant experiencing and constant lessons of blowing up my old dogmatic belief systems from lifetimes past to my present one that finally led the way for me to see Jesus himself manifest before my very eyes in my home.

My dear friends, seeing Jesus in my home for me was more than just seeing him, it represents my own ascension (rapture) in this lifetime – for all aspects of me, including my human self in this lifetime and my own Christ Consciousness are now *one*. Now, it was at that point in time where I discovered who "I truly am" and what the Monks meant by me learning the truth in this lifetime.

We, as man, have forgotten our soul and how our soul works with our human aspect in an effort to awaken us from our sleep so as for us to recognize the Christ within ourselves. However, because of the way we have been taught for so long about fantasizing and seeing spirits as being wrong and evil, it comes hard for us to recognize our truths, and because of it, we do nothing but suffer.

My fellow searchers, it is because of how we have been educated by religion, our parents, governments, big business, and from the people we meet along our path, we all went into a mental state where we took on the perception and the dogmatic beliefs that everything that needs answering must be found outside of ourselves.

So, if you are willing to learn your truths, then I ask you to write down your major events from birth to your now moment and see if you can find what your contract is – for everyone has had life agreements in every lifetime, including the one you are in now. Through life contracts you put together a route that will eventually lead you back to your "I AM Christ" self. These life contracts have been very much embedded within our soul memories to be tapped into at anytime. However, all that we seem to do is just go about our business of living unconsciously because of the way we have been taught.

So, take a look at some of the most important things that have happened in your life from birth to now, and write them down, and you too may see your life contract, and therefore your truth. Also, remember, if you find yourself saying, "Why me oh Lord, why me? What have I done to deserve this?" Then understand, you are never punished by God or even by Satan because it is you that is punishing yourself by calling forth the challenges you are experiencing in order for you to learn the real truth about who you truly are. And now, it is up to you to look at yourself in the eyes and see those challenges as a gift from you and not as a curse.

CHAPTER 23

TRUE FREEDOM

According to the Encarta Dictionary, "freedom" is having the ability to act, speak, and have the capability to exercise free will and choice without restrictions from any external forces. However, religion would say that "true freedom" comes from being obedient to God and his laws. Where others would say that "true freedom" is about not following any laws, not God's, religions, or even the laws of society. Therefore, "true freedom" could have many meanings to many different people.

So, what's your understanding of "true freedom"? Is it having the right to vote, speak, and present your position on any given subject without any fear of reprisal? Is it about having the right to financial freedom, be illness free, or can it be just walking out of prison? However you view "true freedom" there is one thing about it that most everyone would agree. It can be quite difficult to describe or characterize just because of what it means to every person. Unless of course, you know what you are looking for or what you are hoping to accomplish.

From religion's point of view, ultimate freedom comes to a person when they follow God's rules without deviation no matter what, even to the point where the church says eating meat on Friday is a sin. However, before you commit yourself to this view and what "true freedom" means, I would consider how it affects your free will. After all, the meaning of a slave is a person who accepts being ruled by someone or by a rule of law that forces you to submit to an idea, or else pay the penalty.

Well! Don't you think by following God's laws, and how religion views them, is actually being a slave to God and how religion interprets them? How can religion, or any God, say in one hand that He created you with free will and in the other hand say you have to follow His laws, or else? Where is free will in that scenario? How can God create you having free will and then turn right around and say that you have to follow His will (rules), and if you don't, hell becomes your home forever when you die?

If you honestly believe that God created you in His divine image then why do you believe that you have to follow God laws, or for that matter, his divine will? Look, do you believe God's laws are there to protect the innocent and all of what He has created or are God's laws there to protect you, and all humans, from falling into a pit that resembles some type of hell described by man?

Have you ever thought about the concept of God as just an idea, an icon that somehow was created by man in order to understand himself and his surroundings? Look, God has never actually been proven to be real or has been seen by the common man. The only ones that may claim that they have seen God are the ones that are our religious leaders. In fact, if one says that they have seen God they have only seen God in the way He is described by religion anyway. For the common man, all that these religious leaders say is to have faith that He is there.

According to my soul, the concept of God is nothing more than an idea, an icon, and a very strong belief that we, as man, accepted a long time ago because we lacked the understanding of our existence, our surroundings, and how we work with energy. Look at how we all turn to God to save us and yet, because of our lack of understanding God, we, and religion, have come up with many different meanings and methods to describe Him.

For instance: Many of you, because of religious teachings, have this belief that you cannot hide from God. That He knows where you are at all times. Well! You can hide from God even to the point that God cannot find you.

You see, you, as a souled being, and the children of the Spirit of One, can block out your human personality from ever knowing the true identity of God just by believing you are a sinner and that you are somehow lost. You play the old game that many of us play as a child. "Hide and seek, and see if you can find me."

In spite of what religion say about you not being able to hide from God, you can truly hide from Him, which in affect puts a whole new twist on what God can do for you or what you can do for God. Why? It is because of what you have been taught about God for centuries. In fact, you tend to deceive yourself when it comes to knowing God.

Look, most of you pray to some form of God continually for protection, understanding, how to survive, and clarity and yet, most of you will go out of your way to evade God. There is no need for you to evade God because God cannot find you anyway. How can God find you if all that you do is exist and work from out of your rational mind and physical consciousness?

My dear friends, as long as you continue to look for God using your rational mind. You will never find Him nor will God ever find you, for He and you, will be lost to each other forever or until you learn how to get out of your hypnotic sleep state, and see what your deceptive mind of reason has been doing for centuries. Many of you have asked why it is that religion depict God as such a mystery. Well! It is quite simple. So simple that it may surprise you. You see, God is in your expressions and in your experiences. This means you are that God hiding from yourself.

Look, have you ever heard from any of your religious leaders where they have truly found God in their holy books? I don't think so, because I can assure you, none of them have ever managed to find God in their holy books. How can they find God in their holy books if they have never seen or found God outside of themselves? If any of them say that they have found God in the scriptures, or have seen God outside of themselves, then they are lying to you! It is a lie because God is you, God is your consciousness, God is your expressions, and God is your experiences.

My dear friends, God is nothing more than an idea, an icon, and a theory. None of our religious leaders, not even the best of the bible scholars, have a definitive conclusion about discovering God in a book, in their scriptures, or have seen God outside of themselves, and they never will. How can they ever discover God or see God if they continuously look for him using the rational mind as the tool in trying to know and find him?

How can you tell if religions are using the rational mind? Well, as long as they teach their philosophy about how God promotes judgment, sin, and punishment, and therefore hell, then they are using the rational mind and intellectual analysis to understand God. It is impossible to know or find God using the rational mind and the method of reasoning, because they are both tied to drawing to some conclusion that it is all mental, and therefore God becomes mental, limited, conditional, and changeable. The real God is neither limited, mental, nor conditional but is unconditional and therefore, unchangeable.

The only way God can be truly found, and God finding you, is through your consciousness, expressions, and the experiencing of many lifetimes playing out many distressing and painful situations using the energy of positive and negative. Once this is accomplished, that is when you get to a place in consciousness where you ultimately understand that the rational mind is only a place of emotional measures that relate to the mental processing of what is not understood about yourself, your family, the world around you, and how energy works.

By playing with the energy of duality, positive and negative, we all have become so addictive to it we are now stuck in a revolving cycle (circle) that only sees good and bad, right and wrong, light and dark, God and Satan, and ourselves in human form as real. These things my dear friends, along with our dogmatic belief systems and our ties to family, can only come from the rational mind. All of it is not real, just like this God of the bible is not real. Even you in your human form and Satan are not real.

For instance: Do you ever wonder why you pray for peace and yet, the earth is filled with wars, disagreements, and countless opinions about God's word and what God wants for you? Have you ever noticed when you seek the light and good, darkness and evil seems to be right there deciding your fate as well? This is because of the way you understand the word "light" as meaning "good" and yet, forgetting that in order to have "light and good," "dark and bad" exist as part of you as well, all because of the rational mind and how it believes in these things as being real.

Is it hard for you to look at the possibility that there are no such thing as good and bad, right and wrong, light and dark, God and Satan, as well as sin and karma? My fellow searchers, you, along with all humans, have given life to an idea and an idol that requires devotion, sacrifice, and worship, and in return, this idol will presumably give you happiness, abundance, and bliss but only when you're dead! Who needs it after you're dead?

When you hold to the belief that you are a sinner, that you live only one lifetime, and that there is a mythical, all-powerful God outside of you who must be reckoned with and feared, then you have destined yourself to live in an illusion of shortages, grief, worry, drama, and always needing to be saved. However, by looking at yourself as a branch coming from the Spirit of One, you can get in touch with your natural ability to release these old mental and psychological measured beliefs that have kept you trapped within a consciousness of separation.

When you see and trust that you are a God also, equal to Him in all phases of consciousness, and I mean all phases. It allows your human mind and emotional consciousness to open up to the totality of who you truly are and to your relationship to your soul and intuitive consciousness. Your wishes, dreams of health, abundance, and happiness are all at your fingertips. But you give these things away for the mere benefit of holding onto old dogmatic beliefs, traditions, and the idea of some God in a book is going to save you and give you "freedom," but only if you play by His rules.

You continue to forget that you have moved into the land of the Tree of Knowledge of Good and Evil (second circle), not realizing that you, and all souled beings, created this tree of duality (second and third-dimension) on purpose in order to learn responsibility, have soul growth, and to answer the question, "Who am I?"

My dear friends, the religions of the world are selling you a bill of goods when it comes to this God of the Bible. A true and loving God never judges, is jealous, says you are a sinner, and takes action against you because you do not agree with him. Therefore, the God of the Bible, the God that you have been taught to be your creator, is no more than an idea and an icon put in place by those in authority to maintain their control over you.

It is you that is the real God here! It was you who moved outside of the Spirit of One a long time ago, and then forgetting that you still remain part of the tree of life. When you did this you ended up giving a whole new meaning to Spirit (God) and a whole new meaning where you come to know all things through your consciousness, your expressions, and your experiences, including this false God of the Bible.

However, because of feeling separated from your own "I AM Christ" identity, you have created a place of confinement. A confinement so great that it has caused you to give away your "freedom" along with your "energy" to those that hold a belief in some "original sin" and yet, this confinement is not made of iron bars, it is made up of your belief systems. Therefore, in my opinion, for I know who I AM, by submitting to the idea of a God in a holy book. You are actually giving away your "free will" to be controlled by fear and that of others.

Religions say that the human heart is corrupt and therefore will always seek and choose to do bad things. My dear friends, if this is true, then you are already doomed to hell, suffering, and separation from God just because you have accepted the belief in sin and karma. Religions also say by giving your life to God, you will gain your freedom from sin. Not only from sin, but you will be free to do the very thing you were created to do, which is to honor and worship God forever.

However, in spite of all what religions say about surrendering to God's will, you will still not trust Him. Instead, you will continuously worry about being good enough to get into heaven to meet Him. Now, why is that? Why would you continuously worry about getting into heaven to meet and live with God? It is because deep within your soul you can actually feel your soul telling you that you have had many experiences and lifetimes playing with the energy of karma, hence you are already saved. Yet, you still pray, go to church, try to live a proper life, and all that happens is that you continue to worry if you are good enough to get into heaven.

Yes, most of us listen to our religious leaders, give them our money, obey the rules of the church, and we still worry about getting into heaven. Oh, the worry doesn't come from fearing the devil. Often it comes from us not feeling important or worthy enough to meet God face to face. After all, look at all of this duality arguing going on between churches, politicians, and between ourselves about who is right and who is wrong.

It is not about how intellectual or intelligent you are, or how much you go to church and know the Bible, or who you think you know. It is about how conscious you are in knowing "who *you* truly are." Everything that you see and feel right now appears to be confusing and challenging, and it is because you just don't understand who you are, who God is, how your consciousness works with energy, and how you bring it into your life to play. Thus, you look to religion and your beliefs for the assurance that you will be protected and somehow make it to heaven when you die.

When you have consciousness, along with technology, moving at a fast rate and yet, the rational mind limiting you because of your dogmatic beliefs, something has to give or you will get caught in a consciousness of nothing but fear. Where is the freedom in that?

Many of us do not realize that energy exists in many different ways, and it is stored throughout the cosmos and also in the angelic pool of our sub-consciousness, including in the "field of neutrality." Therefore, it is there waiting to serve us, the true creators.

So, take deep breaths and define your prison – a metaphor of course – for mine was that I was hiding from myself and my soul. What happened, I got very mental and intellectual about God, thereby losing my awareness and my freedom to the "knowing of who I truly am." When you see God, the universe, yourself as literal, and you only human and separate from God, all life responds perfectly to support that idea.

You have forgotten that you are a conscious being that has formed and shaped your energy to take on a human form and you did it because you are in the likeness of the Spirit of One. But now, you are stuck in your human form and story as if they are real. That is not "true freedom." It is freedom that comes with a price.

However, you can choose to restructure your energy from all layers of your consciousness and set yourself free from your creations of fear, unworthiness, and from those that control you through man-made rules and conditions. You can do this just by learning that God is a Goddess, and that this Goddess is you, which means you are not a sinner and you never were.

My fellow searchers, even if you believe in the devil, or even in God, there is one thing for certain, it is that they both played their part in hypnotizing you from knowing who you truly are. Otherwise, the "tree of knowledge of good and bad" would not have been in the Garden. Religions of the world overlook this point because the true God, which is you, desired to understand the dual nature of the rational mind that you actually created while you were in our divine state (first creation-garden) and how it worked with your consciousness and with energy.

Therefore, it is not about some God in a book. It is about your soul and spirit and how it desired to understand your choices, and why you chose to come into the physical reality to play them out. Now, after millions, or perhaps billions of years later, your soul-spirit senses that you have the belief that you did something wrong by leaving some Garden that don't even exists.

Perhaps the biggest reason why you keep your soul at bay is because you feel deep within your heart that you have created such a crime against your spirit, that you, in all levels of your consciousness, feel unholy and unworthy of love and forgiveness. Now, because of this, you believe that you have disappointed your soul because you feel that you should have done better with this pure energy that you used since the time you left the Garden. So, in your ignorance of not knowing who God truly is, you have created a mental barrier so strong that you now protect this barrier with your beliefs and with your live.

There is a saying in Scripture, "*God so loved the world that he gave his only begotten Son* (John 3:16)." Well! Who do you think the only begotten Son is? It is all humans. It is you, all humans, which came forth into the physical realm, like Jesus, to introduce life, light, and love. The God within you is the branch and the renowned creator that loved the physical world so much in all of its chaos, its challenges, and its density. It gave its begotten human you (the son) so the "I AM God" of you might know life and its workings of duality, denseness, and how consciousness works with energy.

My fellow searchers, the ascension (rapture) you have long awaited for has come but you keep ignoring the signs because you continue to pray to an idea and an icon to come and rescue you. Wake up! The rapture is here and now. It is just that you have forgotten that you are Christ and the creator of your experiences and your existence.

Look, we all have taken vows of poverty, suffering, servitude, and so much more, trying to atone for what we felt were our sinful ways.

However, the time has come for us to get off that old karmic road and move beyond the guilt and shame embedded so deep within our soul. The time has come to understand that the God of the bible is the most misunderstood and misinterpreted non-being that we have ever attempted to comprehend all because of the way we have been taught by religion and our schools.

My dear friends, if you have come this far in the book, you should know now that there are as many different concepts of God as they are with the meaning of true freedom. Of course, religions tend to assign the concept of a God that lives in a book as the only path to this freedom.

However, what is overlooked by religion, as well as the common man, is that they assigned to it a force that vibrates in a dualistic manner, all because everything we see, taste, smell, touch, and hear bears some type of duality energy to it. Thus, leaving out any possibility of there being something else that exists that we cannot see, taste, smell, touch, or hear, all because of how the rational mind understands it that way.

If you go on the web at: http://www.livescience.com/16284-cern-elena-antiproton-antimatter-experiment.html. There is an amazing discovery that most of us might be familiar with because of hearing it on the news or seeing on the history channel under the title, the Universe. At the time of its airing on the news it caused a controversial concern where the scientists involved were going to blow up the world or create some big dark whole where everything would be sucked into it.

The article is about how the CERN laboratory in Switzerland experimented on colliding matter and anti-matter into each other, and the result was far from the world blowing up or creating a big dark hole for everything to fall into. The test showed that when scientist collided matter and anti-matter together, they both annihilated each other, and the results of it became "pure energy." Yes, this is true, the test showed "pure energy."

You see, when religion talks about God and how it relates to "true freedom," they ignore the composition of duality energy performing in a manner that creates exact opposites. For instance: The composition of the human mind is that it acts or processes everything it sees, tastes, smells, touches, and hears as dualistic and real. As a result of this! A dualistic consciousness philosophy will always deal with everything as a high and a low, light and dark, good and bad, right and wrong, all because that is how duality works.

However, you have some scientists working in Switzerland testing and experimenting with magnets and electromagnetic energies and colliding them together, producing an energy that is faster than the speed of light. How many of you thought that nothing is faster than the speed of light? By religions working from a dualistic consciousness, they overlook things such as the human consciousness, human thoughts, and human intuitive feelings, for all of these things are faster than the speed of light.

Scientists say that when you slow down energy it becomes light, and when you slow down light it reduces into the electromagnetic spectrum, which is the distribution of colored light that was produced by a beam of white light into its components, including positive, negative, and that of neutralized energy. The neutralized energy comes from an equal number of protons and electrons otherwise; it has a positive charge if there are fewer electrons or negative charge if there are more electrons.

Therefore, when light is reduced to positive and negative it eventually becomes harden energy. Thus the Atom becomes dense enough to create a physical body or for that matter anything material.

Now, from this testing of colliding matter into anti-matter, and coming up with "pure energy," the scientists noticed that the particles of the atom moved faster than the speed of light and beyond solid matter. This means something exists beyond duality (positive and negative). This then opened a whole new door where dualistic energy doesn't get denser. Instead, it begins to spiral upward to where it becomes "pure neutral energy."

So, what does this mean? It means that we, as souled beings, did move from a pure neutral energy state of consciousness (faster than then the speed of light) a long time ago to a much slower dualistic energy consciousness (the speed of light), where in the end, it caused us to become part of a denser physical world and a physical body (slower than the speed of light, or a denser frequency). Does this surprise you?

Now, because of this test, it means that we, as souled beings, have locked away deep within our consciousness an innate spirit consciousness of a higher frequency that is much faster than the speed of light. However, my soul calls it the Christ-Gnost consciousness, which by the way has remained pure and neutral. The only way we can tap into it is by spiraling through many different cycles of layered energy bodies (consciousnesses) until we become one with it again.

In other words, since we left the first creation a long time ago, we have, through our creations, layered our consciousness with seven energy bodies that is looked at as the human energy field, and they are:

1. Spirit body (faster than the speed of light)
2. Soul body (faster than the speed of light)
3. Intuitive body (faster than the speed of light)
4. Mental body (the speed of light)
5. Emotional body (the speed of light)
6. Etheric/Astral body (the speed of light)
7. Physical body (less than the speed of light)

I count the physical body as an energy body since we have learned from Einstein that all matter is made up of energy. Therefore, each subtle energy body overlaps and passes through the physical body, even our spirit and soul body, for it is all there waiting for us to awaken to them.

Each subtle body is defined by their different frequency in the same way that we would define radio signals because both are around us in the same space simultaneously. Becoming aware of each subtle body frequency is almost like turning the radio dial to find the ultimate station for us to listen and learn. The only way to dial into the ultimate station is for us to move past the concept of energy that only comes in the form of positive and negative, good and bad, right and wrong (the speed of light).

As we all know, the physical body is the densest form of energy that our human consciousness uses to explore the environment around us and to interact with one another. By the densest, I mean that the vibrational energy design of the physical body is of a frequency (slower than the speed of light) low enough to be seen by our eyes, heard by our ears; in other words, experienced with all of our five senses. Of course, the more we are awakened to this understanding, the more we are able to see the physical body in a greater light, even to the point where we can learn to heal our physical body and choose different realities.

For instance: Let us look at each subtle body from what I mentioned above using the numerical numbers from 1 – 7, of which I assigned to them. Let us use these numbers of 1 – 7 to represent different frequencies, or in our example, different radio signals.

First, you have your spirit representing a frequency of 1, your soul body representing a frequency of 2, your intuitive body representing a frequency of 3, all which travels faster than the speed of light. Then you have your mental body as representing a frequency of 4, your emotional body representing a frequency of 5, and your etheric/astral body representing a frequency of 6, all traveling at the speed of light. Last but not least, you have your physical body representing a frequency of 7, which is less than the speed of light.

Now, let us look at these different frequency numbers 1 - 7 as radio stations that you can dial into once you know they exist. If you only know and believe that radio station number 7 is the only station that exists then what do you think your belief systems are going to consists of? It's simple! Your belief systems are going to be tied to everything of physical, including looking at everything as good and bad, right and wrong, which also means that your consciousness and wisdom will travel less than the speed of light.

Now, can you imagine for a moment what each radio station would provide you, as far as belief systems, awareness, and wisdom if you knew that other stations existed?

Well! Through choosing and experiencing many lifetimes, via the soul creating many "personality-aspects" to play out a story, there are many of you today that have become aware of these different frequencies in the human energy field (different radio stations) where your energy vibrates beyond the physical senses. Beyond what you see with your physical eyes, for you have been placed into a consciousness where you know that your physical senses are only a small portion of the vibrational energies around you. Thus, the physical bodies at the atom, molecule, and cell levels are patterns of vibrating energy that you call matter.

When you become aware that your physical body is really a field of vibrating energy patterns that can merge with all energy fields of your consciousness that surround you, like for instance, your subtle bodies and your many "personality-aspects. You come to understand that each energy field then interacts with each other as one energy field. Because of this, each energy field (frequency) can affect another energy field through your consciousness because each energy field holds its own consciousness and yet, each consciousness (frequency number) is part of the "one consciousness."

This, my dear friends, is another key to understanding how energy works and how you can achieve complete freedom just by coming into awareness and a knowing that your consciousness can travel faster than the speed of light. Thus, you can collect or tap into your past and present experiences, as well as your future potentials, and the wisdom tied to all of them, faster than the speed of light.

Let us now take a look at the Etheric-Astral Body. Your Etheric body is the first energy body frequency that is just above the physical body and yet, it exists within the physical body as well. However, your Etheric body extends outward just outside of the physical body. The purpose of the Etheric body is to form a pattern that serves as a template for you to experience life in a physical body in order for you to expand and grow in consciousness.

The Etheric body contains a vibrational energy of duality that opposes each other, which is why you have many "personality-aspects" of you from the past and present (from clear, gray, to dark and every shade in-between) lingering around in the astral realms waiting for you to integrate them as one with you, for each aspect (lifetime) carries a frequency of different belief systems when you lived out a particular lifetime. However, you have also created several aspects of you to explore future potentials to experience, either in your present lifetime or for some future lifetime.

In other words, your Etheric body contains the energetic blueprint (divine plan) for the pathway that guides the location and development of every "personality-aspect" that you have created to play out a story in a physical lifetime. These "personality-aspects" exist only because of the etheric field of energy behind them that keeps them as part of your physical lifetime of today and yet, they feel separate from you because of your belief systems ring in at different frequency levels.

Since the Etheric body is your physical body's blueprint, the two are very closely related, which is why when you die from physical death, you continue to live in a slightly higher vibration than what your physical body was vibrating at, high enough to where those in the physical cannot see you. This also means you will pick up those belief systems that you didn't even know you had when you where in the physical. This also explains why when a person dies they take on the form of what they looked like when they were on earth.

So, never fear or worry about your loved ones for they still live. You cannot see them because the energy field around them is vibrating a bit higher than your physical body of consciousness. When you die from physical death and move into your Etheric body, you do take with you all that you have believed while you were in the physical. Not only do you bring the beliefs from your current lifetime but also your beliefs from all of your past lifetimes.

Because of this, the energetic vibrations of your Etheric body will then determine the blueprint and the "personality-aspect" that you will play out for your next lifetime. If the vibrations of your past lifetimes have not been cleared or integrated with your present lifetime, then disharmony will be reflected in your next physical lifetime. This is where your accidents, diseases, bad relationships with family or non-family members, and sufferings come from. They do not from some God, devil, or from those that you swear that it's their fault to why you suffer.

Hence, drama, the belief you are only human, your idea of God and Satan, and your wisdom of limitations are then reflected into your Etheric body, unless there is some interceding process that prevents this reflection. By becoming aware of your vibrational energy fields and the frequency that surrounds your physical and etheric body, it becomes the first step for rapid and effective integrating of all frequencies along with your other personality-aspects. This then, allows you to move higher up the energetic ladder.

According to the study of metaphysics, the etheric body is a counterpart to the overall structure of the physical body that extends from one quarter inch (1/4") to about two inches (2") beyond the physical body.

Now, looking at the Emotional body, it contains the emotional patterns of all your past personality-aspects, including your present lifetime, your mind-set that centers on thoughts and feelings about your beliefs, and how you chose to experience life. All of it has determined your personality in this lifetime. It is from your personality that determines how you feel about yourself and how you interact with others.

For instance: If you are always angry, feel alone, or are in constant fear, then you have set up a vibrational pattern that will lock you into an emotional energy field that becomes your personality in this lifetime. Your emotional body generally follows the shape of the physical and etheric bodies but is somewhat more distracted and unstable, and extends from one to about three inches (1" to 3") outside of the physical body.

Your emotional body also contains energy colors of the rainbow; the color it displays depends on your emotional expressions, especially with family and non-family members. Higher energy charged expressions of love, joy, and compassion are associated with energy colors that are bright and clear, while lower energy charged expressions of hate, anger, and dogmatic beliefs are darker and lack clarity.

Now, your mental energy body contains the structure and patterns of all the thoughts and belief systems that you consider your truths. Truths that come from the first time you left the first creation to where you fell to your lowest and densest vibrational level, and to your climb back up the emotional ladder. With this you develop a strong connection between your mental and emotional bodies.

For instance: An idea in of itself is very powerful, and the reaction to the idea can carry a lot of energy, and different people will react differently to the same idea. For example: Consider the idea that only Catholics can get into heaven. What do you think a Baptist, or Jew, or Muslim is going to think?

In fact, they will look upon the idea as being silly, and give it no energy. However, the Catholic person might be very passionate about it and give the idea a lot of energy. Thus, the Catholic's emotional body would then record the intensity of the reaction to the idea therefore becoming part of the mental body and his/her memories. This would be also true for family members because most all family members come together in many lifetimes to work out karma. Thus, the wisdom of those experiences becomes limited to the human consciousness.

On the other hand, the person who thought the idea was silly would add no meaning to it, and therefore no energetic pattern would be part of the mental or emotional body. Thus, leaving this person to a potential of opening up to a vibrational frequency that could connect this person to the wisdom of their own Christ consciousness all because of the person's consciousness moving faster than the speed of light.

Now, the mental body is also connected with the color of the rainbow, as it will show a yellow light radiating around the entire body from head to toe and, according to metaphysics, extends from three to eight inches (3" to 8") beyond your physical body. It is within this area your thoughts and ideas form as small dribbles of light of varying form and strength.

Now, let us talk a bit about your intuitive body. The intuitive body and how it relates to you in expressing your "free will" is what "fell" from your remembrance a long time ago. When you lowered your thoughts, views, and feelings to a judgmental belief consciousness (symbolically taking the bite of the apple) a long time ago, you discovered that you not only lost your intuitive consciousness to memory, you lost your divine will and the wisdom of your Christ consciousness as well.

Because of feeling this loss, your outer, disobedient nature, represented by the servant and Ishmael in the Bible, came up with an alternate will called "free will" or "free choice" that actually became part of your mental nature. Of course, this was a good thing, because "free will" was needed to move you outside of yourself and into the endless nothingness where you would then layer and form your consciousness with multiple layered dimensions, also known as many consciousnesses that hold many belief systems. This resulted in the rational mind accepting a belief that those dimensions, including earth and your free will, were real and made of opposing energies.

Your "free will" not only allowed you to move outside of your divine state (first creation) and enter into this endless nothingness of potentials. It also becomes the key for your awakening later on, for it was required that your intuitive body be a servant to your soul consciousness in order to bring about the illusion of "free will," and that it is separated from your higher "divine will." The illusion of "free will" helps you think, understand, and reason with all the things you experience with for the first time.

The perception of power and having "free will," even though all of what you were choosing came from a mental nature, gave you the capability to define your expressions, experiences, and conditions as good (light) and bad (dark). This includes those immoral and destructive forces that caused you great harm, misfortune, and unpleasant events throughout your many lifetimes. Now, your intuitive consciousness is more connected with your heart center and yet, the vibrational frequency extends just about ten inches (10") beyond your physical body.

Now, let us talk about your spirit and soul body, for their frequency patterns are higher than all of your subtle bodies put together. In other words, it is the perfect radio station to tune into. Why? It is because that is where your true wisdom lies. Within your soul body of consciousness, you contain all the information and wisdom related to your experiences in every lifetime that you have lived.

You see, the frequency of this energy field is faster than the speed of light because it is nothing but "pure neutral energy." Thus, within your soul body, you can reflect all of what you have learned and experienced, for it contains your higher intentions, your true wisdom, your Gnost-Christ consciousness, your purpose, and who you truly are, and it also exposes to you all of your beliefs. Your soul body is about finding you, while in physical form, learning the effectiveness of how you hid your true identity and wisdom for eons of time.

Your spirit and soul body has been part of your consciousness ever since you left the first creation and now, because of your many lifetimes bearing your cross, you have the potential to move from a 2-D and 3-D consciousness to a 4-D and 5-D consciousness that operates faster than the speed of light, even though you still remain part of the physical world. The 4-D consciousness is considered a formless realm much like the 2-D mental consciousness that connects you to the 3-D world of physicality.

However, the difference between the 2-D and the 4-D, even though they are both mental states of consciousness, is that the 4-D is not made up of any judgmental based ideas about good and bad or anything that has a vibrational dualistic energy to it. It operates in a more neutral state. It is through the 4-D where you enter into a 5-D consciousness of physicality.

The 5-D consciousness is the gateway for tapping into New Expansional Energy (New Earth) that carries no limitations, no judgment, and that everything is unconditional. The 4-D mental realm is a consciousness of non-form that becomes the tool to help you rid yourself of all the belief systems in what you took on as your truths when you lived only from out of your 2-D mind of duality and judgment.

In other words, if you want to know where you are when it comes to 3-D versus 5-D living, then you only have to consider what you are thinking about right now at this very moment. If you still have beliefs of judgment, drama, being a sinner, or that one is good and another is bad, or believing that one race of people or religion are better than another, or that God and Satan are separate from you, and that you still have emotional ties to your physical family, then you are obviously living the life of a 2-D and 3-D being.

Only thoughts and beliefs of non-duality, non-judgment, unconditional love, limitlessness, and compassion for yourself and others can survive in a 4-D and 5-D consciousness environment. This means, when you move your consciousness to a non-judgmental philosophy and trust in yourself as an equal to God, and that you are a Christ also, you move from a 2-D to a 4-D consciousness in forming your ideas and expressions (words) into inconceivable magic. You actually can say that the 4-D and 5-D consciousness is what you have learned by journeying through the 2-D and 3-D consciousness.

Now, in the 5-D consciousness, you can live life under the rulership of you being the King of Kings and the Lord of Lords. In other words, you choose what to experience in the flesh, instead of playing games like, "It's your destiny" or "the devil made me do it," or that "I have a disease." The difference between destiny and choice is profound. The difference is actually "true freedom."

These are the seven subtle bodies that make up your human energy frequency field or aura. According to metaphysics, its outer shape appears egg-shaped and extends out to about one and half (1 ½') to about two feet (2') beyond your physical body. However, this can extend even further or become closer to you depending on what you believe as your truths.

For instance: Let's say that you have feelings of unconditional love for yourself, for others, and that you do not participate in any drama. Then your aura could expand to meet up with your soul's frequency level, whereas, if you feel fear and threatened, then your aura could collapse to a much denser frequency where you make choices from a consciousness pattern of only a few inches of the physical body.

So, here you have it, matter and antimatter colliding into each other and creating "pure neutral energy," and it has been proven by scientists. This means that when you release old stuck dogmatic belief systems from its state of dualistic expressions and collide it with new beliefs of you being a divine being, the energy used to create those dualistic dogmatic belief systems explodes and goes back to "pure neutral energy." Thus, your frequency level expands and moves beyond the speed of light, and therefore your memory and wisdom becomes clearer.

You see, when you add awareness, understanding, and a knowing to "all that you are," including that of divine conscious choice, into the many vibrational energy frequencies of duality that surround you, all energy frequencies will move back to their pure neutral state, thus your wisdom is released. I know you would think that by colliding two known energies together (opposing beliefs and that of what it formed into matter) it should still add up to the same two known energies and yet, it turned out to be different, proven by scientist.

Today, we can find people all around the world becoming awakened to this "new pure energy," although it has always been there. According to my soul, this "new pure energy" is now available to all who are willing to wake up to it and have it become part of their reality. As always, there are many right now that are not sure what this "new pure energy" is, or how to use it, or how it is to serve us, and therefore we wait until we see something that will convince us of its existence, thereby missing out on many good miracles.

Of course, let's not forget! This "pure neutral energy" will not work with your old way of thinking. It will not work using dual thought patterns of energy. However, you can choose to bring in this pure energy just by allowing yourself to let go of the old belief that someone has to be right and that someone has to be wrong.

Once you understand that you cannot experience this pure energy in your life if you continue to believe that positive and negative is all that is because all that will happen is that your creations will always consist of dualistic energy. Thus your experiences remain the same. That is living in the old world. Also, there may be some of you that have tried to create your miracles using pure energy but nothing seems to happen. Well, the reason is because pure energy can only be used with the intuitive consciousness and not with your mental or rational consciousness.

For instance: Stop for a moment and think about what you would like to experience right now. Before you know it, your thoughts will automatically move towards associating what you want using dualistic energy. In other words, because of not having the experience in using "pure energy," you will most likely connect to what you are trying to create now with what you have experienced in the past using dualistic energy as its foundation.

You see, because of how we have created a mental network and many personality-aspects (lifetimes) of ourselves since the time we left our divine state, these past personality-aspects of us are always using the same mental patterns, the same logic, and the same skill process to derive at a result. This means we, in our present life, will do the same if these personality-aspects of our past are not integrated with our present self.

When you try to use this "pure energy," even though you are aware of its existence, with your new creations of today, you cannot associate it with your old way of thinking in trying to bring it into your life to experience it unless all aspects of you are integrated, including your emotional ones. You see, "pure energy" cannot be associated with old thinking because there are no patterns for you to follow. It is all about you creating a new route to experience as a sovereign God in your own right.

Bottom line! What it comes down to is that you cannot use or call in this "new expansional energy" by means of the old thought process or using the rational mind as the trigger. It has to be triggered by your imagination, intuition, and your Gnost consciousness, via through the heart center and not your mind center.

However, once you learn how to use this "expansional energy," you will begin to set up a process that will annihilate (like the test showed) all your old memories of duality thinking or what you have been calling your sins. Remember, your spirit/soul is made up only of "pure neutral energy, and it can expand infinitely without limitations."

My fellow searchers, this is the true meaning of washing away your sins. It is your spirit/soul that retains the wisdom of your many lifetime experiences and yet, your soul destroys the emotional memory of the impact that it has caused you for many lifetimes. You see, once you ascend to this level of understanding of "who you truly are," your spirit and or soul doesn't like patterns or structure for no longer than for you to experience them, and then it wants to move onto the next experience. This is very important to understand because it prevents you from getting stuck with belief systems.

For instance: You feel deep within your heart that you want to rid yourself of an illness or that you desire to move out of poverty. Then the first thing that you have to do is make the choice and then trust your spirit or soul completely without adding any duality energy to it. Like for example, mentally asking yourself how you will accomplish it.

Listen to your heart instead of your head in what it is telling you what to do next. What do I mean by "listen"? I am actually talking about feeling your soul responding to you without any emotional ties to what you are feeling. You will know exactly what I mean if you seem to have a problem in letting go God and your emotional ties to friends, family, government, and your church, especially letting go of all attachments to your parents and siblings. Oh, you can love them and be with them, just don't get caught up with the drama that family create.

Also, if you have a hard time seeing yourself equal to God, or that your family comes first, and if it comes hard for you to take the cross of Jesus down of the wall, then know you are still responding to your emotional ties to the past. Once your spirit/soul wipes clean all of your emotional ties to your old ways of thinking, especially when it comes to your family and religion, then you will be able to bring into your creations nothing but "pure expanded neutral energy."

This means, in the remaining time you have on earth in this lifetime, you will not create or experience anymore drama, or play in poverty, or have an illness that devastates you, or many other experiences that are connected to the old energy (old earth) of duality. Even your golf game will improve.

Of course, drama consciousness is very hard to let go because it is so tied to our emotional belief systems about who we are, what we are, and how we are so strongly connected with our families, friends, and the God that we were brought up with. Drama energy is very addictive and many of us have a hard time living without it. The moment we try to let go of our drama addiction, we begin to become very uneasy, to the point we become very desperate to move back into it.

Drama energy is nothing more than someone feeding of the blood of another like some kind of vampire. To those that took vows or have overcome feeding off others, they instead become a vampire that feeds off themselves. You know, feeding off the energy (blood) of your other personality-aspects of the past because you actually believe that they don't exist because you pretend to think you live only one lifetime. All that you are doing is creating more division and disorder within yourself.

You see, when you can finally let all of this go and move into the belief that you are a Christ also, and equal to God in all ways, without doubt, you then set up your two dimensional mind where it will mess you up dearly when it comes to your beliefs and what you can do, which is a good thing.

Look, at first, your two dimensional mind allows you to see things that are invisible, like seeing and communicating with other angels, then out of the blue the two dimensional mind stops it with no apparent reason. I know this to be true because it has happened to me. Once it happened, I became very confused because I thought that I understood my soul and how to bring in this "pure expanded energy" to serve me. Thus, once again, I felt disconnected to "all that I thought I was."

However, this was a good thing! Because once I recovered from my confusion and doubt about "who I am," what happened next was that I began to take a second look at some of the things from my past, including my emotional ties to family, and to all "personality-aspects" of myself and what I (they) created. That was the time when I finally began to integrate all of them with nothing but unconditional love, no judgment, and with no drama or emotional ties to them.

Yes, the thought of losing your platform in life, like losing your God, your family, your church, and many other things that you feel are your truths, even your base of reality, suddenly hits you in the face to make a choice. Believe me, if you make the choice to move forward, then your whole reality will shift. A shift where you will suddenly have your old dogmatic views colliding right into what you have already manifested in your life.

You know exactly what I mean! It is anti-matter and matter, belief and anti-belief, trust and doubt, and every other possible type of duality scenario starting to collide into each other. When you make the choice to move forward with this new expanded energy, you will have an interesting period where you will have energetic and vibrant experiences in your life because of everything and all beliefs coming together, including the building blocks of all your other past personality-aspects.

All colliding together, and in the end, you begin to create your world with nothing but using "pure expanded energy" because everything, including your human consciousness returns back to their original form. Back to where your soul is now one hundred percent part of your physical life instead of your soul only being two to three percent of your physical life.

My dear friends, this means you become free and disconnected from the reservoir of the energetic grid of duality. You become a sovereign "I AM" energy creating being in your own right. This also means, you become an energy creating being of pure expanded energy that doesn't serve the collectiveness group anymore that are still part of the reservoir of the energy grid of duality.

In other words, for the very first time in your life you will create what you desire without using the dualistic field of energy that surround most humans. It will be a time when you begin to focus on "who you truly are" for a change, and not on trying to serve someone else, not even family, for family will always keep you in a drama consciousness because of past karma.

It is about you having compassion for them where they are in life, and then allowing them to earn their own way to heaven because no one can do it for them, not even you. When you begin to love and serve yourself first, it means you have accepted yourself as a divine being that needs no confessional booth to tell your sins. You have bared your cross, and now you have to let go of all your guilt and shame in what you have done, either in this lifetime or in some future lifetime.

It is through totally letting go of your old way of thinking, when you suddenly begin to have compassion for everybody because you begin to understand everyone's journey, including your own. "Freedom" is about learning to re-wire (re-think) your consciousness, and not by the old hardwire of using electrical cables of positive and negative to connect you to some main metaphoric energy box, but to rewire your consciousness that connects you to a new expanded energy stream of "pure energy" that needs no wires.

By moving out of your two dimensional mental energy field of rational thinking and into this new mental quantum type of energy of neutrality and expansion, you dissolve and melt everything away that feels part of the old way of thinking. It is when you learn to trust in yourself to take the leap in consciousness, for it can feel like you are taking a leap of a high building and into a deep dark alley. But when you take the leap, it is no longer a high building or a deep alley. It is whatever you have chosen to experience in that now moment.

True freedom is not about following God, his laws, or anyone else. True freedom is about learning to make a conscious choice to become a sovereign Christ like being in your own right, for you are the God to follow. Choices that will always demonstrate that you are indeed the Christ you have been looking for, and that you are not a sinner. When you learn to do this, you will create your miracles faster than the speed of light. Then suddenly the miracles you create become a real experience and a real joy to you.

Remember, you have the "I AM!" You have the "Rational Mind!" You have the "Ego Personality!" It is like the saying, "Me (ego personality), myself (the rational mind), and I (the, I AM)." The "ego personality" is about your human lifetime (story) and the family you associate yourself with today, and the rational mind is the make-up of your characteristics that you use in this lifetime in determining who you are.

Therefore, you have at least three different choices every time you have a choice or decision to make about who you are. You have the "me personality," the "myself mental personality," and then you have the "I AM God personality" choice or potentiality. The more you are aware of the three in one choice, the more freedom you are going to experience.

It is up to you, and no one else, to make the shift from judgment and disharmony to unconditional love, for that is the key to true freedom.

Epilogue

My fellow seeker, from the soul's perspective, the arrival in accepting and understanding "who you truly are" could not have been better timed because the human you is tired, confused, and worried about its future. Look, are you or are you not filled with questions about your health, well-being, family, the future, and even about the structure of your religious beliefs.

Do you find yourself over stressed because of all the demands placed on you because of family, your job, government, friends, religion, and the thought about how to keep everything from falling apart? When you loudly say to yourself, and to others, that you are your human name, your personality, your body, your religion, and your career, you actually shut out the best of you. Believe me! That is a lot of wisdom to shut out.

The understanding behind why some of you feel depressed and out of touch with God, yourself, family, and who you think you are, is because the human consciousness is departing from the old energy of very dense energy and into the New Expansional Energy.

You can say that we, as humans, are moving from very dense energy to the new Golden Age of Expansional Energy. The vibrational energy of positive and negative, good and bad, have been very challenging to us all because of the energy being so dense and three dimensional. You know this to be true because of how we have been in conflict with each other for many centuries. Also, at this point in time, we, as mankind, are feeling this very dense energy, and as we approach the ending of this opposing cycle of 12/21/2012), this strong dense energy is bringing out the worst within us, all because of our past lifetime demons.

This is why we feel so much anger, jealousies, greed, corruption, and aggressive warlike tendencies within us, as it is mirrored back to us from what we are experiencing in life, what we see from our politicians, and from what is happening around the world, including our fires, floods, and droughts. It is not about global warming as our politicians allege it to be. It is about us, as humans, coming face to face with our demons.

This is why you are experiencing illnesses, accidents, failures, and your discomforts in life because your soul is in the process of gathering together "all that you are," and many of you are fighting hard to ignore your soul. All because of your strong fixed beliefs and the emotional ties you have with your family, your friends, your politics, and your dogmatic beliefs. It is not about destiny or sin, even though you pretend that it is what's guiding your life. It is all those past lifetime personality aspects of you that are guiding your life, which is why what happens to you today is all based on your past without you even realizing it.

Case in point! Haven't you noticed that time seems to be accelerating so fast you cannot keep up with it any longer, as it escapes you in getting anything done? Doesn't it seem like a year passes by very quickly? Well! Time is moving very quickly because you, and the human race, are at the end days where the old vibrational energy of denseness is crossing over to the New Golden Age of Expansional Energy.

In this New Expansional Energy is where we, as a divine human, can literally create New Energy to be used for all the miracles we can stand. It is also an age where we can live up to and over 100 years or more if we wish. However, before we, as humans, can move into this New Golden Age of Expansional Energy, we cannot carry with us all those old dogmatic beliefs, the drama energy of our families, and the baggage of our past lifetimes.

My dear friends, all of you are now fast approaching the time where you must make a choice, to either fall back and go through another spiraling alchemy energy cycle (more lifetimes playing with dense energy) or move forward into the New Golden Age of Expansional Energy, as the Bible calls it the New Earth. The choice is yours if you desire to repeat more lifetimes of drama and ancestral karma (sin) or move forward in consciousness to learn the truth about who you truly are, for you indeed are divine.

The idea of releasing yourself from this very dense dualistic emotional energy caused by religious dogmas and your ties to family keeps you from moving into a "knowing" that there is just "oneness." It is an "oneness" where you begin to understand that the real Christ is you. This "knowing" that everything is "one" automatically shifts your 2-D and 3-D consciousness into the 4-D and 5-D Expansional Energies, thus transforming you as a sovereign "I AM God" in your own right.

My dear friends, the way you think and belief is what creates the density of your veil. If you cannot allow yourself to open up to your own soul, and the wisdom it holds, the more your body becomes solid and unyielding. Thus creating more lifetimes of suffering! The more you allow yourself to let go of your old way of thinking the more the veil is lifted.

Believe it or not, when you were born here on Earth you were born with many types of physical bodies. Some are thinly veiled while others are more dense and solid, and the body that you are experiencing today is where you are on your wisdom ladder. To know which body you are occupying today is to take deep breathes, many of them, and then allow your soul to join you while you are in your human body. Learn to bring in your thinly veiled body by letting go of what you think you know about whom you think you are and where you think you came from.

Just know that in your present lifetime you can indeed experience life but you cannot know life and what it means to live with joy, abundance, and health with your current beliefs. If you are attached to your beliefs like you are attached to your body, than you cannot know life or what it is all about other than what you are experiencing right now. The life that you are living today means nothing if you are not fulfilling what you long to experience. If you continue to live life being attached to your beliefs, then by all means be prepared to undergo more suffering in your life. The choice is yours!

It is about letting go of all that you believed to be your truths including the truths of your parents, their parents before them, and all that you have been taught about this mentalistic God. What do you have to lose by letting go of all your old beliefs and what you think you know about life? Is it that you fear God or that you may not go to heaven? All I can say is, if you desire better health, abundance, and more joy in your life then you are going to have to dissolve all that you have ever believed about yourself and what you have been taught about God and his miracles.

Your religious beliefs and family are just beings that you have learned to love and hate at the same time, and sometimes battled with. You have forgotten that they are just angelic beings like you that you have traveled with for many lifetimes, that you have developed karma with, and that you have come attached to. You owe them, your church, your friends, and your government nothing and they owe you nothing. However, you stay connected to them all because of your beliefs. It actually comes down to what you want to experience in life. Do you want abundance, health, and joy or do you want continues suffering? It is up to you!

It is in the letting go of your old beliefs that you will find the greatest truths. By learning to dissolve who you think you are, even your since of value in life, and the role you play here on earth, the more you will break down the density of your consciousness. It is when you become unattached to your beliefs you come into your soul's wisdom, thus gaining good health, abundance, and great miracles of joy.

So, the time is now to launch yourself from this old dualistic energy to the New Expanded Energy in discovering that truth is not one dimensional but is multi-dimensional.

My fellow seekers, truth is real and meaningful, even though it is an illusion. If someone comes forward spouting off truth to you as only one dimensional then all that was hidden in that one truth must come out because it will not stand the new energy storm of expanded consciousness. For those that will not let go of their old beliefs or those that don't understand that truth is multi-dimensional, it is going to be difficult for them. Why? It is because they will find themselves buried deep into drama, fear, and karma.

That, my dear friends, is where they will create their probability to come back for more lifetimes, and with the same family group members to play out more drama and karma. Therefore, don't you think it would be wise to release your ancestral karma by loving them with compassion, understanding, and unconditional love then out of obligation and duty? They are a souled being just like you trying to find their own way by the choices they make, even the choice to have cancer, live in adversity, or grow old with having no dignity, thus creating demands on family members.

We all pray for truth, health, abundance, and joy but when truth comes our way we ignore it because it doesn't match up with our beliefs and what we have been taught by religion. This is why we repeat our experiences over and over because every time we look in the mirror all that we see is what we believe we are instead of seeing who we truly are. You are not what you see in the mirror but what you don't see.

With that, I trust that this book has given you the potential to unlock the wisdom of your consciousness, revealing to you the deep secrets of you being the designer and the creator of your divine plan to learn "who you truly are" and where "you truly came from." Now, you know it was not from some God outside of you or from your family, for it was your own spirit that opened up the pathway for your soul to create many diverse lifetimes that were crafted with such precision in fulfilling your mission to "know who you truly are." My friends, you are a sovereign divine being in your own right.

Understand that everything you have been taught has been nothing but a big lie, for your soul knows who you truly are, where (and who) you have been, where you are today, and where you would like to be right now. Your soul knows that you are and have been a wonderful creator. It is just that you have forgotten that your real name is "I AM That I AM." Meaning, you have no name. You are the "Ehyeh Asher Ehyeh," the God you seek.

When Moses asked for God's name on the mound that day, he was told, "Ehyeh Asher Ehyeh," "I AM That I AM." "Ehyeh" translated means, "I will be." The name "Asher" is translated as "who or whom," and when the names come together as "Ehyeh Asher Ehyeh," it means "I will be who I will be." Or, "I will become whatever I choose to be" because my name is "I AM," and "I Am the God" who delivers the expressions, energies, and the potentials for me to play and create what I please. Hence, I place no other God before me but me!

My dear friends, you have forgotten that Earth is an amazing place that you, and all souled beings, created so you can pretend that you were not God. That in itself is a great miracle. It gave you the opportunity to reincarnate into a new identity, a new story, and a new name where you could play with free choice to learn about life, love, power, and then come to know who you truly are, for you are indeed a divine being.

You see, your spirit did not know about life, truth, power, or love until it was created by the human you. This is why life, truth, power, and love cannot be taught, lectured about or even rationalized using the human mind. Life, truth, power, and love can only be experienced. How could your spirit know about these things if you have never experienced the implications of their meaning in the flesh?

It was you, and all souled beings working together as the Godhead, who designed and created physical life and the entanglements of what truth, power, and love brought to the meaning of life, and to true freedom. It was you that chose the course you wanted to take to learn about these things, and when you give away your power to someone else you are then a God fighting with yourself.

Therefore, my fellow seekers, it is time now to accept your true identity. The act of forgetting has served you well. It is time to take full responsibility for the God that you are in creating your world of illusions. Feel this wisdom within yourself, stop denying who you truly are, and know that you have been a miracle maker and a creator in designing your many lifetimes as a king, queen, a slave, rich person, a poor person, a person with defects, mentally and physically, as well as a person victimized, and a person that victimized. Know that you have done it all, and now you have a soul consciousness that is filled with limitless power, wisdom, truth, love, and enlightenment.

Don't be afraid to let go of the concept of duality and the God of the Bible because they have been nothing more than how you processed sin and God using the physical senses in understanding yourself as a God. Take a deep breath and let go all of what you think you know about yourself, even your fear of God and what he might do to you if you change your way of thinking about him and his rules.

Learn to understand that those fears came from you when you decided to leave the first creation a long time ago. Also, understand that these fears have come from your many past lifetimes and from how you have been processing them through the alchemy energy cycles of time and space. Understand that you will not go out of existence or go to hell if you let all of these lies go including your dogmatic beliefs and your connection to family. How can that happen if it was your soul that created your divine plan in the first place?

Right now your soul is filled with such overwhelming wisdom, and you can bring this wisdom forth into your current lifetime and into this New Expansional Energy as wonderful miracles to experience. This wisdom that you possess is not about who you were in some past lifetime because they are an expression of your soul and not an expression of you in this lifetime. Oh, you can say that they are related to you like a brother or sister but they are not you in this lifetime. This is very important to understand because it releases you from any karmic baggage that you may be experiencing now.

It is you in this lifetime that is the soul's designee in opening up your heart, mind, and consciousness to "all that you are" with unconditional love and forgiveness. When you do this, it allows your soul to come into your life bringing with it a huge amount of wisdom, multiple layers of truths, and understanding that can lead to healing, abundance, and to all the miracles you can stand, including the resolution to your current conditions no matter what they are, even cancer.

Also remember, it is you that is the point of contact for your soul and not your other lifetimes, for you are the chosen ascendee to bring in your Christ consciousness here on earth. Once you do, you become the standard in bringing into balance your past lifetimes. You do it by setting them free from any concept of ancestral karma and the idea of sin. It takes letting go of your old way of thinking and processing that will create the energy needed for you to release any emotional guilt, shame, or burden that you may feel deep within because of the belief that you did something wrong or that you are obligated to care for your family and religion.

Keep in mind, when you left the first creation your consciousness was just a ball of light. You had no form or physical body at the time, not even a family. Then when you moved into the second creation, you used pure energy (symbolic of God) to form and create what you believed to be true for you, even though it was all an illusion. It was an illusion because "all that you are today is still just a ball of divine light." However, you are a ball of divine light that is now filled with vast wisdom, understanding, and life, all because of your soul and past lifetime experiences.

Look at it this way: When you first left the first creation you designed and created a mental version of yourself that became real to you, which then allowed you to experience your belief systems in order to understand yourself and life. Then you, from the soul level, and knowingly having the ability to create likenesses of yourself, decided to experience as many forms (bodies) and potentials as you could, no matter if those potentials where good or bad made no difference to you because all that your soul desired was to feel and learn the wisdom of each experience, including you joining a family.

So, in order for your soul to accomplish this, your soul created as many personality aspects of yourself as it could, and then your soul called them your physical lifetimes. Now, if you would, imagine for a moment that each of those lifetimes that you have had on earth, good and bad, are now a high ranking General, and at this moment in time, they all live in many different non-physical dimensions while the human you of today is in this physical lifetime. This would make the human you of today the president and chief over all those Generals that are still part of your human consciousness of today.

However, the consciousness of the human you of today would never guess or even conceive that it is the president and chief over your past lifetime personalities and their beliefs because the human you of today feels that it has no power to do anything about it. Now, why is that? The reasons are many however; the two most important ones are that each General (the yous in those past lifetimes) came up with their own belief systems while living out each particular lifetime, and now they all still believe they are the boss in what is best for you in this lifetime.

Since your soul is always with the latest incarnation, making you the president and chief over them, the human you now feel on an emotional level nothing but those beliefs coming from those Generals. This creates within you a deluge of belief systems to the point where you become so confused about who you truly are, where you truly came from, and that you believe you are only human. This is why you hold to a belief that you need someone to save you, heal you of your illnesses, help you with money, or help you with whatever deficiency that you feel is wrong in your life.

Therefore, the human you in this lifetime, without realizing it, gives away its God power to all those high ranking Generals and to their belief systems of the past, as well as to others because you are so blind (asleep) to the truth that you are the God you seek, which is why it is very important to learn how to integrate "all that you are," all those Generals of past lifetimes.

So my fellow seekers, you can choose to be in your "I AM" divine essence or you can choose to be a personality that has no power of your own, and therefore only rely on others to take care of you including what they believe you need for spiritual growth. Remember, earth is the only planet where you have free choice to choose any type of experience, even cancer. Earth is also the only planet that has death, which is why you strive so hard to avoid it. Earth is also the only planet that has the concept of a God that created everything including you, therefore misinterpreting your own "I AM" eternalness, all of your experiences from past lifetimes, and the wisdom you possess as a God unto yourself.

So, when you get to the zero point on your path to cross over to your enlightenment and ascension, you do come to a point where you have to choose to let go "all that is of this old world." For this "old world" of death, suffering, good, bad, and what you have been taught about God and family are now passing away or coming to an end. All that is lift is to learn to let go and become a Christ in your own right that inherits what your heart desires to create because you are the God that will create it for you to experience and no one else.

Understand that real enlightenment is effortless whereas the rational mind loves spiritual complexity that defines you as who you think you are as a human. If you believe you need healing, saving, and that you need money to survive then by all means healing, saving, and money will always escape you. If you honestly believe that some white male Hebrew God can heal you, save you, take you of the poverty ladder, or take you to heaven, than by all means keep up your hope, for hope, my friends, is nothing but wishing someday to be healed in body, in mind, and in your bank account.

My dear friends, it was you that has given yourself the gift of being the creator of your life in an effort to release yourself from stuck energies and old beliefs that identify you as something you are not. So listen, open up your heart and understand that your soul is nudging you right now to bring you to a place of awareness of "who you truly are," and to a place of knowing that you have been a Christ before time began. All that is left is for you to give yourself permission to receive "who you truly are" and stop your rational mind from debating you, denying you, and doubting you as the true creator.

So, take a deep breath and welcome in your soul. It is waiting for you to invite it into your life. It is you that has a seat at the Christ table along with everyone else that chooses to move forward because there is no one higher than you, not even Jesus or those Generals from your past lifetimes. The choice is yours!

Remember, we all have a reason for experiencing something and extending ourselves in a certain way, which means each and every one of us is a master, and therefore cannot interfere with another soul's purpose. However, we can offer to them a new way of looking at things. Learn to trust what has been working within you is also at work within others, and therefore honor the choices and the processes of others, even when it seems that they are moving away from you.

Trust in the divine timing for all people, including your friends and family members. Remind yourself that they are also being guided by their own soul, for each of them may desire to expand in understanding but may have different ideas as to how to accomplish it.

In closing, it is very important to understand and respect personal growth, and that each person is delivered by their own soul. Also remember the rational mind is hard wired for logic and reasoning, and therefore fills the gaps where it does not understand that consciousness is free flowing and not limited to time, space, and a physical persona. Consciousness always evolves and expands infinitely and in the end, it leaves behind everything to which one thinks one was in some past lifetime but the experience and the wisdom learned from the experience always follows.

I hope that my soul has given you, as it did for me, the understanding that you are not a sinner that needs saving. You are worthy of this New Expansional Energy that is coming in today, and all that you have to do is allow it in. It was your soul that committed you to a path of self-discovery and then set the date for your ascension. The question is now, are you ready to let go and ascend?

Remember, as long as you do your deep breathing and acknowledge who you truly are, for you are a God unto yourself, you will flow into a place of unlimited possibilities to experience. However, to receive those unlimited possibilities you cannot allow anyone tell you what your truths are. A person can only tell you what their truths are in perspective to what belongs to them personally. It is up to you in what you want your life to be and how you want to play it out.

My fellow seekers, you are what you reflect outward as your beliefs. Your reality and what you experience in life is a reflection of your consciousness. If you belief in good and bad, God and Satan, then you will see and experience your world around you as good and bad. The choice is yours and yours alone in what you want to experience!

CPSIA information can be obtained at www.ICGtesting.com
Printed in the USA
LVOW122005021112

305411LV00003B/3/P